GW00691170

TRIPS and Developing Countries

TRIPS and Developing Countries

Towards a New IP World Order?

Edited by

Gustavo Ghidini

Professor of Intellectual Property and Competition Law, University of Milan; Director, Observatory on Intellectual Property, Competition and Communications Law, LUISS Guido Carli University, Rome, Italy

Rudolph J.R. Peritz

Professor and Director, IProgress Project, New York Law School, USA

Marco Ricolfi

Professor of Intellectual Property Law, University of Turin; Tosetto Weigmann and Associati, Turin and Milan, Italy

Edward Elgar

Cheltenham, UK • Northampton, MA, USA

Published by
Edward Elgar Publishing Limited
The Lypiatts
15 Lansdown Road
Cheltenham
Glos GL50 2JA
UK

Edward Elgar Publishing, Inc.
William Pratt House
9 Dewey Court
Northampton
Massachusetts 01060
USA

A catalogue record for this book
is available from the British Library

Library of Congress Control Number: 2013949791

This book is available electronically in the ElgarOnline.com
Law Subject Collection, E-ISBN 978 1 84980 494 3

ISBN 978 1 84980 485 1

Typeset by Servis Filmsetting Ltd, Stockport, Cheshire
Printed and bound in Great Britain by T.J. International Ltd, Padstow

Contents

Contributors

Linda Briceño Moraia: Post-Doc researcher, University of Oxford (Centre for Health, Law and Emerging Technologies, HeLEX).

Jorge L. Contreras: Associate Professor of Law at American University Washington College of Law, Washington, D.C.

Lifang Dong: Managing Partner of Dong & Partners Law Firm, Rome; LUISS Guido Carli University, Rome, Italy; University of East Anglia, Norwich, UK; Peking University, Beijing, P.R.C.

Gustavo Ghidini: Professor, University of Milan and LUISS Guido Carli University, Rome. Past President of ATRIP.

Annette Kur: Professor, Senior Researcher, Max-Planck-Institute for Intellectual Property and Competition Law, Munich.

Molly Land: Professor of Law, University of Connecticut School of Law.

Marianne Levin: Professor Emeritus, former Director of the Institute for Market Law and Intellectual Property Law (IFIM) at the University of Stockholm.

Duncan Matthews: Professor, Chair in Intellectual Property Law, Centre for Commercial Law Studies, Queen Mary, University of London.

Charles R. McManis: Thomas & Karole Green Professor of Law, Washington University School of Law, St. Louis, USA.

Justice **James Otieno Odek**: Professor, Judge of Appeal, Court of Appeal, Republic of Kenya.

Rudolph J.R. Peritz: Professor and Director, IProgress Project, New York Law School.

Horacio Rangel-Ortiz: Professor of IP Law and International IP Law at the School of Law of Universidad Panamericana and UNAM, Mexico City. Past President of ATRIP. Chairman of the International IP Committee of the Mexican Bar.

Marco Ricolfi: Professor, University of Turin, Co-Director of the Turn/WIPO LLM.

Introduction

Rudolph J.R. Peritz

Since its inception in 1994, the Agreement on Trade Related Aspects of Intellectual Property Rights (TRIPS) has embodied the orthodox view that enforcing strong intellectual property rights (IPRs) is necessary to solve problems of trade and development. The Doha Declaration of 2001 offered short periods of special dispensation, especially to least developed countries, and proclaimed one goal to be the promotion of "access to medicines for all." Nonetheless, it is important to recognize that the Declaration did not disturb the orthodox view of strong IPRs reflected in TRIPS. The editors of this collection reject this view and the traditional development theory that underlies it, particularly the theory's binary model of the world as comprising developed countries and all the rest who must follow the IPR-laden path to development. The editors share the conviction that the TRIPS regime of strong IPRs is increasingly out of phase with the shifting geopolitical dynamics of multilateralism in international relations, a multilateralism in which human rights has become a progressively more influential factor in shaping trade and development policy.

The editors of this collection ask: How can TRIPS mature further into an institution that supports a view of economic development which incorporates the ensemble of human rights now seen as encompassing a more comprehensive set of collective interests that includes public health, environment, and nutrition? In particular how can this twenty-first century congregation of human rights provide a pragmatic ethic for accomplishing a rapport with IPRs in the new landscape of development policy?

Addressing such questions, the chapters in the first part of the collection shed new light on recent deployments of human rights ethics, international treaty obligations, and domestic law that have had success in reshaping IPRs, deployments made in developing countries and the BRIC (Brazil, Russia, India and China) group. The chapters in the second part make new proposals and recommendations for the further use of human rights and related ethics to resolve conflict over IPRs in ways that can benefit less-developed countries.

Such conflict was inevitable, especially between patent rights, given their continuing expansion in the pharmaceutical and biotechnology sectors, and human rights, which now comprise a wider array of collective interests. The conflict between patent rights and human rights is widely understood as expressing a particularly difficult form of the familiar tension between efficiency and dispersion, between encouraging innovation and promoting fair distribution.[1] This dominant view of the conflict bears scrutiny. Why? Because the economic theory supporting patent rights as the engine of research and development is not well supported. In consequence, it cannot be taken for granted that the moral virtue of wider distribution of patented goods, especially pharmacological products, exacts a high price on research and development.

WHAT IS THE CONFLICT BETWEEN PATENT RIGHTS AND HUMAN RIGHTS?

The rights conflict in mainstream policy debate persists with great force because both sides are supported by international treaties as well as domestic law, whether constitutional or legislative in form. Moreover, on both sides, the rights are doubly justified, first, by economic arguments and second, by natural rights claims. Patent rights are understood as the economic incentive necessary to encourage innovation and, with it, economic growth; they are also seen as a particularly attractive form of natural right, one that not only takes up the Lockean call to protect the fruits of one's labor but also conjures the Romantic ideal of nurturing the individual Imagination.[2] At the same time, human rights are seen as encompassing natural rights to food and shelter, and to health and medicine, rights to some extent reflected in the Lockean proviso of leaving "enough and as good" for those who follow; moreover, the economic logics of efficiency are literally dependent on the scale and scope of distribution in both the short and long terms, in regard to both the microeconomic sense that allocative efficiency is by definition a function of distribution and, second, in the macroeconomic sense that both the consumption and production functions driving economic growth expand in populations that live in conditions of better health and nutrition.

---

[1] And, even more fundamentally, the complex relationship between liberty and equality.

[2] Supporting these forces is the anxious neo-mercantilist insistence, certainly in the United States, that patent (as well as copyright and trade secret) protection must be maximized because it represents the last competitive advantage in global markets.

Yet, the conflict as it has played out in mainstream debate over trade and development does not reflect these double justifications. Instead, patent rights have typically been justified in economic terms while human rights have largely been asserted as natural rights that should curb if not trump patent rights despite their assertedly ill-effects on technological innovation and, with it, on economic growth. In the context of development, global mappings of trade have long shown hemispheric profiles of import and export, whether north–south or east–west. But the emergence of the BRIC countries and their predecessors, including Taiwan and Korea, has not only complicated hemispheric profiles of trade and development but also injected new dynamics into the TRIPS regime of strong patent rights because of those countries' dual interests as both IP importers and exporters, as well as their mercantilist fiscal and trade policies.[3] This complexity amplifies the importance of interrogating the orthodox justification for strong patent rights as the incentive necessary for vigorous innovation and, with it, economic growth and development.

The orthodox scholarly conception of patents as the instrument of economic growth is supported by the intuitively attractive economic tenet that patents provide the financial incentive needed for inventors and their investors to engage in research and development. The assumption is that all society benefits from the economic growth that results. In economic terms, without the incentive of patent rights, new ideas and their embodiments are too quickly and too easily copied, imitated, and reproduced. Inventors and their investors will not profit enough to undertake the risky enterprise of research and development. In the orthodox view that supports TRIPS, patents are justified in economic terms by the need to privatize positive externalities, by the market failure of unfettered competition.

In this light, many scholars and policy makers call for expanded patent protection on the logic that more is better, that maximizing the means of patent protection maximizes the ends of promoting economic progress. This maximalist logic makes intuitive sense insofar as the greater private profits stemming from stronger patent protection are understood as spurring more innovation and, with it, the greater public benefits of increased economic growth.

Although the economic incentive rationale and its maximalist logic are intuitively attractive, the fact is that they simply do not hold together. Indeed, economists and policy analysts have recognized deep problems

---

[3] Of course, the TRIPS Agreement can itself be understood as neo-mercantilist, with IP rather than gold as the marker of wealth and IPRs rather than tariffs as the regulating mechanism.

since the nineteenth century.[4] The problems are both theoretical[5] and empirical. The empirical research is particularly arresting: Despite more than 50 years of studies, economists have not produced empirical evidence to support the claim that the economic benefits of patents are superior to those of patent-free [or open] competition in encouraging innovation or advancing economic growth. In sum, the theoretical critiques and empirical results conclude that increasing the private benefits of patents to inventors and investors tells us nothing about their effects on the public good, particularly on economic growth.

The result is an analytical stalemate that the orthodox view does not acknowledge, a stalemate because both patent protection and patent-free

---

[4] *See, e.g.*, William M. Landes & Richard A. Posner, The Economic Structure of Intellectual Property Law 9–10, 294–333 (Cambridge, MA: Harvard University Press 2003). References for the analysis that follows as well as further discussion can be found in Rudolph J.R. Peritz, *Competition* Within *Intellectual Property Regimes – The Instance of Patent Rights*, in Intellectual Property and Competition Law: New Frontiers, Ariel Ezrahi & Steven D. Anderman, eds (Oxford, UK: OUP 2011); Rudolph J.R. Peritz, *Essay Thinking about Economic Progress: Arrow and Schumpeter in Time and Space*, in Technology and Competition: Contributions in Honour of Hanns Ullrich, Josef Drexl, ed. (Bruxelles: Larcier Pub. 2009); Rudolph J.R. Peritz, *Freedom to Experiment: Toward a Concept of Inventor Welfare*, 90 J. Patent & Trademark Office Society 245 (2008), available at SSRN URL http://ssrn.com/author=75649. For discussion of the European debates, see Fritz Machlup & Edith Penrose, *The Patent Controversy in the Nineteenth Century*, 10 J. Econ. Hist. 1 (1950), analyzed in Rudolph J.R. Peritz, *Patents and Progress: The Economics of Patent Monopoly and Free Access*, in Intellectual Property Rights: Does One Size Fit All?, Annette Kur, ed. (Cheltenham: Edward Elgar Pub. 2009).

[5] The theoretical critiques begin with the general proposition that there is no logical basis for assuming that increasing the means increases the wished-for ends. As a matter of logic, stronger patents do not necessarily lead to more public benefits. Means–ends relationships are determined not by abstract logic but by empirical and moral inquiry. Simply conflating them is a logical category error. Then there are the more focused economic criticisms of equating patent protection with economic growth, the criticism for instance that incentive theory does not take into account opportunity costs and thus overstates the public benefits of patent protection. Why? Because it ignores the lost benefits of alternative investments, public benefits that would have resulted from investment in, for example, more production or more unpatentable research and development. Further, patent rights produce the social cost of monopoly profits that diminishes dispersion of the patented inventions to both consumers and later inventors. As well, proliferating patent rights produce increasing transaction costs of technology transfer, costs encapsulated in the concept of anti-commons. In sum, there is no theoretical basis for claiming that as a general matter the social benefits of a patent regime justify its considerable social costs.

competition contribute to economic growth but to indeterminable degrees. In short, the TRIPS commitment to strong patent rights as the necessary foundation for the success of a global trade and development regime lacks economic support.

Several alternatives to the incentive theory of patents have emerged in the literature, alternatives ranging from tinkering within the strong rights regime to rejecting the entire formulation.[6] Despite disagreements, they all stem from the same recognition that an economic logic of incentive theory cannot provide a technical solution to patent policy questions of economic progress. It turns out that patent policy makers can do no better than "muddle through" hard choices based on economically informed estimates and normative judgments about social welfare, however conceived.

In this economic light, there is no fundamental conflict between patent rights and human rights. There are only overlapping questions whose resolution should take into account the economic and moral dimensions of social welfare. Thus human rights activists need not argue that the economic costs of declining innovation are worth the moral virtue of wider dissemination because, as a general matter, no one can determine whether innovation would decline or, if it would, whether the decline would produce economic costs or benefits.

The policy analysis that emerges, then, calls for identifying and weighing the economic and moral dimensions of social welfare in the particular circumstances. Here, the circumstances involve pharmaceutical and biotechnology patent rights, and human rights to health, nutrition, and medicine. As for the patent rights, a landmark study of data from interviews of research and development directors in the United States supports a claim that patents provide significant incentive to the pharmaceutical industry, apparently because research and development is costly and imitation is cheap in that sector.[7] Still, these findings should be understood for what they are—the importance of patents for private profitability in specific

---

[6] For discussion, see Rudolph J.R. Peritz *Patents and Progress: The Economics of Patent Monopoly and Free access*, in INTELLECTUAL PROPERTY RIGHTS: DOES ONE SIZE FIT ALL?, Annette Kur, ed. (Cheltenham: Edward Elgar Pub. 2009). Of course, tinkering could be extensive, whether by intra-regime measures such as constricting patent scope, expanding the misuse doctrine, or raising the standard of non-obviousness, or by extra-regime measures such as stricter enforcement of antitrust doctrines limiting the opportunities for abuse by dominant firms, patent pools, or holders of patents in industry-standard inventions.

[7] Richard C. Levin, Alvin K. Klevorick, Richard R. Nelson, Sidney G. Winter, Richard Gilbert, Zvi Griliches, *Appropriating the Returns from Industrial Research and Development*, BROOKINGS PAPERS ON ECONOMIC ACTIVITY 783–831(1987) (100-industry survey).

contexts and for specific markets, a finding which has nothing to say about social welfare, defined in terms of economic growth.

However, in these particular circumstances, the impact on social welfare calls for additional analysis. For if social welfare is defined more broadly, then private gains to pharma and biotech companies should not be ignored simply because there is no basis for estimating their impact on economic growth. For example, development of new cancer treatment or virus vaccine advances social welfare regardless of its effect on economic growth; thus social welfare more broadly defined can be affected by this sector's business model for funding research and development, a model that relies on the incentive value of patent rights to produce adequate profits.[8]

In these specific circumstances, social welfare analysis should take into account both the profit-as-incentive claims of pharma and biotech patent holders, and the human rights claims of under-supplied populations because social welfare is advanced both by encouraging patent-seeking research and by supplying life-sustaining needs, because social welfare calls for both sufficiently high profits to patent holders and sufficiently low prices to satisfy demand in the least-developed countries. So it is that pharma and biotech patents present a special case insofar as they involve the supply of basic human needs. What is to be done in these circumstances to resolve what appears to be a true conflict?

In evaluating and addressing economic arguments for strong protection of patent and other IPRs, human rights activists might find useful several principles. First and foremost, TRIPS rules and practices founded on presumptions in favor of strong patent rights as a general matter can claim no economic foundation. In short, general claims about the economic necessity of patent protection cannot be sustained. Second and more specifically, patents as incentives for pharma and biotech research and development require not maximizing profits but matching opportunity costs from competing investments. That is, lower profits can be high enough. One implication is that profitability analysis can proceed on a market-by-market basis. That is, monopoly profits from first world markets are typically sufficient to satisfy the sector's business model. Hence lower prices in the least-developed economies would provide adequate benefits to patent holders, so long as they cover costs of supply and the price discrimination does not lead to widespread arbitrage by grey market imports

---

[8] See, generally, Peritz, *An Essay. Taking Antitrust to Patent School: The Instance of Pay-for-Delay Settlements*, 58 ANTITRUST BULLETIN __ (forthcoming, Spring 2013).

to developed countries. Third, in light of the preceding principles, one size need not fit all. Policy analysis can put differentiated patent protection into play: Patent terms for life-saving medications need not extend a full 20 years, though full terms might be appropriate for lifestyle drugs whose intended consumers populate first world markets; such differentiation in patent rights would permit generic life-saving drugs earlier market entry in less developed countries. Fourth, local production and distribution should be part of the policy solution, along with the necessary technology transfer and export controls. Finally, strong biodiversity protection should be instituted, as it has been in Brazil, to include technology transfer and construction of local sites for research and development as well as production.

These principles can help channel public debate regarding trade and development policy in ways that permit the twenty-first century ensemble of human rights, including access to medicines, to serve as a pragmatic ethic to influence the scope and substance of patent protection that provides adequate incentive to spur research and development of life-saving drugs in the pharma and biotech sector while taking into account those human rights served by their wider dissemination.

RE-SHAPING THE TRIPS REGIME TO PROFIT HUMAN RIGHTS

The four chapters in the first part of the volume re-cast in new light recent deployments of human rights ethics and TRIPS obligations in developing countries and the BRIC group, while the six chapters in the second part put forward new proposals and recommendations for the use of human rights and related ethics to resolve conflict over IPRs in ways that can benefit less developed countries.

Part 1. Re-imagining Current Approaches

In Chapter 1, Duncan Matthews demonstrates that non-governmental organizations (NGOs) have used human rights to "highlight the adverse impacts of IPRs on access to medicines to an extent far greater than previously thought." Matthews describes how over the past decade, emphasizing the links between IP, access to medicines, and human rights has evolved into a key strategy for NGOs seeking to draw attention to the potentially adverse effects of patents for pharmaceutical products for public health, particularly for people living with Human Immunodeficiency Virus/Acquired Immune-Deficiency Syndrome (HIV/AIDS). The chapter describes how NGOs have not only reshaped the international debate about the relationship between IPRs and access to medicines by framing it as a human rights issue, but have also utilized the concrete human rights principles enshrined in national constitutional laws as a practical tool in their campaigns, often to good effect. The chapter focuses on the NGO campaigns in South Africa, Brazil, and India.

In Chapter 2, Lifang Dong seeks to show the extent to which China respects its TRIPS obligations by contrasting its regime with those of its BRIC cohort. While "India, Brazil, and the Russian Federation still rely on domestic policy protection to evade the TRIPS Agreement," in Dong's view the absence of such domestic protections places "IP protection in China almost on a level with the regimes of developed countries." Moreover, in arguing against the mainstream view that China's IP regime is lax, Dong goes even further, seeking to show that "in some respects China's level of IP protection has surpassed that of developed countries." Within this context, the author recommends that, going forward, China should shape its IP protection in accord with the TRIPS provision permitting legislation to "protect public health and nutrition."

In Chapter 3, Horacio Rangel-Ortiz finds virtue in recent bilateral patent and trademark agreements between the United States and Latin American nations, despite bilateralism's poor reputation amongst trade and development policy makers who favor regional and global agreements. Arguing against the common wisdom, Rangel-Ortiz asserts that bilateralism can benefit less-developed countries, although they are "weak negotiators." For one, "less developed countries can benefit from treaties that would not be attractive to their stronger counterparts" and, in consequence, would be rejected in a regional context. Second, bilateralism may eventually "lead to the international or regional uniformity or harmonization" that neither regional nor multilateral approaches have achieved. Moreover, the chapter shows that despite the stricter IP protection in the United States, bilateral agreements with Latin American countries have provided for protection of traditional knowledge and genetic resources as well as equitable sharing of benefits. Finally, the treaties have recognized the importance of taking measures necessary to protect public health under the terms of the Doha Declaration.

In Chapter 4, Charles R. McManis and Jorge Contreras seek to reframe understanding of the controversial Anti-Counterfeiting Trade Agreement (ACTA) in terms that reflect legitimate concerns of developing countries. Responding to broad criticism of the proposed agreement, McManis and Contreras tell another tale, a tale of developing countries, least-developed ones included among them, joining the ACTA negotiations on deepening concerns over "mounting empirical evidence that has linked trade in counterfeit and pirated goods with organized crime and terrorism" in the

Middle East, Latin America, East Africa, and Russia. The authors warn that these concerns should be separated from "the more controversial and quite distinct question of digital file sharing." They conclude that "entanglement of the two issues in the ACTA negotiations serves as its own cautionary tale concerning the virtues of promoting a greater degree of transparency and public participation in these negotiations."

Part 2. Proposing New Approaches

In Chapter 5, Gustavo Ghidini focuses his analysis of TRIPS' impact on least-developed countries (LDCs) by identifying two "normative profiles" that in his view support a double standard to their detriment. First, although the TRIPS provision allowing an additional ten years for compliance seems to reflect special dispensation, in fact developed countries have taken much longer than ten years to adopt strong IP laws, as have developing countries more recently. Second, the TRIPS provision allowing patent-granting countries to require *in situ* production harms LDCs by reducing opportunities for spillover of advanced technological knowledge and associated know-how. To ameliorate this double standard, Ghidini offers "redeeming reforms" of the two normative profiles. First, he introduces the idea that the uniform ten-year period should be replaced by individualized time schedules for compliance, based on the particular LDC's level of development. Second, he proposes that a local working requirement would fit neatly under the TRIPS provision allowing "a limited exception to the exclusive rights" of the patentee, an exception less intrusive than the compulsory licensing or government use already permitted.

In Chapter 6, Molly Land examines the development impact of subjecting the international IP standards established by the TRIPS Agreement to the mandatory dispute resolution process of the WTO. There have been two important consequences for developing countries, in her view. First, countries have foregone flexibilities to which they would otherwise be entitled, concessions that have contributed to the regime's "pro intellectual property climate." Second, adjudicators have tended to give short shrift to the internal balancing properly associated with IP rights. The overly restrictive view of TRIPS flexibilities that has resulted has been particularly problematic for LDCs. To counter this loss of flexibilities, Land seeks to revive provisions available to developing and LDCs but currently disregarded in WTO dispute resolution.

In Chapter 7, Annette Kur and Marianne Levin report on a set of proposals to reform the TRIPS agreement, proposals developed at the Max-Planck-Institute for Intellectual Property, Competition and Tax Law in

Munich under the title 'Intellectual Property law in Transition' (IPT). IPT "set out . . . to explore ways to re-establish the balance between different interests involved, where that equilibrium may have been distorted by a one-sided, inflexible approach towards IP." IPT begins with a guarantee of "a minimum level of free or conditioned access for third parties to protected subject matter. . . . [and thus] to halt a potentially dangerous trend towards ever-stronger protection." The guarantee is founded on two basic principles: First, that "non-trade related values . . . such as public health and nutrition, are of seminal importance . . . in the sense of imposing a 'moral duty' on governments vis-à-vis their own population." Second, that "well-functioning, unimpeded competition figures as an objective of primary importance for the establishment and maintenance of a sound IP system." IPT's broadest intention is to recalibrate IP rights in ways that promote "sound and sustainable socio-economic development."

In Chapter 8, Linda Briceño Moraia proposes reforms for the TRIPS Agreement to accord with the Rio Convention on Diversity (CBD) in light of the Nagoya Protocol, though the protocol is not in force. In Moraia's view, such reforms would go a long way in "correcting the present imbalance of TRIPs," especially "the neglected interests of Developing Countries." The problem, as Moraia sees it, is to "guarantee the fulfillment of the objectives pursued by the CBD, without causing an undue burden to IP right holders." The main proposal calls for "reintroducing the local working requirement in the TRIPs Agreement, since it could have a 'teaching effect'" like that discussed in chapter five. Moreover, this chapter concludes, such a reform would serve the Doha Declaration's call for universal 'access to medicines' by unlocking the door to use of genetic resources.

In Chapter 9, James Odek offers ten policy recommendations to improve innovation in Kenya. These reforms are necessary "from the perspective of developing African countries, [because] the TRIPS Agreement is an illusion and a failed promise to spur technology transfer, creativity and innovation in developing and least developed countries." TRIPS has failed, in this view, because its principles "have no local, cultural or legal roots." Moreover, TRIPS is "tilted towards appropriation of knowledge rather than transfer and diffusion of technology." As a result, "ideational power . . . is weak among developing and least developed countries." Odek's policy recommendations stress the importance of recognizing the interests of LDCs, despite TRIPS pressures to the contrary, and the necessity of political will to implement them. The chapter concludes with sixteen specific recommendations "to improve Kenya's creative and innovative capacity."

In the concluding chapter, Marco Ricolfi analyzes the importance of public sector information (PSI) to both developed and developing countries.

In his view, the critical importance of PSI stems from the new paradigm for innovation that has emerged in the past two decades: Innovation is no longer individual- or organization-based, but rather network-driven. These digital networks face the twin problems of data validity and reliability, and data access. In the absence of a uniform approach, there have developed few solutions, most notably the free access approach within the United States, and the European Union directives on data base and data privacy protection. Ricolfi observes that "developing countries have a totally free hand in determining the IP status of data which are candidates to become PSI." In this light, he assesses the costs and benefits of adopting the United States and European Union approaches, then concludes with two recommendations for developing countries regarding the process of digitization and the importance of selecting "machine readable formats."

1. When framing meets law: Using human rights as a practical instrument to facilitate access to medicines in developing countries

Duncan Matthews

INTRODUCTION

Over the past decade, the debate about the relationship between access to medicines and human rights has, to a large extent, come to define the politics of intellectual property (IP). This chapter describes how Non-governmental Organisations (NGOs) seeking to draw attention to the potentially adverse effects of patents for pharmaceutical products for public health, particularly for people living with Human Immunodeficiency Virus/Acquired Immune-Deficiency Syndrome (HIV/AIDS), not only reshaped the international debate about the relationship between IP rights and access to medicines by framing it as a human rights issue, but have also utilised the concrete human rights principles enshrined in national constitutional law as a practical tool in their campaigns, often to far-reaching effect.[1]

FRAMING

A significant amount of attention has already been paid to the extent that NGOs will increase their gains if they 'frame' or 'reframe' IP-related debates by using the emotive language of human rights to underpin substantive arguments.

[1] This chapter draws on research findings from a project funded by the UK Economic and Social Research Council (ESRC) on NGOs, Intellectual Property Rights and Multilateral Institutions (ESRC grant no. RES-155-25-0038), published in a longer version in *Intellectual Property, Human Rights and Development: The Role of NGOs and Social Movements* (Edward Elgar, 2011) by the same author.

Odell and Sell (2006, p. 87) suggest that in much the same way as powerful transnational firms and their governments had framed intellectual property protection as a trade issue during negotiations leading to the World Trade Organization (WTO) Agreement on Trade-Related Aspects of Intellectual Property Rights (the TRIPS Agreement), using the emotive language of 'piracy' and 'theft' to describe alleged violations of intellectual property rights in developing countries, critics of TRIPS have attempted subsequently to reframe the debate as a public health issue, arguing that strong intellectual property protection could be detrimental to access to medicines (and hence an infringement of human rights).

Reflecting on the negotiating history of the TRIPS Agreement, Braithwaite and Drahos (2000, p. 571–6) even argue that had the property-theft-piracy frame of industry and developed country governments been contested at the time of the negotiations, the TRIPS Agreement might not have taken the final form it did and may have been more sympathetic to the development-orientated concerns of the developing world.

Used in this way, framing becomes a tactic utilised by rights-holders and developed country governments to demonstrate that IP rights should be upheld because it is wrong to steal or, alternatively, to demonstrate that IP rights should be applied in a manner that takes account of the need to avoid preventable deaths (Odell and Sell 2006, p. 88). However, these subjective frames of reference imply different policy responses and the more NGOs do to win this subjective contest and establish the dominant frame, the greater that NGOs' negotiated gains, the framing strategy increasing the NGOs' credibility (Odell and Sell 2006, p. 89).

For Lang (2007, p. 147), the diffusion of human rights language into the work of NGOs must be accompanied by degree of elaboration if it is to provide meaningful guidance to trade policy-makers (see, for example, Abbot 2005, p. 294). Seen in this way, re-framing the debate on the impact of IP rights for development in terms of human rights performs a number of potentially important functions, but does not provide substantial policy guidance, is not a source of new policy ideas, and does not provide a means of choosing between competing ideas. Instead Lang argues that, to the extent that the human rights movement can mobilise actors and groups presently marginalised and provide effective tools to augment their political influence, framing the issue as one of human rights may help NGOs to achieve real change. In this way, human rights add legitimacy, new constituencies and (to a certain extent) further resources to those groups pressuring for change (Lang 2007, p. 147).

Similarly, Deere (2008, p. 169) has described how framing has been deployed as a strategic tool to influence international discourse on IP issues and the outcomes of international negotiations. For Deere NGOs, international organisations and academics work to reframe IP debates to better facilitate discussion of their public interest priorities (Deere 2008, p. 172).

Kapczynski (2008, p. 804) also highlights the role of 'frame mobilisation' in instigating, promoting, and legitimating collective action, creating areas of overlapping agreement within the coalition and establishing a language of common disagreement between itself and opposing groups. For Kapczynski (2008, p. 883), this explains how actors interpret their interests, build alliances, and persuade others to support their cause.

Reflecting back on the TRIPS negotiations, Drahos (2008: 269–70) has suggested that, in retrospect, drawing on public health and human rights expertise, trade negotiators interested in opposing United States (US) and European Union (EU) pharmaceutical hegemony during the TRIPS negotiations should have built a counter-frame around the principles of timely access to medicines, equity in access, and the cost-effectiveness of medicines. However, Drahos has also cautioned against viewing framing as a master mechanism and has argued that it needs the support of other strategies if it is to bring genuine structural gains in intellectual property regimes (Drahos 2008, p. 272).

Taking into account framing strategies in this way, this chapter examines how human rights have permeated the debate about the relationship between IP rights and access to medicines. The chapter then pursues this theme further by highlighting the extent that human rights law (as opposed to human rights rhetoric) has been used as a practical tool by NGOs in developing countries, often with significant results.

FRAMING INTELLECTUAL PROPERTY RIGHTS AND ACCESS TO MEDICINES AS A HUMAN RIGHTS ISSUE

A human rights-based approach to the debate on the relationship between IP rights and access to medicines first came to prominence when international NGOs began to frame the issue by using the emotive language of human rights to underpin substantive arguments that public health, the right to health and the right to life were at risk due to the patent provisions of the TRIPS Agreement. In the run-up to the Doha Declaration on the TRIPS Agreement and Public Health in November 2001 (Matthews 2004, p. 73), international NGOs began to campaign for access to medicines by calling for the full utilisation of flexibilities contained in the TRIPS Agreement. Using human rights to frame the debate, these NGOs ultimately added moral authority to the access to medicines campaign, which in turn contributed to a greater emphasis on the importance of using inbuilt flexibilities in the TRIPS Agreement and the need to permanently amend of the TRIPS Agreement provisions on compulsory licensing, making explicit the link between the protection of pharmaceutical patents with key principled ideas and rhetoric of human rights discourse (see also de Mello e Souza 2005, p. 25).

This strategy proved relatively successful because the public, the media and politicians were able to engage in a relatively straightforward way with the notion that the provision of anti-retroviral drugs (ARVs) to treat people living with HIV/AIDS in the developing world was being hindered by the TRIPS Agreement. This contributed to the ability of NGOs to make explicit the link between the HIV/AIDS crisis and IP rights, an issue that had resonance in both the developed and the developing world (see also de Mello e Souza 2005, p. 28).

That resonance was articulated through the framing of the issue so that IP began to be seen not only or primarily as a trade issue, but also as one relevant to health and human rights (de Mello e Souza 2005, p. 10), rooted in the dignity of the other in relation to the self (Orbinski 2008, p. 373). By framing the TRIPS Agreement in terms of health and human rights, activists were able to resort to accountability politics, gaining moral leverage to pressure governments and international organisations previously committed to upholding such rights (de Mello e Souza 2005, p. 159; Schultz and Walker 2006, p. 8).

In many respects, the reframing strategies of NGOs in the access to medicines campaign mimicked and acted as a counterweight to the framing that corporate activists had employed to such great effect when linking IP to trade in the run-up to the TRIPS Agreement (Matthews 2002, p. 21; de Mello e Souza 2005, p. 25). In the run-up to the TRIPS Agreement corporate interests had portrayed IP not only as a critical public policy tool for encouraging disclosure of inventions and encouraging investment in research and development (R&D), but also as an inalienable private property right. Corporate interests had also equated copying with 'piracy' and 'theft', even when this practice was entirely legal (Sell and May 2001, p. 485; Watal 2001, p. 2, quoted in de Mello e Souza 2005, p. 8).

By replicating the strategies adopted by corporate interests in negotiation of the TRIPS Agreement, the reframing strategies of NGOs weakened the public sense of legitimacy about the achievements of the TRIPS Agreement, especially in the HIV/AIDS context (Sell 2003, p. 182). While, in the 1980s, TRIPS advocates had framed it as an alternative to tolerating piracy of private property, the access to medicines campaign compared TRIPS to a different reference point – saving the lives of poor people suffering from HIV/AIDS (Odell and Sell 2006, p. 93).

The framing strategy also facilitated contestation, with the traditional model of patents as a driver for new drug development challenged by reframing the debate using the language of 'human rights' and 'the right to health' as a threat to public health and access to medicines and, through the mobilisation of moral outrage, helped to generate a widespread sense that the TRIPS Agreement in its current form could not be justified (Lang 2007, p. 147).

NGOs were able to raise awareness that access to medicines was a trade issue, mobilising the press in developed countries and bringing the issue to the attention of the public as a means of pressurising politicians in these countries (Drezner 2005, p. 15). In part this task was made easier by developed country guilt about the post-colonial legacy, particularly in sub-Saharan Africa.

By raising awareness about the link between access to medicines and IP rights issues to an extent hitherto not acknowledged, NGOs created pressure on governments in both the developed and developing world that counterbalanced the role played by industry, opening up the debate on IP rights and development policy. This helped facilitate a more open discussion on the impact of the TRIPS Agreement on public health and access to medicines.

In addition to the international access to medicines campaign, NGOs in a number of prominent developing countries have gone much further than framing the discourse on IP rights in terms of the language of human rights. In large, middle-income developing countries such as South Africa, Brazil and India, NGOs have actually used human rights law in substantive terms hitherto not considered by those emphasising framing strategies. NGOs in these countries have used rights enshrined in national constitutions before national courts as tools with which to challenge the scope and application of IP law in a very real and tangible way.

Framing IP Rights and Access to Medicines as a Human Rights Issue in South Africa

AIDS is the leading cause of mortality in South Africa. In 2001, approximately 200,000 people were dying of AIDS or AIDS-related illness each year (Boulle and Avafia 2005, p.14) and by 2008 there were an estimated 5.7 million adults living with HIV/AIDS in South Africa, about 18 per cent of all people between the ages of 15 and 49 (UNAIDS 2008).

The wider socio-economic costs of HIV/AIDS for South Africa have also had catastrophic implications. HIV/AIDS leads to a loss of household income due to illness or death of a household member and time spent on caring. In economic terms, it is the poor who are the worst affected by

HIV/AIDS since in situations of minimal income these additional costs cannot be absorbed easily by the family, resulting in increasing poverty and deteriorating food security (Boulle and Avafia 2005, p. 14). It is often women who bear the increased responsibilities of caring for ill household members and for orphaned children, in addition to their other domestic and economic responsibilities (SIDA 2001).

The socio-economic costs of HIV/AIDS are exacerbated by AIDS denialism, social stigmatisation, fear of violence and other social realities such as exclusion. Despite the horrendous loss of human life and the socio-economic costs of HIV/AIDS for South Africa, the government's response to the HIV/AIDS crisis was initially controversially slow. South African President Thabo Mbeki, for instance, questioned whether AIDS was caused by HIV and said that it was not certain that ARV drugs were safe and effective. He denied knowing anyone who had died of AIDS, despite so many South Africans succumbing to the virus. This institutional AIDS denialism had terrible implications for the provision of ARVs for people living with HIV/AIDS in South Africa.[2]

The focus for NGO activism to challenge the government's inaction came on 10 December 1998 – Human Rights Day, when a group of about 15 people protested on the steps of St. George's Cathedral in Cape Town, demanding ARVs for people living with HIV/AIDS (Boulle and Avafia 2005, p. 15). By the end of the day a new NGO, the Treatment Action Campaign (TAC) had been created and over 1,000 people had signed up as supporters.

TAC's formation was grounded in on a distinctly post-apartheid period of South Africa's history when human rights issues were particularly to the fore and, by linking the right to health to human rights principles, TAC shared historical continuities with the late 1980s and early 1990s anti-apartheid and gay rights activism. The objectives of TAC were set out in clause 4 of its constitution. These included campaigning for equitable access to affordable treatment for all people with HIV/AIDS and challenging, by means of litigation, lobbying, advocacy, and all forms of legitimate social mobilisation, any barrier or obstacle that limits access to treatment for HIV/AIDS (see also Fourie 2006, p. 130).[3]

To achieve these objectives, TAC's campaigns framed access to ARVs for people living with HIV/AIDS as a human right (Boulle and Avafia

[2] While other large developing countries like Brazil had begun offering large-scale public health treatment programmes as early as the 1990s, the South African Cabinet only announced a national treatment plan in 2003 after years of ever-increasing mortality rates and NGO activism.

[3] *Constitution of the Treatment Action Campaign*. Available at: http://www.tac.org.za/Documents/Constitution/Constitution13Dec04.PDF.

2005, p. 23; Halbert 2005, p. 108; Mbali, 2005, p. 2) using to great effect the language and principles of human rights enshrined in the South African Constitution to do so.

TAC's strategy of utilising the human rights principles enshrined in South Africa's constitution (see also de Waal 2006, p. 36) and framing issues in the language of human rights and constitutional obligations (Fourie 2006, p. 163) is consistent with the personal experiences of Zackie Achmat, its chairperson. Achmat was active in the United Democratic Front (UDF) during the later apartheid years in South Africa and used non-violent methods of political activism that included strikes and demonstrations. While never ceding the legitimacy of the apartheid government, UDF activists used human rights law to challenge every aspect of racist and arbitrary rule (de Waal 2006, p. 36). Informed by experience, TAC has developed its human rights approach from an initial framing of the issues to litigation based on human rights principles enshrined in the South African Constitution, working closely with lawyers based in the Law and Treatment Access Unit of the AIDS Law Project (ALP) to achieve its objectives.

As with TAC, the ALP's human rights approach grew out the experiences of the anti-apartheid struggle. Mark Heywood, project head of the ALP for example, was involved in the anti-apartheid movement for a decade and was also a member of the UDF. Originally based at the University of Witwatersrand in Johannesburg, the ALP believes that the progressive realisation of a set of human rights principles is fundamental to achieving sustainable progress in tackling the HIV/AIDS pandemic. It uses a variety of legal approaches to put these human rights principles into practice in order to protect, promote and advance the rights of people living with HIV/AIDS, and to change the socio-economic and other conditions that lead to the spread of HIV/AIDS and its disproportionate impact on the poor (AIDS Law Project 2007, p. 4).

The most effective ARV for the prevention of mother-to-child-transmission (MTCT) of HIV is Nevirapine, the patent for which is owned by the German pharmaceutical company Boehringer Ingelheim (BI).[4] In 2001 BI had offered to donate Nevirapine to South Africa at no cost. The South African Government had nonetheless declined this offer and refused to adopt a full-scale Nevirapine treatment programme for HIV-infected pregnant women on the grounds that the ARV's efficacy and side-effects had not been adequately studied by the government's pilot programs.

---

[4] Nevirapine is a non-nucleoside reverse transcriptase inhibitor for use against mother-to-child transmission of HIV which has been shown to reduce MTCT of HIV in approximately 50 per cent of cases.

The Ministry of Health also contended that treatment would not prevent infected mothers from transmitting the virus through breast feeding and that it did not have sufficient resources to provide the counselling and monitoring required by treatment programs (de Mello e Souza 2005, p. 247).

As a result, in July 2002, TAC brought a legal action before the Pretoria High Court in *Minister of Health & Others v. Treatment Action Campaign & Others*.[5] The complaint concerned the refusal of the South African Government to make Nevirapine available in the public health sector and not setting out a timeframe for a national programme to prevent MTCT of HIV.

The applicants (TAC, Dr. Haroon Saloojee and the Children's Rights Centre, together with the Institute for Democracy in South Africa, First Amicus Curiae, the Community Law Centre, Second Amicus Curiae, and the Cotlands Baby Sanctuary, Third Amicus Curiae) contended that restrictions on the availability of Nevirapine were unreasonable when measured against the human rights principles of the South African Constitution.

The Constitution commands the state and all its organs to give effect to the rights guaranteed in the Bill of Rights, in particular: sections 27(1), 27(2) and 28(1), see Box 1.1 below.[6]

BOX 1.1

Article 27 of the Constitution of the Republic of South Africa: Health care, food, water and social security

(1) Everyone has the right to have access to –
- *(a)* health care services, including reproductive health care;
- *(b)* sufficient food and water; and
- *(c)* social security, including, if they are unable to support themselves and their dependants, appropriate social assistance.

(2) The state must take reasonable legislative and other measures, within its available resources, to achieve the progressive realisation of each of these rights.

(3) No one may be refused emergency medical treatment.

[5] Constitutional Court of South Africa, *Minister of Health & Others v. Treatment Action Campaign & Others*, Case CCT 8/02, 5 July 2002, 10 BCLR 1033 CC. Available at: http://www.saflii.org/za/cases/ZACC/2002/15.html.

[6] Constitution of the Republic of South Africa, 1996. Available at: http://www.info.gov.za/documents/constitution/1996/a108-96.pdf.

Article 28 of the Constitution of the Republic of South Africa 1996: Children

(1) Every child has the right –
  (a) to a name and a nationality from birth;
  (b) to family care or parental care, or to appropriate alternative care when removed from the family environment;
  (c) to basic nutrition, shelter, basic health care services and social services;
  (d) to be protected from maltreatment, neglect, abuse or degradation;
  (e) to be protected from exploitative labour practices;
  (f) not to be required or permitted to perform work or provide services that –
    (i) are inappropriate for a person of that child's age; or
    (ii) place at risk the child's well-being, education, physical or mental health or spiritual, moral or social development;
  (g) not to be detained except as a measure of last resort, in which case, in addition to the rights a child enjoys under sections 12 and 35, the child may be detained only for the, shortest appropriate period of time, and has the right to be –
    (i) kept separately from detained persons over the age of 18 years; and
    (ii) treated in a manner, and kept in conditions, that take account of the child's age;
  (h) to have a legal practitioner assigned to the child by the state, and at state expense, in civil proceedings affecting the child, if substantial injustice would otherwise result; and
  (i) not to be used directly in armed conflict, and to be protected in times of armed conflict.

(2) A child's best interests are of paramount importance in every matter concerning the child.

(3) In this section "child" means a person under the age of 18 years.

Finding in favour of the applicants, the South African Constitutional Court held that section 27(1) and (2) of the Constitution require the government to devise and implement within its available resources a comprehensive and co-ordinated programme to realise progressively the rights of pregnant women and their newborn children to have access to health services to combat MTCT of HIV. The Court also confirmed that the state is obliged to ensure that children are accorded the protection contemplated by section 28(1)(c) of the Constitution. The South African Government was ordered to remove the restrictions that prevented Nevirapine being made available for the purpose of reducing the risk of MTCT of HIV without delay.

By seeking recourse to the human rights principles enshrined in the South African Constitution, TAC and its allies had succeeded not only in improving access to Nevirapine but also in creating an alternative moral framework for understanding the relationship between patents, access to medicines and human life.

This changed the discourse not only in South Africa but on patents and access to medicines internationally. The rights of people living with HIV/AIDS to have access to ARVs came to be more widely seen as an inalienable human right distinct from the temporary property right associated with IP. Thus, the debate over the implications of IP rights for access to medicines were no longer simply framed in terms of the prevention of piracy and counterfeiting and the benefits of the patent system as a stimulus for innovation, but also about balancing that system with the fundamental human rights to life and to health care.

Framing IP Rights and Access to Medicines as a Human Rights Issue in Brazil

The recent history of democratic struggle in Brazil since the 1980s has had significant implications in terms of how NGOs have embraced and utilised principles of human rights in articulating their concerns. When military dictatorship came to an end in Brazil in 1985, there followed a profound period of national self-reflection. Public policy objectives were gradually restructured around a new social agenda for the country; this social agenda was underpinned by a new democratic constitution, firmly grounded in human rights principles that it was believed should be upheld at all costs to avoid a repeat of abuses experienced during the dictatorship.

This belief in the primacy of human rights, particularly the right to health enshrined in the Brazilian Constitution, impacted subsequently on the decision of NGOs to mobilise in support of the Brazilian Government in its attempts to achieve a balance between the patents for pharmaceutical products and the right to health through the compulsory licensing provisions of federal law. Those provisions were subject to a US complaint to the WTO and in turn led to sustained and detailed engagement with issues relating to patents, public health and access to medicines on the part of the Brazilian NGO community.

The period from 1985 to 1989 saw a rapid growth in the number of NGOs in Brazil acting for and on behalf of people living with HIV/AIDS. In particular, these NGOs made explicit the link between the protection provision of ARVs and the fundamental human rights of people living with HIV/AIDS. This connection had profound resonance in a Brazilian society still recovering from the painful legacy of 21 years of military rule.

Articulate and well-educated people living within the gay community took the lead in these NGOs, advocating that the government make the provision of ARVs for people living with HIV/AIDS a priority (Smallman 2007, p. 80). Prominent amongst these new NGOs was *Grupo de Apoio à Prevenção à AIDS* (GAPA – AIDS Prevention Action Group), founded in São Paulo in 1985, the *Associação Brasileira Interdisciplinar de AIDS* (ABIA – Brazilian Interdisciplinary AIDS Association) and *Grupo pela Valorização, Integridade e Dignidade do Doente de AIDS* (Grupo pela *VIDDA* – Group for Life), founded in Rio de Janeiro in May 1989. This was followed, in 1995, by the founding of the Brazilian Network of People Living with HIV/AIDS (RNP+), which today has a membership in excess of 2,500 people. In total there are now more than 600 different NGOs working on issues related to HIV/AIDS in Brazil under the umbrella of the State Forum of AIDS NGOs (Távora dos Santos Filho 2000).

These Brazilian NGOs are responsible for a number of significant initiatives that advocate improved access to ARVs. In the early 1990s, for instance, the *Grupo pela VIDDA* and GAPA sued the federal and state governments to assure access to medication for HIV/AIDS patients in hospitals (Távora dos Santos Filho 2000).

A key strategy of the NGOs campaigning for improved access to ARVs in Brazil was Article 196 of the 1988 *Constituição da República Federativa do Brasil* (Constitution of the Federal Republic of Brazil) which enshrined the right to health in federal law, see Box 1.2 below.

BOX 1.2

Article 196 of the Constitution of the Federal Republic of Brazil.

Health is a right of all and a duty of the State and shall be guaranteed by means of social and economic policies aimed at reducing the risk of illness and other hazards and at the universal and equal access to actions and services for its promotion, protection and recovery.

Using strategies that had worked to such good effect in opposition to the previous military regime, these HIV/AIDS NGOs began to use human rights principles to frame the health policy on the right to health care as a right for all (see also Galvão 2005, p. 112). The right to health enshrined in Article 196 of the Brazilian Constitution quickly became the focus of attention for NGOs representing people living with HIV/AIDS seeking to articulate the universal right of access to ARVs.

In order to fulfil the constitutional right under Article 196, the *Sistema Único de Saúde* (SUS – Unique Health System) was set up to provide healthcare to approximately 123 million Brazilians (74 per cent of the total population) who cannot afford private health care plans (Cohen and Lybecker 2005, p. 216) and is regulated by Laws 8.080/90 and 8.142/90. These laws also established the three founding principles of the SUS.[7] First, that it should be universal, meaning that no citizen could be excluded from SUS coverage. Second, that it should be characterised by equality of access with no discrimination regarding the public health services and products provided to users. Third, that it should provide full health care coverage, from the most basic to the most complex health care needs.

These three principles of universality, equality and integrated health care define the Brazilian state's promotion of health as a fundamental social right and, although the Brazilian Constitution does not mention specifically access to medicines as part of the right to health, it is generally acknowledged that the right to access to medicines is derived from this implementing legislation (see, for instance, Rosina et al 2008, p. 170). Specifically, Article 6(I)(d) of Law 8.080/90 provides that SUS 'must be responsible for promoting full medical assistance, which includes pharmaceutical assistance'.

In line with this obligation, in 1990 the federal government began free delivery of Azidothymidine (AZT), one of the first ARVs, to the citizens of Brazil. Initially, the AZT was purchased from Burroughs-Wellcome Company (now GlaxoSmithKline), the multinational pharmaceutical

---

[7] Public health service delivery is shared equally by the different levels of government: federal, state, municipal and the national health system (Sistema Único da Saúde – SUS). In practice, the delivery and management of health services is increasingly being decentralised to the state and municipal levels, reflecting the government's sensitivity to the population's preference for more local governance. The federal level of government defines the policies and regulations, grants technical and financial support for the states and municipal governments and provides some service delivery. These governments in turn contribute the remainder of the health budget and share responsibility for health service delivery (Cohen and Lybecker 2005, p. 214).

company that had undertaken research and development work and had subsequently been granted patents on the drug.

As the number of people living with HIV/AIDS increased and demand for treatment became more pressing, the federal government struggled to provide free ARV treatment to its citizens. The high prices of patented pharmaceutical products then started to come to the fore. Given the costs associated with purchasing large consignments of these patented pharmaceutical products at the market price, in 1993 the federal government instead began to purchase ARVs manufactured by Brazilian pharmaceutical companies which produced cheaper, equally effective, generic versions of AZT and other patented medicines.

By November 1996, this policy of universal access to ARVs at no cost to patients had become a legislative right for all Brazilian citizens as a result of Federal Law 9.313/96. This guaranteed that the SUS had a federal responsibility to provide ARV treatment to all Brazilian citizens and made it mandatory for the SUS to provide ARV treatment to all citizens living with HIV/AIDS (see also Galvão 2005, p. 112; Rosina et al 2008, p. 189). As a result, Brazil became one of the few countries in the world with a policy of universal free access to ARV treatment.

While 1996 saw the adoption of Federal Law 9.313/96 and marked the beginning of a policy of universal access to ARVs in Brazil, it also marked the point at which awareness grew about the relationship between IP rights, public health and access to medicines. This occurred with the adoption of Industrial Property Law 9.279/96, which introduced patent protection for an area of technology – pharmaceutical products – not previously patentable in Brazil.

Until 15 May 1997, when Law 9.279/96 came into force, Brazilian pharmaceutical manufacturers were permitted to legally reverse-engineer and manufacture cheaper, generic versions of pharmaceutical products that were subject to patent protection elsewhere in the world. This practice was permitted prior to 1997 under previous legislation, Industrial Property Law 5.772/71 that came into force on 21 December 1971 and, as a result, during the 1970s many private firms, such as Aché, Farmasa, Libbs, Sintofarma and public sector manufacturers, such as Fiocruz in Rio de Janeiro and FURP in São Paulo, were able to supply generic pharmaceutical products in this way (Cohen and Lybecker 2005, p. 215).

In the pre-TRIPS era, this was permissible under international law because countries were not required to grant patents to all areas of technology, such as pharmaceuticals. This changed with Article 27.1 of the TRIPS Agreement which required all WTO Members, after the expiration of transitional periods, to make available patents in all fields of technology (including pharmaceutical products).

Only a year after the TRIPS Agreement had come into force and well in advance of the applicable transitional period coming to an end, Law 9.279/96 was introduced in Brazil to provide for the protection of pharmaceutical products by patent law (see also Rosina et al 2008, p. 183). In fact, the legislation was introduced despite concerns that patent protection for pharmaceutical products would increase the financial burden on the SUS, given its obligation to purchase ARVs and provide these drugs free of charge to all citizens living with HIV/AIDS. Nevertheless, Law 9.279/96 also sought to achieve a balance between the patents accorded to pharmaceutical products and the right to health, in particular, the need to ensure the adequate provision of ARVs to people living with HIV/AIDS in Brazil.

The mechanism used to achieve this balance was compulsory licensing. Law 9.279/96 allowed the government to issue a compulsory licence where a patent holder exercises patent rights in an abusive manner, or by means of an abuse of economic power proven by an administrative or court decision. Other instances were also specified where compulsory licences may be issued, particularly under Article 68 and 71.

Under Article 68, the holder of a patent in Brazil was required to 'work' the subject matter of a patent, either by producing the patented good in the country, or by allowing the patented process to be used in Brazil. If this requirement was not met within three years of the issuance of the patent, the government could issue a compulsory licence allowing others to utilise the patent against the patent holder's wishes. Article 68 also stated that if a patent owner chose to utilise the patent through importation rather than the local working of the patent, then others besides the patent holder would be allowed to import the patented product or products obtained from the patented process.

Under Article 71, compulsory licences could also be issued by the federal government in cases of national emergency or public interest (see also Shadlen 2009, p. 48). A Presidential Decree on Compulsory Licensing 3.201/99 was subsequently issued in 1999 to define, in Article 2, what might constitute such situations of national and public interest in which compulsory licences could be issued for patented products.[8] Yet despite

---

[8] In 2003 an additional Presidential Decree 4.830/03 clarified the scope of these situations under Article 71 further. These revisions provided clearer definitions of national emergency and public interest and simplified the mechanism for issuing compulsory licences by giving the Ministry of Health greater authority to act. According the Shadlen (2009, p. 48), Presidential Decree 4.830/03 crucially stipulates that private firms supplying the government constitutes 'public use' and is thus acceptable under Article 71, and also requires patent owners to transfer

these legislative developments, in policy terms the relationship between IP rights and access to medicines at that time remained a topic largely unknown to NGOs in Brazil, particularly given the legal complexity of the issues involved.[9]

This changed in 2001 when, faced with the challenge of carrying on its HIV/AIDS programme at a considerably higher cost,[10] the Brazilian federal government opted to initiate negotiations with a number of the major pharmaceutical companies designed to reduce the price of ARVs. These negotiations were backed by the threat of compulsory licensing, with the possibility of using in particular the procedures mandated by Articles 68 and 71 of Law 9.279/96.

Using the threat of compulsory licences as a negotiating tool, by 2001 the Brazilian federal government had been able to agree substantial price reductions for ARVs with several pharmaceutical manufacturers, including a 64.8 per cent price reduction for Indinavir, 59 per cent for Efavirenz, 40 per cent for Nelfinavir and 46 per cent for Lopinavir. In addition, a technology transfer agreement was established between Merck and the Ministry of Health's main national laboratory Farmanguinhos (Love 2006, p. 2) to enable local working of some of Merck's patented pharmaceutical products.

Then, on 9 January 2001, the US requested that the WTO Dispute Settlement Body (DSB) establish a panel to resolve its complaint against Brazil in relation to the provisions of Law 9.279/96 that authorised the use of compulsory licences and parallel importation to promote the local working of patents.[11] In what was widely viewed as a reaction to the

---

technological knowledge in the case of compulsory licences, thus increasing the Ministry of Health's capacity to leverage price reductions from patent-holding pharmaceutical firms.

[9] A notable exception was the statement made by then Minister of Health the previous year *Statement of José Serra, Minister of Health, to the 2001 USTR Special 301 Report*, 3 May 2001. Available at: http://www.cptech.org/ip/health/c/brazil/serra05032001.html.

[10] The Ministry of Health's budget for purchasing antiretroviral drugs in 2007 was R$984 million. Authoritative estimates demonstrate that 80 per cent of this money is used to acquire patented medicines and 20 per cent is spent on generic drugs that are manufactured domestically by Brazilian companies. The fact that such a huge portion of the budget is being spent on patented medicines has put the sustainability and universality of this healthcare policy in jeopardy.

[11] *Brazil – Measures Affecting Patent Protection. Request for the Establishment of a Panel by the United States*. WTO Document WT/DS199/3, 9 January 2001. Available at: http://www.wtocenter.org.tw/SmartKMS/fileviewer?id=73103. See also *Press Communique by the Government of Brazil*, 25 June 2001, in which Brazil maintained its conviction that Article 68 is fully consistent with the TRIPS

Brazilian federal government's interference in the production and pricing of highly profitable ARV drugs patented by or exclusively licensed to US-based pharmaceutical multinationals, the US Government then began consultation procedures.

The US complaint focused on Article 68 of the 1996 Brazilian Industrial Property Law 9.279/96. The US complained that Article 68 violated the TRIPS Agreement which set out the principle of non-discrimination in the protection of patent rights and the exclusive rights to be enjoyed by patent holders by discriminating against US owners of Brazilian patents whose products are imported into Brazil but not locally produced and curtailing the rights of these owners to utilise the patents.[12] The US demanded from Brazil written guarantees that it would not issue compulsory licenses for products patented or exclusively licensed to US companies. Following the refusal of the Brazilian Government to meet these demands, the US requested the opening of a WTO panel against Brazil, on 1 February 2001. The DSB then established a WTO dispute settlement panel to report on this matter on 30 May 2001 (see also de Mello e Souza 2005, p. 201).

For HIV/AIDS NGOs in Brazil, the US complaint was a catalyst that focused attention on the fact that IP rights can act as a barrier to access to medicines, particularly for people living with HIV/AIDS in developing countries.[13] Brazilian NGOs such as GIV and ABIA articulated their opposition to the US complaint by using the language of human rights and the right to health enshrined in Article 196 of the Brazilian Constitution to claim that the complaint by the US to the WTO had the potential to infringe the human rights of people living with HIV/AIDS. In recognition of the fact that the Brazilian HIV/AIDS programme had been a success and should be protected, HIV/AIDS NGOs in Brazil were quick to support their federal government, and, on 7 March 2001, began to demonstrate against the US outside the US Embassy in São Paulo.

This was the first time that the relationship between IP rights and access to medicines had been discussed openly by NGOs in Brazil and the timing of this meeting was significant. Faced with the need to respond to the US complaint against Brazil at the WTO, Brazilian HIV/AIDS NGOs began

Agreement and an important instrument available to the government, in particular in its efforts to increase access of the population to medicines and to combat diseases such as AIDS. Available at: http://www.cptech.org/ip/health/c/brazil/brazilstatement06252001.html.

[12] WTO Reporter, "United States Drops WTO Case against Brazil Over HIV/AIDS Patent Law" (June 26, 2001). Copyright 2001 by The Bureau of National Affairs, available at: http://www.cptech.org/ip/health/c/brazil/bna06262001.html.

[13] Jorge Beloqui, interview with the author, 19 March 2006.

to act and, driven by the objective of protecting human rights, they began to collaborate with their international counterparts, particularly *Mèdecins Sans Frontiéres* (MSF) and Oxfam, on the implications of the TRIPS Agreement for public health and access to medicines.

Academic experts brought in by international NGOs were able to highlight the fact Articles 204 and 209 of Title 35 of the US Patent Code, which specified local manufacturing of publicly financed patented products and products patented by the US Government, were remarkably similar to those that the US had challenged Brazil on at the WTO.[14] The US countered this by arguing that, whereas the aforementioned articles of its Patent Act referred to contractual terms for publicly financed projects, Article 68 of Brazil's Law 9.279/96 was a blank requirement applicable to all patented goods, regardless of their origin. Nevertheless, international NGOs and the academic experts associated with them had provided crucial information on the US Patent Code and had also brought pressure to bear on the US by means of protests with ample media coverage.

On 25 June 2001 in the face of enormous negative publicity from international and Brazilian NGOs and legal arguments about the similarity between Articles 204 and 209 of Title 35 of the US Patent Code and Article 68 of Brazilian Law 9.279/96, the US withdrew the complaint. It did so after receiving assurances that it would be notified before any products patented by or exclusively licensed to US companies were subject to compulsory licensing in Brazil (de Mello e Souza 2005, p. 203). Brazil and the US also agreed that, before using the disputed provision in Article 68 of Brazilian Law 9.279/96 against a US patent holder, a 'Consultative

---

[14] Section 204 U.S.C. *Preference for United States Industry*:

> Notwithstanding any other provision of this chapter, no small business firm or nonprofit organization which receives title to any subject invention and no assignee of any such small business firm or nonprofit organization shall grant to any person the exclusive right to use or sell any subject invention in the United States unless such person agrees that any products embodying the subject invention or produced through the use of the subject invention will be manufactured substantially in the United States. However, in individual cases, the requirement for such an agreement may be waived by the federal agency under whose funding agreement the invention was made upon a showing by the small business firm, nonprofit organization, or assignee that reasonable but unsuccessful efforts have been made to grant licenses on similar terms to potential licensees that would be likely to manufacture substantially in the United States or that under the circumstances domestic manufacture is not commercially feasible.

USPTO Manual of Patent Examining Procedure (MPEP): http://www.uspto.gov/web/offices/pac/mpep/documents/appxl_35_U_S_C_204.htm.

Mechanism' would be initiated in an attempt to resolve the matter bilaterally (see also Deere 2008, p. 166).[15]

Alongside the technical inputs from academic experts brought on board by international NGOs, Brazilian NGOs proved adept at framing the dispute in terms of the human rights of people living with HIV/AIDS who would be adversely affected by the continued use of patents for pharmaceutical products in Brazil. With public perception that the human rights of people living with HIV/AIDS in Brazil would be undermined by the US complaint to the WTO, the US WTO case against Brazil looked increasingly unsavoury (Sell 2003, p. 158).

In June 2001 the US announced that it was officially withdrawing its case against Brazil on the first day of the first United Nations Special Session devoted to a public health issue – the context was HIV/AIDS. The session culminated in 'The Declaration of Commitment' on HIV/AIDS on June 27, 2001. The declaration framed the issue in terms of access to medicines and human rights to explain why it was of such crucial significance (Sell 2003, p. 158; de Mello e Souza 2005, p. 214).[16] The US and Brazil subsequently notified the WTO DSB that a mutual agreed understanding had been reached to settle the dispute but, in effect, the US had stepped back from further confrontation on this issue, subject to a bilateral understanding to the effect that, should Brazil seek to issue a compulsory licence on grounds of failure to work the patent locally, it would consult the US before doing so.[17]

The continued existence of the safeguard provisions on compulsory licences in Articles 68 and 71 of Law 9.279/96 in Brazil has been described by the Report of the UN High Commissioner on the impact of the TRIPS Agreement as helpful in improving the implementation of the country's HIV/AIDS treatment programme.[18] Moreover, while no compulsory licence was actually issued under Brazilian Law 9.279/96 until 2007, the provisions were nevertheless instrumental in negotiating lower prices with

---

[15] *Brazil – Measures Affecting Patent Protection.* Notification of Mutually Agreed Solution WT/DS199/4, G/L/454, IP/D/23/Add.1, 19 July 2001. See also Joint US-Brazil Statement, 25 June 2001, available at: http://www.cptech.org/ip/health/c/brazil/statement06252001.html.

[16] Ultimately, however, Oxfam retained its distance from the core group. ActionAid, meanwhile, subsequently withdrew from access to medicines issues in Brazil altogether in a move described by some Brazilian HIV/AIDS activists interviewed for this book as 'pitiful'.

[17] C. Raghavan (2001) *US to withdraw TRIPS dispute against Brazil, South-North Development Monitor* (SUNS). Available at: http://www.twnside.org.sg/title/withdraw.htm.

[18] United Nations Commission on Human Rights (2001) at para 56.

the owners of patents on pharmaceutical products.[19] The Report of the High Commissioner concluded that:

> on the facts that have been provided by the Government of Brazil, it is possible to say that the Brazilian case demonstrates how the provisions of the TRIPS Agreement can be implemented in ways that respect, protect and fulfil the right to health. Through careful legislative implementation of TRIPS provisions . . . the Brazilian IP law supports the implementation of national health policy aimed at providing essential drugs to those who need them.[20]

Framing IP Rights and Access to Medicines as a Human Rights Issue in India

Human rights have also played an important role in defining the way that Indian NGOs have engaged with the impact of IP rights on access to medicines. When India's struggle for independence from British colonial rule ended in 1947, human rights and in particular the right to life enshrined in the Indian Constitution formed the basis of the report on the future of the patent system prepared by the Committee on the Revision of the Patents Laws (1957–1959), known as the Ayyangar Committee. The committee looked more specifically at poverty issues, noted the high mortality rates in India[21] and recommended that granting patents in critical areas such as

---

[19] On 4 May 2007, Brazil finally issued a compulsory licence for the ARV Efavirenz after failing to reach agreement with the patent owner, Merck, to lower prices of the drug. Announcing the compulsory licence, the Ministry of Health said that the action would reduce the cost of purchasing Efavirenz, currently used by 75,000 of the 180,000 people living with HIV/AIDS in Brazil, by up to US$240 million between 2007 and 2012, when Merck's patent expires. Meanwhile President Luiz Inácio Lula da Silva, signing the decree granting the compulsory licence, said, 'between our business and our health, we are going to take care of our health'. *Brazil Issues Compulsory Licence for AIDS Drug*, Bridges Weekly Trade Digest, vol. 11 No 16, 9 May 2007. In other instances, the Brazilian Government has opted for voluntary agreements with multinational pharmaceutical companies. On 9 May 2006, for instance, Minister of Health Agenor Álvares and the Vice-President of Gilead Science, Joseph Steele, signed an agreement that resulted in a 51 per cent price reduction of the ARV drug tenofovir. The price of each capsule consequently reduced from US$7.68 to US$3.80, representing an immediate saving to the Brazilian National STD and AIDS Programme of US$31.4 million per annum. *Brazilian deal on tenovofir – translation of Ministry of Health Press Release of 9th May*, posting on IP-Health list server by Michel Lotrowska, MSF, 16 May 2006.

[20] United Nations Commission on Human Rights (2001) at para 58.

[21] High mortality rates had been identified in India's First Five-year Plan in 1950.

food and medicines be curtailed since the high price of patented products could deny Indian citizens access to resources and violate the right to life, enshrined in Article 21 of the Constitution of India (Ragavan 2006, p. 285), see Box 1.3 below.[22] The Committee's reasoning for this recommendation was that the prohibitively high price of patented products could violate the right to life.

> **BOX 1.3**
>
> *Article 21 of the Constitution of India: Protection of Life and Personal Liberty*
>
> No person shall be deprived of his life or personal liberty except according to procedure established by law.

Of particular concern to the Ayyanger Committee was the fact that, at that time, foreign pharmaceutical companies supplied almost 85 per cent of medicines in India and, according to the US Senate Subcommittee on Anti-Trust and Monopoly (the Kefauver Subcommittee), by 1961, prices for pharmaceutical products in India were amongst the highest in the world (Keayla 2005, p. 2).

The Ayyanger Committee, therefore, recommended that, in order to protect the constitutional right to life and promote industrial development in India, product patents should not be granted in critical areas such as food and pharmaceutical products.[23] Instead, patent protection should be limited to the method of making food, pharmaceuticals and chemicals, leaving the final products free from patent protection and consequently allowing local generic drug companies to manufacture without infringing patent rights (Ragavan 2006, p. 286). The Ayyanger Committee also

---

[22] The Supreme Court has held subsequently in *Bandhua Mukti Morcha v. Union of India* (AIR 1984 SC 802) that the right to life in Article 21 includes the right to health. The Supreme Court has also made clear in *State of Punjab v. Mohinder Singh Chawla* (1997 2 SCC 83) and that the Indian Government has a constitutional obligation to provide health facilities. It stated in *Paschim Banga Khet Mazdoor Samity v. State of West Bengal* (AIR 1996 SC 2426 at 2429 para 9) that failure to provide a patient timely medical treatment a violation of the patient's right to life, and in *State of Punjab v. Ram Lubhaya Bagga* (1998 4 SCC 117) that there is an obligation on the State to maintain health services (Mathiharan 2003).

[23] N. Rajagolala Ayyangar, Report on the Revision of the Patents Law (1959), paragraph 101.

recommended that India ensure that patented inventions were worked locally to facilitate industrial development, with the government giving powers to revoke patents or issue compulsory licenses in order to redress instances where foreign patent owners were not working the invention locally (Ragavan 2006, p. 287).

As a result of the committee's recommendations, the Patents Act of 1970, which came into force on 20 April 1972, was designed as a response to growing concerns in India about how best to strike a balance between patents rights as incentives to innovate on the one hand and how best to protect the public interest and promote industrial development in India on the other. In line with the Ayyanger Committee's recommendations, section 5 of the Act introduced differential treatment of food, pharmaceutical and chemical inventions by making available patent rights only for the processes of manufacture (Chaudhuri 2005, p. 37). By excluding protection of the end product, several manufacturers could each own patents for different processes of manufacturing the same pharmaceutical products (Rangnekar 2005, p. 4; Ragavan 2006, p. 289).

The Indian Patents Act of 1970 also limited the term of protection for process patents on food, pharmaceutical and chemical inventions to five years,[24] with a license of right authorising any person to manufacture a patented product,[25] notwithstanding the patentee's approval, available for food, pharmaceutical or chemical inventions after three years.[26] With the objective of encouraging local manufacturing of inventions, this Act also introduced powers for the Comptroller of Patents to issue compulsory licences based on the patent owner's ability to work the invention in India to the public's advantage.[27]

This system of not granting patents for inventions that related to food, pharmaceutical or chemical products prevailed until the coming into force of the TRIPS Agreement and allowed the Indian pharmaceutical industry to develop considerable expertise in reverse engineering and developing new methods of manufacture in order to become highly efficient producers of generic medicines.

This human rights approach in turn informed the subsequent strategy of NGOs working to ensure that amendments to India's patents legislation utilised to the full extent flexibilities contained in the TRIPS Agreement. In the post-TRIPS implementation period, as other NGOs become

---

[24] Indian Patents Act 1970, section 53(1)(a).
[25] Indian Patents Act 1970, section 88 .
[26] Indian Patents Act 1970, section 87(1).
[27] Indian Patents Act 1970, section 84.

involved with patents and access to medicines issues, it was once again an underlying concern that the human rights of people living with HIV/AIDS were being abused which informed their approach.

The Indian Government did not seek the views of NGOs or other stakeholders before undertaking initial negotiations on the TRIPS Agreement in the late 1980s (Daz 2003, p. 38). Nevertheless, a number of well-informed individuals came forward to articulate concern about the increased cost of pharmaceutical products that would result from new international norms requiring patent protection regardless of the products in question (Matthews 2002, p. 31). In particular, the National Working Group on Patent Laws provided the focal point for informed debate in India (Rangnekar 2005, p. 7).

In 1993 the National Working Group on Patent Laws convened the first People's Commission. It consisted of three former judges of the Supreme Court, together with a retired chief justice of the Delhi High Court.[28] Crucially, the Commission's report made explicit reference to the fact that the impact of the TRIPS Agreement on drug prices and access to medicines in India could conflict with the right to life enshrined in Article 21 of the Constitution of India (see Krishna Iyer et al 1996, p. 61). Pointing out that the Supreme Court of India had concluded that the right to health, including access to medical treatment, is a fundamental right,[29] the report argued that the Indian Patents Act 1970 could not be rewritten to allow the grant of patents for pharmaceutical products since this would constitute a violation of Article 21 of the Constitution (see Krishna Iyer at al 1996, p. 62). So, from the outset, the National Working Group on Patent Laws was adept at framing concerns about the impact of the TRIPS Agreement on access to medicines as a human rights issue.

This in turn led to NGOs originally versed in human rights law to engage to a greater extent with the technical aspects of patent law. They began initiating pre-grant patent oppositions against pharmaceutical product patent applications in a way these groups could not have foreseen when they originally began campaigning on human rights issues associated with HIV/AIDS some years earlier.

As NGOs in India began to use human rights to good effect in framing their arguments about the impact of IP rights on access to medicines, this in turn, contributed to a policy-making climate in which, since 2006, the Indian Government has been markedly more receptive to concerns

---

[28] Justice V.R Krishna Iyer, Justice O. Chinnappa Reddy, Justice D.A. Desai and Justice Rajinder Sachar.

[29] *Vincent v. Union of India* (AIR 1987 SC 990).

raised by NGOs on these issues. By framing the issue in terms of human rights, NGOs are of the opinion that their viewpoints are now taken more seriously by the Indian Government.

CONCLUSION

This chapter has sought to demonstrate that the extent that human rights have been used by NGOs seeking to highlight the adverse impacts of IP rights on access to medicines is far greater than was previously thought.

This human rights-based approach first came to prominence a decade ago when international NGOs began to frame IP-related issues by using the emotive language of human rights to underpin substantive arguments that public health, access to medicines, the right to health and the right to life were at risk due to the patent provisions of the TRIPS Agreement. International NGOs began to campaign for access to medicines through the full utilisation of flexibilities contained in the TRIPS Agreement and framed the issue in terms of human rights. By so doing, the human rights frame ultimately added moral authority to the access to medicines campaign, which in turn contributed to a greater emphasis on the importance of using inbuilt flexibilities in the TRIPS Agreement and the need to permanently amend of the TRIPS Agreement provisions on compulsory licensing.

However, while the strategy of international NGOs in framing the access to medicines campaign as a human rights issue has been recognised widely, rather less attention has been paid to the parallel activities of NGOs that have been using similar human rights-based approaches in developing countries. NGOs representing people living with HIV/AIDS in South Africa, for instance, have used strategies that had worked previously to such good effect during the anti-apartheid struggle and highlighted primacy of human rights principles under the country's constitution. In *Minister of Health & Others v. Treatment Action Campaign & Others*, human rights principles enshrined in the South African Constitution were used to overturn the decision of the South African Government's refusal to make Nevirapine available in the public health sector and to set out a timeframe for a national programme to prevent MTCT of HIV.

Similarly, following the ending of military rule in Brazil, NGO activists used their knowledge of human rights acquired during the struggle for democracy to campaign successfully for universal access to ARVs for people living with HIV/AIDS. This belief in the primacy of human rights, particularly the right to health enshrined in the Brazilian Constitution, impacted subsequently on the decision of NGOs to mobilise in support of the Brazilian Government in its attempts to achieve a balance between the patents for pharmaceutical products and the right to health through the compulsory licensing provisions of federal law. Those provisions were subject to a US complaint to the WTO and in turn led to sustained and detailed engagement with issues relating to patents, public health and access to medicines on the part of the Brazilian NGO community.

Human rights have also played an important role in defining the way that Indian NGOs have engaged with the impact of IP rights on the poor, the disadvantaged and vulnerable sectors of society. When India's struggle for independence from British colonial rule ended in 1947, human rights and in particular the right to life enshrined in the Indian Constitution formed the basis of the Ayyangar Committee's recommendation that granting patents in critical areas such as food and medicines be curtailed. The committee's reasoning for this recommendation was that the prohibitively high price of patented products could violate the right to life. This human rights approach in turn informed the subsequent approach of NGOs working to ensure that amendments to India's patent's legislation utilised to the full extent flexibilities contained in the TRIPS Agreement. In the post-TRIPS implementation period, as other NGOs become involved with patents and access to medicines issues, it was once again an underlying concern that the human rights of people living with HIV/AIDS were being abused which informed their approach. This led NGOs originally versed in human rights law to engage to a greater extent with the technical aspects of patent law, particularly by initiating pre-grant patent opposition proceedings against pharmaceutical product patent applications in a way that they could not have foreseen when they originally began campaigning on human rights issues associated with HIV/AIDS some years earlier.

Over the past decade, therefore, NGOs have played a critical role in reappraising the relationship between intellectual property and access to medicines through the frame of human rights principles in a range of ways that will continue to have profound implications for many years to come.

BIBLIOGRAPHY

Abbott, F. M. (2005), 'The 'Rule of Reason' and the Right to Health: Integrating Human Rights and Competition Principles in the Context of TRIPS, in Cottier, T., Pauwelyn, J. and Bűrgi, E. (eds.) *Human Rights and International Trade*, Oxford: Oxford University Press, 279–300.

AIDS Law Project (2007), *18-Month Review: January 2006 to June 2007*, Johannesburg and Cape Town, South Africa: AIDS Law Project, http://www.alp.org.za/pdf/Publications/ALP%20Annual%20Reviews/ALP_2006-2007_Review.pdf.

Boulle, J. and Avafia, T. (2005), *Treatment Action Campaign (TAC) Evaluation*, http://www.tac.org.za/Documents/FinalTACEvaluation-AfaviaAndBoulle-20050701.pdf.

Braithwaite, J. and Drahos, P. (2000), *Global Business Regulation*, Cambridge: Cambridge University Press.

Chaudhuri, S. (2005), *The WTO and India's Pharmaceuticals Industry: Patent Protection, TRIPS and Developing Countries*, New Delhi: Oxford University Press.

Cohen, J.C. and Lybecker, K.M. (2005), 'AIDS policy and pharmaceutical patents: Brazil's strategy to safeguard public health', *World Economy*, 28(2): 211–30.

Daz, K. (2003), 'The Domestic Politics of TRIPS: Pharmaceutical Interests, Public Health, and NGO Influence in India,' Paper prepared for the Research Project on 'Linking the WTO to the Poverty-Reduction Agenda', Part of the DFID-Funded Globalisation and Poverty Research Programme, Gujarat Institute of Development Research, Ahmedabad, India.

Deere, C. (2008), *The Implementation Game: The TRIPS Agreement and the Global Politics of Intellectual Property Reform in Developing Countries*, Oxford and New York: Oxford University Press.

Drahos, P. (2008), Does dialogue make a difference? Structural change and the limits of framing, *The Yale Journal Pocket Part*, 117: 268–73.

Drezner, D.W. (2005), *Gauging the Power of Global Civil Society: intellectual property and public health*, mimeo.

Fourie, P. (2006), *The Political Management of HIV and AIDS in South Africa: One Burden too Many?*, Basingstoke and New York: Palgrave Macmillan.

Galvão, J. (2005), Brazil and access to HIV/AIDS Drugs: A question of human rights and public health, *American Journal of Public Health*, 95(7): 1110–6.

Halbert, D.J. (2005), *Resisting Intellectual Property*, Abingdon, Oxon and New York, NY: Routledge.

Kapczynski, A. (2008), The access to knowledge mobilization and the new politics of intellectual property, *The Yale Law Journal*, 117: 804–85.

Keayla, B.K. (2005), Amended Patents Act: A critique, *Combat Law*, 4(2), http://www.indiatogether.org/cgi-bin/tools/pfriend.cgi.

Krishna Iyer, V.R., Chinnappa Reddy, O., Desai, D.A. and Sachar, Rajinder (1996), *People's Commission on the Constitutional Implications of the Final Act Embodying the Results of the Uruguay Round of Multilateral Trade Negotiations*, New Delhi, India: Centre for Study of Global Trade System and Development.

Lang, A. (2007), The role of the human rights movement in trade policy-making: Human rights as a trigger for social learning, *New Zealand Journal of Public and International Law*, 5: 147–72.

Love, J.P. (2006), 'TRIPS, TRIPS+, and new paradigms: the role of NGOs in shaping the debate', paper prepared for the Chicago-Kent College of Law conference on *Intellectual Property, Trade and Development: Accommodating and Reconciling Different National Levels of Protection*, Chicago, Illinois, 12–13 October 2006.

Mathiharan, K. (2003), 'The fundamental right to health care', *Indian Journal of Medical Ethics*, October–December, 11(4).

Matthews, D. (2002), *Globalising Intellectual Property Rights: the TRIPS Agreement*, London and New York: Routledge.

Matthews, D. (2004), 'The WTO decision on implementation of paragraph 6 of the Doha Declaration on the TRIPS Agreement and Public Health: A solution to the access to essential medicines problem?', *Journal of International Economic Law* 7, 1: 73–107.

Mbali, M. (2005), The Treatment Action Campaign and the History of Rights-Based, Patient-Driven HIV/AIDS Activism in South Africa, Research Report No. 29, University of Kwazulu-Natal Centre for Civil Society, http://ccs.ukzn.ac.za/files/RReport_29.pdf.

de Mello e Souza, A. (2005), The Power of the Weak: Advocacy Networks, Ideational Change and the Global Politics of Pharmaceutical Patent Rights, unpublished doctoral thesis, Stanford University.

Odell, J.S. and Sell, S.K. (2006), 'Reframing the issue: The WTO coalition on intellectual property and public health, 2001', in Odell, J.S. (ed.) *Negotiating Trade: Developing Countries in the WTO and NAFTA*, Cambridge: Cambridge University Press, pp. 85–114.

Orbinski, James. (2008), *An Imperfect Offering: Dispatches from the Medical Frontline*, London: Rider Books/Ebury Publishing/Random House.

Ragavan, S. (2006), Of the inequals of the Uruguay Round, *Marquette Intellectual Property Review*, **10**(2): 273–304.

Raghavan, C. (2001) *US to Withdraw TRIPS Dispute against Brazil*, *South-North Development Monitor* (SUNS). Available at: http://www.twnside.org.sg/title/withdraw.htm.

Rangnekar, D. (2005), No Pills for Poor People? Understanding the Disembowelment of India's Patent Regime, *CSGR Working Paper No. 176/05*, University of Warwick: Centre for the Study of Globalisation and Regionalisation.

Rosina, M.S.G., Wang, D. and de Campos, T.C. (2008), Access to Medicines: Pharmaceutical Patents and the Right to Health, in Shaver, L. (ed.) *Access to Knowledge in Brazil: New Research on Intellectual Property, Innovation and Development*, New Haven, CT: Information Society Project, Yale Law School, 166–214.

Schultz, M.F. and Walker, D.B. (2006), The new international intellectual property agenda, in *Are Intellectual Property Rights Human Rights?* Washington DC: The Federalist Society for Law and Public Policy Studies.

Sell, S.K. (2003), *Private Power, Public Law: The Globalization of Intellectual Property Rights*, Cambridge and New York: Cambridge University Press.

Sell, S.K. and May, C. (2001), Moments in law: Contestation and settlement in the history of intellectual property, *Review of International Political Economy*, **8**(3): 467–500.

Shadlen, K. (2009), The politics of patents and drugs in Brazil and Mexico: The industrial bases of health policies', *Comparative Politics*, **42**(1): 41–58.

SIDA (2001), AIDS: The Challenge of this Century – Prevention, Care and Impact Mitigation, Swedish International Development Cooperation Agency Report.

Smallman, S. (2007), *The AIDS Pandemic in Latin America*, Chapel Hill: The University of North Carolina Press.

Távora dos Santos Filho, E. (2000), 'Real challenges for real actors: the role of advocacy and activism in the fight against AIDS in Brazil', *Sexual Health Exchange*, Issue 4, http://www.kit.nl/ils/exchange_content/html/2000_4_real_challenges_asp?.

UNAIDS (2008), *Report on the global AIDS epidemic.* Geneva, Switzerland: UNAIDS.

de Waal, A. (2006), *AIDS and Power: why there is no political crisis – yet*, London & New York: Zed Books.
Watal, J. (2001), *Intellectual Property Rights in the WTO and Developing Countries*, The Hague, Netherlands: Kluwer Law International.

2. Issues and strategies of China IP protection after the TRIPS Agreement

Lifang Dong

1. THE CURRENT SITUATION RELATING TO THE IMPLEMENTATION OF THE TRIPS AGREEMENT IN CHINA

1.1 The Influence of the TRIPS Agreement on Chinese IP Law

On December 11, 2001, China formally joined the World Trade Organization (WTO).

According to WTO basic rules, a member state must accept the "Agreement on Trade-Related Aspects of Intellectual Property Rights" (TRIPS), which is the most comprehensive international agreement on intellectual property to date. When China entered the WTO, it promised to "wholly comply with the WTO Agreement, by way of changing the existing national law and promulgating new legislation, thus implementing the WTO Agreement in an effective and unified way". To this end, and in order to comply with the requirements of the TRIPS Agreement, China has substantially changed its national legislation on intellectual property law, in particular the China Patent Law, China Trademark Law, and China Copyright Law.

1.1.1 Amendment of the China Patent Law

On March 12, 1984, China promulgated the China Patent Law (Patent Law), which entered into force on April 1, 1985. At that time, the law complied, to a moderate degree, with the system of the Paris Convention for the Protection of Industrial Property. On September 4, 1992, China revised the Patent Law for the first time, a revision that became effective on January 1, 1993, when China was the observer of the General Agreement on Tariffs and Trade (GATT) held in the Uruguay Round. In 1994, during the negotiations, TRIPS came into being. On August 25, 2000, after China decided to join the WTO, the Patent Law was amended a second time, with that amendment entering into force on July 1, 2001. On December 27, 2008, China revised the Patent Law for the third time, with the revision coming into effect on October 1, 2009. Several changes of the China Patent Law reduced the slight discrepancies from the international standard, mainly in relation to the following:

A) The third revision of the China Patent Law further specified the scope of protection of the exclusive rights of the patent owner. This protection was introduced in the second revision of the Patent Law by establishing "the promise of the right to sell or import the patented product or the promise of the right to sell or import the product directly obtained from the patented process for production or business purposes" (section 11 of the third revision of the Patent Law). In this way the patent owner can seek damages for infringement of its exclusive patent rights, even if the damage has not yet occurred, as long as a third party exploits his patent without his permission.
B) In accordance with section 50 of TRIPS, the new law further detailed the "provisional measures" that were introduced in the second revision of the Patent Law, that is, property preservation and evidence preservation measures required before the patent owner brings a lawsuit to the Chinese Court (section 66 of the China Patent Law).
C) The new law maintained the provision that clarifies that a person shall not be considered liable for infringement of patent rights when he can prove that the product was obtained from a legal source (section 70 of the third revision of the Patent Law), which conforms with section 45 TRIPS.
D) In accordance with TRIPS, the new law maintained the provision added by the second revision of the Patent Law that allows an applicant who is not satisfied with the administrative decision of the Patent Re-examination Board to bring an action before the Chinese Court for a judicial review (section 41 of the third revision of the Patent Law).

1.1.2 Amendment of China Trademark Law

The China Trademark Law, which entered into force on March 1, 1983, was revised for the first time in 1993 and for the second time in 2001. In order to comply with the rapid economic change of the Chinese market, the current Trademark Law is under review for the third time, a revision should be promulgated in late 2013. This chapter, therefore, only addresses the current second revision of the Trademark Law, as follows:

A) The second revision of the China Trademark Law extended the subjects entitled to exercise trademark rights in line with the principle of national treatment of TRIPS. In fact, section 4 provides that Chinese individuals who are registered at the State Administration of Industry and Commerce (SAIC) may file trademarks and obtain exclusive trademark rights, as can foreign individuals.

B) The second revision of the Trademark Law extended the scope of protection. Besides the filing of trademarks and service marks, the new law has introduced the filing of three-dimensional trademarks, collective trademarks, and certification marks, so that the protection of trademarks has been improved.

C) The second amendment has also inserted a provision for the protection of well-known trademarks in conformity with the Paris Convention and TRIPS. Indeed, section 13 of the second revision of the Trademark Law expressly provides that the protection of a well-known trademark extends to include non-identical or non-similar classes of products and services whether or not the owner has already registered the well-known trademark in China. In addition, section 14 provides that a judge should take into account the following five factors in order to determine whether a trademark is well known:

   1. How well is that trademark known by the relevant public;
   2. The period during which that trademark has been in use;
   3. The period, extent and geographic scope of any publicity of that trademark;
   4. The record of protection of that trademark as a well-known trademark; and
   5. Other factors for which that trademark is well-known.

   This provision not only facilitates the judicial system, but also encourages enterprises to be aware of the concept of trademarks.

D) The second revision has also included protection of a product's geographical indication. Whereas TRIPS provides that the geographical indication is intangible property, section 16 of the second revision of the Trademark Law further specifies that:

   > if a trademark contains the geographic indication of the goods while the products do not come from the region indicated by that mark, and thus misleading the public, the trademark shall not be registered and shall be prohibited from use; however, those that have been registered in good faith shall continue to be valid.

E) The second revision of the Trademark Law stresses the "prior right" and deletes the subjective factor of the person who infringes the prior right. In 1993, the China Trademark Implementing Regulations relied on the prior right, but only the person "who obtained the registration through artifice or other means" can be sued for infringement of the prior right of the rightful owner. This subjective factor of the person who infringes does not comply with TRIPS, and the second revision of the Trademark Law deleted this requirement. In fact, section 9 of the second amendment expressly sets forth that "a trademark registration application shall not be in conflict with prior rights lawfully acquired by another person", whereas section 31 provides that, "[A]n application for the registration of a trademark shall not create any prejudice to the prior right of another person, nor unfair means be used to pre-emptively register the trademark of some reputation another person has used."

1.1.2.1. The third revision of the China Trademark Law of 2013 After two years of consultations, on August 30, 2013 the Standing Committee of the National People's Congress promulgated the third amendment to the Trademark Law of the People's Republic of China, which will enter into force on May 1, 2014.[1]

This chapter will analyze the principal innovations[2] introduced by the third revision above, as follows:

A) In compliance with international common practice, section 8 of the third revision opens the door to a new type of non-traditional trademark, i.e. *sounds marks*, whereas single colours, scents and moving images are not registerable. In addition, the third amendment inserts a new section 10 that explicitly provides signs identical with or similar to the *national anthem*, *military emblem*, *military song* of the People's Republic of China, or identical with the *names or symbols* of China's

---

1 Please find the official text in Chinese of the *Trademark Law of the People's Republic of China* (as amended up to Decision of August 30, 2013) at http://www.wipo.int/wipolex/en/details.jsp?id=13198.

2 Concerning the significant changes to PRC Trademark Law, see, inter alia, the following interesting legal opinions: "*Latest draft of revised Chinese Trademark Law released for public comment*", in *World Trademark Review*, April/May 2013 – also available on line at: www.WorldTrademarkReview.com; LOU Cecilia and DING Xianjie, "*China: Five Issues You should be Aware of in the Latest Draft of the Revision of PRC Trademark Law*", March 9, 2013, available at http://www.mondaq.com; HUANG Hui and RANJARD Paul, "*Trademark Law Revision: More Work Needed*", in *Managing Intellectual Property*, March 1, 2012, available on line at http://www.managingip.com.

central organizations of the State or the Party, cannot be used or registered as trademarks.

B) In order to improve the efficiency and economy of trademarks filings, this third new amendment provides for electronic filing of trademark applications as well as multiclass filings (section 22 of the third revision). Therefore, it will be possible to file one registration application for a trademark covering multiple classes, with a considerable decrease of the costs for trademark owners. Conversely, under the current law, one trademark application can protect a trademark only in respect of one class of goods or services, so if an applicant is willing to register the same trademark in more than one class, he has to file separate applications with the Chinese Trademark Office (CTO), paying separate fees for each application.

C) The third revision introduces significant innovations to the opposition procedure, as follows:

1. In order to avoid oppositions in bad faith against any third-party registration, the third revision strictly limits the opposing party and the grounds for their opposition. The current legislation establishes that any party could oppose any trademark on any grounds (i.e., absolute ground or relative ground). According to the section 33 of the third amendment, only prior rights owners or other interested parties will be entitled to file an opposition against the registration of a trademark with the CTO on a relative ground before the trademark is registered. The legal ground of the opposition will be based only on the fact that the registration of the trademark might infringe the prior right of the opposing party. These changes will reduce the number of opposition cases and contribute to solve the unfaithful opposition problem;
2. Moreover, this revision eliminates the opposition appeals. In fact, according to section 35, once an unfavorable opposition decision has been issued by the CTO and the trademark has been registered, the said decision will have immediate effect. Thus, the opposing party can only file a cancellation with the TRAB, rather than an appeal (as it is currently the case);
3. The third amendment extends the deadlines to appeal to TRAB from 15 days to 30 days.

D) This third revision introduces also important changes to strengthen civil and administrative *enforcement procedures*, increasing penalties and damages against infringement acts. These innovations are the following:

1. Administrative Fines and Penalties (section 60 of the third revision). Under the current law, local Administrations for Industry and Commerce (AICs) discretionally impose fines up to five times the "illegal business amount" or total revenue of the infringer. When this amount is difficult to determine, statutory fines up to RMB 100,000.00 may be imposed. However, in practice, these fines rarely reach the higher ranges, while the statutory fines are rarely applied at all. Section 60 of the third amendment effectively increases statutory fines up to RMB 250,000.00 by allowing fines up to this amount even in cases where there is no evidence of prior sales by the infringer or the total illegal revenues reach as high as RMB 50,000.00.
2. Increased statutory civil damages and burden of proof (section 63 of the third amendment). The current section 56 of the China Trademark Law of 2001 states that the amount of actual damages for a trademark infringement can be the benefits gained by the infringer (Illegal Benefits), or the losses suffered by the right holder (Actual Losses) during the period of infringement as a result of the infringement. If both the Illegal Benefits and the Actual Losses are difficult to calculate, the court may at its own discretion award damages in the amount up to RMB 500,000.00 ("Statutory Damages"). Under the third revision, in addition to the Illegal Benefits and the Actual Losses, the actual damages can be calculated by reference to the amount of royalty payment. Moreover, the amount of the Statutory Damages is increased from yuan RMB 500,000.00 to RMB 3,000.000.00.
3. With regard to the burden of proving the damages suffered by the trademark's owner, the third revision introduces a presumption in favor of the trademark owner's damages claims in the case of the defendant failing to file evidence of its prior transactions or providing false documentation. The China People's Court is now empowered to request the infringer to provide its accounting books or other information relevant to the trademark infringement. If the latter refuses to comply with the above request, the China People's Court shall order the infringer to compensate the damages claimed by the right holder.

1.1.3 Amendment of the China Copyright Law

China promulgated its Copyright Law in 1991. In 2001, China joined the WTO and revised its Copyright Law for the first time, mainly with respect to the following nine points: 1) the principle of "national treatment"; 2) the scope of protection; 3) the conformity of the copyright law; 4) the restrictions of the copyright law in line with international standards; 5) the improvement of copyright-related rights; 6) the establishment of "collective management" of the copyright; 7) the "assignment" of the copyright; 8) the improvement of the copyright law protection; and 9) copyright protection relating to new technology.

In 2007, the United States of America (USA) sued China before the WTO in order to settle a dispute arising out of an issue relating to access to the publication market. The USA believed that the Chinese Government was examining the content of only some works, thus leaving no opportunity for punishment in relation to many other works that have been infringed in China. For example, even though some movie and television works had not yet passed the examination process lead by the Chinese Government and lawful audio and video appliances were prevented from entering the Chinese market, pirated editions of compact discs were circulating in China. The American owners of the copyright-related rights had no grounds to punish these acts of infringement because the China Copyright Law of 2001 provided that "the publication or dissemination of works, which are prohibited by the law, shall not be protected by this Law". On March 20, 2009, WTO ruled on the case brought by the USA against China for the protection of intellectual property law and its implementation. The ruling was in favor of China. The USA brought before the WTO experts a total of seven charges, but only two of them were accepted. The main content of these two charges was that section 4 of the China Copyright Law violated "the Berne Convention for the Protection of Literary and Artistic Works" (Berne Convention) and the TRIPS Agreement.

As a consequence, China revised its Copyright Law in 2010 for the second time and completely changed three provisions, among them section 4, which was revised in line with Berne Convention and the TRIPS Agreement. Section 4 now provides that, "when the copyright owner exercises the copyright, he shall neither violate the Constitution and the law, nor damage the public interest. The State shall supervise and manage the publication and dissemination of works".

1.1.3.1 Towards a third amendment of the China Copyright Law In order to improve the coherency of the China Copyright Law and strengthen the position of copyrights owners, the National Copyright Administration of China (NCAC) officially issued three proposals for the revision of the third amendment of the China Copyright Law. The first two drafts[3] were both

[3] *"Notice of the National Copyright Administration on Publicly Soliciting Opinions on the Copyright Law of the People's Republic of China (Revised Draft)"*

publicly submitted for opinions and suggestions from all sectors of society, while the third one, released in October 2012, has only been presented to the State Council Legislative Affairs Office for further legal comments; it will then be confidentially submitted to the Standing Committee of China National People's Congress for the final content of China Copyright Law. The following points highlight the most significant changes by comparing the second and third revised drafts;[4]

- Both drafts extend the scope of copyrightable works by introducing the independent new category of "works of applied art", referring to works of art that have a practical use and are of aesthetic significance,[5] without any protection under the existing law. However, with regard to the scope of protection, contrary to the second draft, the third draft introduces the following important innovations: A) the substitution of the terms "cinematographic work and works expressed by a process analogous to cinematographic works" for one single term: the audiovisual works;[6] and B) the introduction of a new definition of "Computer Programs" as "the instruction expressed by either source program or object program that is used with computers or other information solution devices";

---

officially released by the National Copyright Administration on March 31, 2012; "*Notice of the National Copyright Administration on Publicly Soliciting Opinions on the Copyright Law of the People's Republic of China (Second Revised Draft)*", promulgated by the National Copyright Administration on July 6, 2012 and submitted for public comments, both available on the westlaw database. Please also find relevant comments in the following articles: "*NCAC's Explanations on the Draft of 3rd Revision of Copyright Law*", March 31, 2012, at http://www.ncac.gov.cn/cms/html/309/3502/201203/740608.html; XUE Hong, "*One Step Ahead Two Steps Back: Reverse Engineering 2nd Draft for 3rd Revision of the Chinese Copyright Law*", in *Digital Commons @ American University Washington College of Law. PIJIP-Research Paper Series Program on Information Justice and Intellectual Property*, January 7, 2012, available at: http://digitalcommons.wcl.american.edu/research; "*NCAC's Explanations on the 2nd Draft of 3rd Revision of Copyright Law*", July 6, 2012, at http://www.ncac.gov.cn/cms/html/309/3517/201207/759867.html.

[4] For further legal comments on the third draft revision of the China Copyright Law please see: FENG Chao and RANJARD Paul, "*Final draft of proposed PRC Copyright Law amendment released by NCAC*", January 7, 2013, available at http://www.lexology.com.

[5] Article 3, par. 9 of 2nd Draft.

[6] This new terminology is in line with the provisions of Article 12 of the *Beijing Treaty on Audiovisual Performances* adopted by the Diplomatic Conference of the World Intellectual Property Organization on June 24, 2012.

- Concerning the exploitation of the audiovisual works and distribution of profits, the second draft submits the exploitation above to the authorization from both the owner of the audiovisual work and the owners of its components; therefore the authors of such component works enjoy the right of authorship and remuneration. In order to strengthen the protection of the copyright's owners of component works, the third draft specifies that an agreement between the producer of the audiovisual work and the authors of the component works will determine both rights (authorship and remuneration). In the absence of a clear agreement, the authors of the component works shall enjoy a "reasonable remuneration" deriving from the exploitation of the audiovisual work. The third draft also provides that the author of those component works enjoys the exclusive right to his own work embodied in the audiovisual work unless it is stipulated otherwise in the agreement.
- The third draft introduces an important restriction to the employer's exclusive right to use the works created by the employees. In fact, contrary to the second draft, which provided that the employer enjoys the right to use the works made by the employee without paying any fees, the new draft limits the employer's exclusive right for a period of two years. In particular, the draft authorizes the employer, only during the employment relationship, to exclude others, including the authors, from using the work during the two-year period, in exchange of a reward in favor of the employee-author.
- The third draft also contains significant provisions on widely discussed "Orphan Works", i.e., any picture, book or creative endeavor where the author is unknown or untraceable, especially with regard to the creation of a digital library. Under the second draft, the copyright in an orphan work, except for the right of attribution, may be exercised by the owner of an original of the work.[7] The new third draft removes "the owner of an original of the works" from the list of right owners, providing that if the copyright owner is unidentifiable after a diligent search on the original authorship of the work, this work can be used in digital form with the payment of a fee to the NCAC, who carry out the above-mentioned search.
- With regard to the "Fair-Use", the second draft[8] provided a series of circumstances in which a work might be used without permission of the copyright owner and without payment of a remuneration,

---

[7] Article 25, 26 of 2nd Draft.
[8] Article 42 of 2nd Draft

as follows: (1) for the purpose of school education or scientific research; (2) for the purpose of non-profit use by blind persons or (3) for the purpose of public work by administrative or judicial organs. The new draft adds the following two circumstances as fair-use, if it is for (1) research of encryption or (2) reverse engineering of a computer program.

1.2 The Status of the China IP Law Within BRIC Countries

BRIC is an acronym that refers to Brazil, the Russian Federation, India, and China. Because the acronym sounds like the English wording "brick", the Chinese define the four countries as "Jinzhuang Siguo", i.e., "Gold brick four countries".

As far back as 1994, India, Brazil, and other developing countries' representatives (other than China) were against the TRIPS Agreement. In fact they believed that GATT had jurisdiction over the trade liberalization of tangible property, but the rules for the protection of intellectual property (IP) rights and their implementation fell within the scope of protection of the World Intellectual Property Organization (WIPO). Therefore, the prevention of the trade of counterfeit goods should be kept separate from the extensive protection of IP rights. Moreover, if developing countries bore the same obligations as developed countries with respect to the most recent and advanced technology, the former would lose the possibility of setting up systems of IP protection that took into account their own societies and levels of economic development. In addition, a protection standard that was too high would place a serious burden of financial and administrative responsibility on developing countries. Currently, India, Brazil, and the Russian Federation still rely on domestic policy protection to evade the TRIPS Agreement. For example, the Brazilian Government has canceled the patent protection for medicines against AIDS, allowing domestic pharmaceutical factories that have not yet obtained patent protection to produce and sell these medicines; the Russian Federation has imitated patented medicines extensively, therefore its national law is not really being implemented; and India has abolished the license of medicines' main patented components and recognizes only the method of manufacturing, thus allowing pharmaceutical factories to use the main component of patented medicines to manufacture large quantities of not yet patented medicines. Consequently, these countries have a low level of IP protection.

On the other hand, China holds a positive attitude on this matter. After its entry into the WTO, China was willing to improve its export environment in order to expand its exports. China also enjoys the status of a member of the WTO, and over 100 member states of the WIPO have accorded to China most-favored-nation trading status. Furthermore, with regard to most-favored-nation trading status, China will not encounter annual criticism by the USA if it improves the export environment and expands its exports. The customs duty that should originally comply with the provisions of the bilateral agreements conversely enjoys a generalized system of preferences. For example, textile products enjoy no quota restrictions. Secondly, entrance to the WTO is advantageous for China in that it allows China to participate in global competition under equal rules as well as being beneficial for the development of the socialist market economy. After the implementation of national treatment of foreign investors, there has been an improvement in the investment environment, an increase of foreign capital and the enterprises' management level, technology and living conditions. China's entry into the WTO has been beneficial and in particular has improved the industrial and economic structure, promoting the Open Door Policy[9] and thus cultivating the system of the socialist market economy and improving the Chinese population's living conditions. To this end, the Chinese Government has always energetically supported its entry into the WTO by changing its domestic law to conform to the TRIPS Agreement requirements. Currently, with respect to the level of protection of intellectual property rights, China has a leading position among the four BRIC countries. The level of protection of IP rights in China is almost the same as that in developed countries, and in some respects China's level of IP protection has surpassed even that of developed countries.

1.3 The Current Situation Relating to the Protection of IP Rights in China

China has been a member of the WTO for more than ten years, and the laws and regulations relating to IP have seen significant developments. On April 21, 2011, the China State Council News Bureau held a conference entitled "2010 the China intellectual property protection situation". The participants included the Director of the State Intellectual Property Office of the People's Republic of China (SIPO), the Director of the State Administration for Industry & Commerce of the People's Republic

[9] The "Open Door Policy" refers to Deng Xiaoping's economic reforms launched in 1978, when he opened the door to foreign businesses who wanted to set up in China, considering that the Country needed Western technology and foreign investments to modernize its economic system.

of China (SAIC), the Section Chief of the Head Office of the News and Publication Bureau, and the Vice Director of the National Copyright Administration of the People's Republic of China (NCA), who explained to the worldwide media the current situation regarding the protection of intellectual property in China.

First, the Chinese Government challenged foreigners' beliefs that IP protection in China is unsuccessful or that there is still a discrepancy between the law and its implementation.

In reality, the Chinese Government, compared with other countries, takes the protection of IP seriously, putting a lot of effort into strengthening its protection. In this regard, Mr. Tian Lipu, director of SIPO, firmly stated that:

> [T]he Chinese government including the judicial system is taking active anti-counterfeiting actions against the infringement of intellectual property rights; on the other hand, the Chinese government is fully aware of the fact that in certain geographical areas, industrial areas and classes of products the phenomenon of the violation of intellectual property rights is increasing dramatically.

However, since the Open Door Policy, China has significantly improved the implementation of IP rights. For instance, in 2010, the Criminal Court heard 3992 criminal cases and issued 3942 judgments involving 6001 persons, 6000 of whom were convicted of crimes. For civil cases enforcement is even more significant, in 2010 the Civil Court received 42931 cases, an increase of 40 percent.[10]

In October 2010, the Chinese Premier Mr Wen Jiabao stated that:

> many cases of violation of intellectual property rights involve foreign parties, in particular the foreign offenders bring counterfeited samples to China, ordering Chinese manufacturers to produce locally counterfeited products, then to export them to foreign countries for sale. This is an actual issue that passes through the control and examination of Chinese Customs.

Secondly, on April 20, 2011, the Chinese Government announced the beginning of IP propaganda activities to increase the awareness of IP throughout society and to spread the culture of intellectual property.

Also the courts, following the key tasks determined by the central government, pursued judicial activism in particular in adjudicating IP matters. In fact, in 2011, civil hearing was a dominant method for IP protection.

---

[10] *"White Paper of Intellectual Property Protection by Chinese Courts in 2010 released"*, available on line at: http://www.cpahkltd.com/UploadFiles/20110509082512655.pdf.

The percentage of civil IP cases of first instance concluded within time limit increased from 97.93 percent in 2010 to 98.57 percent in 2011.[11]

With respect to trademark law, China's Twelfth Five-Year Plan of Trademark Strategy, the "Shi er wu", has comprehensively increased the level of trademark registration, use, protection, and management, strengthened the legislation, and improved the trademark legal system. In fact, the State Council has already included the third revision of the Trademark Law in the schedule of the works in 2011 that has been promulgated on August 30, 2013, and will be effective on May 1, 2014. Therefore, under the third revision, a trademark examination will be carried out within nine months, and the re-examination of a trademark case will be performed within nine months. Consequently, after the end of the Twelfth Five-Year Plan of Trademark Strategy, China will have effectively increased the number of registered trademarks to 8 million, hence continuing to maintain a leading position worldwide.

The number of IP cases has increased substantially in 2012, particularly significant is the double increase in the number of criminal cases. As for the first instance IP cases accepted in 2012, there were 87419 civil cases, 45.99 percent more than 2011; 2928 administrative cases, 20.35 per cent more than 2011; and 13104 criminal cases, 129.61 percent more than 2011.[12]

2. THE ISSUES THAT CHINA SHOULD TAKE INTO ACCOUNT AFTER THE TRIPS AGREEMENT

2.1 The Influence of the TRIPS-plus Agreement in China

In recent years, efforts to improve the standard of protection of IP have turned from multilateral negotiations to regional or bilateral agreements or agreements on the protection of investments. The USA and the EU have played a key role in this development by using the "elastic clause" of the TRIPS Agreement to encourage developing countries to adopt a higher level of protection of IP while market access and transnational investments have become more and more attractive. In such circumstances, the developing countries, to a certain extent, were arguably forced

[11] *"White Paper of Intellectual Property Protection by Chinese Courts in 2011"*, available on line at: http://www.iam-magazine.com/files/People's%20Supreme%20Court%20Intellectual%20Property%20Protection%20in%20China.pdf.

[12] *"IP Protection by Chinese Courts in 2012"*, available on line at:http://chinaipr2.files.wordpress.com/2013/04/ip-protection-by-chinese-courts-in-2012_en.pdf.

by developed countries to sign Free Trade Agreements (FTAs), which included provisions for the improvement of the standard of protection of IP. As a consequence, because many of the new provisions added into the FTAs surpassed the standard of protection of the TRIPS Agreement, they were referred to as TRIPS-plus Agreements (TRIPS-plus).

The TRIPS-plus Agreement expands and exceeds the requirements of protection laid down by the TRIPS Agreement, in some cases revising and even overturning the TRIPS Agreement. The TRIPS-plus Agreement not only further elaborates on the content of the TRIPS Agreement, but it also attempts to improve the standard of protection of the IP of the contracting countries by significantly enhancing their legislative and the judicial systems. The standard of the TRIPS-plus Agreement is based on the lowest degree of protection set forth by the TRIPS Agreement, which firmly established an even lower level for the standard of protection of IP. In other words, the TRIPS-plus Agreement sets forth a higher standard of protection than the standard of protection provided for in the TRIPS Agreement without the "elastic" provisions of the TRIPS Agreement.

Although the TRIPS-plus Agreement provides a higher level of protection of IP, it also, to some extent, heavily burdens developing countries with obligations relating to the protection of IP. In addition, the USA, the EU, and other developed countries use the TRIPS-plus Agreement indirectly to reach objectives that would not be reachable through the TRIPS Agreement.

There are not as yet any multinational agreements for the protection of investments, only bilateral FTAs, including TRIPS-plus Agreements. This is the main pattern of "TRIPS-plus" today.

Generally speaking, effective protection of IP is one of the main requirements that developed countries impose upon developing countries in the agreements for the protection of investments. To this end, the protection of IP in these agreements reflects the protection of the interests of investors as well as the protection of investments of the developed countries themselves.

In these agreements for the protection of investments, the definition of investments is "based on assets", the principles of fairness and impartial treatment, the criteria of levy and compensation, the obligation of transparency, the mechanism of resolving disputes relating to investments, and other issues. All these provisions have influenced the protection of IP and the development of the TRIPS-plus Agreement. In addition, if the developing countries sign bilateral trade agreements, the developed countries will more easily be able to apply trade sanctions against contracting countries in the event the latter violate their obligations; hence the TRIPS-plus

Agreement has become a political tool for the protection of trade and investment in IP.

The TRIPS-plus Agreement expands and restricts the TRIPS Agreement in order to improve the standard of protection of IP. This is particularly evident in the field of medicines. TRIPS-plus Agreements have negatively affected the accessibility of drugs in developing countries. China, as a developing country, should maintain a high degree of awareness, in domestic legislation and when it signs FTAs and other international conventions, of the TRIPS-plus Agreement and should be prudent in the introduction of the system of patent linkage.[13] It should also restrict the monopolization by developed countries of data protection for high technology, retain compulsory licenses, and keep the parallel importation and other privileges that are permitted by the "elastic clause" set forth by the TRIPS Agreement in order to maintain flexibility in its domestic policy.

Now that more and more developing and developed countries have signed FTAs that include the TRIPS-plus Agreement, especially in the field of protection of patented medicines, the expansion of TRIPS-plus appears inevitable. The TRIPS-plus was developed for the protection of IP, but it corrodes the existing multilateral trading system. In other words, the recent introduction of the TRIPS-plus Agreement has destroyed the original system of protection of IP set up as the foundation for the multilateral trading system by the TRIPS Agreement, which has been signed by many international contracting parties. On the other hand, the TRIPS-plus Agreement is only a bilateral agreement. The TRIPS-plus Agreement prohibits developing countries from manufacturing patented medicines in the absence of a license, purchased at great cost, from the manufacturer of that medicine in a developed country. This requirement affects not only the existence of the pharmaceutical industry in China, but also the patentability of medicines made in developing countries.

According to the American Office of the United States Trade Representative (USTR), the USA, Australia, Bahrain, Canada, Chile, Costa Rica, Israel, Jordan, and more than 20 other countries or areas have signed the FTA Agreement. Because the USA and the EU have not yet signed a bilateral FTA with China, the TRIPS-plus Agreement issues currently do not exist. However, when China concludes FTAs with the USA or the EU, it may face TRIPS-plus pressure; it is therefore necessary to

---

[13] In fact, the FTAs require that the drug inspection authorities of developing countries prohibit the registration of medicines that imitate patented medicines if the patent owner has not yet authorized their use.

analyze the TRIPS-plus Agreement to address the issues that China may face in the near future.

2.1.1 A broader scope of protection of the TRIPS-plus Agreement compared to the TRIPS Agreement

The TRIPS-plus Agreement raises the standard of protection of intellectual property in different ways, but mainly by inserting new provisions and introducing a new system of protection, thereby enlarging the scope of protection of the TRIPS Agreement. This concern is clearly evident in the comments on the provisions of the FTAs concerning, for example, the introduction of the system of the patent linkage, the monopolization of data protection for high technology, and the extension of the time limit of patent protection.

In the Chinese pharmaceutical sector, according to the national standard, SIPO (the Patent Office) decides whether the medicines have inventiveness and originality and whether they satisfy the requirements for patentability of one country, whereas the Drug Inspection Authority evaluates whether the medicines have the necessary quality, safety, and effectiveness for sale purposes. However, when a manufacturer applies to the Drug Inspection Authority to obtain authorization for the sale of medicines that imitate patented medicines, the authority does not even ascertain whether these medicines violate the interests of other patent owners; hence the process of approval for granting the authorization to sell these medicines will not be affected.

On the other hand, the TRIPS Agreement does not contain clear provisions as to whether manufacturers, applying to the drug inspection authority to obtain the authorization for the sale of medicines that imitate patented medicines before the expiry of a patent held by a third party, enjoy the right to use patented medicine rights belonging to others. In this regard, however, section 30 of the TRIPS Agreement sets forth limited exceptions that do not constitute violations of the exclusive patent rights of other owners: (i) the use in restricted quantities of medicines that imitate patented medicines for research purposes; and (ii) the prior use of the medicines as long as the use started before the patent owner applied for the registration of his medicines at state IP office.

However, many FTAs that have already been signed provide for patent linkage and for an authorization procedure for the sale of medicines. In other words, pursuant to the FTAs, both the consent of the drug inspection authority and the review of the state patent office as to whether the medicines violate the exclusive patent rights of another patent owner are necessary in order to obtain approval for the sale of medicines in a developing country. These provisions not only delayed the market entry of medicines that imitate patented medicines, but hindered the implementation of the compulsory license system that TRIPS Agreement permits.

Under the TRIPS Agreement, the government of a member state may allow manufacturers to produce medicines that imitate patented medicines by granting them a compulsory license under certain circumstances. Under the FTAs, however, not only must the medicines be registered with the drug inspection authority before their production and sale, but they must be assessed by the state patent office to determine whether they infringe the exclusive rights of other patent owners. Moreover, if prior to the expiration of the patent on patented medicines, the drug inspection authority restricts the registration of medicines that imitate patented medicines, the compulsory license cannot be even implemented.

2.1.2 The restrictions of the TRIPS-plus Agreement compared to the TRIPS Agreement

The TRIPS-plus Agreement has not only expanded the effectiveness and the scope of protection of the TRIPS Agreement, but it has also achieved an even stronger level of protection of IP by restricting the rights that had been enjoyed by the member states of TRIPS.

The TRIPS Agreement permits the use of the compulsory license, allowing the governments of developing countries to use patents of other rights owners temporarily, such as when national or extreme emergencies occur, and authorizing the production of medicines that imitate patented medicines to promote access to affordable medicines in the interest of public health.

In this regard, in 2001, the Doha Declaration reaffirmed that "*the TRIPS Agreement does not and should not prevent Members from taking measures to protect public health*", namely, that WTO Members retain the right to make full use of the safeguard provisions of the TRIPS Agreement in order to protect public health and enhance access to medicines in developing countries. In fact, the Doha Declaration refers to several aspects of TRIPS, including the right to grant compulsory licenses and the freedom to determine the grounds upon which licenses are granted, the right to determine what constitutes a national emergency and circumstances of extreme urgency, and the freedom to establish the regime of exhaustion of IP rights. Therefore, TRIPS clearly permits developing countries to use broadly the "elastic clause" in order to protect public health and enhance access to medicines in their countries.

However, in the time since the implementation of the TRIPS Agreement, the USA, through the FTAs, has instead started to restrict the "elastic clause" lawfully allowed by TRIPS. In particular, the FTAs have restricted the use of the compulsory license by inserting a provision concerning the monopolization of data protection for high technology and have limited the freedom to determine the grounds upon which compulsory licenses may be granted and used by developing countries.

Generally speaking, developed countries charge very high royalties to developing countries for the right to sell patented high technology. Patent owners in developed countries would not in any case license to manufacturers of poor countries the right to produce such high technology. Hence, developing countries pay excessive consideration to developed countries in order to sell patented high technology.

Parallel importation is the importation without the consent of the patent holder of a patented product marketed in another country either by the patent holder or with the patent holder's consent. The principle of exhaustion states that once a patent holder, or any party authorized by him, has sold a patented product, he cannot prohibit the subsequent resale of that product because the original sale exhausts his rights with respect to that market. Provision 6 of the TRIPS Agreement explicitly states that practices relating to parallel importation cannot be challenged under the WTO dispute settlement system. In addition, the Doha Declaration has reaffirmed that member states do have this right, stating that each member is free to establish its own regime for such exhaustion without challenge; therefore parallel importation does not violate the TRIPS Agreement. In other words, it is very unlikely that contracting states will be in agreement on this issue, so they prefer not to address it.

Because many patented products are sold at different prices in different markets, the rationale for parallel importation is to enable the importation of lower-priced patented products. Parallel importation can be an important tool in enabling access to affordable medicines, because there are substantial price differences for the same pharmaceutical product sold in different markets.

However, in recent years the USA, through FTAs, has restricted and to some extent even forbidden parallel importation. This will certainly damage the interests of developing countries, because the latter will not be able to implement parallel importation in order to protect public health and enhance domestic access to medicines.

2.2 The Issues that China Should Take into Account when Signing the TRIPS-plus Agreement

Considering the previous paragraphs, it is obvious that the USA and the EU use the TRIPS-plus Agreement as a political tool and that the developed countries indirectly use the FTAs, including the TRIPS-plus Agreement, as a means of obtaining benefits that it would not be possible to obtain through the TRIPS Agreement.

For instance, the USA often offers financial aid or technological cooperation in order to convince developing countries to enter into bilateral trade agreements that contain the TRIPS-plus Agreement. However, this kind of bilateral agreement often oversteps the developing countries' needs.

On the other hand, many developing countries have accepted these TRIPS-plus provisions in order to obtain extra financial aid, as well as to avoid being included on the watch list under "Special Section 301" set forth unilaterally by the USA, but have found themselves subject to potential trade sanctions instead. In fact, the USA, when signing free trade agreements with foreign countries still continues to implement the "Special Section 301" to a certain extent; hence the developing countries that have been included on the watch list must observe the requirements for the protection of intellectual property set forth in the FTAs. In addition, if the developing countries sign individual bilateral trade agreements, the USA will be able to more easily apply trade sanctions against contracting countries in the event that the latter violate their obligations. As a result the international multilateral agreements in the field of intellectual property that have already been signed by the member states have been negatively affected by the FTAs.[14]

During the negotiation of the FTAs, the developed countries will probably continue to insist on the provision known as the "WTO additional pattern", which requires that the developing countries commit themselves to more prohibitive and stricter conditions than those set forth by the WTO. Therefore the FTAs will reaffirm an additional pattern against developing countries.

On the one hand, the developed countries will certainly require China to insert the provisions of the WTO into the FTAs as obligations which have not yet been implemented. On the other hand, the WTO Agreement does not impose any conditions of this sort upon contracting states; only countries that have concluded FTAs are subject to such restrictions.

During the negotiation of regional trade agreements or bilateral FTAs, the developed countries may introduce the Agreement on Government

---

[14] ZHANG Zhengyi, "*TRIPS-plus Agreement toward the inspiration of the policy of intellectual property*", in *Rule by law essays* (fa zhi lun cong), vol. 25, fifth weekly, September 2010, p. 65.

Procurement (GPA) in the context of the FTAs. The GPA, set out by the WTO, is a multilateral trade agreement that the member states of the WTO need not implement domestically. This agreement is therefore in line with the principle of the "most-favored-nation treatment" (MFN) set out by the WTO, that is, every time a country lowers a trade barrier or opens up a market, it has to do so for the same goods or services from all its trading partners – whether rich or poor, weak or strong.

China must be very prudent in this regard, because as a contracting state it has not yet implemented the GPA as laid down by the WTO. In addition, if China enters into an agreement with one country, for instance signs a FTA with the USA in which the GPA is a binding obligation, then China will not be able to freely choose whether to purchase goods from Russia or Europe. In fact, pursuant to the MFN treatment principle, countries cannot normally discriminate among their trading partners. When a country grants a special favor to another country, such as a lower customs duty rate for one of its products, then it has to do the same for all other WTO members. Consequently, when China purchases goods from Russia, opening up its market, it must give this special favor to all the trading partners of the WTO, including the USA and the EU, otherwise any other contracting party, such as the USA, will claim a violation of the GPA provision of the FTA. In other words, if China signs a FTA that includes a GPA provision, China would be required to give to the USA the same special favor it grants to any other contracting party of the WTO or risk infringing the principle of the MFN and having to pay damages to the USA.

Many countries have already signed FTAs. These countries will certainly refer to the previously successful experience of negotiation with other countries to impose the same conditions in their negotiations with China. In addition, these countries will try to impose upon China the "standard clause" or "classic pattern". In these circumstances, China should be especially vigilant when weighing up the pros and cons of this situation so as to avoid falling into the "standard clause" pitfall.

Finally, developing countries, which have a lack of experience in the negotiation of sections and chapters of the service trade provisions contained in the FTAs, may easily fall into the so-called "Spaghetti Bowl Effect".

The "Spaghetti Bowl Effect" is a phenomenon of international economic policy that refers to the complications that arise from the application of domestic rules of origin in the signing of FTAs. The effect leads to discriminatory trade policy because the same commodity is subject to different tariffs and tariff reduction trajectories based on domestic preferences. With the increase in FTAs throughout the international economy, the phenomena has led to paradoxical, and often contradictory, outcomes among bilateral and multilateral trade partners.[15]

The effect is seen as a measure of political risk for firms that seek to invest in nations with complex measures relating to IP rights and contract law. The term was first used by Jagdish Bhagwati in his 1995 paper, US Trade Policy: "The Infatuation with Free Trade Agreements".[16] Subsequently, Bhagwati has used the term on various occasions in describing the problem of FTAs. He named it the " Spaghetti Bowl Effect", referring to the manner in which half-finished products and parts are delivered through various FTA networks using tariff differentiation in an effort to export finished products to consumer countries at the lowest price. He visualized criss-crossing lines and likened these lines to strands of spaghetti tangled in a bowl.

More recently, the term has been used by scholars to explain the difficulties in using East Asian Free Trade Agreements to solve the intertwined mass of preferential trading arrangements among ASEAN members.

In other words, if China enters into many bilateral FTAs with different countries, each FTA will impose different detailed lists of obligations. Because the contracting parties of the FTAs are also member states of the WTO, according to the MFN principle, and notwithstanding the fact that China has signed different bilateral FTAs with various countries, China will be obligated to grant the same special favor to any member country of the WTO, even a country with which China has not yet concluded a bilateral FTA, or risk violating its obligations. This is the "Spaghetti Bowl Effect".

To cite an example, if China does not wish to sign a FTA with the USA, but is willing to conclude a FTA with India, there will be a "Spaghetti Bowl Effect". In accordance with the FTA, China would be required to allow India to enter into the Chinese financial market as a consequence of MFN. If we suppose that afterward India signs a FTA with the USA, the latter will enjoy special favored status not only with India, but can also claim the same special treatment with a third country, in this instance, China, with which the USA has not yet concluded a bilateral FTA, because they are all contracting states of the WTO. In fact, because the USA has signed a FTA with India, the former will enjoy the special favored treatment that India enjoys with China, arising out of the bilateral FTA previously entered into

---

15 CHENG Jianming, "*The issues of the international trade*", dealing with pitfall and principles of being on guard during the negotiation of FTA, please see http://www.cacs.gov.cn/maoyijiuji (Information network on China trading relief).

16 BHAGWATI Jagdish, "*US Trade Policy: The Infatuation with FTAs*", April 1995, Columbia University, Discussion Paper Series No. 726.

between China and India. Hence, even if China does not want to sign a FTA with the USA, it must open its domestic market to the USA and its enterprises, causing negative effects on the Chinese market.

3. STRATEGIES PROPOSED BY CHINA AFTER THE TRIPS AGREEMENT

3.1 Strategies Proposed by China in Respect of the TRIPS-plus Agreement

The USA and the EU have implemented the TRIPS-plus Agreement through FTAs, and at some point the USA adopted this tool as a countermeasure against developing countries, in particular against those that are strong, powerful, and self-confident. In fact, the USA and the EU have now realized that it has become more and more difficult to achieve the objectives discussed during the multilateral negotiations of the WTO; therefore they have turned from a multilateral system to a bilateral system.

However, when the TRIPS-plus Agreement reaches a certain level, the multilateral system will inevitably come into being, and the TRIPS-plus Agreement will also embody the multilateral negotiation system. Hence the TRIPS Agreement can be considered to be only one phase and not the final stage of the multilateral legislation for the international protection of IP.

Because China has a very large population, the system of medical safeguards is not perfect. More than 97.4 percent of western medicines used in China are imitations of patented medicines, and the production of 90 percent of organic medicines has been protected by foreign companies through patent registration. Even though the research and development of new medicines are the best way for China to change from a big country that produces medicines that imitate patented medicines to a powerful country that invents medicines and owns its IP rights, China will be still be faced with the challenge of drug accessibility.

In recent years, many sudden and continuous outbreaks of diseases dangerous to public health and safety, such as SARS (Severe Acute Respiratory Syndrome), Bird Flu, and H1N1 Flu, have occurred in China, and these dramatic circumstances have significantly influenced China to improve drug accessibility. The investment of huge amounts of capital necessary for the development and creation of new patented medicines seems to be unrealistic for many domestic companies, however, and imitation patented medicines still occupy a predominant position in the Chinese market.

It is possible to say that, before the TRIPS-plus Agreement, China substantially raised its capability to cure diseases that affect public health and significantly improved the research and development of new medicines. In this context the higher degree of protection of IP set forth in the TRIPS-plus Agreement will certainly affect China negatively. Consequently, China should maintain a prudent approach, in particular with regard to future patent legislation, before the conclusion of any bilateral agreements (FTAs) and international conventions that contain the TRIPS-plus Agreement. China should be aware of the following issues:

3.1.1 To introduce the patent linkage system cautiously

In order to prevent acts of infringement, some developed countries that have carried out original research and development of new medicines have implemented the system of patent linkage, setting up a link between the registration of a patent and further assessment in order to establish whether the manufacture of a medicine constitutes a violation of the patent rights of other owners. In this way, the patent owner can bring an action for the protection of his interests.

To this end, the USA has implemented the system of patent linkage not only domestically, but internationally through FTAs, because it is the leading developed country in the research of new medicines. These FTAs have not only delayed market entry of medicines that imitate patented medicines, but they may also hinder the use of the compulsory license that has been already recognized by TRIPS. Thus FTAs will not safeguard public health or improve the accessibility of high-quality medicines because the introduction of the patent linkage system creates a link between market access and patent status. It is relevant to note that the current Provisions for Drug Registration (Drug Provisions) in China have retained the requirement that the applicant submit the declaration of the prescription, technology, use, and explanation of the patent for medicines, as well as a declaration as to whether the patent being applied for constitutes an infringement of the rights of another patent owner. The Drug Provisions have also kept open the possibility for a third applicant to apply for the registration of a medicine that has already been registered and protected by an earlier applicant in the same territory within two years prior to the expiry of the patent belonging to the earlier applicant.

However, the Drug Provisions do not set out whether it is possible for a patent owner to bring an administrative action before the Medicines Management Administration for the annulment of a license granted to a patent infringer to produce medicines that imitate a patented medicine. In the absence of such provisions, the only way for the patent owner to seek damages would be by bringing a civil action for the invalidation of the license to produce the infringing medicines.

3.1.2 To restrict the monopolization of data protection relating to high technology

Even in the absence of a patent license, the exclusive right to data protection for high technology may also prevent the manufacture and sale of medicines that imitate patented medicines.

The system of data protection for high technology and the system of patent protection provide different ways of ensuring IP protection, and a medicine can be protected by both systems at the same time. As a result, even though patent protection expires after 20 years, the same medicine can be still protected for a further six years by data protection for high technology. For example, an applicant that files for and receives patent registration of its medicine from the Patent Office in 1980 will have patent protection for 20 years (1980–2000). Suppose then that in 1999, the 19th year of patent protection, China signed the FTAs and promised to allow six years of data protection relating to high technology. This medicine would continue to be protected from 1999 to 2005. In other words, the data protection provisions would restrict the sale of the medicine for a further five years following expiry of the patent.

If China joins the FTAs and complies with an even higher standard of protection of IP with regard to the pharmaceutical sector, its access to high technology will be restricted, preventing its medicine manufacturers from imitating the patented medicines belonging to the producers of developed countries. This situation will certainly negatively affect drug accessibility. In fact, when the monopolization right of data relating to high technology is dominated by the multinational enterprises of developed countries, it is even more difficult for the governments of developing countries to implement the compulsory license.

Pharmaceutical manufacturers that have carried out research and development and have produced medicines that imitate patent medicines whose protection has already expired will encounter difficulties in selling these medicines because of the right of monopolization of data relating to high technology because they cannot rely on the original patented medicines with regard to the data on clinical trials.

As for data protection relating to high technology, we note the experience of India as an example. The right of monopolization of data protection for high technology was omitted from the revision of the Indian Patent Law in 2005 because that provision would seriously have affected the prosperity of the pharmaceutical industry of India.

China, however, agreed to allow six years of data protection for high technology to comply with WTO rules. But the TRIPS Agreement is broadly drafted with regard to the provision on data protection for high technology. Member states can limit the scope of data protection to very sensitive data, leaving outside the scope of protection data that is not of high importance. In other words, the TRIPS Agreement allows the use of non-sensitive data relating to high technology. Developing countries can use this loophole to restrict the monopolization of data protection for high technology, which is set forth in favor of the developed countries by the TRIPS-plus Agreement (FTAs).

Some Latin America countries that were forced to accept the TRIPS-plus Agreement in the FTAs they signed with the USA were able to obtain the provision to restrict the monopolization of data protection for high technology. Therefore, when China signs FTAs with developed countries, such as the USA and the EU, it can also set forth conditions with respect to the monopolization of data protection for high technology, because such a provision violates neither a country's obligations towards the WTO nor the TRIPS Agreement.

3.1.3 To maintain the "elastic clause" that is permitted by the TRIPS Agreement

The TRIPS-plus Agreement has restricted developing countries from lawfully using the "elastic clause". Under the TRIPS Agreement, developing countries enjoy a certain level of freedom with respect to their own laws and policies. However in the TRIPS-plus Agreement, these elastic clauses have been limited, so that the developing countries' freedom to enact legislation has been heavily restricted. Even though China's Patent Law to some extent has reached the standard set out by the TRIPS-plus Agreement, China's adherence to the TRIPS-plus Agreement will largely limit its freedom to promulgate legislation and choose its own policies. A country that was previously free to enact legislation will be restricted by the binding rules of the international conventions even in the event of changes in its domestic situation. For instance, after signing the FTAs with the USA and introducing the system of patent linkage and other requirements of TRIPS-plus Agreement, Australia changed its domestic law to reduce the negative effects of the TRIPS-plus Agreement, only to face strong criticism and condemnation from the USA.[17]

---

[17] As regards the broader meaning of the TRIPS-plus Agreement and the strategies proposed by China, please see http://www.chinalawedu.com.

3.2 The Improvement of Chinese IP Law under the Framework of the TRIPS Agreement

If we analyze the TRIPS Agreement in depth, we realize that the special treatment given to developing countries is illusory and unbalanced. Because the developing countries seek a balance of interests, they must implement flexibly the "elastic clause" detailed in the TRIPS Agreement through specific provisions, exceptions and restrictions, and extensively using the right to make one's own decisions as permitted by the TRIPS Agreement.

In other words, in line with the principles set out by the TRIPS Agreement, China should take advantage of the scope of protection permitted by the TRIPS Agreement by using the "elastic clause" to defend the public interest of its own country and challenge the predominant position of the developed countries.[18]

3.2.1 The establishment of a uniform intellectual property code

China's current system of IP tends toward special regulations; even so, economic knowledge has increased, and IP has reached a conspicuously important position. In fact, the IP law itself and its system of rights have been significantly revised, leading to the establishment of a uniform code and the improvement of the system of IP law protection.

The TRIPS Agreement updated previous international conventions in areas including copyright, trademark, geographical indication, integrated circuit design, trade secrets, and all types of IP, but the biggest breakthrough lies in the introduction of strategies for the protection of IP and the mechanism for the resolution of disputes. Not only has the TRIPS Agreement become the widely accepted parameter for the multilateral protection of IP, it symbolizes the improvement in its international protection, making the TRIPS Agreement more influential than previous conventions. It has been a milestone in the development of the legislative and judicial systems of IP protection in many countries. These circumstances have influenced China to establish its IP code according to international standards in order to set out legislation that harmonizes with that of the international community.

---

[18] SHUAI Hua and HUANG Xian Ling: "*The elastic clause of the TRIPS Agreement and the improvement of the intellectual property law in China*", in Economic Issues, vol 10, 2003. (协议弹性条款与中国知识产权立法的完善 作者：师华、黄羡玲，《经济问题》 2003年第10期).

3.2.2 The emphasis on persisting in stressing outstanding public interest and the principle of using pluses and ignoring minuses (the so-called "yang chang bi duan" principle)

China's IP laws should adhere to the following principles:

3.2.2.1 To stress outstanding public interest The provisions of the TRIPS Agreement are based on the level of protection required for the intellectual property of the developing countries, which unavoidably affects the purposes of the USA and the other developed countries. The following principle has been inserted, however, into the TRIPS Agreement:

> Members may, in formulating or amending their laws and regulations, adopt measures necessary to protect public health and nutrition, and to promote the public interest in sectors of vital importance to their socio-economic and technological development, provided that such measures are consistent with the provisions of this Agreement.

In the overall spirit of the TRIPS Agreement, therefore, China should strengthen its sense of patriotic awareness for the safeguarding of the public health and the interests of the country by fully using domestic legislation, such as provisions that "restrict or make an exception to exclusive patent rights". Because the TRIPS Agreement has not yet set forth detailed provisions, but rather grants the power to members to make their own decisions, China should flexibly implement those decisions in line with the principle of upholding the public interest. It should not, however, set out a higher level of protection for IP than that of the developed countries.

3.2.2.2 The principle of "yang chang bi duan" China's entry in the WTO does not imply that China should change the law passively. But the TRIPS Agreement not only protects the interests of the developed countries; it also allows countries to take the initiative and strengthen the protection of IP to a certain extent, for example, with regard to the Chinese traditional medicine sector. China should take legislative initiatives to increase the level of protection and strengthen the patent protection of its traditional medicines, defend its treasures, and stress the importance of the status of protection of these subjects in the domestic legislation.[19]

---

[19] CHEN Xiao Yu: "*Theory on the TRIPS Agreement and the development and improvement of the intellectual property law*", Liao Ning Normal University Magazine, Social Science Edition, January 2010, Vol. 33, first quarterly.

3.3 The Leading IP Cases after China's entry into the WTO

3.3.1 *HISENSE vs. SIEMENS* for infringement of trademark right

In 2004, HiSense, the leading Chinese home electronic appliance company, exported its flat-screen TV and frequency conversion air conditioner into the German market and was sued by Siemens for infringement of its "HiSense" trademark. The Chinese HiSense brought a legal action to annul the trademark "HiSense" registered by the German Bosch-Siemens Company (BSH) at the German Trademark Office.

The trademark "HiSense" registered by HiSense Company is not only the original trademark of this Chinese company, but it is also the trade name of its enterprise. After the creation of this trademark, HiSense applied for the registration of its trademark in China. On December 14, 1993, after the examination procedure at the competent Chinese Trademark Office, the Chinese company obtained the registration of its trademark. A few years later, the Chinese character "海信" (that phonetically indicates HiSense) and the Latin characters "HiSense" became famous Chinese trademarks. However just six days after the official recognition by the Chinese Trademark Office of the status of the famous trademark of "HiSense", on January 11, 1999, Siemens's subsidiary company, BSH intentionally filed for registration of the trademark "HiSense" at the German Trademark Office, a trademark that was identical to the original "HiSense" trademark created by the Chinese company and used by BSH for the production of its dishwashers.

In 2001, HiSense Company carried out negotiations with BSH with regard to the act of infringement by the latter and to buy back the trademark "HiSense" unlawfully registered by BSH. BSH requested payment of the enormous amount of 40 million euros in exchange for the trademark "HiSense", and the Chinese company refused to continue negotiations. HiSense Company maintained that the Paris Convention set out very clear provisions for the protection of a famous trademark. Both China and Germany are member states of the Paris Convention and the Chinese Trademark Office firmly believed that the famous trademark "HiSense", bearing original features and economic value, should receive identical protection and respect in Germany. However BSH maintained its position that it had not infringed the trademark rights of the Chinese HiSense Company. After the negotiations between the parties failed, HiSense Company registered a new trademark, "Hsense", in the European market, and at the same time it announced this new brand in Northern Europe in 2004 through western mass media.

In March 2005, BSH proposed a settlement between the parties, as follows: 1) BSH will not insist on its position; 2) HiSense will acknowledge that BSH has lawfully registered the trademark "HiSense"; 3) HiSense will pay a reasonable price for the transfer of this trademark; and 4) both parties will withdraw their respective legal actions. Since BSH believed that the profits to be made in the Chinese market would be much higher than those attainable in the German market, it was certainly not worth falling out with a Chinese company for the "HiSense" trademark, because this would negatively affect BSH's reputation and business in the Chinese market.

Finally, following pressure from the Chinese Ministry of Commerce, in March 2005, the HiSense Company and BSH entered into an agreement for the settlement of the dispute and HiSense Company bought back the trademark "HiSense" for the more reasonable price of 500,000.00 Euros.

3.3.2 *GM DAEWOO vs. CHERY* for design patent infringement

In May 2005, the American company GM Korea (GM) (formerly GM Daewoo Auto and Technology Company, which changed its trade name as of 2011) brought an action for design patent infringement against the Chinese company, Chery Automobile Co Ltd. (Chery) at the Beijing Intermediate People's Court, on the grounds that Chery produced a car called "QQ", which was exactly the same as the model named "Matiz" produced by GM. For that reason, GM sought to obtain an order from the judge ordering Chery to stop the infringement, make a public apology, pay damages amounting to 8 million, 22000 euros (equal to RMB 75 million), bear legal expenses amounting to 540 000 euros (equal to RMB 5 million), and assume the responsibility for the illegal turnover made by Chery.

During the legal proceedings, GM affirmed that: "the reason for which we brought an action is not to make a profit, but to confirm the basic principle of protecting the healthy growth of the automobile industry, the respect of intellectual property and to create a market based upon fair competition rules."

As far back as May 2002, GM learned that Chery was developing a mini-car. The possibility of entering into partnership was discussed, but GM's proposal was rejected by Chery. Chery's investigation determined that GM had not registered any patent in China that could support its assertion of an alleged patent violation by Chery. On the contrary, Chery was lawfully protected by the patent covering the QQ car.

In November 2003, notwithstanding the fact that GM did not have any IP rights or evidence to support its claim in China, GM informed Chinese political leaders that Chery had infringed its IP rights. In February 2004, the Chinese Ministry of Commerce organized a team composed of the State Industry and Commerce Head Office, SIPO, the Academy of Social Sciences, Peking University, Chery, and other experts to investigate the alleged infringement of a patent right by Chery. All the experts unanimously believed, however, that the process of the research and development of the QQ car did not constitute an act of infringement of the patent right as claimed by GM. In April 2004, the Chinese Government convened a negotiation to settle the dispute between GM and Chery, but this settlement attempt failed.

An analysis of the controversy between GM and Chery shows that GM's behavior involves, to a certain extent, an abuse of IP rights. For instance, notwithstanding the fact that GM did not have any lawful evidence to prove its claim, it sent many warning letters to Chery claiming that Chery had infringed GM's design patent rights. In addition, GM announced its suit against Chery through mass media, greatly exaggerating the situation, causing a huge loss to Chery and negatively affecting its reputation and business, not to mention distorting and hampering competition in the market.

On November 18, 2005, GM and Chery entered into a settlement regarding the dispute by publishing a joint statement that resolved the controversy between them.

3.4 The Newly Promulgated 2011 Intellectual Property Action Plan

In order to implement effectively the State Intellectual Property Strategies in 2011, a joint conference was organized in which 28 experts participated in drafting the "2011 China Intellectual Property Action Plan". This Action Plan reformulates and revises the law, regulations, and documents with regard to intellectual property, strengthens the level of enforcement of IP law, expands the services relating to intellectual property, raises the standards of training with regard to IP education and the building of teams of talented people, and spreads the dissemination of IP awareness and culture, as well as expanding cooperative exchange with other countries. Experts from six different areas have suggested 100 specific strategies, giving functional guidance to all the work that should be carried out to protect China's intellectual property rights in 2011.

At the same time, the Joint Conference also proposed the "2011 China Intellectual Property Implementing Strategies Work Propulsion Plan". This Propulsion Plan precisely focuses on the attempt to require the Chinese Central Government to change overall conditions to accelerate economic growth and the "Twelfth Five-Year" (Shi Yi Er Wu) Plan, in line with the principles to "consolidate the foundation, separate tasks, develop all aspects, drive ahead focal point", by specifically planning all the work necessary to implement the National Intellectual Property Strategies in 2011.

This Propulsion Plan includes the strategies set forth in the 2011 China Intellectual Property Action Plan and fosters the implementation of these strategies by organizing and coordinating seven categories, comprising 176 specific measures. In addition, each measure clearly sets out the department responsible for ensuring the implementation of these strategies.

In order to implement the emphasized strategies, the Propulsion Plan fixed 13 important measures, mainly involving strategic and growth industries, to promote the creation and use of intellectual property in such industries, to strengthen the national science and technology plan and improve IP management, to develop actions against acts of infringement of intellectual property and the making and selling of counterfeit and poor quality goods, to advance the work of lawful software companies, and to reduce the publication of pirated works on the Internet, as well as to make strong efforts to improve services relating to intellectual property, build teams of talented people, spread culture, and promote international cooperative exchange.

4. CONCLUSION

It has been more than ten years since China joined the WTO, and although there is an improvement in the level of trade liberalization and the compliance of China with international standards, trade protectionism still exists. The trade barrier coming from the Western developed countries with regard to IP protection is the main obstacle to the "Going Out Policy" being carried out by the Chinese Government and its enterprises today.

The TRIPS-plus Agreement, imposed by developed countries through the execution of bilateral Free Trade Agreements, is the vehicle for a higher level of protection of intellectual property. At the same time, however, TRIPS-plus, to some extent, burdens developing countries with regard to the protection of intellectual property. In fact, the USA, the EU, and other developed countries use the TRIPS-plus Agreement indirectly in order to reach objectives that it would not otherwise be possible to achieve through the TRIPS Agreement, which enables the implementation of the "elastic clause" in the domestic law of each member state in order to safeguard its public health and national interests.

China, as the world's largest developing country, should seriously take into account the challenges it will face and create strategies to meet these serious challenges before signing any Free Trade Agreement and accepting the TRIPS-plus Agreement with most developed countries.

I would like to thank Prof. Gustavo Ghidini, Prof. Zhang Lihong, Prof. Fei Anling, Prof. Xue Hong, Ms. Xie Lina, Prof. Chen Han, Prof. Renzo Cavalieri, Prof. Amalia Diurni, Prof. Marina Timoteo, Prof. Giovanni Casucci, Mr. Umberto Zamboni di Salerano, Mr. Joseph Simone, Mr. Fabrizio De Benedetti, Mr. Danny Friedmann, others friends and colleagues, my team of lawyers, my family, who gave me continuous support throughout the years.

BIBLIOGRAPHY

"2011 nian zhong guo bao hu zhi shi chan quan xing dong" (2011年中国保护知识产权行动计划), at http://www.gov.cn (中国政府门户网站).

CAO Yang (曹阳): "TRIPS xie yi yu fa zhan zhong guo jia de zhi shi chan quan" (TRIPS协议与发展中国家的知识产权)，zhi shi chan quan li lun yu shi wu-2006 nian zhi shi chan quan zheng wen huo jiang wen ji, (知识产权理论与实务-2006年知识产权征文获奖文集).

CHEN Xiao Yu (陈晓宇): "Lun TRIPS xie yi yu zhong guo zhi shi chan quan fa de fa zhan yu wan shan" (论TRIPS 协议与中国知识产权法的发展与完善), liao ning shi fan da xue xue bao (she hui ke xue ban, Liao Ning Normal University Magazine, January 2010, Vol 33, first quarterly.

CHENG Jianming: "The issues of the international trade", http://www.cacs.gov.cn/maoyijiuji (Information network on China trading relief).

FENG Chao and RANJARD Paul: "Final draft of proposed PRC Copyright Law amendment released by NCAC", January 7, 2013, at http://www.lexology.com.

FRAUNCE, Thomas A. and LEXCHI Joel: "Linkage Evergreening in Canada and Australia, Australian and New Zealand Health Policy" [EB/OL]•[2009-08-25], at http： //www. anzhealth-policy. com /content/4/1/8.

FRIEDMANN, Danny: "Paper Tiger or Roaring Dragon, China's TRIPS Implementation and Enforcement", Thesis of Master Degree, University of Amsterdam, 2007.

GHIDINI Gustavo: "On the impact of TRIPS on 'least developed countries: a tale of double standards?", *Queen Mary Journal of Intellectual Property*, Vol 1 No. 1, April 2011.

HUANG Hua Jun and ZHANG Bin Min (黄华钧,张秉民): "WTO gui ze dui xi bu di qu zhi shi chan quan fa zhi de ying xiang ji dui ce"(WTO 规则对西部地区知识产权法制的影响及对策), in "ning xia she hui ke xu" (宁夏社会科学), 2001, vol. 5

HUANG Hui and RANJARD Paul: "Trademark Law Revision: More Work Needed", in *Managing Intellectual Property*, March 1, 2012, at http://www.managingip.com.

"IP Protection by Chinese Courts in 2012", at http://chinaipr2.files.wordpress.com/2013/04/ip-protection-by-chinese-courts-in-2012_en.pdf.

KOTERA Akira: "What is the "Spaghetti Bowl Phenomenon" of FTAs?" at http://www.rieti.go.jp/en/columns/a01_0193.html, May 23, 2006.

"Latest draft of revised Chinese Trademark Law released for public comment", in *World Trademark Review*, April/May 2013, at http://www.WorldTrademarkReview.com.

LI Feng Qin (李凤琴): "Shuang bian mao yi zhong de TRIPS-plus biao zhun yan jiu" (双边贸易协定中的TRIPS-plus标准研究), shi jie mao yi zu zhi dong tai yu yan jiu》(世界贸易组织动态与研究), 2009, vol. 3.

LOU Cecilia and DING Xianjie: "China: Five Issues You should be Aware of in the Latest Draft of the Revision of PRC Trademark Law", March 9, 2013, http://www.mondaq.com.
"NCAC's Explanations on the Draft of 3rd Revision of Copyright Law", March 31, 2012, at http://www.ncac.gov.cn/cms/html/309/3502/201203/740608.html.
"NCAC's Explanations on the 2nd Draft of 3rd Revision of Copyright Law", July 6, 2012, at http://www.ncac.gov.cn/cms/html/309/3517/201207/759867.html.
"Notice of the National Copyright Administration on Publicly Soliciting Opinions on the Copyright Law of the People's Republic of China (Revised Draft)" officially released by the National Copyright Administration on March 31, 2012.
"Notice of the National Copyright Administration on Publicly Soliciting Opinions on the Copyright Law of the People's Republic of China (Second Revised Draft)", promulgated by the National Copyright Administration on July 6, 2012.
SHENG Jian Ming (盛建明): "FTA tan pan zhong de xian jing ji fan fang yuan ze" (FTA谈判中的陷阱及防范原则), at http://www.cacs.gov.cn/maoyijiuji.
SHI Hua and HUANG Xian Ling (师华、黄羡玲): "TRIPS xie yi tang xing tiao kuang yu zhong guo zhi shi chan quan li fa de wan shan" (TRIPS协议弹性条款与中国知识产权立法的完善), jing ji wen ti (经济问题), 2003, vol 10.
THELEN Christine: "Carrots and Sticks: Evaluation the Tools for Securing Successful TRIPs Implementation", *Temple Journal of Science, Technology & Environmental Law* (Fall 2005).
"TRIPS-plus tiao kuang de kuo zhang ji zhong guo de ying dui ce lue" (TRIPS-plus条款的扩张及中国的应对策略) http://www.chinalawedu.com, fa lv jiao yu wang（法律教育网）.
"White Paper of Intellectual Property Protection by Chinese Courts in 2010 released", at http://www.cpahkltd.com/UploadFiles/20110509082512655.pdf.
"White Paper of Intellectual Property Protection by Chinese Courts in 2011", at http://www.iam-magazine.com/files/People's Supreme Court Intellectual Property Protection in China.pdf.
WU Xue Yan (吴雪燕): "TRIPS-plus tiao kuan de kuo zhang ji zhong guode ying dui ce lue" (TRIPS-plus条款的扩张及中国的应对策略), xian dai fa xue (现代法学), 2010, vol. 32, 5 weekly.
XUE Hong: "One Step Ahead Two Steps Back: Reverse Engineering 2nd Draft for 3rd Revision of the Chinese Copyright Law", in Digital Commons @ American University Washington College of Law. PIJIP-Research Paper Series Program on Information Justice and Intellectual Property, January 7, 2012, at http://digitalcommons.wcl.american.edu/research.
ZHANG Li Na (张丽娜): "WTO yu zhong guo zhi shi chan quan fa lv yan jiu" (WTO与中国知识产权法律制度研究) zhong guo min zhu fa zhi chu ban she (中国民主法制出版社).
ZHANG Nai Gen (张乃根): "Guo ji mao yi de zhi shi chan quan fa" (国际贸易的指示产权法), fu dan da xue chu ban she (复旦大学出版社), 1999.
ZHANG Zheng yi (张正怡): "TRIPS-plus tiao kuang dui zhong guo zhi shi chan quan zheng ce de qi shi" (TRIPS-plus条款对中国知识产权政策的启示), fa zhi lun cong (法治论丛), 2010, Vol 25, 5th weekly.
ZHENG Cheng Si (郑成思): "TRIPS xie yi de zhong wen wen ben" (TRIPS协议的中文文本), zhong guo fang zheng chu ban she (中国方正出版社), 1999.
ZOELLICK Robert: (2009) Letter to Vaile M, Australian Minister for Trade, [EB/OL]. [2009-10-05] at http://www. dfat. gov. au/trade/negotiations/us_fta/ index. htm.1.

3. Patent and trademark rights in commercial agreements entered by the United States with Latin American nations in the first decade of the twenty-first century: *Divide et vinces*

Horacio Rangel-Ortiz

INTRODUCTION

It is established contemporary philosophy that the way patent and trademark rights are treated in a given jurisdiction has an impact on the way commercial activities are carried out in that jurisdiction. It has been submitted that failure to recognize and enforce patent and trademark rights pursuant to certain rules and criteria expected by patent and trademark owners, can operate as a trade barrier, and therefore the rules applicable to the way patent, trademark and related rights should be treated by reason of the existence of a commercial understanding are often discussed and agreed upon as part of the negotiations for the adoption of a trade agreement whether a trade promotion agreement, a free trade agreement or other forms of commercial understandings meant to reduce or completely remove barriers to trade, both tariff and non-tariff barriers.

The first decade of the twenty-first century is a period during which several countries of the Americas started and completed negotiations between and among themselves towards the adoption of several forms of commercial understandings to eliminate or reduce trade barriers, including engagements on the way the parties agreed to treat patent, trademark and related rights.

Some of the trade agreements completed in the Americas in the first decade of the twenty-first century, tend to attract the attention of participants and of the public in general in a more evident fashion than others.

From an intellectual property standpoint, those that have attracted the attention of specialists in a more evident fashion are the agreements where the United States (US) is one of the parties. This is not only because of the commercial and economic reasons behind the adoption of a commercial understanding with the US, but also to the innovative and at times surprising character of some of the provisions found in trade agreements but rarely seen in other international instruments where intellectual property rights are treated differently or where certain intellectual property issues are simply not addressed. It is apparent that the mutual benefits sought by the negotiators of free trade instruments tend to create an atmosphere that does not exist when intellectual property rights are discussed in isolation, and thus the possibility of adopting engagements that form a part of a global understanding meant to reduce or eliminate trade barriers in whatever forms these barriers may come into view. Also, the environment created in discussions with a reduced number of participants tends to favor the adoption of understandings more difficult to reach in a multinational arena or in a regional context where negotiations are pursued in rather different circumstances.

The following paragraphs will focus on the trade agreements adopted by the US with a Latin American nation including those that were negotiated and completed in the first decade of the twenty-first century.[1]

---

[1] At the beginning of 2013, the US has free trade agreements in force with 20 countries. These are:

- Australia (entered into force in 2005)
- Bahrain (entered into force in 2006)
- Canada (entered into force in 1994)
- *Chile (entered into force in 2004)*
- *Colombia (entered into force in 2012)*
- *Costa Rica (entered into force in 2009)*
- *Dominican Republic (entered into force in 2007)*
- *El Salvador (entered into force in 2006)*
- *Guatemala (entered into force in 2006)*
- *Honduras (entered into force in 2006)*
- Israel (entered into force in 1995)
- Jordan (entered into force in 2001)
- Korea (entered into force in 2012)
- *Mexico (entered into force in 1994)*
- Morocco (entered into force in 2006)
- *Nicaragua (entered into force in 2006)*
- Oman (entered into force in 2009)
- *Panama (entered into force in 2012)*
- *Peru (entered into force in 2009)*
- Singapore (entered into force in 2004)

After adoption of the North American Free Trade Agreement (NAFTA) by Canada, the US and México in December 1993, other Latin American nations have also completed a commercial agreement with the US, all of which include an intellectual property chapter that contains commitments and engagements dealing with specific issues that generally did not appear in previous international instruments where the parties to these agreements were already members. What is more, examination of the new provisions incorporated into the new commercial agreements executed in the Americas shows that many of them were already a part of a draft for the Free Trade Agreement of the Americas that has not come to a successful completion after several years of negotiations.[2] Therefore, it is apparent that what has not been achieved in a regional commercial instrument where the US is one of the parties negotiating the adoption thereof, it has been possible to obtain with some of the commercial partners of the South through the adoption of separate commercial agreements all of which do now contain certain novelties on the way the parties agree to treat various aspects of intellectual property rights.

Formally speaking, the negotiating processes involving the US and these Latin American nations were completed with the signature of the respective trade agreements between 2003 and 2007. These agreements have already gone through the respective congressional approval processes in the two jurisdictions involved, as a condition precedent in order for same to become effective. This is the case of Chile (January 2004), Colombia (May 2012), El Salvador (March 2006), Honduras (April 2006), Nicaragua (April 2006), Guatemala (July 2006), Dominican Republic (March 2007), Costa Rica (January 2009), Panama (October 2012) and Peru (February 2009). That is to say, all the trade agreements signed by the US with a Latin American nation in the first decade of the twenty-first

---

A condition precedent in order for the free trade agreements entered by the US with other nations, the US Congress must enact legislation to approve and implement each individual agreement in order for them to go into effect. *See* http://www.ustr.gov/trade-agreements/free-trade-agreements More than half of these agreements have been adopted by the US with nations of the Americas, specifically with 12 nations of North, Central and South America. With the exception of the agreements with Canada and Mexico, signed in 1993, and the agreement with Israel, signed in 1985, the remaining agreements were all signed in the first decade of the twenty-first century between 2001 and 2009.

[2] (*See* FTAA.TNC/W/133/Rev3 at www.ftaa-alca.org/FTAADraft03/ChapterXX_e.asp and http://www.ftaa-alca.org/FTAADraft03/TOCWord_e.asp. *See also* http://www.uschamber.com/international/policy/drcafta.htm and http://www.state.gov/r/pa/ei/bgn/2019.htm

century are already in force including those which became effective in the second decade of the twentieth century represented by the last two agreements signed with Colombia in 2006 and Panama in 2007, both of which became effective in 2012.

1. Trade Agreements Adopted Between US and Latin American Nations in the Twenty-first Century

Table 3.1 Trade agreements adopted between US and Latin American nations in the twenty-first century

United States	Latin America	Signature	In force
United States	Chile	2003	2004
United States	El Salvador CAFTA – D.R.	2004	2006
United States	Honduras CAFTA – D.R.	2004	2006
United States	Nicaragua CAFTA – D.R.	2004	2006
United States	Guatemala CAFTA – D.R.	2004	2006
United States	Dominican Rep. CAFTA – D.R.	2004	2007
United States	Costa Rica CAFTA – D.R.	2004	2009
United States	Peru	2006	2009
United States	Colombia	2006	2012
United States	Panama	2007	2012

All these bilateral instruments include a number of developments that were not in the text of a previous trade agreement, and thus pertain to the post-NAFTA times where clear differences are evident in the way patent, trademark and related rights are treated. This chapter includes references to these bilateral agreements as well as to similar instruments adopted at about the same times in other regions of the world with a view to examining, *i.a.*, the ways and manners in which US law and policy applicable to international trade – which encourage uniformity on the way intellectual property rights are treated – has been implemented in Latin America and other regions of the world like North Africa, the Persian Gulf and Oceania represented by Morocco, Bahrain and Australia with whom the US signed similar agreements in the year 2004.

2. Trade Agreements US – Latin America

The tradition of incorporating patent and trademark provisions as part of the language contained in free trade agreements (FTAs) executed between the US and other nations began with the adoption of Chapter XVII of

NAFTA executed by the US, Canada and Mexico in December 1993.[3] This was the first FTA a Latin American nation had executed with the US, and the Mexican side therefore had little experience in negotiating intellectual property issues as part of FTAs; this would change in the next decade when Mexico adopted similar trade instruments with more than 40 nations.[4] Under the circumstances, the parties adopted the practical approach and relied on a draft for the TRIPS Agreement which would later be adopted by General Agreement on Tariffs and Trade (GATT) members in April of 1994 when the Marrakech Agreement was completed (WTO). This is why the patent and trademark provisions of NAFTA and TRIPS bear a close resemblance to each other.[5]

NAFTA is the only FTA executed by the US with a Latin American nation before the twentieth century came to an end. At that time, TRIPS standards as generally reflected in NAFTA seemed to be the appropriate framework on which negotiators could rely in search for objective standards of protection at the time patent and trademark provisions were discussed in the context of bilateral trade. The remaining commercial

---

[3] The Spanish version of NAFTA (North American Free Trade Agreement – Tratado de Libre Comercio de América del Norte) was Publisher *Diario Oficial de la Federación* of December 20, 1993, Mexico. The adoption of intellectual property provisions in NAFTA is discussed in RANGEL-MEDINA David, *Normatividad de la propiedad intelectual en el Tratado de Libre Comercio de América del Norte*, in *Panorama jurídico del Tratado de Libre Comercio II*, Departamento de Derecho, Universidad Iberoamericana, México, 1993, pp. 83–93. *See also* RANGEL-ORTIZ Horacio, *La propiedad intelectual en el Tratado de Libre Comercio de América del Norte*, Actas de Derecho Industrial, Tomo XV, Instituto de Derecho Industrial , Departamento de Derecho Mercantil y del Trabajo, Universidad de Santiago, España, 1993, pp. 787–98.

[4] The incorporation of intellectual property provisions in FTAs adopted by Latin American nations is discussed in RANGEL-ORTIZ Horacio, *Aspectos de propiedad industrial relativos al proyecto para un acuerdo de libre comercio de las américas (ALCA): el caso de las marcas*, in *Estudios sobre propiedad industrial e intelectual y Derecho de la competencia. Colección de Trabajos en Homenaje a ALBERTO BERCOVITZ RODRÍGUEZ-CANO ofrecida por el GRUPO ESPAÑOL DE LA AIPPI*, Barcelona, marzo 2005 at pp. 873–93.

[5] Consequently, both the defects and the merits of the TRIPS draft both as to form and substance were integrated into NAFTA. On the question of the defects and the merits of TRIPS both as to form and substance, *see* GOMEZ SEGADE José Antonio, *El Acuerdo ADPIC como nuevo marco para la protección de la Propiedad Industrial e Intelectual*, Actas de Derecho Industrial, Tomo XVI, Año 1994–1995, Instituto de Derecho Industrial, Universidad de Santiago, España pp. 33 y ss. *See also* BOTANA AGRA, *Las normas sustantivas del A-ADPIC (TRIP'S) sobre los derechos de Propiedad Intelectual*, Actas de Derecho Industrial, Tomo XVI, pp. 109 y ss.

instruments adopted by the US with other Latin American nations were executed in the first decade of the twenty-first century, specifically between the years 2003 and 2007.

A. PATENTS IN COMMERCIAL AGREEMENTS ADOPTED IN THE AMERICAS IN THE TWENTY-FIRST CENTURY

1. The Doha Declaration (2001) and the US Trade Promotion Act (2002)

The post-NAFTA-TRIPS times show significant changes with respect to the way patent rights had been treated in the past. The understandings and engagements applicable to patent rights were influenced by domestic and international developments such as the US Trade Promotion Authority Act of 2002 and the Doha Declaration on the TRIPS Agreement and Pubic Health of 2001.[6]

---

[6] The genesis of these changes is discussed in CORREA Carlos M, *Intellectual Property Rights, the WTO and Developing Countries. The TRIPS Agreement and Policy Options*, Zed Books Ltd (London and New York) and Third World Network (Penang, Malaysia), 2000. *See also* ZHANG Shu, *DE L'OMPI AU GATT, La protection internationale des droit de la propriété intellectuelle*, Editions Litec, Paris 1994, pp. 51–74 y 251–309. After five years of troubled negotiations, the Doha Development Round, aimed at freeing global trade and at extending the benefits of globalization to developing countries, was suspended following the failure of negotiators to reach a compromise about reducing farming subsidies and lowering import tariffs. This was not the first time one of the WTO negotiation rounds has broken down. Negotiations are inevitably complicated as each member has a veto over the final deal. The Uruguay Round, which began in 1986 and led to the replacement of the General Agreement on Tariffs and Trade (GATT) by the WTO in 1995, was frozen for over a year in 1990, due to antagonism between the EU and the US; although it was never formally suspended. The broad trade authority granted under the Trade Promotion Act (TPA) of 2002 to former US President George W Bush expired in July 2007. Past that date, observers believed that US Congress would resume its power to make amendments to any trade deal presented to it, thereby making it less attractive for other WTO members to participate in negotiations as they are unsure of obtaining any real commitments from the US. Before the July 2007 expiration date, the US administration signalled that it could attempt to extend the TPA to make an agreement more feasible. The key players in the negotiations, known as the G6, were Brazil and India (representing the G20 group), the EU, the US, Australia (representing the Cairns group of agricultural exporters) and Japan (representing the G10 group of net agricultural importers). Intellectual property is not expressly identified among the major sticking points in their discussions. *See: The Doha Development Round, EurActiv.com,*

In 2002, the US Congress enacted the Trade Promotion Authority Act stating that "any agreement governing intellectual property rights that are entered by the United States (must) reflect a standard of protection similar to that found in United States *law" (*Trade Promotion Authority Act of 2002, section 2102*).* In various issues, the standards of domestic US law are higher and stricter than those of TRIPS, this being the reason why some refer to them as *TRIPS-plus* standards. The Trade Promotion Authority Act was in force until July 2007.[7]

Consequently, after 2002, the standards that Latin American nations should have expected to be incorporated in commercial agreements including FTAs by US negotiators were those contemplated in US law. At least during the period when the Trade Promotion Authority Act of 2002 was in force (2002–2007). To a more limited extent, and only as far as certain health and patent issues are concerned, this is also true with respect to the understandings contained in the Doha Declaration on the TRIPS Agreement and Public Health adopted the year before the US Trade Promotion Authority Act was adopted by the US Congress.

2. Patent Law Provisions: Post-NAFTA Innovations

Examination of the intellectual property chapters of the commercial agreements entered by the US with these nations of the South in the first decade of the twenty-first century shows the adoption of innovations that did not appear in those types of instruments before the year 2003, where clear differences are evident in the way patent, trademark and related rights are treated, specifically in the area of pharmaceutical and agricultural chemical products. New issues now addressed in international patent law, specifically in bilateral commercial agreements, may be summarized as follows:

- Protection of undisclosed information involved in marketing approval proceedings.

EU New & Policy Positions Newsletter, August 1, 2006. http://www.euractiv.com/en/trade/doha-development-round/article-157082.

[7] For a discussion on these issues *see* MORIN Jean-Frédéric, *Tripping up TRIPS Debates: IP and Health in Bilateral Agreements*, in: *Propriètè intellectuelle: entre l'Art et l'argent*, ATRIP – Centre de Recherche en Droit Public – Faculté de droit, Université de Montréal, Les Éditions Thémis, Montreal 2006, pp. 322 *et seq. See also* DESAI Manisha A., *Free Trade Agreements in the Americas: Positive and Negative Impact*, 8 April 2008, ASIPI, AIPPI and IPO, Intellectual Property in the Americas: Free Trade Agreements, Current Issues and the future of IP, Mexico City, April 6–8, 2008.

- Obligation not to grant marketing approval to third parties prior to the expiration of the patent term of pharmaceutical patents (*patent linkage*).
- Obligation to make available to the patent owner the identity of a third party requesting marketing approval during the term of the patent (*patent linkage*).
- Extension of the patent term to compensate for unreasonable delays at the patent office.
- Extension of the patent term to compensate for unreasonable delays resulting from the marketing approval process.
- Patentability of new uses or methods of using known products.
- Exhaustion of patent rights.
- Traditional knowledge, genetic resources and equitable sharing of benefits.
- Ability of Latin American nations to take necessary measures to protect public health in terms of the Doha Declaration.

Protection of undisclosed information involved in marketing approval proceedings

The agreement signed in 2003 between the US and Chile includes a provision that appears for the first time in this type of bilateral trade agreement in Latin America: the protection of undisclosed information concerning the safety and efficacy of a pharmaceutical or agricultural chemical product which utilizes a new chemical entity, which product has not been previously approved. In situations involving products in these circumstances, the authorities of the respective countries agree not to permit third parties to market a pharmaceutical or agricultural chemical product based on this new chemical entity, on the basis of the approval granted to the party submitting such information, unless, of course, such party grants the necessary consent (Article 17.10.1, Chile – US).

This protection is granted for a five-year period from the date of approval of a pharmaceutical product and for a ten-year period from the date of approval of an agricultural chemical product.

A similar provision is found in the agreement with Central America and the Dominican Republic (Article 15.10.1 (a), CAFTA-DR) signed in 2004, as well as in the agreement with Peru (Article 16.10.1) signed in April 2006, the agreement with Colombia signed in November 2006 (Article 16.10.1), and the agreement with Panama signed on June 28, 2007 (Article 15.10, 1. and 2).

Similar bilateral agreements adopted by the US with other countries from regions other than Latin America reflect consistency with the rationale of the US Trade Promotion Act passed the year before (2002) the bilateral agreement with Chile was completed (2003). Therefore, the restrictions shown in the agreements with Latin America are also found in the trade agreements executed the following year (2004) by the US with Australia (Article 17.10.1, Australia–US), Bahrain (14.9.1) and Morocco (Article 15.10.1, Morocco–US).

Unlike other areas where no uniformity exists, this is an area suggesting that, in spite of the strong conflicting interests involved, this issue was not subject to negotiation or debate as evidently shown not only in the Latin American instruments adopted in 2003 (Chile), 2004 (CAFTA-DR), 2006 (Peru and Colombia) and 2007 (Panama) but also in the commercial agreements entered by the US in 2004 with nations as geographically distant as Australia, Morocco and Bahrain:

Article 17.10.1, Chile – US 2003
Article 15.10.1 (a), CAFTA-DR – US 2004
Article 16.10.1, Peru – US 2006
Article 16.10.1, Colombia – US 2006
Article 15.10.1, 2 Panama – US 2007
Article 17.10.1, Australia – US 2004
Article 14.9.1, Bahrain – US 2004
Article 15.10.1, Morocco – US 2004

Note that these bans apply irrespective of whether or not there is a patent involved. The source of the five-year and ten-year exclusivity is not found in patent rights, but is found instead in three requirements contemplated in these agreements:

- the undisclosed nature of the information supplied by the applicant of marketing approval;
- the novelty of the pharmaceutical or agricultural product involved in the marketing approval; and
- the absence of a previously granted marketing approval for the same product.

Where a patent is involved, a different independent rule – which is contemplated in the agreements – will apply.

Obligation not to grant marketing approval to third parties prior to the expiration of the patent term of pharmaceutical patents (*patent linkage*)

There are situations where marketing approval and sanitary authorities have granted marketing approval to third parties not having the consent of the patent owner in order for such parties to make and sell the pharmaceutical product claimed in the patent, even in the absence of the express consent on the part of the patent owner.

There are also situations where this way of proceeding is neither allowed nor forbidden by domestic health legislation and therefore patent owners are aware of situations where marketing approval and sanitary authorities have granted the corresponding permit to such third parties arguing *i.e.* that marketing approval and sanitary authorities are not patent enforcement authorities, and that therefore they are not bound to reject the marketing approval of products on the basis of the existence of a previously granted patent to a party other than the applicant of the marketing approval for a pharmaceutical product.

A marketing approval is only that, and is not an authorization to make and sell the pharmaceutical product involved in violation to exclusivity rights derived from a patent. It is difficult to imagine a patent enforcement authority who genuinely believes that a marketing approval is an authorization to infringe a patent, and the latter notwithstanding, patent owners are aware of situations where patent enforcement authorities at a given stage have accepted as a defense the marketing approval granted to an alleged infringer in a patent infringement law suit, thus superseding the exclusivity rights flown from a patent.

Anticipating the existence of patent enforcement authorities who *genuinely* believe that the plaintiff's patent rights cease to exist in a situation where the defendant raises as a defense the grant of a marketing approval or sanitary permit involving the patented pharmaceutical product, US patent owners have been inflexible and firm in incorporating a provision that prevents this kind of defense being raised and accepted by the courts where patent owners may exercise little control once the matter reaches the level of legal interpretation and construction, specifically in administrative proceedings where the patent owner formally is not one of the parties.

A pragmatic way of avoiding these ways of interpreting and applying the law is by preventing the law from being interpreted, specifically by preventing a marketing approval from being granted in a situation where the marketing approval involves a pharmaceutical product claimed in a patent that would be used as the basis of a patent infringement action. If the marketing approval is never granted to a party with no entitlement to receive the authorization, then such marketing approval can never be raised as a defense in patent infringement lawsuits. Also, if the marketing approval was granted to an unauthorized third party in violation of both patent rights and an engagement contained in an international instrument forbidding this conduct, then this sort of defense would be an invalid defense for being grounded on illegal conduct on the part of the marketing approval authority of the country where the patent infringement situation takes place.

This is certainly a resourceful approach and US negotiators have been inflexible in adopting it at the same time as a bilateral trade agreement is drafted. Since the year 2003, all countries who have completed such a bilateral FTA with the US in the Americas have acceded to the incorporation of a commitment whereby local authorities engage in not granting a marketing approval of a pharmaceutical product claimed in a patent. This is the case of the bilateral trade agreements executed by the US with Latin American countries like Chile, the Central American nations, the Dominican Republic, Peru, Colombia and Panama. The same commitment exists in terms of the bilateral trade agreements executed in 2004 by the US with other nations outside the Americas such as Australia, Bahrain and Morocco. This is an area where clear uniformity exists as shown in the text of these bilateral trade agreements recently executed by the US with nations from Latin America, North Africa, the Persian Gulf and Oceania:

Article 17.10.2 (c) Chile – US
Article 15.10.2 (a) CAFTA-DR – US
Article 16.10.3 (a) Peru – US
Article 16.10.3 (a) Colombia – US
Article 15.10.4 (1) Panama – US

Article 17.10.4 (a) Australia – US
Article 14.9.4 (a) Bahrain – US
Article 15.10.4 (a) Morocco – US

What the provision really intends is to prevent the grant of a marketing approval before the expiration of the patent term without the consent of the patent owner, as well as the unauthorized marketing of a product where that product is claimed in a patent.

Obligation to make available to the patent owner the identity of a third party requesting marketing approval during the term of the patent (*patent linkage*)

The language of the bilateral trade agreements to make patent rights effective is not limited to rejecting the marketing approval of a product recited in a patent to a party other than the patent owner. The marketing approval authority is now legally compelled to give notice to the patent owner of the identity of the party who applied for the respective marketing approval of a patented product without the consent of the patent owner.

The realism and practicality of this engagement depends in the first place on the information available to the marketing approval authority regarding the existence of a patent to cover the product involved in the marketing approval application filed by the unauthorized third party. Expressed differently, the marketing approval authority will be able to comply with this obligation only if the operation of the approval includes a mechanism that allows patent owners to inform the marketing approval authority of the existence of a patent where a pharmaceutical or an agricultural chemical has been claimed, but also the timely identification of the patented product that has been the subject of a marketing approval application. The engagement is contained in all trade agreements executed by the US with Latin American nations and other nations of the world:

Article 17.10.2 (b) Chile – US
Article 15.10.2 (b) CAFTA D.R. – US
Article 16.10.3 (b) Peru – US
Article 16.10.3 (b) Colombia – US
Article 15.10.4 (b) and 15,10.3 (b) Panama – US

Article 17.10.4 (b), (ii) Australia – US
Article 14.9.4 (b) Bahrain – US
Article 15.10.4 (b) Morocco – US

Extension of the patent term to compensate for unreasonable delays at the patent office

The common practice of patent offices around the world to take their time in examining and prosecuting patent applications, including the inevitable delays caused up to the time when prosecution is completed, is expressly addressed in all bilateral trade agreements entered by Latin American nations with the US.

All bilateral trade agreements provide for the obligation of the parties to adjust the term of the patent, at the request of the patent owner, to compensate for unreasonable delays that occurred in granting the patent.

An unreasonable delay is understood to include a delay in the issuance of the patent of more than five years from the date when the patent application was filed or more than three years from the date when the request for examination was filed, whichever is later.

Periods of time, *i.e.*, delays, attributable to actions of the patent applicant need not be included in the determination of such delays. This would be the case of continuous requests for extensions of a term to comply with any particular requirement, a common practice among patent applicants.

It is not totally clear whether the five-year term is intended to cover only the time of prosecution at the patent office or if this term also includes the time devoted to appeals of a rejection which in a best scenario would not take less than two years. But it is apparently not so, the absence of express references to these situations to court proceedings and the language used by the drafters suggest that the five-year term is restricted to prosecution at the patent office, the appeal's time not being included in this five-year term.

The specific mechanics on how the adjustments to the patent term will be made, *i.e.*, how the delays will be actually compensated, is not expressly addressed in the texts of the Latin American bilateral agreements, all of which contain the obligation to adjust and compensate for delays occurred at the Patent Office for which the Patent Office and not the applicant can be held responsible.

The treaty provisions where this issue is addressed are:

Article 17.9.6 Chile – US
Article 15.9.6 (a) CAFTA – DR – US
Article 16.9.6 (a) Peru – US
Article 16.9.6 (a) Colombia – US
Article 15.9, 6 (a) Panama – US

Article 17.9.8 (a) Australia – US
Article 14.8.6 (a) Bahrain – US
Article 15.9.7 Morocco – US

Extension of the patent term to compensate for unreasonable delays resulting from the marketing approval process

Similar delays to those found on the occasion of the prosecution of a patent application are often found during the marketing approval process. For this reason, the representatives of the US delegation in these works have succeeded in incorporating into the bilateral trade agreements the obligation on the part of the Latin American nations to make available an extension of the patent term to compensate the patent owner for unreasonable curtailment, shortening or reduction of the patent term as a result of the marketing approval process.

The obligation to make available this extension is contained in all bilateral trade agreements executed by the US with other Latin American nations beginning with the agreement with Chile in 2003. The same obligation also shows up in the other bilateral agreements examined in this study:

Article 17.10.2(a) Chile – US
Article 15.9.6 (b) CAFTA – D.R.-US
Article 16.9.6 (b) Peru – US
Article 16.9.6 (b) Colombia – US
Article 15.9.6 (b) Panama – US

Article 17.9.7 (b) Australia – US
Article 14.8.6 (b) (i) Bahrain – US
Article 15.10.3 Morocco – US

Patentability of new uses or methods of using known products
Recently adopted bilateral agreements between the US and other countries include express references to the obligation of the parties to grant patents involving new uses or new methods of using known products. This is the case of the agreements with countries like Australia (Article 17.9.1), Morocco (Article 15.9.2) and Bahrain (Article 14.8.2). These three agreements were signed in 2004, shortly after the US had signed a similar bilateral agreement with Chile (June 6, 2003) which does not include similar provisions. It may therefore seem that the obligation to grant patents for new uses is a development introduced in all bilateral agreements signed in 2004, but this is not the case. Another bilateral agreement signed the same year 2004 with Central America (*i.e.*, with a group of Central American nations) does not address the obligation to grant patents for new uses or methods of using known products as in the other bilateral agreements signed the same year with Australia, Morocco and Bahrain. The bilateral agreement signed with Peru on April 12, 2006 does not address the issue, and this is also the case of the agreement with Colombia signed on November 22, 2006, which does not address the issue of patentability of new uses. The agreement with Panama addresses some obligations applicable to patent claims that cover an approved pharmaceutical product or its approved method of use. Nevertheless, this agreement does not contain an express engagement to accept patent claims for new uses or methods of using methods of known products as explicit as in the agreement with Morocco, Bahrain and Australia also signed in 2006.

Exhaustion of patent rights
The TRIPS Agreement includes a provision where the drafters stipulated that *for the purposes of dispute settlement under the Agreement, nothing in TRIPS would be used to address the issue of exhaustion of intellectual property rights* (Article 6, TRIPS). Subsequently, on the occasion of the Doha Declaration on the TRIPS Agreement and Public Health adopted seven years after TRIPS, WTO members ratified the notion generally addressed

in TRIPS and eliminated room for interpretation by introducing new language in the sense that, "The effect of the provisions in the TRIPS Agreement that are relevant to the exhaustion of intellectual property rights is to leave each Member free to establish its own regime for such exhaustion without challenge."[8]

This means that, in their domestic legislation, WTO members are free to adopt a system of national, regional or international exhaustion of intellectual property rights including patent rights and that whatever measure is adopted by members on this issue and the issue of whether or not parallel imports are allowed, may not be regarded as a TRIPS violation.

Exercising this right, the bilateral trade agreements US – Australia (Article 17.9.4) and US – Morocco reflect ideas that not only incorporate the adoption of a system of national exhaustion of patent rights by statute but also by contract. Not unlike the school of thought adopted in 1994 through the TRIPS Agreement, the language chosen by the drafters to address this issue is strange and unnecessarily complicated, perhaps with the idea of leaving some room for more than one interpretation or even with the idea of hiding plain language, *i.e.*, the language generally used to address exhaustion of rights and parallel imports is in more precise terms. In spite of this, the underlying principle that parallel imports of patented products are not allowed in these bilateral relationship is clearly there.

The bilateral US agreement with Chile was executed in 2003 and does not include provisions on parallel imports of the nature apparently adopted for the first time in 2006 in the bilateral agreements executed by the US with Australia and Morocco. Interestingly, the bilateral agreement executed the same year 2004 with Central America and the Dominican Republic does not refer to this topic. The bilateral agreement signed two years later in April of 2006 between the US and Peru does not address this issue either, and this is also the case of the agreement with Colombia (signed on November 22, 2006) and the agreement with Panama (signed on June 28, 2007) where the issue of parallel imports of patented products is not addressed. As far as these countries are concerned, the TRIPS standards generally contemplated in Article 6 remain.

---

[8] *Subject to the MFN and national treatment provisions of Articles 3 and 4.* WORLD TRADE ORGANIZATION, WT/MIN(01)/DEC/2, 20 November, 2001 (01-5860), MINISTERIAL CONFERENCE, Fourth Session, Doha, 9–14 November, 2001, *DECLARATION ON THE TRIPS AGREEMENT AND PUBLIC HEALTH* Adopted on 14 November, 2001. http://www.worldtradelaw.net/doha/tripshealth.pdf.

Traditional knowledge, genetic resources and equitable sharing of benefits
For the first time in bilateral official understandings in the region, the agreements with Peru signed on April 12, 2006 and Colombia signed on November 22, 2006 reflect the concern of these nations on subjects that had never been included in bilateral trade agreements in the region. This is the case of topics like traditional knowledge, genetic resources and equitable sharing of benefits, which have been on the international agenda for several years at the request of developing countries. Some of the concerns relative to these three issues appear for the first time in the agreements with Peru and Colombia under the heading: "Understanding regarding biodiversity and traditional knowledge" (for text see below Box 3.1)

BOX 3.1 UNDERSTANDING REGARDING BIODIVERSITY AND TRADITIONAL KNOWLEDGE

"The Governments of the United States of America and the Republic of Colombia **have reached the following understandings** concerning biodiversity and traditional knowledge in connection with the United States – Colombia Trade Promotion Agreement signed this day:

The Parties recognize the importance of traditional knowledge and biodiversity, as well as the potential contribution of traditional knowledge and biodiversity to cultural, economic, and social development.

The Parties **recognize the importance** of the following:

(1) obtaining informed consent from the appropriate authority prior to accessing genetic resources under the control of such authority;
(2) equitably sharing the benefits arising from the use of traditional knowledge and genetic resources; and
(3) promoting quality patent examination to ensure the conditions of patentability are satisfied.

The Parties recognize that access to genetic resources or traditional knowledge, as well as the equitable sharing of benefits that may result from use of those resources or that knowledge, can be adequately addressed through contracts that reflect mutually agreed terms between users and providers.

Each Party shall endeavor to seek ways to share information that may have a bearing on the patentability of inventions based on traditional knowledge or genetic resources by providing:

(a) publicly accessible databases that contain relevant information; and
(b) an opportunity to cite, in writing, to the appropriate examining authority prior art that may have a bearing on patentability."

Note that the understanding relative to biodiversity and traditional knowledge is not a legal provision on which Peru and Colombia may eventually rely to compel US companies or the US Government to observe any particular commitment. That is to say, the understanding does not embody the text of an engagement but a mere recognition that these topics are important and only that. The reality is that even if there was good faith in searching for compliance of a true engagement by the parties in any particular sense, the nature of the legal issues involved would in most cases make the implementation of such understanding a mere declaration of good faith unless the parties agreed in specific mechanisms to implement an engagement in this difficult area of the law, that is often associated with intellectual property rights but where little resemblance to these rights are available with a view to relying on them in search for implementation of a legal engagement by the parties. The recognition of the importance of these topics as contained in the agreements with Peru and Colombia may eventually give the parties the basis to discuss contractual understandings that may be influenced by the experience in dealing with commercial transactions and licensing operations that involve the exploitation of intellectual property rights even if, in the strict sense, no intellectual property right is involved in a transaction of this nature.

The agreement with Panama signed on June 28, 2007, also includes an acknowledgement of the importance for each party of traditional knowledge and folklore to its people. Unlike the agreement with Peru and Colombia executed the previous year, the agreement with Panama includes two provisions not read in these two instruments, namely:

> Accordingly, the Parties will seek to work together in consulting on issues and positions in the World Intellectual Property Organization Intergovernmental Committee on Intellectual Property and Genetic Resources, Traditional Knowledge, and Folklore in addressing matters related to traditional knowledge and folklore.
>
> If the United States and another government sign a free trade agreement that contains provisions addressing traditional knowledge or folklore, the

United States and Panama shall promptly consult after that agreement enters into force on whether to apply similar provisions, as appropriate, between the United States and Panama.

Ability of Latin American nations to take necessary measures to protect public health in terms of the Doha Declaration

Another area not previously incorporated in the text of a trade agreement in the Latin American region, specifically in a bilateral trade agreement where the US is one of the parties, has to do with the incorporation of language which makes clear that no understanding contained in the intellectual property chapter of the bilateral trade agreement may be construed as derogating between the parties' previous international understandings in the context of the Doha Declaration on the TRIPS Agreement and Public Health. In the Latin American region, these understandings were first introduced through CAFTA-DR in 2004 and afterwards in the Peruvian agreement signed in 2006.

Unlike the understanding included in the agreement with Colombia on traditional knowledge, genetic resources and equitable sharing of benefits where no true engagement exists but only a mere recognition of the importance of these topics, the understanding on the ability to take necessary measures to protect public health of CAFTA and the agreement with Peru includes an express engagement in the sense that the text of the bilateral trade agreement does not derogate the previously adopted understandings in the context of the Doha Declaration on the TRIPS Agreement and Public Health limited, of course, to the specific situations addressed in CAFTA–DR – USA and the recently executed bilateral agreement between the USA and Peru in the following terms (see Box 3.2 below):

BOX 3.2 CAFTA-DR
"UNDERSTANDING REGARDING
CERTAIN PUBLIC HEALTH MEASURES
AUGUST 5, 2004

The Governments of the Republic of Costa Rica, the Dominican Republic, the Republic of El Salvador, the Republic of Guatemala, the Republic of Honduras, the Republic of Nicaragua, and the United States of America **have reached the following understandings** regarding Chapter Fifteen (Intellectual Property Rights) of the Dominican Republic – Central America – United States Free Trade Agreement signed this day (the "Agreement"):

The obligations of Chapter Fifteen do not affect a Party's ability to take necessary measures to protect public health by promoting access to medicines for all, in particular concerning cases such as HIV/AIDS, tuberculosis, malaria, and other epidemics as well as circumstances of extreme urgency or national emergency.

In recognition of the commitment to access to medicines that are supplied in accordance with the Decision of the General Council of 30 August 2003 on the Implementation of Paragraph Six of the Doha Declaration on the TRIPS Agreement and public health (WT/L/540) and the WTO General Council Chairman's statement accompanying the Decision (JOB(03)/177, WT/GC/M/82) (collectively the "TRIPS/health solution"), ***Chapter Fifteen does not prevent the effective utilization of the TRIPS/health solution.***

With respect to the aforementioned matters, if an amendment of a pertinent provision of the WTO Agreement on Trade-Related Aspects of Intellectual Property Rights (1994) enters into force with respect to the Parties and that amendment is incompatible with Chapter Fifteen, our Governments shall immediately consult in order to adapt Chapter Fifteen as appropriate in the light of the amendment.

FOR THE GOVERNMENT OF COSTA RICA:
FOR THE GOVERNMENT OF THE DOMINICAN REPUBLIC:
FOR THE GOVERNMENT OF EL SALVADOR:
FOR THE GOVERNMENT OF GUATEMALA:
FOR THE GOVERNMENT OF HONDURAS:
FOR THE GOVERNMENT OF NICARAGUA:
FOR THE GOVERNMENT OF THE UNITED STATES OF AMERICA."

Based on the text of CAFTA signed in 2004, the Peruvian negotiators succeeded in introducing a similar text as part of the understandings contained in the bilateral trade agreement with the US executed two years later (see Box 3.3 below).

BOX 3.3 "PERU – UNDERSTANDINGS REGARDING CERTAIN PUBLIC HEALTH MEASURES APRIL 12, 2006

The Governments of the United States of America and of the Republic of Peru have reached the following understandings regarding Chapter Sixteen (Intellectual Property Rights) of the United States – Peru Trade Promotion Agreement ("Agreement") signed this day:

The obligations of Chapter Sixteen of the Agreement do not affect a Party's ability to take necessary measures to protect public health by promoting access to medicines for all, in particular concerning cases such as HIV/AIDS, tuberculosis, malaria, and other epidemics as well as circumstances of extreme urgency or national emergency.

In recognition of the commitment to access to medicines that are supplied in accordance with the Decision of the General Council of 30 August 2003 on the Implementation of Paragraph Six of the Doha Declaration on the TRIPS Agreement and Public Health (WT/L/540) and the WTO General Council Chairman's statement accompanying the Decision (JOB(03)/177, WT/GC/M/82) (collectively the "TRIPS/health solution"), ***Chapter Sixteen does not prevent the effective utilization of the TRIPS/health solution***.

With respect to the aforementioned matters, if an amendment of the WTO Agreement on Trade-Related Aspects of Intellectual Property Rights (1994) enters into force with respect to the Parties and a Party's application of a measure in conformity with that amendment violates Chapter Sixteen of the Agreement, our Governments shall immediately consult in order to adapt Chapter Sixteen as appropriate in the light of the amendment.

FOR THE GOVERNMENT OF THE UNITED STATES OF AMERICA: THE REPUBLIC OF PERU."

The same is true with respect to the agreement with Colombia of the same year 2006, and the agreement with Panama completed in 2007. This is an area where uniformity tends to be established as from 2004 at the evident action of the Latin American nations involved in the adoption of this kind of bilateral trade agreement with the US.

B. TRADEMARKS IN COMMERCIAL AGREEMENTS ADOPTED IN THE AMERICAS IN THE FIRST DECADE OF THE TWENTY FIRST CENTURY

Post-NAFTA Innovations

The legal institutions that show up for the first time in the Americas, specifically in bilateral agreements executed by the US with Latin American nations in the first decade of the twenty-first century discussed in this chapter, may be summarized as follows:

- Obligation to register not visually perceptible trademarks.
- Obligation to protect sound and scent marks.
- Well-known marks must be protected in situations involving goods and services that are not similar to a well-known unregistered trademark.
- Obligation to be guided by World Intellectual Property Organization (WIPO) Joint Recommendation of Well-known Trademarks.
- Obligation to adopt the international classification contained in the Nice Agreement.
- Class does not govern confusing similarity (but actual similarity or lack of similarity of the goods or services involved).
- No party may require recordation of trademark licenses.
- Common procedural provisions applicable to trademark registration proceedings.
- Members are compelled to Adopt a System of Certification Marks.
- Geographical Indications, Collective Marks and Certification Marks.
- Engagement to Join the Protocol Relating to the Madrid Agreement Concerning the International Registration of Marks (1989).
- Engagement to Join the Trademark Law Treaty (1994).

Not all provisions addressing the new issues contained for the first time in commercial agreements concluded in the Americas appear in each and all of the agreements signed by the US with a Latin American nation in the first decade of the twenty-first century, specifically between 2003 and 2007. Many of them are common to various agreements in the region, and have definitely influenced the adoption of subsequent commercial agreements where the US is one of the parties. What matters for purpose of this discussion is that many of the provisions in question appear for the first time whether in multinational instruments – such as TRIPS – or in a bilateral agreement like the one executed by the US with a Latin American nation in recent times.

Obligation to register not visually perceptible trademarks

In 1993 NAFTA provided that "a Party may require, as a condition for registration, that a sign be visually perceptible" (Article 1708, 1).[9] Under this principle, NAFTA members were free to reject the registration of a mark on the sole grounds that the mark consisted in a sound or a scent. The drafters of the new agreements have departed from these criteria when providing that "trademarks must not be visually perceptible" as a condition for registration. That is to say, must not *necessarily* be visually perceptible as a condition for registration. This means that the option available for NAFTA members as adopted in 1993, is no longer available for the Latin American nations who have entered a commercial agreement with the US during the first decade of the twenty-first century, where parties are bound to accept for registration trademarks that are not visually perceptible. This new provision shows up in the agreements between the US with Chile, Peru and Colombia, but not in those with the Dominican Republic and CAFTA countries which still follow the NAFTA rule.

Obligation to protect sound and scent or smell marks

Under the old NAFTA criteria, members were free to reject the registration of a mark on the sole grounds that the mark consisted in a sound or a scent. This alternative is no longer available under the new commercial agreements. These contain an express indication in the sense that the parties may not reject the registration of a mark on the sole grounds that it consists in a sound or a scent. This is simply a ratification of the new rule whereby parties to the new treaties are compelled to accept for registration marks that are not visually perceptible as in the case of the agreement with Chile, Panama, Peru and Colombia, but not in CAFTA-DR.[10]

---

[9] "*Article 1708: Trademarks (NAFTA). 1.* For purposes of this Agreement, a trademark consists of any sign, or any combination of signs, capable of distinguishing the goods or services of one person from those of another, including personal names, designs, letters, numerals, colors, figurative elements, or the shape of goods or of their packaging. Trademarks shall include service marks and collective marks, and may include certification marks. A Party may require, as a condition for registration, that a sign be visually perceptible."

[10] The idea to extend trademark protection to all forms of signs including traditional and non-traditional trademarks has not been welcome in the same way in all parts of the world. This is the case of Japan where a group on *Non-Traditional Trademarks* formed by local trademark specialists, a few years ago recommended against the adoption of a system to protect smell or scent marks which should

Well-known marks must be protected in situations involving goods and services that are not similar to a well-known unregistered trademark

TRIPS provides that members are bound to apply Article 6*bis* of the Paris Convention *mutatis mutandis* to situations involving goods and services that are not similar to those covered by a registered trademark.

The requirement that there be a registered mark as a condition precedent in order for the well-known trademark owner to attack the unauthorized use of the same or similar mark as applied to different goods from those covered by the registration has been expunged from the text of the new commercial agreements. In other words, under the new agreements, it should suffice to establish that the mark is well known for certain goods or services, and that the third party has used the same or a similar mark for goods or services that are not similar, in order for the well-known trademark owner to have the stand to attack the unauthorized use of the third party. What controls is that the moving party be able to establish:

- that the unauthorized user indicate a connection between those goods or services and the owner of the well-known trademark, and
- that the interests of the owner of the trademark are likely to be damaged by such use.

The requirement that there should exist at least a registration for the mark sought to be protected in a situation involving different goods or services has been eliminated in all commercial agreements executed by the US with Latin American nations in the first decade of the twenty-first century specifically between 2003 and 2007, namely, CAFTA-DR, Chile, Panama, Peru and Colombia.

In the absence of at least one registration to cover certain goods or services, one has to wonder which is going to be the subject matter that will play the role of a frame of reference to determine whether the third

---

be excluded from trademark protection under current policy applicable to non-traditional trademarks in Japan. The latter, for two basic reasons. First the legal difficulties in determining the scope of the right granted to this type of trademarks, and second, the reduced number of applicants for the registration of smell marks at the Japanese Trademark Office. Report of the author's colleague AOKI Hiromichi, a partner with the YUASA and HARA law firm in Tokyo, member of the Non-Traditional Trademarks Group in Japan where the reported decision was reached. International Trademark Association, Regional Update – ASIA, Monday, May 24, 2010, Boston, Mass. (132nd Annual Meeting May 22–26, 2010).

party's use is in relation to the same, similar or different goods or services. Everything indicates that such subject matter need not to be a registration but rather appropriate evidentiary material attesting the existence of a well-known mark in relation to certain goods or services. Whether this well-known mark is registered to cover certain goods or services that are neither the same nor similar to those of the third party is immaterial. What is relevant is that the moving party or the authority be able to establish the existence of a well-known mark that is notorious in respect of certain goods or services that are neither the same nor similar to those the third party applies. Having established this, the moving party should further establish the two requirements referred to above.

Expressed differently, what the new agreements require as conditions to access the extended protection to goods or services that are not the same nor similar to those distinguished by the well-known mark are not only the two conditions expressly contemplated in recent treaty law. Instead, what the moving party should establish is a series of requirements that can be best identified in four categories, namely:

- the existence of a well-known mark which became notorious prior to the unauthorized adoption of the same or a similar mark by a third party;
- the fact that the well-known mark was a notorious mark in relation to certain goods or services whether or not a trade or service mark registration exists for such well-known mark in relation to certain goods or services;
- that the unauthorized user indicate a connection between those goods or services and the owner of the well-known trademark; and
- that the interests of the owner of the trademark are likely to be damaged by such use.

The language and notions adopted by the drafters of treaty law adopted in the Americas in the first decade of the twenty-first century endorse the old orthodox principle of trademark and unfair competition law that appreciates notoriety as a source of rights independent of trademark use and trademark registration. Under this strict principle of the law governing notoriety, all that the party arguing notoriety as a source of trademark rights is bound to establish is that the mark sought to be protected against the unauthorized adoption thereof by a third party was a well-known mark prior to the adoption of the same or a similar mark by the third party, in the circumstances inscribed in the new commercial instruments adopted in the Americas in recent times. Under this line of thinking, no obligation to show trademark registration or trademark use may be required to the party relying on notoriety as a source or trademark rights.

Obligation to be guided by WIPO Joint Recommendation of Well-known Trademarks

In 1999, the General Assembly of WIPO and the Assembly of the Paris Union adopted a *Joint Recommendation Concerning Provisions on the Protection of Well-known Marks*, which is merely a recommendation that Paris Union and WIPO Members are not necessarily bound to follow, depending on a number of factors including the way local jurisprudence has developed and on the way international law is construed and interpreted by national courts. At least one of the Latin American countries who have executed a commercial agreement with the US in the first decade of the twenty-first century has agreed to use the principles of the Joint Recommendation on well-known marks of 1999 *to guide* the resolutions and decisions involving these issues. While the Joint Recommendation has been in existence since 1999, an engagement of the tone adopted in the agreement between the US and Chile had never been introduced as shown in the commercial agreement executed in 2003.

Obligation to adopt the international classification contained in the Nice Agreement

All agreements contain an engagement in the sense of adopting the International Classification of Goods and Services for the Purposes of the Registration of Marks at the time the registrations granted by members are published, specifically at the time the goods and services covered by each registration are identified in public records. The agreements do not compel the parties to join the Nice Agreement, but only compel the parties to use the classification contained therein for purposes of identification of the goods and services covered by local registrations. Unlike the other agreements, the agreement with Chile does not contain an express engagement but simply an understanding whereby the parties are encouraged to use the international classification when the subject matter covered by each registration is identified.

Class does not govern confusing similarity (but actual similarity or lack of similarity of the goods or services involved)

It has been common practice throughout the world to assume that the goods or services that fall into the same class of the international classification should be regarded as similar goods or services simply for the reason that the goods or services fall into the same class. Likewise, practitioners and authorities frequently assume that the goods or services are not similar for the reason that they do not fall into the same class. Abundant precedents in many countries of the world established several years ago that while this may be the case in many situations, it is not necessarily the rule for all as there may be cases involving goods or services that fall into the same class that are not necessarily similar goods or services in a trademark sense. This has also been the case where it appears that even if the goods or services do fall into different classes, the reality is that there is a similarity between the goods or services involved from a trademark standpoint. It has, therefore been sustained that it is the actual similarity between the goods or services involved, and not the fact that they pertain to the same class, that really controls similarity of goods or services for purposes of establishing whether or not two trademarks are confusingly similar. The new commercial agreements include an express provision in the sense that these latter criteria should govern the determination of similarity and likelihood of confusion, and not the fact that the goods in question fall into the same or different class. All agreements discussed in this chapter adopted in the first decade of the twenty-first century in the Americas include a similar provision.

No party may require recordation of trademark licenses

National legislations – like Mexican trademark law – often require the recordation of a trademark license at the trademark office as a condition precedent in order for the use made by a licensee to inure into the benefit of the trademark owner-licensor. Lack of record of the licensee is followed by lack of trademark use and therefore makes the respective registration vulnerable to third-party attack on non-use grounds even if in reality the registered mark is being used by an authorized licensee who has not been registered at the trademark office as an authorized user of the registered mark.

The new agreements include a new provision not *expressis verbis* included in previous international instruments in the region whereby the parties to the commercial agreements recently executed by the US with other Latin American nations are prevented from requiring the recordation of the licensee to establish validity of the license, to assert any rights in a trademark or for other purposes.

All commercial agreements but the one between US and Chile include an engagement to this effect.

This forms a part of what seems to be a trend implemented by local trademark offices to get rid of paper and paper work, a trend that does not necessarily operate in the best interest of the public. There are day-to-day situations clearly showing the negative impact that may follow the absence of registration of an exclusive licensee in situations where a good-faith licensee is granted a license by a licensor who has already engaged into not doing so. The availability of legal tools, resources and remedies to cope with this type of situation by a good-faith licensee is not disputed. What is suggested here is that, from a trademark law standpoint, the interest of all those involved, including licensors and licensees, would be better served if the parties to a transaction as described were under an express legal obligation to give notice to the trademark office of the existence of a license, particularly when the license is exclusive in nature. Apart from what recent treaty law in the Americas indicates with respect to these issues, trademark licensees will always be well advised to handle the transaction in a way that third parties are legally informed of the existence of an exclusive license, instead of having to implement complex and expensive litigation mechanisms to correct something that should have been avoided by diligently giving notice to the trademark office about the existence of an exclusive license in terms not totally dissimilar to those that should be implemented in situations involving the assignment of a trademark registration.

Common procedural provisions applicable to trademark registration proceedings

All agreements contain a procedural provision generally addressing the way trademark applications should be prosecuted by members, including the right of the applicant to appeal any final decision on the part of the trademark office. The reason for the US having had the initiative to incorporate these provisions in the commercial agreements is not that basic principles governing these issues were not contemplated in the local law and practice of the members to these instruments. Instead, it appears that the resistance to adopting these sort of provisions in other *fora* such as FTAA-ALCA (Free Trade Area of the Americas-Área de Libre Comercio de América) has to do with the Latin American nations opposing uniformity where it is not actually needed or desired, particularly in areas involving procedural questions where international instruments should not be insisted on as long as the basic principles governing questions such as the right to be heard and similar notions are respected, observed and implemented.

Members are compelled to adopt a system of certification marks

NAFTA included a reference to reflect that members were compelled to adopt a system of protection of collective marks, but were free to adopt a system of certification marks if that was their desire. The alternative available under NAFTA standards for the adoption of certification marks is no longer available for Latin American nations who have entered a commercial agreement with the US in the first decade of the twenty-first century. Agreements now provide that each member shall provide that trademarks shall include collective and certification marks.

Geographical indications, collective marks and certification marks
Commercial Agreements executed by the same nations with the US in the last decade now include an express engagement to the effect that signs that may serve, in the course of trade, as a geographical indications, *may* constitute certification or collective marks. Note that members are not bound *expressis verbis* to protect geographical indications either as collective marks or certification marks. The alternative to protect geographical indications under trademark principles still appears to be there. If the member decides to go for this trademark approach, then the member still has another alternative consisting in implementing the collective mark approach or the certification mark approach. Not to be confused with the obligation to adopt a system of protection both of collective marks and certification marks, which is indisputably there. Whether the system is subsequently used to protect geographical indications, is up to the parties. The whole idea is that members do not have the excuse that a geographical indication cannot be protected either as a collective mark or a certification mark for the reason that domestic legislation does not contemplate a system of protection of collective marks and certification marks. But again, the texts are vague enough that allow an interpretation in the sense that whenever a sign may serve in the course of trade as a geographical indication, members are bound to protect that sign either as a collective mark or as a certification mark.

Engagement to join the Protocol Relating to the Madrid Agreement Concerning the International Registration of Marks (1989)
All trade agreements executed by the US with a Latin American nation in the first decade of the twenty-first century include some sort of engagement in order for the Latin American partner to join the Madrid Protocol. While the engagement is essentially the same in all cases, the wording varies from case to case ranging from an actual commitment to be a part of the Madrid Protocol within a certain period of time to the obligation to exercise all reasonable efforts to join the Madrid Protocol.

Engagement to join the Trademark Law Treaty (1994)
Not unlike the engagement to join the Madrid Protocol, all trade agreements executed by the US with a Latin American nation in the first decade of the twenty-first century, include the engagement of the Latin American partner to exercise all reasonable efforts to join the Trademark Law Treaty (TLT) (1994). The wording varies from case to case from the actual commitment to join TLT by a certain date to the obligation to exercise all reasonable efforts to join this treaty. No reference is made to the TLT of Singapore adopted in 2006 in any of these trade agreements.

FINAL REMARKS

This final section attempts to draw some further general conclusions.

a. Examination of trade agreements executed by the US with Latin American nations in the first decade of the twenty-first century shows that the adoption of these instruments has been the occasion to introduce patent law innovations with a direct impact in the way pharmaceutical inventions are treated in the territory of the commercial partners of the South including Latin America.
b. The new language introduced in the agreements recently executed represents an innovation not only with respect to the texts read in commercial agreements, both regional and multinational, adopted by the end of the twentieth century like NAFTA and TRIPS, but also with respect to the way pharmaceutical inventions are regulated in most domestic statutes of the region.
c. A comparison of the patent law innovations introduced in the new commercial agreements shows that some of them remained within brackets in previous attempts implemented towards obtaining harmonization in the region, such as FTAA (ALCA), where no agreement was reached on the adoption of some of the new provisions later adopted in bilateral commercial agreements.
d. The negotiation and adoption of bilateral commercial instruments is a clear implementation of Julius Cesar's philosophy *divide et vinces*: divide and rule, and also as a pragmatic organizational tool that recognizes plurality where uniformity cannot be achieved, at least not in the short term.
e. Acknowledging that new patent law institutions are now regulated through regional and bilateral trade law recently adopted in the Americas, examination of the pertinent texts shows that in some instances all that the Latin American agreements have in common is the incorporation of an institution previously unknown in international instruments in the region, and that the new institution is not always regulated in the same way in all commercial instruments. This is the case of new patent law institutions where provisions have been adopted to clearly engage the parties in a particular conduct, whereas in other cases the issue is addressed only to make it clear that no such engagement exists and that the parties are free to act in the way that best fits their domestic interests, goals or policies.
f. Examination of bilateral trade law recently adopted in the Americas shows that during the first decade of the twenty-first century, partial harmonization has been achieved in the Americas through the

implementation of bilateral mechanisms on issues where regional efforts headed by those implemented by the US have failed to obtain such harmonization, specifically in the context of a project to create FTAA. What observers are witnessing in the second decade of the twenty-first century in the Americas is a process of harmonization through a variety of bilateral efforts successfully implemented by the US negotiators in patent areas having an impact on the pharmaceutical industry on issues such as

- Protection of undisclosed information involved in marketing approval proceedings.
- Obligation not to grant marketing approval to third parties prior to the expiration of the patent term of pharmaceutical patents (patent linkage).
- Obligation to make available to the patent owner the identity of a third party requesting marketing approval during the term of the patent (patent linkage).
- Extension of the patent term to compensate for unreasonable delays at the patent office.
- Extension of the patent term to compensate for unreasonable delays resulting from the marketing approval process.

g. Unlike the above areas which are regulated in all the bilateral agreements included in this study, there are other topics which only show up in some of the agreements. This is the case of the following topics
   - Patentability of new uses or methods of using known products.
   - Exhaustion of patent rights.
   - Traditional knowledge, genetic resources and equitable sharing of benefits.
   - Ability of Latin American nations to take necessary measures to protect public health in terms of the Doha Declaration and the work resulting therefrom.

h. Three agreements contain language that for the first time appear in a commercial agreement where the US is a party, namely the provisions stressing the importance of:
   - prior informed consent to access genetic resources,
   - equitable sharing from use of genetic resources and
   - traditional knowledge.

   The wording chosen by the drafters allows for more than one interpretation of the new provisions on these three issues, but the new texts are there, ready to be interpreted in specific situations pursuant to applicable law including that contained in the Vienna Convention on the Law of Treaties.

i. Whether as an obligation or as a mere statement expressed in good faith by the parties, the new century has brought to the South and to the North new legal obligations and attitudes that have to do with sensitive health and patent law issues with which patent owners, practitioners, negotiators, advisors and academics involved in international trade law and international intellectual property law should become familiar for indicators exist suggesting that they could be here to spread both in the South and North. This could be particularly true in cases involving TRIPS-*plus* issues that appear to be reasonable symbols of respect to third-party rights irrespective of the nature of such rights, and irrespective of whether the demand comes from the North or the South.
j. Not unlike the patent law situation, in the case of trademarks, many of the trademark provisions that show up in the commercial agreements entered by the US with Latin America in the first decade of the twenty-first century, specifically between the years 2003 and 2007, have been within brackets in the drafts for an intellectual property chapter (XX) of FTAA. In the last draft that relates back to the year 2003, such trademark provisions remained within brackets, meaning that the negotiators for the adoption of this regional instrument had not reached an agreement on whether or not these specific trademark issues should be included in the FTAA, and the conditions in which such issues should be incorporated into the FTAA draft.[11]
k. It is interesting to note that all the commercial agreements entered by the US with a Latin American nation in the first decade of the twenty-first century between 2003 and 2007, were executed as from the time when the parties stopped the negotiations that led to the final draft of a Chapter XX on Intellectual Property in FTAA that relates back to November 21, 2003.[12]
l. It has been submitted that Latin America will be able to improve its bargaining position on IP and other trade matters in negotiations

[11] For a discussion on the trademark provisions of the Free Trade Agreement of the Americas (FTAA-ALCA) see RANGEL-ORTIZ Horacio, Aspectos de propiedad industrial relativos al proyecto para un acuerdo de libre comercio de las Américas (ALCA): el caso de las marcas, in Estudios sobre propiedad industrial e intelectual y Derecho de la competencia. Colección de trabajos en Homenaje a Alberto BERCOVITZ Rodríguez-Cano Ofrecida por el Grupo Español de la AIPPI, pp. 874–93.

[12] *See* FTAA.TNC/W/133/Rev3 at www.ftaa-alca.org/FTAADraft03/ChapterXX_e.asp and http://www.ftaa-alca.org/FTAADraft03/TOCWord_e.asp. *See also* http://www.uschamber.com/international/policy/drcafta.htm and http://www.state.gov/r/pa/ei/bgn/2019.htm.

with the US, the European Union or Japan only when members of this region of the world are willing to negotiate as a group and not as isolated separate countries. This makes a lot of sense and, in an ideal world – for Latin America – this strategic approach could have been implemented by the Latin American community, or any other community formed by several countries wishing to complete a trade agreement with another nation. The problem with achieving the desired results sought by implementing this negotiating approach is that large and powerful economies like the US are aware of the immediate benefits of implementing Julius Cesar's philosophy *divide et vinces*, divide and rule, divide and govern, as suggested in the *modus operandi* implemented by the US that allowed in bilateral negotiations what remained in brackets in the context of FTAA exercises.

m. The philosophy of *divide and rule* may be seen in two possible ways. First, as an opportunistic attitude adopted to make the other side smaller and weaker, and therefore less dangerous as an adversary; and second, as an organizational strategy to provide a solution to a complicated problem in a way not totally different from the way intellectual property specialists solve complex questions, beginning by detecting the different components of the problem and attacking them part by part individually, until it is found that the solution of the problem was not as complicated as it appeared when it was first looked at in its entirety, as a whole.
n. The line of thinking that suggests dividing to govern is both pragmatic and romantic. It acknowledges the existence of a plurality where uniformity is only apparent, thereby giving respect to individuality, that is to say, to the different individualities that exist in the international community, whether regional, sub-regional or bilateral.
o. It is suggested that the position of the US as a skilled negotiator of bilateral and sub-regional trade agreements with 20 nations of different regions of the world is not either of these two possible extreme approaches. As happens each time a decision has to be made between two extreme positions, it is always easier to find the eclectic route, and this will not be the exception. For good or bad, bilateral instruments – and to a certain extent, sub-regional instruments like CAFTA-DR – tend to depart from certain multinational propositions and positions, as in the case of FTAA, but this is never free. Something – that never shows up *expressis verbis* in the text of international instruments, but is invariably present – was negotiated in exchange. To assert that results that failed in the regional context succeeded in a bilateral context because the strong party prevailed over the weaker

individual negotiator may be true, but is clearly a simplistic approach. Something that could not be negotiated regionally, that could be attractive to the weak negotiator, was most probably introduced into a bilateral negotiation in circumstances that could never be present in a regional or multinational context.

p. With the noted exceptions, all countries in Latin America who have entered into a bilateral trade agreement with the US in the first decade of the twenty-first century have adopted provisions along the lines and trends noted in this chapter. These trends are evident in the agreements with Chile (2003), Costa Rica, El Salvador, Guatemala, Honduras, Nicaragua, Dominican Republic (CAFTA-DR 2004), Peru (2006), Colombia (2006) and Panama (2007), all of which are in force at this time. This suggests that if a country, whether from Latin America or any other region of the South, wishes to enter into a bilateral trade agreement with the US, such a country should be prepared to adopt an engagement in the same sense as in the bilateral agreements executed by ten Latin American nations with the US between 2003 and 2007, all of which entered into force at different times between 2004 and 2012, once the respective domestic congressional approvals were obtained.

q. This is not an area for improvised negotiators unfamiliar with precedents of what has taken place in situations involving the drafting and adoption of similar instruments intended to be executed with the same country who has already entered into similar agreements with other countries, whether in the same region or sub-region, or in regions and sub-regions of other continents. Familiarity with texts previously adopted in not totally dissimilar situations may contribute to achieve similar results as those achieved by one of the parties in a similar agreement, or to try to depart from them. Whether a licensing operation between two private parties or a bilateral agreement between two governments, information on the terms of a transaction previously completed by the same licensor with other licensees or those present in a commercial agreement executed by the same country with other business partner may give immediate and perceptible tangible results in negotiating international instruments of a private or official nature. If obtaining private information on the terms of a licensing operation implies the use of peculiar skills in the law and business of licensing operations, accessing the terms in which a bilateral trade agreement was completed by any nation with the US within a certain period of time, simply implies the need to check the webpage www.ustr.gov. What the country of the South receives in exchange for switching to the position consenting to what remained within brackets in an FTAA context, is information not found at www.ustr.gov. Presumably, this switch was not gratis.

r. The difficulties in achieving uniformity and consensus in substantive and procedural patent and trademark law in multinational instruments dealing with these topics is known by all who are involved in international intellectual property law. It is interesting to note once again the implementation of the advice to *divide and rule* as an organizational tool in the sense of solving in part the small problems that form a part of a big problem, and to take the approach of little by little and part by part instead of attempting to solve the big problem as a whole.

s. At this pace, it is not a totally disproportionate expectation that one day all nations (of the South) who have executed a bilateral trade agreement with the US contribute to international or regional uniformity or harmonization in international patent and trademark law, not necessarily through regional instruments – which have clearly failed to achieve this goal in the Americas (i.e., FTAA) – but rather through the adoption of a number of bilateral trade agreements as is clearly the case in various sensitive issues of international patent and trademark law which have been examined in this chapter.

t. Bilateralism may eventually contribute to the achievement of the international or regional uniformity or harmonization that neither regional nor multilateral approaches have realized. But this will only happen provided participants in the international community continue to sympathize with the adoption of legal and commercial instruments towards the reduction or elimination of trade barriers both tariff or non-tariff.[13] Economic and business history, however, show that economic trends and behaviors do not last forever and that they tend to remain in business and economic life for no more than a few decades. The strict approach favoring low standards of protection of intellectual property rights present in nations of the South – fostered

---

[13] In the past, examination of the participants in bilateral exercises where the US is one of the parties has made some observers of the international situation to assert that *apparently, with an increasing number of countries concluding such agreements, it will become more difficult for outsiders to resist the economic pressure to sign as well.* It has also been submitted that with the adoption of bilateral instruments including TRIPS-*plus* standards, *will make it increasingly likely that one day TRIPS-plus rules will be incorporated as multilateral TRIPS standards.* See DREXEL Joseph, *IP in Bilateral Trade Agreements. Some Ideas on How They Promote Market Power and Distort International Competition*, (ATRIP PAPERS 2006–2007). Editors GHIDINI Gustavo and GENOVESI Luis Mariano, Ed. Eudeba, Universidad de Buenos Aires, 2008, pp. 534 and 535.

by the work of specialized agencies within UN like UNCTAD and UNIDO – in the late sixties and seventies of the twentieth century did not last more than two decades.[14] The new trend evident in the eighties reversing what lawyers and legal commentators called *anti-intellectual property* positions, included statements by UN agencies – which in the past favored low levels of protection of intellectual property rights – expressly admitting the need of a switch to a more tolerant and favorable attitude towards intellectual property rights. By the mid and late eighties, nations of the South were already considering and implementing switches to more flexible – and favorable – approaches towards intellectual property protection in exchange for commercial deals of interest to those nations of the South. The finishing touch of this switch that started in the eighties is put two decades later with the adoption of bilateral intellectual property legislation in the twenty-first century along the lines discussed in this paper, whether Latin America, North Africa, the Persian Gulf or Oceania. The adoption of intellectual property legislation in these bilateral instruments adopted in more than ten nations of the South is a clear illustration of a successful implementation of TRIPS-*plus* criteria on more than 20 issues that do not show up either in regional or multinational instruments. Bilateralism in the Americas has not only contributed to harmonization, but also to a successful implementation of TRIPS-*plus* standards in this part of the world.

u. The adoption of TRIPS marked the beginning of a new age as far as standards of intellectual property protection are concerned, and contributed to increasing such standards in five continents as they existed before this understanding was reached by 130 nations of the world in 1994. Less than one decade before TRIPS was adopted, Doha re-introduced the discussion on the need to make intellectual property protection, specifically patent protection, compatible with public health in developing countries. This, together with other signs such as the failure to adopt TRIPS-*plus* standards in the context of a project for a FTAA, and the need to look for bilateral solutions, are

---

[14] *See* CONFERENCIA DE LAS NACIONES UNIDAS SOBRE COMERCIO Y DESARROLLO, *La Función de Sistemas de patentes en la Transferencia de Tecnología en los Países en Desarrollo*, Junta de Comercio y Desarrollo. Comisión de Transferencia de Tecnología. Primer Periodo de Sesiones. Ginebra 24 de noviembre de 1975. Tema 5 del Programa Provisional. TD/B/C612, at p. 2. *See also* RANGEL ORTIZ Horacio, *Evaluación del sistema de patentes*, Revista de la Escuela Libre de Derecho, Año 11, Número 11, México 1987 at 431 *et seq.*

additional indicators that observers of the way intellectual property rights are treated internationally should be attentive to what takes place in the various regional, sub-regional and bilateral patterns that are developing in the world in the second decade of the twenty-first century. It is not suggested here that a switch to the seventies is approaching nor anything close to that, for it is almost certain that TRIPS standards are here to stay. The question is whether the trend to look for alternative means to implement TRIPS-*plus* standards through mechanisms like bilateral trade instruments is here to stay or if this evident trend in the first decade of this century will be limited to the legal instruments adopted only by the US with the nations of the South with whom the relevant commercial and IP understandings have already been reached. Changes in this area are not put into effect radically one day. In the past, it has taken approximately one decade of transition in order for policy makers to influence the departure to other approaches towards doing business in the international community. Again, economic and business history shows that having reached the second decade of developments in international IP protection, observers, advisors, negotiators and commentators, would be well advised to be attentive to what takes place in the world in the way businesses are conducted and the way intellectual property rights are treated by policy makers, parliaments and national courts in the years to come.

v. Acknowledging that the bilateral approach implemented by the U.S. in the first decade of the twenty-first century threw interesting results as far as raising standards of IP protection is concerned, the second decade of the twenty-first century shows the implementation of a different method. At this time, everything suggests that the bilateral scheme successfully implemented by the U.S. in Latin America during the first decade of the twenty-first century is exhausted, or at least put into rest, for the time being. Instead, what U.S. policy makers have done in the second decade of this century is to switch to transnationalism in a rather broad sense, in search for multiple ties and interactions across the borders of a number of nations in the Pacific and the Atlantic. The device for this second decade of the twenty-first century comprises two transnational exercises represented by the initiation of Trans Pacific Partnership negotiations (TPP) in November 2011, and the initiation of the first round of Transatlantic Trade and Investment Partnership (TTIP) negotiations in Washington, D.C. on July 8, 2013. At this time, only the U.S. and the European Union are involved in TTIP. Of direct interest, at this time, as far as Latin America is concerned, is TTP, and not TTIP.

w. At the beginning of the second decade of the twenty-first century, specifically on November 12, 2011, the leaders of nine countries in the Asia Pacific area, namely Australia, Brunei Darussalam, Chile, Malaysia, New Zealand, Peru, Singapore, Vietnam and United States, announced the completion of the broad guidelines that should be present in the negotiations for the adoption of a trade instrument among these nations, under the name of Trans-Pacific Partnership Agreement (TPP). Shortly thereafter, the two NAFTA countries not included in the original discussions, i.e., Canada and Mexico, joined the negotiations. On July 23, 2013 the United States and the other TPP countries welcomed Japan as the 12th member of the negotiations. Nothing specific may be said at this time on the way intellectual property rights are considered in this project. Most relevant provisions still are within brackets, and thus there is no point in discussing the proposals and counterproposals shown in the relevant texts and drafts. For purposes of this discussion, it is reasonable to expect that the standards recently achieved in the bilateral instruments between the U.S.A. and the Latin American nations participating in TPP, namely Mexico, Chile and Peru, should not only remain in TPP, but will most likely enhance even further (for further developments see the official TPP site http://www.ustr.gov/tpp).

4. Compulsory licensing of intellectual property: A viable policy lever for promoting access to critical technologies?

Charles R. McManis and Jorge L. Contreras

Responding to violent anti-globalization protests and the tear gas-beclouded collapse of its 1999 Ministerial Conference in Seattle, a chastened World Trade Organization (WTO), in its 2001 Doha Ministerial Declaration, stressed the importance of putting the needs and interests of developing countries at the heart of the work program adopted in that Declaration.[1] In an accompanying declaration, the WTO stressed in particular the importance of interpreting and implementing the WTO Agreement on Trade-Related Aspects of Intellectual Property Rights (the TRIPS Agreement)[2] in a manner supportive of the right of WTO members to protect public health and, in particular, to promote access to medicines for all.[3] This Declaration on the TRIPS Agreement and Public Health

[1] World Trade Organization, Doha Ministerial 2001: Ministerial Declaration, adopted 14 November 2001, WT/MIN(01)/DEC/1, 41 I.L.M. 746 (2002), *available at* http://www.wto.org/english/thewto_e/minist_e/min01_e/mindecl_e.htm. For an account of the 1999 WTO Ministerial in Seattle, *see* http://en.wikipedia.org/wiki/World_Trade_Organization_Ministerial_Conference_of_1999_protest_activity, accessed 30 December 2010.

[2] World Trade Organization, Agreement on Trade-Related Aspects of Intellectual Property Rights, Marrakesh Agreement Establishing the World Trade Organization, Annex 1C, 15 April 1994, in World Trade Organization, The Legal Texts: The Results of The Uruguay Round of Multilateral Trade Negotiations 321 (1999) [hereinafter TRIPS Agreement], *available at* http://www.wto.org/english/docs_e/legal_e/27-trips.pdf.

[3] *See* World Trade Organization, Doha Ministerial 2001: Declaration on the TRIPS Agreement and Public Health [hereinafter Declaration on TRIPS and Public Health], adopted 14 November 2001, WT/MIN(01)/DEC/2, 41 I.L.M. 755 (2002), *available at* http://www.wto.org/english/thewto_e/minist_e/min01_e/mindecl_trips_e.pdf.

emphasized that TRIPS contains various "flexibilities" that could be used to achieve that goal,[4] including compulsory licensing – *i.e.* a governmental authorization for a third party, against or regardless of the patent owner's will, to perform acts that would otherwise legally require a license or other authorization from the patentee, and to do so at compensation rates that are typically less than those prevailing on the market.[5] At the same time, paragraph 6 of that Declaration conceded that the existing TRIPS provision governing compulsory patent licensing (Article 31) was insufficiently flexible to enable developing countries with little or no domestic pharmaceutical manufacturing capacity to make effective use of this particular policy lever, as Article 31 (f) requires that compulsory licensing be "predominantly for the supply of the *domestic* market of the Member authorizing such use."[6] Accordingly, the WTO instructed the Council for TRIPS to find an expeditious solution to the problem.[7]

In its Decision of 30 August 2003 (the Waiver Decision),[8] the WTO

---

[4] *Ibid.* The flexibilities enumerated in the Declaration on the TRIPS Agreement and Public Health include 1) applying the customary rules of interpretation of public international law so as to read each provision of the TRIPS Agreement in light of the stated object and purpose of the Agreement, which – according to TRIPS Article 7 – is to "contribute to the promotion of technological innovation and to the transfer and dissemination of technology, to the mutual advantage of producers and uses of technological knowledge and in a manner conducive to social and economic welfare, and to a balance of rights and obligations"; 2) the right to grant compulsory licenses and the freedom to determine the grounds upon which such licenses are granted; 3) the right to determine what constitutes a national emergency or other circumstance of extreme urgency sufficient to suspend the obligation to make reasonable efforts to seek authorization of the right holder on reasonable commercial terms and conditions; and 4) the freedom of each WTO member to establish its own regime as to what constitutes an exhaustion of intellectual property rights.

[5] *See* NUNO PIRES DE CARVALHO, THE TRIPS REGIME OF PATENT RIGHTS, 230 (2002) [hereinafter Carvalho], who goes on to note that compulsory licenses are granted by governments to government agencies, their contractors, or other private third parties, thereby substituting the government's authority for the consent of the patentee. Compulsory licensing regimes exist in many different contexts. The focus of this chapter is primarily on compulsory licensing of patent rights, but compulsory licenses also apply routinely in the U.S., for example, in the context of copyrights in musical compositions. *See* U.S. Copyright Act, Sec. 115.

[6] TRIPS Agreement, *supra* note 2, Article 31(f) (emphasis added).

[7] Declaration on TRIPS and Public Health, *supra* note 3, ¶ 6. TRIPS Article 68 mandated the creation of a Council for TRIPS to monitor the operation of the TRIPS Agreement and carry out responsibilities assigned to it by the WTO members.

[8] World Trade Organization, Decision of the General Council of 30 August 2003, Implementation of paragraph 6 of the Doha Declaration on the TRIPS

adopted a proposed solution, which consisted of waiving, for patent-protected pharmaceuticals, the obligation of WTO members to limit compulsory licensing to uses predominantly for the supply of the domestic market of the member invoking compulsory licensing, though subject to compliance with certain additional procedural safeguards (the Paragraph 6 system).[9] That is, under the Waiver Decision, pharmaceutical manufacturers *outside* the country invoking compulsory licensing could supply the needs of the invoking country, even if the country lacked a domestic pharmaceutical industry suited to take advantage of the compulsory licensing regime. This Waiver Decision and the accompanying Paragraph 6 system could become a permanent part of the TRIPS Agreement (in the form of a new Article 31*bis*), upon ratification of a proposed Protocol Amending the TRIPS Agreement (the Amendment), which is currently under consideration by members of the WTO.[10]

Since the WTO adoption of the Waiver Decision, however, only one prospective exporting country (Canada) and one prospective importing country (Rwanda) have notified the TRIPS Council of their intent to invoke the Paragraph 6 system,[11] and even this may have been a contrived test case, as it was initiated by parties in the exporting country, rather than by the beneficiary importing country, and appears to have been designed to demonstrate the practical difficulties likely to inhibit use of the Paragraph 6 system, at least as that system has been implemented in Canada's domestic Access to Medicines Regime (CAMR).[12] Although the office of the United States Trade Representative (USTR) hailed the adoption of the Waiver Decision and Paragraph 6 system,[13] the United States (U.S.) has generally viewed compulsory patent licensing by other

Agreement and public health, WT/L/540 and Corr.1 (1 September 2003), 43 I.L.M. 509 (2004), *available at* http://www.wto.org/english/tratop_e/trips_e/implem_para6_e.htm.

[9] *Ibid.* at 511.

[10] World Trade Organization, General Council: Amendment of the TRIPS Agreement, Decision of 6 December 2005, WT/L/641 (8 December 2005), *available at* http://www.wto.org/english/tratop_e/trips_e/wtl641_e.htm.

[11] World Trade Organization, *Canada is First to Notify Compulsory Licence to Export Generic Drug* (2007), *available at* http://www.wto.org/english/news_e/news07_e/trips_health_notif_oct07_e.htm.

[12] *See* World Trade Organization, *Members Ask: Is the 'Par. 6' System on Intellectual Property and Health Working?*, WTO 2010 News Items, *available at* http://www.wto.org/english/news_e/news10_e/trip_02mar10_e.htm. *See also* Richard Elliot, *Pledges and Pitfalls: Canada's Legislation on Compulsory Licensing of Pharmaceuticals for Export*, 1 Intl J. Intell. Prop. Mgmt. 94, 96 (2006).

[13] *See, e.g.*, Conan Grames, *U.S. Welcomes New WTO Compulsory Licensing Policy* (2005), *available at* http://www.iibulletin.com/kmclaw/12_05/article2.html.

countries with considerable distrust and suspicion.[14] Indeed, even as the Waiver Decision was being negotiated and implemented, the U.S. negotiated a number of bilateral trade agreements with various developing countries which have agreed not to take full advantage of the compulsory licensing flexibilities permitted under TRIPS.[15]

During this same time period, health ministries in various developing countries apparently began using informal threats of compulsory licensing to negotiate more favorable prices for pharmaceuticals intended for domestic consumption.[16] Then, in 2006 and 2007, two leading developing countries, Thailand and Brazil, formally invoked their authority under Article 31 of the TRIPS Agreement and granted domestic compulsory licenses on various antiretroviral treatments for HIV-AIDS (and in Thailand on a major cardiovascular treatment as well), thereby unleashing a torrent of criticism and a number of explicit or veiled threats of retaliation, not only by multinational pharmaceutical companies, but also by the USTR.[17]

More recently, in a sign that the international debate over compulsory patent licensing is expanding as well as intensifying, leading developing countries have proposed that an international system of compulsory licensing similar to the WTO Paragraph 6 system be adopted pursuant to the UN Framework Convention on Climate Change (UNFCCC) to facilitate access to technologies designed to combat climate change – a

---

[14] For a discussion of the U.S. position on compulsory licensing during the TRIPS negotiations, *see* Colleen Chien, *Cheap Drugs at What Price to Innovation: Does the Compulsory Licensing of Pharmaceuticals Hurt Innovation?* 18 BERKELEY TECH. L. J. 853, 860 (2003); Anja Eikermann, *Article 31 Other Use Without Authorization of the Right Holder* [hereinafter Eikermann] in PETER-TOBIAS STOLL, JAN BUSCHE & KATRIN AREND (Eds.), WTO—TRADE-RELATED ASPECTS OF INTELLECTUAL PROPERTY RIGHTS, 554, 560 (2009) [hereinafter Stoll et al.] (who notes that the first US proposal in the TRIPS negotiations was for a general prohibition of compulsory licenses, while the second US proposal would have limited compulsory licensing to addressing a declared national emergency or to remedy an adjudicated violation of antitrust laws).

[15] *See, e.g.*, Joseph E. Stiglitz, *Economic Foundations of Intellectual Property Rights*, 57 DUKE L.J. 1693, fn 22 (2008).

[16] *See, e.g.*, Donald G. McNeil Jr., "As Devastating Epidemics Increase, Nations Take on Drug Companies", N.Y. Times, July 9, 2000, at A8; Michael Wines, "Agreement Expands Generic Drugs in South Africa to Fight AIDS", N.Y. Times, Dec. 11, 2003, at A24.

[17] *See, e.g.*, Ed Silverman, "*A New US Trade Rep and Compulsory Licensing*", *available at* http://www.pharmalot.com/2008/12/a-new-us-trade-rep-and-compulsory-licensing/, last accessed January 1, 2011.

proposal that sparked immediate and strong opposition from the U.S.[18] Meanwhile, on the pharmaceutical front, Brazil and India in May 2010 invoked the WTO's dispute settlement process against the European Union (E.U.) and the Netherlands to complain about alleged seizures of generic drugs manufactured (and apparently unpatented) in India but transiting through ports and airports in the Netherlands (where they are patented) for Brazil and other developing country destinations.[19] WTO members are also now debating anew whether the Paragraph 6 system for international compulsory licensing of patent-protected pharmaceuticals is in fact working.[20]

While the spirited North-South debate over compulsory licensing of intellectual property (IP) has thus far focused primarily on compulsory patent licensing under Article 31 of TRIPS, some commentators have noted that a more limited form of compulsory patent licensing (not subject to the procedural constraints imposed by Article 31 or the Paragraph 6 system) could conceivably be based on TRIPS Article 30,[21] which

---

[18] *See* Tessa J. Schwartz & Sarah Tierney Niyogi, *Special Feature—Technology Transfer and Intellectual Property Issues Take Center Stage in UNFCCC Negotiations, Intellectual Property Today* (Dec. 16 2009), *available at* http://www.iptoday.com/news-article.asp?id=4743.

[19] *See* World Trade Organization, Dispute Settlement: Dispute DS 408, 11 May 2010 (India), European Union and a Member State—Seizure of Generic Drugs in Transit, *available at* http://www.wto.org/english/tratop_e/dispu_e/cases_e/ds408_e.htm; and *see* World Trade Organization, Dispute DS 409, 12 May 2010 (Brazil) European Union and a Member State—Seizure of Generic Drugs in Transit, *available at* http://www.wto.org/english/tratop_e/dispu_e/cases_e/ds409_e.htm.

[20] *See* WTO 2010 News Item, *supra* note 12.

[21] *See* Frederick M. Abbott & Jerome H. Reichman, *The Doha Round's Public Health Legacy: Strategies for the Production and Diffusion of Patented Medicines under the amended TRIPS Provisions*, 10 JOURNAL OF INT. ECON. L. 921, 957 (2007), arguing that "Because exports of patented products under a compulsory license to assist another country lacking manufacturing capacity inflict no harm to the patentee in the former's domestic market, a case can be made for invoking the exceptions clause of Article 30 rather than the provisions of Article 31. . . [at least if] the patent holder's expectations in the export market . . . [are] offset by the importing country's particular circumstances and WTO-consistent legal policies." *See also* Jerome H. Reichman, *Comment: Compulsory Licensing of Patented Pharmaceutical Inventions: Evaluating the Options*, 37 J. L. MED. & ETHICS 247, 250 (2009), citing to J. Debrulle, L. De Cort, and M. Petit, *La license obligatoire beige pour raison de santé publique*, *in* GENE PATENTS AND PUBLIC HEALTH, 159 (G. van Overwalle, ed., 2007) (English translation and summary available at 199), who report that in 2005 the Belgian Government enacted broad new measures allowing authorities to grant compulsory licenses in the interest of public health generally, and did not purport to derive its authority from Article 31 of TRIPS, but claimed

articulates a three-step test permitting WTO members to adopt "limited exceptions" to exclusive patent rights, so long as such exceptions "do not unreasonably conflict with a normal exploitation of the patent and do not unreasonably prejudice the legitimate interests of the patent holder, taking account of the legitimate interests of third parties."[22] Because Article 30 authorizes limited exceptions to exclusive rights, rather than compulsory licensing of those rights, it is conceptually distinguishable from Article 31, requiring neither a specific governmental *authorization* nor any kind of *compensation* to the patentee, as Article 31 does.[23] On the other hand, nothing in Article 30 explicitly bars a WTO member from limiting an exception in one or both ways as a means of meeting the second or third requirements of the three-step test.[24] If this reading of Article 30 is correct, analogous TRIPS provisions governing limited exceptions to other forms of exclusive IP rights could likewise be relied on by developing countries to fashion suitably limited compulsory licensing schemes designed to promote access to unpatented but nevertheless IP-protected innovations, such as copyrighted software.[25] Notwithstanding the longstanding U.S.

---

its actions were justified under Articles 8 and 30 of the TRIPS Agreement. *Contra:* Susanne Reyes-Knoche, *Article 30 Exceptions to Rights Conferred*, in Stoll et al., *supra* note 14, 534, 537 (2009), who states that Articles 30 and 31 of TRIPS "are mutually exclusive"— thus, "a national regulation that allows the use of a patent without the consent of the patent owner may **either** be permitted as a **limited exception** pursuant to Art. 30 **or** represent a **compulsory license** in accordance with the stricter requirements of Art. 31." For a critique of the latter view, *see infra* notes 24 and 25 and accompanying text.

[22] TRIPS Agreement, *supra* note 2, Article 30.

[23] *See* Eikermann, *supra* note 14, in Stoll et al., *supra* note 14, at 564.

[24] *See* note 4 *supra* and accompanying text, noting the emphasis in the Doha Declaration on the TRIPS Agreement and Public Health on the various "flexibilities" built into the TRIPS Agreement, including applying customary rules of interpretation of public international law so as to read each provision of TRIPS in light of the stated object and purpose of the Agreement. For examples combining limitations on certain exclusive copyrights and compulsory licensing of same, *see infra* notes 33 and 34 and accompanying text.

[25] Analogous and similarly worded provisions apply to both copyright and to industrial designs, articulating the same three-step test. TRIPS Agreement, *supra* note 2, Articles 13 and 26.2. These provisions for patent, copyright, and industrial designs are distinguishable from the similarly worded Article 17, which pertains to trademarks, as Article 17 is constrained by Article 21, which states that "compulsory licensing of trademarks shall not be permitted." TRIPS Agreement, *supra* note 2, Articles 17 and 21. A distinct type of compulsory licensing format also exists for designs for integrated circuits. TRIPS Agreement, *supra* note 2, Article 37. Under Article 37, a system is expressed in which it is not unlawful to incorporate in a design an;

suspicion and distrust of the practice of compulsory IP licensing when practiced by other countries, the U.S. legal system itself turns out to offer a well-developed body of law governing compulsory licensing of copyrights as well as patents.[26]

As this brief chronology suggests, compulsory licensing of intellectual property is a widely recognized, yet extremely controversial, policy lever for promoting access to technology. Given the growing intensity and expanding parameters of the international debate over compulsory IP licensing, this chapter will examine not only the legal, but also the economic and political considerations surrounding a WTO member's decision to employ this controversial policy lever.

I. AN OVERVIEW OF TRIPS AND COMPULSORY LICENSING OF INTELLECTUAL PROPERTY

Although Article 31 of the TRIPS Agreement eschews use of the term "compulsory licensing," it nevertheless effectively defines the practice as any legally authorized use of a patent (other than a use allowed under Article 30) "without authorization of the right holder, including use by the government or third parties authorized by the government[.]"[27] The distinction drawn between uses allowed under Article 30 and those that

---

> unlawfully reproduced layout-design or any article incorporating such an integrated circuit where the person performing or ordering such acts did not know and had no reasonable ground to know, when acquiring the integrated circuit or article incorporating such an integrated circuit, that it incorporated an unlawfully reproduced layout-design.

On notification of unlawful reproduction, however, a compulsory license is activated which applies to stock on hand and that ordered before notification:

> after the time that such person has received sufficient notice that the layout-design was unlawfully reproduced, that person may perform any of the acts with respect to the stock on hand or ordered before such time, but shall be liable to pay to the right holder a sum equivalent to a reasonable royalty such as would be payable under a freely negotiated licence in respect of such a layout-design. TRIPS Agreement, *supra* note 2, Article 37.1.

[26] *See, e.g.*, 17 U.S.C. § 115 (2006) (establishing compulsory license for "mechanical reproduction" of copyrighted musical compositions); 35 U.S.C. § 203 (2006) (granting the government march-in rights in which the government can grant a license when "health and safety needs" are not being met by the patent holder of a federally-funded invention).

[27] *See* TRIPS Agreement, *supra* note 2, Article 31, fn 7.

may be authorized pursuant to Article 31 is crucial for understanding the permissible scope of compulsory patent licensing under the latter provision and also helps illuminate the permissible scope of compulsory licensing of other forms of intellectual property protection mandated by the TRIPS Agreement.

As we have seen, the three-step test of Article 30 permits 1) "limited exceptions" to the exclusive rights conferred by a patent, provided that such exceptions do not 2) "unreasonably conflict with a normal exploitation of the patent" and 3) "do not unreasonably prejudice the legitimate interests of the patent owner, taking account of the legitimate interests of third parties."[28] Although its wording is different, Article 30 is clearly modeled on TRIPS Article 13,[29] which governs limitations and exceptions to the various exclusive copyrights that are enumerated in the 1886 Berne Convention for the Protection of Literary and Artistic Works (Berne Convention) and are incorporated by reference in Article 9 of the TRIPS Agreement.[30] Article 13, in turn, simply expands on Article 9.2 of the Berne Convention, which permits limitations on the exclusive reproduction right "in certain special cases, provided that such reproduction does not conflict with a normal exploitation of the work and does not unreasonably prejudice the legitimate interests of the author."[31]

The TRIPS negotiating history offers no explanation for why TRIPS Article 30 (and its analog, Article 26.2, governing limited exceptions to the protection of industrial designs) authorizes "limited exceptions" that do not "unreasonably conflict with a normal exploitation of the patent," while Article 13 speaks rather of confining "limitations or exceptions" to "certain special cases" that do not "conflict with a normal exploitation of the work."[32] The most plausible explanation seems to be that Article 13

---

[28] *See supra* note 22 and accompanying text.

[29] *See* TRIPS Agreement, *supra* note 2, Article 13.

[30] *See* TRIPS Agreement, *supra* note 2, Article 9.

[31] Berne Convention for the Protection of Literary and Artistic Works art. 9(2), Sept. 9, 1886, revised at Paris July 24, 1971, 25 U.S.T. 1341, 828 U.N.T.S. 221 [hereinafter Berne Convention], *available at* http://www.law.cornell.edu/treaties/berne/overview.html.

[32] In addition to Article 30's substitution of "limited exceptions" for Article 13's "certain special cases," and the insertion of the qualifier that these limited exceptions need only avoid *unreasonably* conflicting with the legitimate interest of the patent holder, the third important linguistic difference between Article 30 and Article 13 is that Article 30 mandates that any inquiry into unreasonable prejudice to the legitimate interests of the patent holder take into account "the legitimate interests of third parties." For a discussion of the importance of this third linguistic

is tracking the language of Article 9.2 of the Berne Convention as closely as possible because both are authorizing limitations and exceptions to exclusive rights in the same subject matter – namely literary and artistic works. By contrast, Articles 30 and 26.2 are concerned with limited exceptions to exclusive rights in "industrial property" – *i.e.* subject matter historically governed by the Paris Convention for the Protection of Industrial Property – and thus should not be too closely tethered to the language of the Berne Convention.[33]

In any event, all three of these TRIPS provisions recognize that certain limited uses of another's intellectual property can properly be defined as exceptions to, rather than infringements of, exclusive intellectual property rights, so long as the use does not conflict with a normal exploitation of the protected subject matter and does not unreasonably interfere with the legitimate interests of the exclusive right holder.[34] Conversely, the clear implication of Article 31's applicability to any use "other than that

---

variation, and its relation to the second linguistic variation, *see supra* notes 21 and 22 and accompanying text.

[33] *See*, e.g., Anthony Taubman, *Rethinking TRIPS: 'Adequate Remuneration' for Non-Voluntary Patent Licensing*, 11 J. INT. ECON. L. 927, 956 (2008) [hereinafter Taubman], noting that "Article 30 concerns exceptions, not limitations (in contrast with the analogous provision on copyright, Article 13.2, which covers both limitations and exceptions)" and concluding that the "analogy with copyright should not be forced." *Ibid.* fn 135. *But cf. supra* note 25 and accompanying text.

[34] The three-step tests articulated in TRIPS Articles 30 (for patents) and 13 (for copyrights) have each been the subject of a WTO Dispute Panel decision. *See* World Trade Organization, Dispute Settlement: Dispute DS 153, 2 December 1998 (Canada), European Communities — Patent Protection for Pharmaceutical and Agricultural Chemical Products, *available at* http://www.wto.org/english/tratop_e/dispu_e/cases_e/ds153_e.htm; World Trade Organization, Dispute Settlement: Dispute DS 160, 7 January 2002 (European Commmunities), United States — Section 110(5) of US Copyright Act, *available at* http://www.wto.org/english/tratop_e/dispu_e/cases_e/ds160_e.htm. Each Panel decision considered two separate exceptions, one of which was found to be overbroad, while the other was found to be sufficiently "limited" or "certain" and "special," respectively, to meet the requirements of the relevant three-step test. While these Panel decisions are important guides to interpreting Articles 30 and 13, neither decision was reviewed by the WTO Appellate Body, both predate the 2001 Declaration on TRIPS and Public Health, and both have been criticized. For a critique of the panel decision interpreting Article 30, *see* Christopher Garrison, "Exceptions to Patent Rights in Developing Countries" 40–42, Issue Paper No. 17 (August 2006)[hereinafter Garrison], UNCTAD-ICTSD Project on IPRs and Sustainable development, *available at* http://www.unctad.org/en/docs/iteipc200612_en.pdf. For a critique of the panel decision interpreting Article 13, see MARTIN SENFTLEBEN, COPYRIGHT, LIMITATIONS AND THE THREE-STEP TEST: AN ANALYSIS OF THE THREE-STEP TEST IN INTERNATIONAL AND EC COPYRIGHT LAW 140–4 (2004).

allowed under Article 30" is that Article 31 governs legally authorized uses that *do* conflict with a normal exploitation of the patent or otherwise prejudice the legitimate interests of the patent owner – albeit not unreasonably so – and that such uses will be permitted so long as the specific requirements of Article 31 are met.[35]

The distinction between uses permitted under Article 30 and uses that may be authorized pursuant to Article 31 also aids in the interpretation of Articles 13 and 26.2, as the language of Articles 30, 13 and 26.2, as noted above, is quite similar, albeit not identical. Interpreting these articles to permit suitably limited compulsory licensing schemes for patents, copyrighted works and legally protected industrial designs seems particularly warranted in light of two more specific TRIPS provisions governing compulsory licensing of trademarks and integrated circuit designs, respectively. On the one hand, TRIPS Article 21 explicitly bars compulsory licensing of trademarks, thereby limiting the scope of Article 17, which appears to adopt a "two-step test" for limited exceptions to the rights conferred by a trademark.[36] On the other hand, Article 37.2 makes no mention of limited exceptions to exclusive rights in integrated circuit designs but specifically permits "non-voluntary licensing" of same, so long as conditions analogous to those specified in Article 31 for compulsory licensing of patents are met.[37]

To understand why Article 31 of TRIPS authorizes compulsory patent licensing that may interfere with the normal exploitation of the patent or prejudice the legitimate interests of the patent owner, one must look to history, as the practice has long been recognized as "a way to preserve the benefits of the patent system while minimizing its evils."[38] The underlying economic premise of the patent system, after all, is that the grant of patents is necessary to create incentives to invent, disclose, and commercialize innovations; but it is equally well recognized that these incentives come at a cost, including the potential for "abuse" of a patent holder's exclusive

---

[35] See Carvalho, *supra* note 5, 251, noting that Article 31 deals with non-authorized uses that "do not meet one of the three conditions established by Article 30." Arguably, it is this functional distinction, rather than Reyes-Knoche's purely formal distinction between "limited exceptions" to rights and "compulsory licensing" of rights, *see supra* note 21, that distinguishes uses governed by TRIPS Article 30 and those governed by Article 31. For a discussion of what constitutes a conflict with the normal exploitation of a patent and an interference with the legitimate interests of the patent owner, taking account of the legitimate interests of third parties, *see supra* notes 21 through 24 and accompanying text.

[36] *See* TRIPS Agreement, *supra* note 2, Articles 21 & 17.

[37] *See* TRIPS Agreement, *supra* note 2, Article 31 & 37.2.

[38] See Chien, *supra* note 14, at 858.

rights.[39] International recognition of compulsory patent licensing as a permissible policy lever to curb potential patent abuse can be traced back to Article 5 A. (2) of the Paris Convention for the Protection of Industrial Property, which authorizes member countries of the Paris Union to provide for the grant of compulsory licenses "to prevent the abuses which might result from the exercise of the exclusive rights conferred by the patent, for example, failure to work."[40]

Article 31 of TRIPS, in turn, recognizes that the practice of compulsory licensing is itself subject to potential abuse[41] and should thus be subject

---

[39] *Ibid.*, noting in particular the costs associated with potential abuse of monopoly power by patentees, the use of patents to block inventive activity by third parties, the diversion of productive activity disproportionately towards patentable activity, as well as the substantial administrative costs of operating a patent system. *See also* Eikerman, *supra* note 14, at 558, quoting C.M. Correa, "Intellectual Property Rights and the Use of Compulsory Licenses: Options for Developing Countries" at 24, South Centre T.R.A.D.E. Working Paper No. 5 (1999), for the proposition that a system of compulsory licenses may be a useful instrument "in order to mitigate the restrictive effect of exclusive rights and strike a balance between the title-holders' interests and those of the public."

[40] Paris Convention for the Protection of Industrial Property, art. 5, P A(2), Mar. 20, 1883, revised July 14, 1967, 21 U.S.T. 1583, 828 U.N.T.S. 305, *available at* http://www.wipo.int/export/sites/www/treaties/en/ip/paris/pdf/trtdocs_wo020.pdf. Although Article 5 A. (4) places certain legal constraints on compulsory licenses for failure to work a patent – *e.g.* an application for such a license may not be filed before the expiration of four years from the date of filing of the patent application or three years from the date of its grant, whichever is longer, such a compulsory license may not be granted if the patentee justifies his or her inaction by legitimate reasons, and any compulsory license granted for failure to work must be non-exclusive and non-transferable, except as a part of the enterprise or goodwill which exploits such license—these constraints do not apply to compulsory licensing as a remedy to curb potential abuses other than a failure to work. For a discussion of what those potential abuses may be, *see infra* note 45 and accompanying text.

[41] *See* Carvalho, *supra* note 5, at 231, pointing out that the problem with compulsory licenses is that they harm both patentees and the countries where they are granted, as they tend to discourage the development of an independent, research-based industry that can meet the demands of the local market. Carvalho notes that in those few countries where, before the TRIPS Agreement was implemented, a compulsory licensing scheme was used extensively (*e.g.* Canada's compulsory licensing scheme for pharmaceutical production), the local research-based industry affected by the licenses vanished. *Ibid.* For a history of compulsory licensing of pharmaceuticals in Canada, *see* Margaret Smith, *Patent Protection for Pharmaceutical Products*, BP-354E (Law and Government Division, Government of Canada, November 1993), *available at* http://dsp-psd.pwgsc.gc.ca/Collection-R/LoPBdP/BP/bp354-e.htm. *But cf.* CARLOS M. CORREA & ABDULQAWI A. YUSOF, INTELLECTUAL PROPERTY AND INTERNATIONAL TRADE: THE TRIPS AGREEMENT 245 (2nd ed. 2008), noting that at the time TRIPS was negotiated 96 countries allowed

to more stringent legal constraints than the Paris Convention imposes.[42] Rather than enumerate a specific catalogue of *substantive* patent abuses for which compulsory licensing is an appropriate remedy, however, Article 31 provides a system of 12 specific *procedural* safeguards designed to curb the potential for compulsory licensing abuse,[43] while at the same time offering an illustrative list of four key circumstances in which certain of these procedural safeguards may be waived or modified or must be supplemented in the interest of either more effectively curbing or more precisely defining potential patent abuse.[44]

Although these four key circumstances could be characterized as prototypical occasions for potential patent abuse, Article 31 makes it clear that the "abuse" in question can amount to nothing more than asserting the full range of one's exclusive patent rights in circumstances where a more modest exercise of those rights is called for in the public interest. Indeed, the first two of the four enumerated circumstances – namely, national emergencies or other circumstances of extreme urgency and public non-commercial use of a patent – seem to be primarily concerned with promoting the public interest. The third circumstance—exercise of patent rights to block exploitation of an improvement patent – seems equally concerned with promoting the public interest and preventing potential patent abuse. Only the fourth circumstance – use of compulsory licensing as a remedy for anti-competitive practices – is primarily concerned with

---

for one form or another of compulsory licensing and that, although the actual application of compulsory licenses has been rather limited, the existence of such a system has been deemed an important factor to ensure a fair exercise of patent rights. For a detailed discussion of the economics and politics of compulsory licensing, *see* Part II, *infra*.

[42] For the limited constraints imposed by the Paris Convention, *see supra* note 40. For the objective of Article 31, *see* Carvalho, *supra* note 5, at 239 (stating that the objective of Article 31 (as well as that of the TRIPS Agreement as a whole) is "not to facilitate compulsory licenses, but rather to submit them to conditions of predictability and legal security").

[43] Article 31(c) does place substantive constraints on the circumstances in which patented semi-conductor technology can be the subject of compulsory licensing, but Article 31 does not otherwise substantively constrain the practice of compulsory patent licensing, though an implicit limitation can arguably be extrapolated from the objectives and principles of TRIPS enunciated in Articles 7 and 8 which would bar the grant of compulsory licenses on frivolous grounds or no grounds at all.

[44] For a discussion of these four key circumstances, as well as other circumstances in which compulsory patent licensing might be appropriate, *see* notes 45 and 46 *infra* and accompanying text.

remedying specific abuses of patent rights.[45] In other words, just as Article 30 authorizes WTO members to protect the public interest by creating limited *substantive* exceptions to exclusive patent rights, so Article 31 specifies the procedures whereby WTO members can protect the public interest by imposing certain *remedial* limitations on the exercise of patent rights.[46] The WTO's Waiver Decision and the accompanying Paragraph 6 System, in turn, waive one of Article 31's procedural requirements, where patented pharmaceuticals are involved, but impose additional procedural requirements of their own.

In short, it is possible to speak of three tiers of TRIPS-compliant compulsory IP licenses: 1) compulsory patent, copyright, and industrial design licenses that comply with the relevant TRIPS three-step test; 2) compulsory patent or integrated circuit licenses that comply with the procedural requirements of Article 31; and 3) compulsory pharmaceutical patent licenses that comply with all but one of the procedural requirements of Article 31, plus the procedures specified in the Waiver Decision and Paragraph 6 System. Given that the TRIPS Agreement clearly seems to authorize compulsory IP licensing in these circumstances, it is important to consider the economic and political circumstances in which a country might choose to invoke this controversial policy lever.

II. ECONOMIC PERSPECTIVES ON COMPULSORY LICENSING

As noted above, one of the primary functions of the patent system is to promote innovation and technology development by granting inventors limited exclusive rights to their inventions.[47] Indeed, this sentiment is reflected in the patent clause of the U.S. Constitution, which authorizes

---

[45] *See*, e.g., Taubman, *supra* note 33, at 931, 947, noting that an important distinction should be drawn between (even though under the rubric of "compulsory licensing" general discourse tends to conflate): 1) compulsory licenses as interventions to safeguard market competition (the third and fourth key circumstances), and 2) government use authorizations for public non-commercial use (the first and second key circumstances).

[46] Note, however, that nothing in the language of Article 30 explicitly bars a WTO member's decision to substitute remedial for substantive limitations on patent rights, so long as those limitations otherwise meet the requirements of the three-step test. For a discussion of circumstances that might lead a WTO member to adopt remedial rather than substantive limitations pursuant to Article 30, *see infra* notes 59–63 and accompanying text.

[47] *See* note 39, *supra*, and accompanying text.

Congress to "promote the progress of science and useful arts, by securing for limited times to authors and inventors the exclusive right to their writings and discoveries."[48] Under the laws of most jurisdictions, the exclusive rights granted to a patent holder include the rights to "make, use and sell" the patented article and to exclude those not authorized by the patent holder from doing so.[49] Accordingly, the patent holder, during the term of the patent, has great flexibility to determine the price that it charges for patented articles, flexibility that is limited, in the absence of governmental regulation, solely by consumer demand.[50] Thus, in markets in which ready substitutes for a patented article do not exist (as is the case with many pharmaceutical products), a patent holder will typically raise prices to a level that maximizes profit in view of the demand characteristics of the market, as illustrated by Figure 4.1.

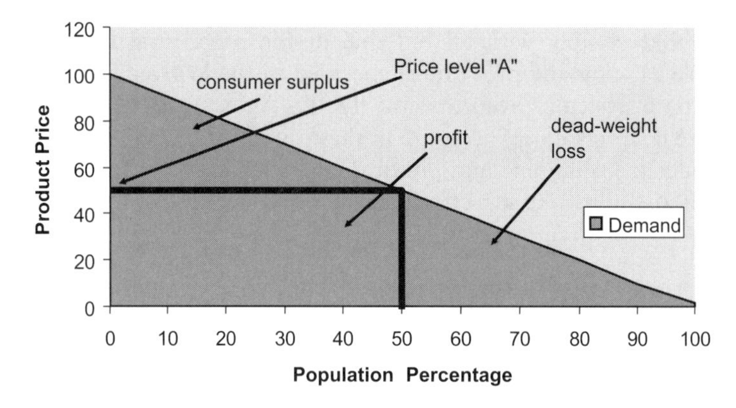

Figure 4.1 Straight-Line Demand Curve

Thus, in Figure 4.1, the y-axis represents the patent holder's price for the patented article above marginal cost (assumed for the sake of simplicity to be zero) and price level "A" (the "profit-maximizing price") represents the level at which the patent holder maximizes its surplus based on demand for the article ("profit"). The area above the profit-maximizing price represents the surplus enjoyed by consumers who otherwise would have paid a higher price for the patented article, and the area to the right of the profit-maximizing price represents the loss to consumers who are

---

48 U.S. Constitution, Art. 1, Sec. 8.

49 *See, e.g.*, 35 U.S.C. § 271.

50 *See* WILLIAM M. LANDES & RICHARD A. POSNER, THE ECONOMIC STRUCTURE OF INTELLECTUAL PROPERTY LAW (2003) [hereinafter ECONOMIC STRUCTURE].

unwilling or unable to purchase the patented article at price "A" (otherwise known as "dead weight loss").

In this model, the producer's profit is viewed as an incentive to promote innovation and inventive activity.[51] According to the theory, in order to induce an inventor to invest substantial time and resources in creating useful inventions, society must offer a reward, or at least the ability for the inventor to recoup his or her research and development investment, presumably with some return on that investment. In the case of pharmaceutical products, which are currently estimated to cost between $500 million and $1 billion to bring to market in the U.S.[52], this argument has been made quite forcefully.

The patent holder's ability to charge a profit-maximizing price and to extract a profit, however, necessarily entails a dead weight loss. Thus, in a market with free competition among perfectly substitutable products, pricing is naturally driven toward the producer's marginal cost and dead weight loss likewise approaches zero.[53] However in the market for a patented product as to which there are few and/or imperfect substitutes, the patent holder will increase its price up to the profit-maximizing price, above which further increases would result in diminished demand and lower overall profit. Dead weight loss is experienced by those consumers who are willing to pay more than marginal cost but do not obtain the product because it is priced above the price they are willing or able to pay.

In terms of pharmaceutical products, dead weight loss can be equated to a reduction in access: *i.e.* consumers who cannot afford to purchase the patented articles at the profit-maximizing price are denied access to them.

---

[51] *See* Robert C. Bird, *Developing Nations and the Compulsory License: Maximizing Access to Essential Medicines while Minimizing Investment Side Effects*, J.L. MED. & ETHICS, Summer 2009, at 209, 211 (citing various studies assessing the effects of patenting and compulsory licensing on pharmaceutical innovation); Frederick M. Abbott, *Protecting First World Assets in the Third World: Intellectual Property Negotiations in the GATT Multilateral Framework*, 22 VAND. J. TRANSNAT'L L. 689, 697–98 (1989); Jerome H. Reichman, *From Free Riders to Fair Followers: Global Competition Under the TRIPS Agreement*, 29 N.Y.U. J. INT'L L. & POL. 11, 53 (1996); Alan O. Sykes, *Public Health and International Law: TRIPS, Pharmaceuticals, Developing Countries, and the Doha "Solution,"* 3 CHI. J. INT'L L. 47, 49, 62 (2002).

[52] *See, e.g.*, Joseph A. Dimasi, Ronald W. Hansen, and Henry G. Grabowski, *The Price of Innovation: New Estimates of Drug Development Costs*, 22 J. HEALTH ECON. 151 (2003).

[53] The result is that each consumer that desires the product can purchase it. In the real world, however, the producer's marginal cost is not zero, and there will always be a set of consumers that cannot afford a given product at any non-zero price.

Thus, when products are life-saving medications, there is significant social benefit derived from minimizing this dead weight loss. Yet eliminating the dead weight loss caused by patent protection, and thus the producer's surplus, could also reduce the producer's incentive to create new innovations, which would also redound to society's detriment.[54] Moreover, it has been suggested that eliminating or limiting patent protection in developing countries would stymie the growth of innovative enterprises *within* those countries, also diminishing future consumer welfare.[55] Thus, as observed by Flynn, Hollis and Palmedo,[56] a natural trade-off exists between present consumer benefit (greater access to medicines) and future consumer benefit (new products developed through innovation).

It has been argued that the current 20-year patent term, even taking into account the lengthy pre-market pharmaceutical approval process, over-compensates producers who, in theory, could recoup their R&D investments over a shorter exclusive period.[57] Proponents of this theory, particularly with respect to pharmaceuticals, argue that profit is unduly high and imposes unnecessary dead weight losses on society (with direct adverse impacts on health and mortality). These negative social effects are exacerbated in the developing world, in which the theoretical "straight line" demand curve illustrated in Figure 4.1 does not accurately reflect the realities of developing economies. As shown by Flynn, Hollis and Palmedo, many such economies exhibit "highly convex" demand curves with respect to products such as pharmaceuticals (Figure 4.2).[58]

In an economy characterized by the highly convex demand curve illustrated by Figure 4.2, a small percentage of wealthy consumers are relatively price-insensitive and will be willing to purchase a patented article at almost any price (particularly if the article is a life-saving medication). The vast majority of the population, however, cannot afford the product, except at the very lowest price. Both theory and empirical data show that the producer can thus maximize its surplus by charging a high price for the

---

[54] *See* Landes & Posner, Economic Structure, *supra* note 50 at 22.

[55] *See* Sykes, *supra* note 51; Robert M. Sherwood, *The TRIPS Agreement: Implications for Developing Countries*, 37 IDEA 491 (1996).

[56] Sean Flynn, Aidan Hollis & Mike Palmedo, *An Economic Justification for Open Access to Essential Medicine Patents in Developing Countries*, 37 J.L. Med. & Ethics 184, 185 (2009).

[57] *See, e.g.*, Richard Posner, "Pharmaceutical Patents", *available at* http://www.becker-posner-blog.com/2004/12/pharmaceutical-patents--posner.html, last accessed 1 January 2011.

[58] *See* Flynn, *supra* note 56 at 187–8.

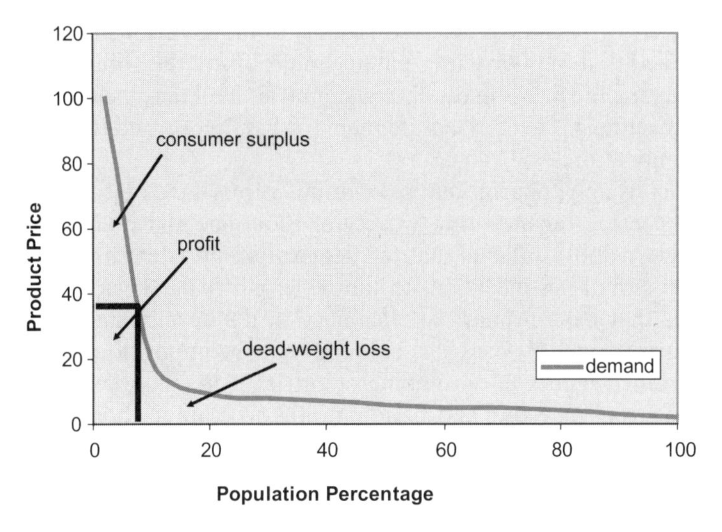

Figure 4.2 Highly-Convex Demand Curve

product and selling it only to the wealthy minority, leaving the majority of the population without access.[59]

This situation has contributed to calls for compulsory licensing of essential medicines at the WTO negotiations leading up to the Doha Declaration.[60] Under a compulsory licensing regime, the patent holder's exclusive rights are extinguished or limited, opening the market to competitors. In the pharmaceutical industry, in which marginal costs of production are relatively low,[61] such competition is likely to drive prices to near-zero per-unit levels. As a result, even in a market characterized by a highly convex demand curve, dead weight loss will be reduced substantially and product will be made available to much larger segments of the population. Proponents of compulsory licensing have attempted to justify the resulting reduction, if not outright elimination, of the producer's surplus in such cases[62] by pointing to the offsetting increase in social

---

[59] *See* Flynn, *supra* note 56 at 187–8. *See also* Abbott & Reichman, *supra* note 21, at 971 for additional theories put forward to explain pharmaceutical companies' pricing practices in developing countries.

[60] *See* Abbott & Reichman, *supra* note 21 at 928–9.

[61] *See, e.g.*, Kevin Outterson, *Pharmaceutical Arbitrage: Balancing Access and Innovation in International Prescription Drug Markets*, 5 YALE J. HEALTH POL'Y L. & ETHICS 193, 253–5 (2005).

[62] While some compulsory licensing schemes seek to compensate producers for the exploitation of their patent rights, such compensation could be below market

welfare derived from the greater availability of life-saving medicines. They also contend that in many cases patent holders have the ability to charge profit-maximizing prices in developed countries, and that these profits are more than sufficient to compensate them for R&D costs and to incentivize further innovation.[63]

Not surprisingly, pharmaceutical manufacturers have objected to compulsory licensing regimes on a variety of economic and policy grounds. They argue, as noted above, that the deprivation of patent protection for medicines diminishes incentives to innovate, particularly with respect to medicines that have primary applicability in the developing world (*e.g.* anti-malarial drugs).[64] They also contend that the imposition of compulsory licensing regimes in developing countries is likely to deter Western companies from investing and building infrastructure in those countries, either as retaliation for the imposition of compulsory licensing or due to fear of continuing expropriation of proprietary rights.[65] Arguments have also been made that, particularly under the Doha regime, compulsory licensing arrangements serve to facilitate the creation of "gray" markets in products, enabling low-priced products manufactured for the developing world to flow back into the developed world at reduced prices in direct competition with products sold by the producer.[66] In some cases, the mere threat of a compulsory licensing regime has been used to persuade producers to lower their pricing in order to avoid the draconian and unpredictable effects of a compulsory license.[67]

The positions of the pharmaceutical industry opposing compulsory licensing have largely been echoed by governments in the developed world,

---

rates (*see* Abbott & Reichman, *supra* note 21, at 971–2 (noting the argument that recoupment of marginal costs plus 5 percent might be viewed as reasonable by proponents of compulsory licensing)).

[63] *See* Flynn, *supra* note 56 at 185 (suggesting that compulsory licensing may be a "justifiable policy response" in such economies).

[64] *See* Pharmaceutical Research and Manufacturers of America, "Compulsory Licensing Trend Dangerous", Press Release, May 14, 2007, *available at* http://www.phrma.org/node/669, last accessed 31 December, 2010.

[65] *See* Bird, *supra* note 51. A number of commentators hold the view that strong patent rights encourage the transfer of technology and innovation to developing countries. *See* Keith E. Maskus, *Intellectual Property and the Transfer of Green Technologies: An Essay on Economic Perspectives*, 2009 WIPO J. 1, 133, 135.

[66] *See* Dana Zilker, *Facilitating Access of AIDS Drugs While Maintaining Strong Patent Protection*, 42 Duke L. & Tech. Rev. 17 (2001); David Finegold, *Merck: Staying the Course*, in David L. Finegold et al., BIOINDUSTRY ETHICS 45 (2005); *see also* Friedman et al., *Out-licensing: A Practical Approach for Improvement of Access to Medicines in Poor Countries*, 361 THE LANCET 341, 341 (2003).

[67] *See* Abbott & Reichman, *supra* note 21 at 970.

including that of the U.S. The U.S. Department of State, in particular, has applied pressure through diplomatic channels to dissuade developing countries from implementing compulsory licensing regimes including, as discussed below, through the imposition of so-called TRIPS-Plus agreements in bilateral free trade agreements. As a result, only a handful of compulsory licensing regimes have been formally implemented since the conclusion of the Doha Declaration.[68]

As noted above, some participants in the UNFCCC climate change debate have argued that compulsory licensing schemes should be applied to hasten the dissemination of "clean technology" innovations in the developing world, adopting the reasoning employed in the debate over essential medicines. They reason that mitigating global climate change is an urgent worldwide requirement that must be addressed in both developed and developing countries; and thus, as with essential medicines, patent protection in developing countries should be sacrificed to the extent necessary to achieve this greater social good. These arguments, while appealing at a superficial level, overlook several key distinctions between the technologies, markets and patent coverage for medicines and clean technologies and make it unlikely that an international accord modeled on the Doha Declaration is achievable or desirable in the area of clean technologies.

Capital-Intensive Markets

Unlike essential medicines, many clean technologies are not consumer products, but infrastructure improvements and capital projects such as wind farms, nuclear reactors, transmission grids and carbon recapture retrofitting of existing factories. While aspects of the design and operation of these facilities may be covered by patents, it is likely that technical skill and know-how will be more critical in implementing these technologies in the developing world.[69] As compulsory licensing has no effect on these forms of intellectual property and, in fact, may make it *less* likely that knowledgeable producers will be willing to provide their expertise within the imposing country, developing countries may be better off by foregoing

---

[68] *See* notes 11 through 13 and 18, *supra*, and accompanying discussion.

[69] *See* Carlos M. Correa, *Can the TRIPS Agreement Foster Technology Transfer to Developing Countries?* in INTERNATIONAL PUBLIC GOODS AND TRANSFER OF TECHNOLOGY UNDER A GLOBALIZED INTELLECTUAL PROPERTY REGIME 227, 229–30 (Keith E. Maskus & Jerome H. Reichman, eds., 2005) and Sherin M. Rashedi, *The Role of Intellectual Property Rights in Addressing International Climate Change*, SCITECH LAW. 16, 17 (Winter 2011).

compulsory licensing in favor of policies (*e.g.* tax incentives or tariff relief) designed to attract foreign capital and know-how relevant to clean technology. Accordingly, even if compulsory licensing were established for clean technologies in developing countries, it is not likely these measures would result in the production of more clean energy in such markets.

Availability of Alternatives

To the extent that clean technologies are consumer products (*e.g.* solar panels, biofuels, etc.), consumer demand in the developing world is likely to be driven primarily by price, rather than features. That is, unlike the pharmaceuticals market, in which an AIDS drug is not a substitute for a malaria drug and a particular manufacturer often enjoys a monopoly in a broad field of therapeutics or diagnostics, different clean technology alternatives both exist and compete with one another.[70] A consumer, particularly in the developing world, has no real reason to favor one over the other beyond price (*i.e.* electricity is fungible, and the means of generating it, assuming that "green" considerations are not predominant, are likewise fungible). Thus, even when patent protection remains intact for clean technology products, the producer's ability to charge an elevated profit-maximizing price is reduced due to the presence of alternatives and competition, and the convex demand curve exhibited in the market for pharmaceuticals in the developing world is unlikely to apply in the market for clean technologies. As a result, it is not likely that the imposition of compulsory licensing would significantly increase dissemination of such clean technologies in the developing world.

Patent Coverage

Despite the attention given to patents in the debate concerning international dissemination of clean technology, the actual number of patents claiming such technologies is comparatively low. One study identifies a total of 823 U.S. patents issued in 2009 covering clean technologies across a broad range of categories,[71] representing less than 0.5 percent of the

---

[70] See John H. Barton, *Intellectual Property and Access to Clean Energy Technologies in Developing Countries, An Analysis of Solar Photovoltaic, Biofuel and Wind Technologies*, Int'l Centre for Trade and Sustainable Dev., Issue Paper No. 2 at viii (2007) *available at* http://ictsd.net/downloads/2008/11/intellectual-property-and-access-to-clean-energy-technologies-in-developing-countries_barton_ictsd-2007.pdf, last accessed 31 December, 2010.

[71] John M. Lazarus, Cleantech Energy Patent Landscape Annual Report

total 167,349 U.S. patents issued in 2009.[72] For purposes of comparison, in the same year 2,710 patents issued for molecular biology inventions (class 435) and 841 patents issued for multicellular organisms (class 800).[73] Thus, there is a stark difference between the *quantity* of patents being issued for clean technologies and for biotechnology/pharmaceutical inventions.[74]

Moreover, scholars, most notably the late John Barton of Stanford Law School, have pointed out key *qualitative* differences between patent coverage in the pharmaceutical and clean technology industries.[75] In particular, Barton notes that in the fields of solar photovoltaic, biofuel and wind technologies, patent protection is typically far narrower than in the pharmaceuticals sector. Many of these clean technologies are "old", meaning that early broad patents have expired, leaving producers with patents primarily directed to minor improvements and differentiating features. As a result market entry is not blocked by patents, as it is with pharmaceuticals, and competition exists, both among vendors of products within the same technology categories (*e.g.* competing photovoltaic cells) and among different product categories (*e.g.* wind versus solar). In a market characterized by such competition, a patent holder is unable to extract monopoly rents and pricing is adjusted downward in accordance with competitive pressures. Accordingly, the imposition of compulsory licensing of clean technology

2010: Investment and Licensing Opportunities May Arise in New Areas 5 (2010) (identifying the following clean tech categories: solar, wind, hydro/wave/tidal, geothermal, biomass/biogas/biofuel, nuclear, hybrid vehicle, fuel cells for hybrid vehicles, utility metering, smart grid and CO2 storage or sequestration).

[72] United States Patent and Trademark Office, "U.S. Patent Statistics Calendar Years 1963–2009", *available at* http://www.uspto.gov/web/offices/ac/ido/oeip/taf/us_stat.pdf, last accessed December 31, 2010.

[73] United States Patent and Trademark Office, "Patent Counts By Class By Year 01/01/1977–12/31/2009", *available at* http://www.uspto.gov/web/offices/ac/ido/oeip/taf/cbcby.pdf, last accessed December 31, 2010.

[74] While the absolute quantity of patents in a given technical area does not necessarily indicate the amount of innovation in the area, or even the strength of patent protection in the area (as some patents have few claims, and some have many, and even the strength and breadth of claims varies dramatically from one to the next), patent quantity does indicate, at least, the number of patents that would need to be licensed or subject to a compulsory license in such a technical area.

[75] Barton, *supra* note 70; John H. Barton, *Mitigating Climate Change Through Technology Transfer: Addressing the Needs of Developing Countries*, Chatham House Energy, Env't and Dev. Programme: Programme Paper 08/02 (2008), *available at* http://www.chathamhouse.org.uk/files/12357_1008barton.pdf, last accessed 31 December 2010.

patents would not necessarily reduce consumer prices, nor achieve the benefits otherwise sought.[76]

III. COMPULSORY LICENSING ALTERNATIVES, HYBRIDS AND THE WAY FORWARD

Given the high profile of the debate over compulsory licensing for essential medicines and the reprise of the same arguments in the brewing confrontation over clean technology and climate change, it is not surprising that numerous alternatives to compulsory licensing have arisen. From the perspective of the industrialized world, one approach to addressing (if not wholly eliminating) the prospect of compulsory licensing is the so-called TRIPS-Plus agreement, a bilateral treaty that imposes on its signatories IP obligations exceeding minimum TRIPS levels (and negating the parties' ability to impose compulsory licensing regimes).[77] TRIPS-Plus agreements have been included in free trade agreements negotiated by the U.S. with countries including Jordan (2001), Chile (2003), Morocco (2004) and the DR-CAFTA group (2005, including the Dominican Republic, Costa Rica, El Salvador, Guatemala, Honduras, and Nicaragua).[78] Japan and the E.U. have also concluded free trade agreements including TRIPS-Plus agreements. One consistent criticism of TRIPS-Plus agreements is that they neutralize the pro-developing country provisions of TRIPS, including the compulsory licensing authorization granted under the Doha Declaration, and are thus unfavorable for developing countries.[79]

---

[76] *See* Maskus, *supra* note 65 at 136–7 (noting a dearth of empirical data and research investigating the effects of intellectual property rights and exclusions such as compulsory licensing on incentives to innovate and access to patented technologies, particularly with respect to differing types of technologies).

[77] The TRIPS Agreement established a "floor" for international intellectual property protection, but allows members to adopt "more extensive protection" at their discretion. For a discussion of the rise of TRIPS-Plus agreements, *see generally* Matthew Turk, *Bargaining and Intellectual Property Treaties: The Case for a Pro-Development Interpretation of TRIPS but not TRIPS Plus*, 42 N.Y.U. J. INTL. L. & POL. 981, 1004–5 (2010); Ruth L. Okediji, *Back to Bilateralism? Pendulum Swings in International Intellectual Property Protection*, 1 U. OTTAWA L. TECH. J. 125 (2004).

[78] *See* www.ustr.gov.

[79] *See, e.g.*, Peter K. Yu, *The International Enclosure Movement*, 82 IND. L.J. 827 (2007). *But see* Turk, *supra* note 77, at 1010 (concluding that a cost-benefit analysis of TRIPS-Plus agreements yields uncertain results and does not conclusively weigh against developing countries).

Other commentators have approached the issue of compulsory licensing from a developing world perspective. Abbott and Reichman have proposed a private ordering system whereby developing countries could pool their procurement activities, with or without price regulation, to encourage patent-holding pharmaceuticals producers to lower prices.[80] Under such a system, the pooling countries would offer to enter into joint supply contracts with low-bidding pharmaceuticals producers, thus increasing their leverage (with the threat of multilateral compulsory licensing) but also making available favorable economies of scale to the prospective supplier.[81] Bird and Cahoy have proposed a similar "collective bargaining" approach that would be coordinated by regional trade associations rather than individual countries.[82] Yet another variant has been proposed by Anderson, who develops a "co-op" compulsory licensing approach that emphasizes "shared investment, shared work, and shared participation in future benefits" and is derived from traditional game theory models.[83] Other proposals, including a recent one by Maitra, suggest abandoning the compulsory licensing model in the clean technology area and moving toward a two-tiered system of global subsidies funded by developed countries whose companies profit from sales to the developing world.[84] While none of these innovative approaches has yet been adopted or tested in the market, each offers interesting and potentially valuable insights for the next chapter of the compulsory licensing debate.

---

[80] Abbott & Reichman, *supra* note 21, at 973–4.

[81] *Ibid.*

[82] Robert Bird & Daniel R. Cahoy, *The Impact of Compulsory Licensing on Foreign Direct Investment: A Collective Bargaining Approach*, 45 Am. Bus. L.J. 283 (2008).

[83] Horace E. Anderson, *We Can Work it Out: Co-Op Compulsory Licensing as the Way Forward in Improving Access to Anti-Retroviral Drugs*, 16 B.U. J.Sci. Tech. L. 167, 170 (2010). This proposal was made in the specific context of anti-retroviral drugs, and its broader applicability to patented technologies, in general, is not clear.

[84] Neel Maitra, *Access to Environmentally Sound Technology in the Developing World: A Proposed Alternative to Compulsory Licensing*, 35 Colum. J. Envtl. L. 407, 433–8 (2010).

5. On TRIPS' impact on 'least developed countries': The effects of a 'double standards' approach

Gustavo Ghidini

FOREWORD

It is undisputed evidence that the dynamics of trans-national economic integration have altered the traditional dialectic 'Developed vs. Developing' countries. The qualification itself of countries as 'developing' is under continuous revision in the face of the growth of emerging economies like Brazil, Russia, India, China and others. Accordingly, even the debates on IPRs-related issues must be re-oriented in the light of the new balances of power, first of all to reckon with the prospective decline of 'unilateralism' in international relations, so far largely framed by a traditionally dominant (and even diplomatically boosted) 'Washington consensus'. (As Graham Dutfield has asked, "Will the United States government be so pro-patent when the proportion of domestic patents granted to Indian and Chinese inventors increases dramatically?")[1]

However, the hypothesis that the progress of international economic integration might per se ensure a *general* 'rebalancing' of the traditionally dominant IP law patterns, is far from settled, in particular as concerns the *least* developed countries (art. 66 TRIPs; henceforth: LDCs), which constitute today's real frontier of the geopolitical trade competition issue that has historically divided the 'two worlds' emerging from the colonial era. On one hand the 'double speed' of the dynamics of exit from underdevelopment is all too evident. On the other, even the present global financial and economic crisis might play ambiguously on the emerging countries' assessment of their own geopolitical interests and consequent

[1] Dutfield, G., *Knowledge Diplomacy and the New Intellectual Property Fundamentalism*, in Malbon J. and C. Lawson (eds.), Interpreting and Implementing the TRIPS Agreement—Is it Fair?, Cheltenham, U.K., 2008, 31, at 32.

IP policies. Will they act as drivers of the progress of the least developed, or will they 'forget their past' and coalesce with the developed world in maintaining, and indeed expanding the scope of the deep 'asymmetries' of terms of trade, as also enhanced by existing international (TRIPs', in particular) regulation of IP, versus many countries (African, first and foremost, but not alone) still struggling to achieve a reasonable economic and technological standard in vital societal sectors?

All this suggests a specific focus on these very countries and the questions how and with what effect the rules governing intellectual property rights (IPRs) intervene in relations between developed and developing countries.

In exploring this perspective, the reader's attention is called to two specific normative profiles of the Agreement that, evidencing an historical Western 'double standard' approach to IP regulation and enforcement in favour of developed countries, can work to aggravate the LDCs' weak position, especially as concerns the sharing of advanced technologies. After examining such profiles, this chapter will briefly attempt to outline a couple of 'redeeming' reforms of present TRIPs' text. Reforms that are deemed profoundly coherent with the overall system of the Agreement's basic (official) principles and objectives.

1. 'ONE TERM FITS ALL' FOR COMPLIANCE – IT DIDN'T FOR 'US'

As is well known, the TRIPs Agreement (art. 65) has obliged developing countries to apply its provisions within a *short period* (very short from a historical perspective: five years from the signing of the WTO Agreement) that is furthermore *fixed and equal* for all – save for a limited (from a historical perspective) delay of a further five years (art. 66) in favour of the LDCs – this term being further extended in 2001 in Doha to 2016 as concerns the rules on pharmaceutical product patents. (However, the Council for TRIPs may, upon a duly justified request by a LDC member, accord further extensions.)

Let us dwell for a while on the geopolitical significance of this unification of models and time limits for compliance – particularly as regards the latter. In the view of the author,[2] it reflects a double standard in the framing of the rule: since, by putting a short *and fixed* term to developing

[2] Ghidini, G., Innovation, Competition and Consumer Welfare in Intellectual Property Law, Cheltenham, 2010, *Appendix*.

countries to toe the line with Western IP law standards, today's industrialised countries 'have done unto others' what they themselves refused be 'done unto them' in the initial stages of their own industrial development.

It is an undeniable fact, indeed, that contemporary established powers *themselves* determined, based on *their own* stage of development, how and when to apply strong models for the protection of intellectual property. For example, at the beginning of the 19th century the German states were considered by France as havens for plagiarists. And Germany introduced legislation against unfair competition between the end of the 19th and the beginning of the 20th centuries, when it recognised that it could afford the 'luxury of fairness'.[3] It is also fair to recall that before its rapid industrial reconstruction after World War II, Japan was famous for its eagerness to copy almost anything new produced in Western countries.

As for the U.S., current aggressive champion of the need for worldwide stringent protection of intellectual property, Professor Jane Ginsburg[4] reminds that, as concerns copyright, they grew and flourished, till the end of the 19th century, as a "pirate nation", *i.e.* free riding on the works of English and Irish authors (Dickens's exasperated protests have remained famous). This continued till the end of the 19th century, when the American publishing industry produced 'enough' successful *own* authors to 'sell' even on the international market (just think of Beecher Stowe, Twain, Hawthorne, Melville, James, Thoreau, Emerson, Whitman, Alcott, Fuller, etc.)[5], thereby eventually accepting the principle of reciprocal international copyright protection. But please note: even under those circumstances, the Chace Act 1891, which acknowledged foreign authors' and publishers' copyright – and which remained in force for decades – granted such protection on condition that foreign texts were printed in the U.S.), banning the import of editions published abroad.[6]

---

[3] *'Die deutsche Industrie steht heute auf einer solcher Höhe, sie ist so reich und kräftig, das sie sich den Luxus der Ehrlichkeit gestatten kann'*, said the distinguished German jurist Wassermann, in a speech held in Berlin, in 1912, at the constitution of a commission for the study of indications of origin (source: L. COQUET, *Les indications d'origine et la concurrence déloyale*, Paris, 1913, 317; emphasis added).

[4] GINSBURG, J.C. and J.M. KERNOCHAN, *One Hundred and Two Years Later: The U.S. Joins the Berne Convention*, in MERGES, R.P. and J.C. GINSBURG (eds), *Foundations of Intellectual Property*, New York, 2004, 298 *et seq.*

[5] See also YU, P. K., *The Global Intellectual Property Order and Its Undetermined Future*, in The WIPO Journal, 1/2009, vol. 1, 13.

[6] See BUGBEE, B., *Genesis of American Patent and Copyright Law*, Washington D.C., 1967, 43–4. This is substantially what the Venetian authorities did in the late 15th century, *i.e.* granting privileges to printers aimed at fostering the growth of the local publishing industry after the emergence of the Gutenberg revolution.

(The less said about Italy the better. Suffice it to say that while the industries of the author's country's northern regions clamour for protection against counterfeit goods, a huge amount of such goods is produced and/or distributed by 'entrepreneurs' rooted in southern regions.)

In the final analysis, those 'one-sized' deadlines, willy-nilly accepted by developing countries for applying Western models of IP protection, objectively risk to 'stick' the same countries to the disadvantaged economic situation mentioned above: precisely because the value of high-tech products that, in international exchanges, flows from the protection of IPRs, mostly relates to the production of 'the others'.

'No, the contrary is true!' outright supporters of the present system proclaim. Quick legal unification tends to speed up recourse to R&D by developing countries, they say. These optimists argue that a healthy lash of the whip does help 'backward' countries to escape their long dependence on the primary sector, as well as the clutches of technological stagnation. It is a serious objection, certainly convincing when it refers to the 'innovation divide' that still characterises the relations between countries which have however attained a reasonable level of development – take. *e.g.* the technological gap existing in several sectors between Northern European and Mediterranean European industrial systems. But as regards relations between developed and developing countries in strict sense, that objection draws little comfort from experience: and in any case the historical reality contradicts its underlying assumption.

First of all, the prophesy of the healthy whiplash has come true for a limited number of developing countries (BRICs, and a few others) whose levels of industrial investment have grown over time enough to marshal sufficient resources to give birth to advanced productions.

Even more significant is the fact that the countries in question have reached that capacity also thanks to a previous *refusal* – and not a previous *acceptance*! – of strong intellectual property protection models.

In short, these emerging 'technologically proficient' developing countries[7] have extensively done what today's many industrialised countries did in the 1800s and part of the 1900s, when they effectively ignored or got around an effective enforcement of IPRs *until* their own industries were no longer in their infancy. By contrast, some countries started to effectively respect and enforce IPRs *as they in turn* became producers of advanced technologies (often acquired through imitation) and it became in their own

---

[7] Basheer, S. and T. Prashant Readdy, *The 'Efficacy' of Indian Patent Law: ironing out the creases in Section 3(d)*, Vol. 5, Issue 2, August 2008, available at: http://papers.ssrn.com/sol3/papers.cfm?abstract_id=1086254

interests to adopt a policy of safeguarding intangible assets in domestic and above all international trade.

Così fan tutte in the initial stages of industrial development.

2. THE REPUDIATION OF THE 'LOCAL WORKING REQUIREMENT'. WHO GAINS, WHO LOSES

The second normative profile of TRIPs referred to above highlights a relevant development introduced by the TRIPs Agreement in the domain of patents. It concerns the repudiation, expressly sanctioned by article 27.1 of the TRIPs Agreement, of the historical principle (enshrined in the Paris Convention 1883, article 5A.2, and adopted by the vast majority of the emerging industrial States of the 19th century) that allowed Member States granting a patent to request that said patent be (industrially) worked, *i.e.* manufactured, *in situ*.[8] The obvious objective, and rationale, of the principle was the fostering of technology sharing and thus the acceleration of domestic industrial growth.

With regard to historical principle, long before the 1883 Universal Convention, it had characterised the very early stages of Western economic development. Already in late medieval and Renaissance Europe,

---

8 Article 5A of the Paris Convention, incorporated in the TRIPs Agreement via article 2.1 TRIPs, requires a patentee to produce the patented goods in the country where protection is sought if the country issuing a patent so desires and treats a failure to work the patent locally as an *abuse* of the patentee's exclusive rights. On the other hand, article 27.1 TRIPs makes 'patent rights enjoyable without discrimination as to the place of invention [. . .] and whether products are imported or locally produced'. The need to reconcile these two provisions has led scholars like Straus, J. (*Implications of the TRIPs Agreement in the Field of Patent Law*, in Beier, F.-K. and G. Schricker (eds), *From GATT to TRIPs*, in *ICC*, 1996, 18, 204) to assume that WTO Members can no longer consider patentees' failure to work a patent locally as a *per se* abuse. They would commit such abuse (and thus become subject to a compulsory licence under the same article of the Paris Convention) *only* if they should undersupply the country that granted the patent, that is, they would not provide, even by mere exports, enough products to the country itself. Albeit not universally shared (see, for example, Reichman, J.H. and C. Hasenzahl, *Nonvoluntary Licensing of Patented Inventions: Historical Perspective, Legal Framework under the TRIPs Agreement, and an Overview of the Practice in Canada and the United States*, Draft, UNCTAD/ICTDS, 2002, II, C.2), even such an interpretation – upholding the repeal of the local working requirement – can be reconciled with our argument and thesis. The former indeed provides for a general rule, while the latter refers to a limited exception in the meaning of article 30 TRIPs.

privileges and franchises, the ancestors of modern patents, were issued primarily to induce the transfer, even by mere import, of foreign technologies. Thus, under Elizabeth I, a monopoly right was granted to introduce the manufacture of hard white Spanish soap, and another for the manufacture of saltpeter, a component of explosive powders previously imported from Antwerp.[9] This policy was shared *i.e.* by early American legislators. Addressing Congress on 8 January 1790, George Washington called for legislative attention to IP, 'giving effectual encouragement, as well to the introduction of new and useful inventions from abroad, as to the exertions of skill and genius in producing them at home'.[10]

Returning to today's economic and legal scenario, it is agreed that within the contemporary framework of trade relations *between developed countries* – *i.e.* countries that have already achieved industrial maturity and are endowed with sufficient financial means to invest in technology-driven competition – the repudiation, at the very end of the 20th century, of the local working requirement, after over a century of honoured service, represents a convincing anti-protectionist stance. At *that* stage of development, indeed, the requirement implied greater costs in terms of freedom of industrial establishment than benefits in terms of local acquisition of technology.[11]

It is doubted, however, that this equally applies to relations between such countries and developing countries. In this context, the abandonment of the requirement to work the patent locally curtails the *spill-over* of advanced technological skills, and hence the sharing by LDCs of both the patented technologies and the know-how that typically accompanies them. Thus, at the stroke of a pen, the international protection of IPRs has dropped a decisive instrument for supporting developing countries, and especially LDCs, in their efforts to bridge the gap with advanced countries. An instrument, repeat, that industrially advanced countries largely employed in the past, precisely to enhance, to their own benefit, the sharing of technological knowledge. See, for example, article 53 of the Italian

---

[9] FEDERICO, J., *Origin and Early History of Patents*, in *J. of the Pat. Off. Soc.*, 1929, 11, 293–7.

[10] DAVID, PAUL A., *The evolution of intellectual property institutions* in AGANBEGYAN, A., O.BOGMOLOV AND M. KASER , *System Transformations: Eastern and Western Assessments (Proceedings of the Tenth Congress of the International Economic Association)*, Vol. I, London, 1994.

[11] As a matter of fact, the repudiation of the principle had for a long time been advocated by a few countries, first and foremost the U.S., as a means of enhancing 'industrial freedom' (freedom of choice of industrial setting) at an international level.

Patent Act in force *till 1996*, stating that 'the import into or sale in the State of objects produced abroad does not constitute working of the invention'.

Again, a double standard: this, even in the light of two further remarks.

First, at the time the TRIPs Agreement began to be negotiated, both the normative features we have just discussed were no longer of interest for the already developed countries. On the contrary, establishing a standard short term for enacting the TRIPs 'Western-style' standards, and abolishing the local working requirement altogether provided a dual benefit for same countries: 1) as concerned their mutual (developed to developed) relations, the establishment of a level playing field for innovation-oriented competition between countries that had already reached the economic (and financial) stage that enables competition through innovation; b) as concerned their relations with DCs, the enactment of legal solutions, such as the two we have just discussed, which, in their synergy, would work for 'sticking' said countries – LDCs in particular – to their historical (substantially colonial) basic status of importers of advanced (patented) technology and exporters of raw or semi-processed materials and low-tech local products.

Second (or in fact first?): until WWII, the stages of industrial development were determined by national governments that exercised effective power over economic policies. This no longer holds in contemporary scenario (in which the TRIPs Agreement is also rooted), where economic sovereignty – and sometimes more than that – lies to a significant extent in the hands of multinational enterprises which are typically insensitive, in the absence of specific political or/and economic motivations, to support the efforts of single developing nations to fill their technological gap.

3. TWO SIMPLE 'REDEEMING' REFORMS

The adverse impact on LDCs of the two normative profiles discussed above can realistically be overcome only by solutions *de lege ferenda*, *i.e.* explicit reforms to the present legal framework. Indeed, the norms' text (articles 65 and 66, as integrated by the Doha resolution) and article 27.1) seems so clear and univocal that there do not seem to be any reliable 'wiggle rooms' or 'flexibilities' allowing redeeming interpretations. Thus the effort here will focus on outlining reforms to TRIPs' text which might efficiently prevent the distorting effects of present regulation while complying with the Agreement's system of principles and objectives: in particular those set forth in Part. I, General, arts 7 and 8.[12]

---

[12] Art. 7: '*protection and enforcement of IPRs*' is not an end in itself, but rather a means to '*contribute to the promotion of technological innovation and to the trans-*

As 'basic principles' – also highlighted by WIPO's in-progress 'Development Agenda'[13] – these norms should also guide the definition of type and scope of those 'measures' that the system of TRIPs allows Members to adopt when the need arises to conciliate IPRs holders' 'legitimate interests' with third parties' [*equally*!] 'legitimate interests' (article 30).

Thus, as concerns the 'time schedule' for complying with TRIPS' substantive rules, an incisive and efficient reform might envisage that LDCs (whose official list is of course 'fluid') be bound to adopt said rules not at a standard, one-size-fits-all date, but on an individual basis, so to say, i.e. as each different country effectively reaches a certain level of economic development, expressed by *a bundle of objectively measurable indexes*, such as per capita income, basic infrastructural assets, export/import balance, gross national product (GNP)and other significant ones.

As to the faculty of reintroducing the local working requirement (in industrial sense), articles 30 and 31 of the Agreement come into play as concerns, respectively, the possibility to 'provide limited exceptions to the exclusive rights conferred by a patent' ('provided that such exceptions do not unreasonably conflict with a normal exploitation of the patent and do not unreasonably prejudice the legitimate interests of the patent owner'), and the possibility of allowing 'other uses' ('other', i.e. different from the measures envisaged in article 30: see official Note to article 31) 'of the subject matter of a patent, without the authorisation of the right holder, including use by the government or third parties authorized by the government' – thus: 'Government use' and 'compulsory licenses' (article 31).

In this framework, it is submitted the following argument: that the imposition of a local working requirement inflicts a *much more limited restriction* on the patentee's rights and freedom of action, than that stemming from a compulsory licence (or government use). The former only weighs upon the choice between exporting and producing *in situ*, leaving *all* other faculties of the patentee fully intact – including the choice

---

fer and dissemination of technology' (emphasis added); and then see, in connection, art. 8 'Members may, in formulating or amending their laws and regulations, adopt measures necessary . . . to promote the public interest in sectors of vital importance to the socio-economic and *technological development*' (emphasis added).

[13] See in particular proposals and recommendations Nos. 19, 25 28 by WIPO's *Provisional Committee on Proposals Related to a WIPO Development Agenda* (Fourth Session, 11–15 June 2007, at http:// www.wipo.int?ip-development/en/agenda/pcda07_session4.html. Further references in A. Kur & H. Grosse Ruse-Kahn , *Enough Is Enough—The Notion of Binding Ceilings in International Intellectual Property Protection*, in *Max Planck Papers on Intellectual Property, Competition and Tax Research*, No. 09-01, available at http://papers.ssrn.com/sol3/papers.cfm?abstract_id=1326429

between producing directly or through a local licensee of her own trust and appointment. In fact, quite unlike the local working requirement, the imposition of a compulsory licence (or government use) 'reduces' the patentee's position to little more than that of a simple *rentier*.

In short: in more exists less. If the system of TRIPs explicitly allows the compulsory transfer to a third party of the exercise of practically all basic patentee's rights, affecting patterns of production, distribution, pricing – and this, albeit in exceptional cases, even without requiring a previous attempt to negotiate a contractual licence with the patentee (article 31(b)) – why shouldn't same system equally allow LDCs to request a local working requirement, as 'a limited exception to the exclusive rights' of the patentee (article 30)? So limited, that it would leave in the patentees' hands, unlike compulsory licenses, the exercise of all patent holder's fundamental faculties basic – just limiting the option to 'work' the patent by means of mere export. (And limiting it not indefinitely: just until the objective indexes recalled above will certify that the country is no longer 'least developed').

Further, and conclusively, this chapter hints at some further reasons in favour of the proposed reform.

First, allowing LDCs to reintroduce the local working requirement (in the industrial sense, *i.e.* of manufacturing) might be highly supportive, as hinted, of those countries' *industrial policies* aimed at 'catching up' with innovation even beyond those socio-economic and humanitarian emergencies which usually justify the granting of compulsory licences and government use. Thus LDCs would profit from the chances offered by the reintroduction of the local working requirement in other sector of high relevance for overall economic development – *e.g.*, production and saving of energies, cost-saving construction techniques, transportation and logistics, etc.

Second, as concerns the effective technological 'spill-over' effect, that patentees might more eagerly, hence more 'abundantly' in quality as well as in quantity, 'keep feeding' *their own* local plant, or *their own* local licensee with the know-how associated to (but not included in) the patent, and quite often useful for the best implementation thereof. Indeed, it seems all too reasonable to assume that this would much more likely occur in a cooperative context than in cases where, by contrast, patentees would be obliged to surrender their patent to an unrelated, much less controllable (even vis-à-vis re-export to affluent markets) licensee, imposed by a foreign government.

Third, the basic costs of working the patent would accrue to patentees and their licensees rather than weigh on the local governments or government-subsidized local firms.

Thus, it is finally submitted that the overall benefits associated to the reintroduction of the (industrial) local working requirement – fulfilled directly by patent holders or by licensees appointed by them – might often significantly surpass those expected by LCDs' straight recourse to compulsory licences or 'Government use'.

6. Adjudicating TRIPS for development

Molly Land[*]

I. INTRODUCTION

The conclusion of the Agreement on Trade-Related Aspects of Intellectual Property (TRIPS Agreement)[1] in 1994 heralded two important changes for global intellectual property regulation. First, the agreement made compliance with certain minimum intellectual property standards a requirement of membership in the World Trade Organization (WTO). Second, it subjected these standards to the WTO's mandatory dispute resolution process. This chapter focuses on the development impact of the second of these changes.

The decision to enforce intellectual property standards through the WTO's dispute resolution process has had several consequences for developing nations. The threat of litigation has contributed to the creation of a "pro IP climate" in which countries have foregone flexibilities to which they would otherwise be entitled.[2] Locating intellectual property in the dispute resolution mechanism of the international trading system has also led adjudicators to miss the unique need for internal balancing associated with intellectual property and TRIPS, resulting in overly restrictive

* I am grateful to Patricia Judd and Rudy Peritz for their very helpful feedback on this chapter and to Harlan Cohen, Evan Criddle, Rochelle Dreyfuss, and Joel Trachtman for their comments on the larger project of which this is a part. My thanks to Beulah Chou and David Rodrigues for their outstanding research assistance.

1 Agreement on Trade-Related Aspects of Intellectual Property Rights, Apr. 15, 1994, Marrakesh Agreement Establishing the World Trade Organization, Annex 1C, 108 Stat. 4809, 869 U.N.T.S. 299 [hereinafter TRIPS Agreement].

2 Carolyn Deere, The Implementation Game: The TRIPS Agreement and the Global Politics of Intellectual Property Reform in Developing Countries 156–9 (Oxford, Oxford University Press, 2009).

interpretation of TRIPS flexibilities.[3] For the least-developed countries (LDCs), the loss of flexibilities is particularly problematic.

This chapter seeks to revive the special and differential provisions of the treaty governing WTO dispute resolution as a way of countering the potential loss of flexibility under TRIPS. Specifically, the chapter recommends using a little-known provision of the Understanding on Rules and Procedures Governing the Settlement of Disputes (DSU), Article 24.1, to benefit LDCs in TRIPS disputes. Article 24.1 requires that "[a]t all stages of the determination of the causes of a dispute and of dispute settlement procedures involving a least-developed country Member, particular consideration shall be given to the special situation of least-developed country Members." The chapter argues that Article 24.1 could and should be used in TRIPS disputes to provide LDCs with greater flexibility in implementing their obligations under the treaty, including through a more lenient standard of review, shifting the burden of proof with respect to exceptions and limitations, and requiring injury as part of a prima facie case against an LDC.

As the transitional periods for LDCs to implement TRIPS come to an end, it is an appropriate time to consider the treatment of LDCs in TRIPS litigation. Although no LDCs have been the subject of complaints under TRIPS thus far, the expiration of these transitional periods on July 1, 2013 (in general) and January 1, 2016 (for pharmaceuticals)[4] opens LDCs up to the possibility of litigation. Special and differential treatment in dispute resolution would encourage LDCs to use the TRIPS flexibilities available to them to tailor their national innovation policies in ways that respond to local needs. Knowing that their actions would be viewed with greater deference in the event of a TRIPS complaint might provide them with the reassurance they need to experiment.

II. TRIPS ADJUDICATION AND DEVELOPMENT

In the context of intellectual property, flexibility in implementation is critical. Intellectual property policies can play an important role in

---

[3] *See* Molly Land, *Rebalancing TRIPS*, 33 MICH. J. INT'L L. 433 (2012).

[4] Council for Trade-Related Aspects of Intellectual Property Rights, *Extension of the Transition Period under Article 66.1 for Least-Developed Country Members*, IP/C/40 (Nov. 30, 2005); Council for Trade-Related Aspects of Intellectual Property Rights, *Extension of the Transition Period Under Article 66.1 of the TRIPS Agreement for Least-Developed Country Members for Certain Obligations with Respect to Pharmaceutical Products*, IP/C/25 (July 1, 2002).

fostering innovation and development, but to do so, they require tailoring.[5] The intellectual property policies that will promote development in one context are different from those necessary in another. For example, states may need to vary across industries the strength of the intellectual property protection they provide. China may want strong rights for its software industry but weaker rights for pharmaceuticals in order to ensure sufficient access to medicines.[6] Stronger intellectual property rights may also be advantageous with respect to fields in which the country possesses domestic resources. For example, data exclusivity may provide incentives for research into traditional medicines in countries that have significant indigenous knowledge resources.[7]

Flexibility in implementation is particularly important for LDCs. Although countries in transition, such as Brazil and India, may benefit from strong rights in some instances,[8] empirical research indicates that developing countries as a whole do not see significant economic growth associated with the adoption of strong intellectual property protection.[9]

---

[5] *See, e.g.*, Daniel J. Gervais, *TRIPS and Development*, *in* INTELLECTUAL PROPERTY, TRADE, AND DEVELOPMENT: STRATEGIES TO OPTIMIZE ECONOMIC DEVELOPMENT IN A TRIPS-PLUS ERA 3, 51–2 (Daniel J. Gervais ed., Oxford, Oxford University Press, 2007); Henrique Choer Moraes & Otávio Brandelli, *The Development Agenda at WIPO: Context and Origins*, *in* THE DEVELOPMENT AGENDA: GLOBAL INTELLECTUAL PROPERTY AND DEVELOPING COUNTRIES 33, 42 (Neil Weinstock Netanel ed., Oxford, Oxford University Press, 2009); Peter K. Yu, *The International Enclosure Movement*, 82 IND. L.J. 827, 896 (2007).

[6] Peter K. Yu, *Intellectual Property, Economic Development, and the China Puzzle*, *in* INTELLECTUAL PROPERTY, TRADE AND DEVELOPMENT, *supra* note 5, at 173, 208.

[7] Shamnad Basheer & Annalisa Primi, *The WIPO Development Agenda: Factoring in the "Technologically Proficient" Developing Countries*, *in* IMPLEMENTING WIPO'S DEVELOPMENT AGENDA 100, 108 (Jeremy DeBeer ed., Wilfrid Laurier University Press, CIGI, IDRC, 2009) (describing the recommendation of an Indian governmental committee that "data exclusivity for a term of five years is a good way to create incentives for more research and development into traditional medicines").

[8] Rochelle C. Dreyfuss, *The Role of India, China, Brazil and Other Emerging Economies in Establishing Access Norms for Intellectual Property and Intellectual Property Lawmaking* 2–3 (NYU School of Law Public Law & Legal Theory Research Paper Series, Working Paper No. 09-53, 2009), *available at* http://papers.ssrn.com/sol3/papers.cfm?abstract_id=1442785 (although the emerging economies of India, Brazil and China "suffer from the same access problems experienced by less developed economies," they also "have growing creative sectors that are beginning to enjoy the benefits of strong intellectual property protection").

[9] Robert L. Ostergard, Jr., *Economic Growth and Intellectual Property Rights Protection: A Reassessment of the Conventional Wisdom*, *in* INTELLECTUAL PROPERTY, TRADE AND DEVELOPMENT, *supra* note 5, at 115, 140.

Implementation is also more expensive in relative terms for countries with poor legal infrastructure.[10] Further, the costs of implementation have not been offset by the economic growth, increased foreign direct investment, and technology transfer that proponents of the TRIPS Agreement had anticipated.[11] "For the poorest developing countries, . . . there are questions regarding the degree to which IP laws are relevant at all."[12]

The TRIPS Agreement offers states several different ways in which they can tailor intellectual property policies to domestic needs. These "flexibilities" include explicit exemptions, balancing provisions, procedural flexibilities, ambiguous standards, and textual silence.[13] Articles 13, 17, and 30, for example, empower states to impose exceptions and limitations on copyright, trademark, and patent rights.[14] Many countries, however, including many of the least-developed states, have explicitly foregone flexibilities (*e.g.*, declining to implement compulsory licensing) or have adopted national laws beyond what is required by TRIPS (*e.g.*, adopting

---

[10] *See, e.g.*, Rochelle C. Dreyfuss & Andreas F. Lowenfeld, *Two Achievements of the Uruguay Round: Putting TRIPS and Dispute Settlement Together*, 37 VA. J. INT'L L. 275, 302–3 (1997) (discussing costs of setting up systems to grant, monitor, and enforce intellectual property rights as well as costs associated with loss of comparative advantage); Hon. Jean R. Homere, *Intellectual Property, Trade and Development: A View From the United States*, *in* INTELLECTUAL PROPERTY, TRADE AND DEVELOPMENT, *supra* note 5, at 333, 344.

[11] *See* Peter K. Yu, *Are Developing Countries Playing a Better TRIPS Game?* 5 (Drake University Law School Research Paper No. 12-06, 2011), *available at* http://papers.ssrn.com/sol3/papers.cfm?abstract_id=1915117## (noting that the "gains by less developed countries in the areas of agriculture and textiles would not make up for losses in the intellectual property and information technology areas" particularly given that "developed countries thus far have refused to honor their promise to reduce tariffs and subsidies in the areas of agriculture and textiles"); *see also* Peter K. Yu, *TRIPs and Its Discontents*, 10 MARQ. INTELL. PROP. L. REV. 369, 379 (2006); Dreyfuss, *supra* note 8, at 4.

[12] DEERE, *supra* note 2, at 103.

[13] *See* Land, *supra* note 3, at 439–42 (describing flexibilities).

[14] Each of the articles governing exceptions and limitations is drafted somewhat differently. Article 13 provides that "Members shall confine limitations or exceptions to exclusive rights to certain special cases which do not conflict with a normal exploitation of the work and do not unreasonably prejudice the legitimate interests of the right holder." TRIPS Agreement, *supra* note 1, art. 13. Article 17 allows "limited exceptions to the rights conferred by a trademark, such as fair use of descriptive terms, provided that such exceptions take account of the legitimate interests of the owner of the trademark and of third parties," while Article 30 provides for "limited exceptions to the exclusive rights conferred by a patent, provided that such exceptions do not unreasonably conflict with a normal exploitation of the patent and do not unreasonably prejudice the legitimate interests of the patent owner, taking account of the legitimate interests of third parties." *Ibid.* arts. 17, 30.

copyright terms that exceed those required by the treaty).[15] These decisions were often made pursuant to bilateral trade and investment agreements in which states bound themselves to provide such "TRIPS-plus" protection.[16] Although most of these "TRIPS-plus" agreements were concluded with states that had markets of commercial significance for the United States or European Union, "[e]ven LDCs that mattered little from a commercial viewpoint attracted some interest."[17] Developed countries pushed for strong intellectual property laws in small countries to help isolate the "larger, more competitive and less-malleable developing countries" and marshal support for TRIPS-plus agreements.[18]

The availability of mandatory dispute resolution through the WTO also played a role in over-compliance with the TRIPS Agreement. The DSU is a treaty negotiated as part of the creation of the WTO in 1994 that provides a mechanism for states to bring complaints against one another for violations of covered agreements. Through the procedures established by the DSU, member states can obtain a binding decision on a complaint from an adjudicatory panel.[19] The DSU also establishes a standing body, called the Appellate Body, that hears appeals of panel decisions.[20] A panel can sanction a member state for violating the TRIPS Agreement by authorizing the complaining state to suspend trade benefits to which the violator state is otherwise entitled.[21] If the violator state does not comply with a panel's recommendations,[22] the DSU allows the complaining state to "request authorization . . . to suspend the application to the Member concerned of concessions or other obligations under the covered agreements."[23]

The decision to subject TRIPS to dispute resolution through the WTO system was controversial. Several developing nations initially opposed applying the DSU to the TRIPS Agreement, fearing that it would result in significant litigation against developing countries.[24] On the other hand,

---

15 *See, e.g.*, DEERE, *supra* note 2, at 73, 81, 91–4, 98.

16 *Ibid.* at 151–5.

17 *Ibid.* at 116.

18 *Ibid.*

19 Understanding on Rules and Procedures Governing the Settlement of Disputes, arts. 4, 16.4, Apr. 15, 1994, Marrakesh Agreement Establishing the World Trade Organization, Annex 2, 1869 U.N.T.S. 401, 33 I.L.M 1226 [hereinafter DSU].

20 *Ibid.* art. 17.

21 *Ibid.* art. 22.1.

22 *Ibid.* art. 19.

23 *Ibid.* art. 22.2.

24 U.N. CONF. ON TRADE & DEV.–INT'L CTR. FOR TRADE & SUST. DEV.

developing countries also hoped that "legalization"[25] of dispute resolution at the WTO would help "insulat[e] them against the pressures of power politics" and "limit the scope of the debate to the legal merits."[26] As the WTO Secretariat notes, the system of compulsory multilateral dispute settlement can be viewed as "empower[ing] developing countries and smaller economies by placing 'the weak' on a more equal footing with 'the strong.'"[27] Developing countries also anticipated that the DSU's monopoly on trade retaliation would eliminate the possibility of unilateral sanctions.[28] Although unilateral pressure continues,[29] David Evans and Gregory Shaffer have observed that WTO dispute resolution has "helped to level the playing field between weaker and stronger WTO Members."[30]

Nonetheless, the decision to subject intellectual property standards to trade dispute procedures has had the effect of constraining some of the bargained-for flexibilities of the TRIPS Agreement. The threat of litigation has contributed to a "pro IP climate" that has discouraged states from

---

[UNCTAD-ICTSD], RESOURCE BOOK ON TRIPS AND DEVELOPMENT 659–64 (2005) [hereinafter TRIPS RESOURCE BOOK].

25 The reforms of the dispute settlement process associated with the creation of the WTO have been characterized as a process of "legalization." *See, e.g.*, Gregory Shaffer, *How to Make the WTO Dispute Settlement System Work for Developing Countries: Some Proactive Developing Country Strategies* 9 (ICTSD Resource Paper No. 5, 2003).

26 Hansel T. Pham, *Developing Countries and the WTO: The Need for More Mediation in the DSU*, 9 HARV. NEGOT. L. REV. 331, 347 (2004).

27 WORLD TRADE ORGANIZATION SECRETARIAT, A HANDBOOK ON THE WTO DISPUTE SETTLEMENT SYSTEM 109 (2004) [hereinafter HANDBOOK].

28 *See* TRIPS RESOURCE BOOK, *supra* note 24, at 663, 686; Karen Kaiser, *Article 64: Dispute Settlement*, *in* WTO—TRADE-RELATED ASPECTS OF INTELLECTUAL PROPERTY RIGHTS 798, 800 (Peter-Tobias Stoll et al. eds., Leiden, Martin Nijhoff Publishers, 2009).

29 The United States has continued to employ threats of sanctions through its "Special 301" process, *see* Donald Harris, *TRIPS After Fifteen Years: Success or Failure, As Measured by Compulsory Licensing*, 18 J. INTELL. PROP. L. 367, 373 (2011), although the impact of this threat has been limited by the United States' position in litigation before the WTO that it would not use this process in ways inconsistent with TRIPS, *see* Panel Report, *United States—Sections 301–310 of the Trade Act of 1974*, ¶¶ 7.125–7.126, 7.131, 7.135, WT/DS152/R (Dec. 22, 1999) (although Section 304 constituted a prima facie violation of Article 23.2(a), the United States had expressed an "unambiguous and official position" that prevented it "from making a determination of inconsistency contrary to Article 23.2(a)" and which rendered the process consistent with the DSU).

30 David Evans & Gregory C. Shaffer, *Conclusion*, *in* DISPUTE SETTLEMENT AT THE WTO: THE DEVELOPING COUNTRY EXPERIENCE 342, 342 (Gregory C. Shaffer & Ricardo Meléndez-Ortiz eds., 2010); HANDBOOK, *supra* note 27, at 109.

taking advantage of flexibilities.[31] Clearly, there are a variety of reasons why states implemented levels of protection higher than what was required by the treaty,[32] and the direct threat of litigation does not explain over-compliance by LDCs not yet required to implement the treaty. Yet dispute resolution did play a role in creating a culture of over-compliance. As Deere notes in her study of TRIPS implementation:

> Developed countries deployed a suite of economic pressures on developing countries, using bilateral trade, IP and investment deals, WTO accession agreements, trade sanctions, the threat of sanctions, and the WTO DSU Process. . . . Even for countries not directly subjected to them, economic pressures reinforced an international policy climate in which it was clear that taking steps toward stronger IP protection would be favoured by powerful donors, foreign companies, and trading partners.[33]

This "pro-IP" climate was exacerbated by the polarized rhetoric used by proponents and opponents of strengthened intellectual property protections worldwide.[34] Although the availability of dispute resolution did not result in the explosion of litigation that many had feared,[35] the very lack of precedent (and particularly precedent involving developing countries) has meant that "there has been no opportunity to generate the norms that would provide developing countries with guidance on what sorts of moves they can safely regard as compatible with international obligations."[36]

The climate of over-compliance fostered by economic pressure and the availability of mandatory dispute resolution has been exacerbated by overly restrictive interpretations of TRIPS flexibilities. As I have argued elsewhere,[37] situating intellectual property disputes within a trade dispute resolution mechanism has led at least one WTO panel to develop crucial jurisprudence that is both internally incoherent and inconsistent with the goals of intellectual property balancing and the TRIPS Agreement. In *U.S.–Copyright*, the only case thus far interpreting the provision of TRIPS governing exceptions and limitations to copyright (Article 13),

---

[31] DEERE, *supra* note 2, at 156.

[32] These include, among others, the state's domestic capacity for intellectual property policy making, unilateral economic pressure, and public engagement. *See generally ibid.*

[33] *Ibid.* at 306.

[34] Joost Pauwelyn, *The Dog That Barked But Didn't Bite: 15 Years of Intellectual Property Disputes at the WTO*, 1 J. INT'L DISP. SETTLEMENT 389, 425 (2010).

[35] *Ibid.* at 395.

[36] *See* Dreyfuss, *supra* note 8, at 7.

[37] Land, *supra* note 3, at 450–61.

the panel declined to consider the purpose of the challenged exception, citing Appellate Body cases interpreting the national treatment clauses of the General Agreement on Tariffs and Trade (GATT) and the General Agreement on Trade in Services (GATS).[38] Not only does the rationale of these cases fail to apply in the context of Article 13, but an approach that disclaims consideration of purpose is fundamentally at odds with the instrumental nature of intellectual property law and its consideration of the burdens imposed by granting monopoly rights and the objectives those grants are designed to achieve.[39] The panel's textual and dictionary-driven interpretive approach has read much of the treaty's flexibility out of the agreement.

In the short term, over-compliance with the treaty may have been a net gain for developing countries, bringing significant benefits with trade partners and costing little given inadequate domestic enforcement. Yet while lack of enforcement may currently mitigate the absence of flexibilities in many cases, inadequate enforcement is not a long-term solution to protecting the TRIPS flexibilities necessary for development and human rights, particularly in light of international efforts designed to bolster enforcement efforts worldwide.[40]

Further, as transitional periods expire, there is reason to believe that developing countries and LDCs in particular may be especially sensitive to concerns about litigation. First, the consequences of losing a dispute are higher for developing countries: "For trade-dependent, IP-importing developing countries, the prospect that failure to implement TRIPS could result in trade retaliation is one of the Agreement's most pernicious aspects."[41] Further, as Niall Meagher explains, a "developed country can more readily spread the financial costs of failure (whether involving the loss of any anticipated trade gains or the cost of implementation or

---

[38] Panel Report, *United States—Section 110(5) of the US Copyright Act*, ¶ 6.111, WT/DS160/R (June 15, 2000) [hereinafter *U.S.–Copyright*].

[39] *See, e.g.*, Jon O. Newman, *Considering Copyright*, 40 Hous. L. Rev. 613, 615 (2003) ("The dominant issue in all of copyright law is striking an appropriate balance between the maintenance of an adequate incentive for authors to create new works and the vital interest of the public in having adequate access to the works that are created—limited access via the fair use doctrine during the copyright term and general access once the work has entered the public domain.").

[40] *See, e.g.*, Sean Flynn & Bijan Madhani, *ACTA and Access to Medicines* 2–3 (Washington College of Law, Research Paper No. 2012-03, 2011), *available at* http://papers.ssrn.com/sol3/papers.cfm?abstract_id=1980865 (discussing enforcement measures required by the Anti-Counterfeiting Trade Agreement that could restrict access to medicines).

[41] Deere, *supra* note 2, at 65.

counter-measures imposed by a complainant WTO member) throughout its economy."[42] Given limited resources available for implementation, developing countries may also assume that they are more likely to lose on the merits of a dispute if challenged.[43] Marc Busch and Eric Reinhardt's empirical study of early settlement has also shown that developing countries tend to lack the legal capacity needed to take advantage of the opportunity to extract full concessions during early settlement.[44]

Second, WTO dispute resolution is expensive, and these costs are, in relative terms, "much higher for developing than developed countries."[45] Legalized adjudication "demands increasingly sophisticated legal talent" thereby "driv[ing] up the cost of formal dispute settlement, which is disproportionately burdensome to developing countries."[46] Developing nations also tend to possess less domestic legal expertise in the area of intellectual property and have access to fewer resources necessary to initiate or defend against suits.[47] The start-

---

[42] Niall Meagher, *Representing Developing Countries in WTO Dispute Settlement Proceedings*, *in* WTO LAW & DEVELOPING COUNTRIES 213, 220 (George A. Berman & Petros C. Mavroidis eds., 2007). Although the views in the essay are his own, Meagher's observations are based on his "personal experience as senior counsel at the ACWL [Advisory Centre on WTO Law]." *Ibid.* at 213.

[43] *Ibid.* at 221.

[44] Marc L. Busch & Eric Reinhardt, *Developing Countries and GATT/WTO Dispute Settlement*, *in* WTO LAW AND DEVELOPING COUNTRIES, *supra* note 42, 195, 196. Busch and Reinhardt argue that the threat of litigation benefits WTO members by encouraging early settlement, which is associated with securing full concessions. *Ibid.* Countries with more limited legal capacity, however, have greater difficulty securing early settlement. *Ibid.*

[45] Meagher, *supra* note 42, at 218–19 (discussing the costs of initiating and defending a complaint); *see also* South Centre, *Issues Regarding the Review of the WTO Dispute Settlement Mechanism* 23 (Trade-Related Agenda, Development and Equity Working Papers, 1999), *available at* http://tinyurl.com/ctcyd6m (noting that cost is one of the main complaints developing countries have raised with respect to the DSU); Mohammad Ali Taslim, *How the DSU Worked for Bangladesh: The First Least Developed Country to Bring a WTO Complaint*, *in* DISPUTE SETTLEMENT AT THE WTO, *supra* note 30, 230, 240 (discussing the costs of bringing a complaint as a disincentive to make use of the dispute resolution procedures); Tshimanga Kongolo, *The WTO Dispute Settlement Mechanism: TRIPS Rulings and the Developing Countries*, 4(2) J. WORLD INTELL. PROP. 257, 260–1 (2001).

[46] Timothy Stostad, Note, *Trappings of Legality: Judicialization of Dispute Settlement in the WTO, and Its Impact on Developing Countries*, 39 CORNELL INT'L L.J. 811, 826 (2006).

[47] Gregory C. Shaffer, *Recognizing Public Goods in WTO Dispute Settlement: Who Participates? Who Decides?*, 7 J. INT'L ECON. L. 459, 472–73 475 (2004). In 2004, Shaffer estimated the average cost of a WTO claim at $300,000–$400,000. *Ibid.* at 473.

up costs of litigation are significantly more burdensome for countries without domestic capacity. Such states must obtain legal expertise on an ad hoc basis, a process that can take time, and they might lack the assistance of a Geneva mission.[48] Because they are less likely to be repeat players, developing nations also "benefit from fewer economies of scale in deploying legal resources."[49] Although the Secretariat provides developing countries with experts, there has historically been an insufficient number of experts to fill the need, and the Secretariat's commitment to neutrality has hindered the ability of these experts to act as advocates for developing countries.[50]

III. PROCEDURAL PROTECTIONS FOR DEVELOPING COUNTRIES

The WTO dispute resolution mechanism contains several provisions designed to mitigate some of the costs for LDCs associated with introduction of TRIPS standards and the potential loss of TRIPS flexibility resulting from over-compliance with the treaty. Panels and the Appellate Body can provide developing and least-developed countries with additional flexibility in their implementation of the agreement by taking advantage of provisions in the DSU providing special and differential procedural protections to developing state and LDC litigants.

A. Special and Differential Treatment Under the DSU

Developing WTO members are entitled to a range of special and differential treatment under the covered agreements. As the Secretariat notes, special and differential treatment provisions in the WTO agreements tend to fall into five categories—increasing trade opportunities, requiring other countries to safeguard developing country interests, allowing flexibility in rules governing trade measures, providing for transitional periods, and guaranteeing technical assistance.[51] Many of these rules are "substantive" in the sense that they reduce or eliminate specific obligations for developing or least-developed members. For example, in the Agreement

---

48 Meagher, *supra* note 42, at 219.
49 Shaffer, *supra* note 47, at 474.
50 Pham, *supra* note 26, at 356.
51 Note by the Secretariat, *Special and Differential Treatment for Least-Developed Countries*, ¶ 1, WT/COMTD/W/135 (Oct. 5, 2004).

on Agriculture, LDCs are exempt from commitments to reduce export subsidies.[52]

The TRIPS Agreement does not explicitly provide special and differential treatment for developing nations in the form of exemptions or more flexible rules.[53] The 20-year patent term required by the TRIPS Agreement, for example, applies to all countries regardless of their stage of development.[54] In addition, the intent of at least some of the negotiating members—the United States, in particular—was to impose common substantive standards for all member states. These states desired to eliminate "special and differential treatment" in TRIPS and instead to provide only increased transitional periods for developing and least-developed nations.[55] By and large, this position was successful, and TRIPS does not include the kinds of substantive "special and differential" treatment present in the other covered agreements.[56]

The DSU, however, does provide for special and differential treatment for developing and least-developed countries in the context of dispute settlement, including in TRIPS cases.[57] Broadly characterized, special and differential treatment provisions in the DSU fall into three categories—consultation, implementation, and adjudication.[58] First, the DSU provides additional protections for developing countries and LDCs in the context of consultation. Article 3.12 offers developing countries alternative procedures for consultation that allow recourse to the good offices

---

[52] Agreement on Agriculture, art. 15.2, Apr. 15, 1994, Marrakesh Agreement Establishing the World Trade Organization, Annex 1A, 1867 U.N.T.S. 410 (1994).

[53] Kongolo, *supra* note 45, at 258.

[54] TRIPS Agreement, *supra* note 1, art. 33.

[55] Judith H. Bello, *Some Practical Observations About WTO Settlement of Intellectual Property Disputes*, 37 VA. J. INT'L L. 357, 364 (1997).

[56] *See* Constantine Michalopoulos, *Special and Differential Treatment of Developing Countries in TRIPS* 2 (TRIPS Issues Papers No. 2, 2003) (noting the "lack of substantial SDT" in the TRIPS Agreement and the problems this poses for developing countries). As I argue elsewhere, however, much of the flexibility needed for developing nations is already encompassed in the "standard-like" norms that the treaty provides. *See* Land, *supra* note 3, at 440–1.

[57] *See generally* South Centre, *supra* note 45.

[58] The DSU also requires transparency concerning the use of the provisions for special and differential treatment under other covered agreements. Article 12.11 of the DSU asks panels to indicate, in disputes involving developing countries, "the form in which account has been taken of relevant provisions on differential and more-favourable treatment for developing country Members that form part of the covered agreements which have been raised by the developing country Member in the course of the dispute settlement procedures." DSU, *supra* note 19, art. 12.11.

of the Director-General and shortened time frames. Article 4.10 calls for "special attention to the particular problems and interests of developing country Members" during consultations. Article 24.2 provides that in cases involving a LDC, the LDC member state can request the assistance of the Director-General or Chairman of the Dispute Settlement Body in settling a dispute. Under Article 10, parties are entitled to additional time to engage in consultations regarding measures undertaken by developing countries.

Second, the DSU includes several provisions designed to address developing country concerns with implementation. Article 21.2 requires that in the context of implementation, "[p]articular attention" be paid "to matters affecting the interests of developing country Members with respect to measures which have been subject to dispute settlement." To address the specific challenges that developing country members face in making effective use of the dispute settlement mechanism given their weaker capacity for retaliation,[59] Articles 21.7 and 21.8 the DSU require panels to consider "further action" in implementation and to "take into account not only the trade coverage of measures complained of, but also their impact on the economy of developing country Members concerned." Article 24.1 provides that "[i]f nullification or impairment is found to result from a measure taken by a least-developed country Member, complaining parties shall exercise due restraint in asking for compensation or seeking authorization to suspend the application of concessions or other obligations pursuant to these procedures."

Third, the DSU also provides specific procedural protections for developing country members designed to reduce the burden on such members associated with the adjudicatory process itself. Developing countries can request a panelist from a developing country (Article 8.10) and are entitled to legal advice and assistance from the Secretariat (Article 27.2).[60] When "examining a complaint against a developing country Member," panels "shall accord sufficient time for the developing country Member to prepare and present its argumentation" (Article 10).

Despite these strong statements about the special consideration required for developing and least-developed member states, states have made little use of the provisions in the DSU offering special and differential treatment

---

[59] TRIPS Resource Book, *supra* note 24, at 687–8.

[60] DSU, *supra* note 19, art. 21.2; TRIPS Resource Book, *supra* note 24, at 684 (noting that this is in some tension with the obligation of WTO experts to be neutral). Article 21.2 explicitly notes that the expert "shall assist the developing country Member in a manner ensuring the continued impartiality of the Secretariat." DSU, *supra* note 19, art. 21.2.

in dispute resolution.[61] In part, this may be a function of the ambiguity of many of these provisions.[62] Articles 4.10 and 21.2 require "special attention," "particular attention" and "particular consideration" to the needs of developing countries without providing any indication of what this additional attention and consideration might include. As the South Centre noted in discussing Article 4.10, provisions "of a declaratory nature," without further guidance, "have not been of any practical use to developing countries."[63] Lack of reliance on these provisions also appears to be related to a desire to avoid the perception of special treatment. Frieder Roessler observes that "there is a reluctance of developing countries to invoke the DSU provisions according them special privileges and of the judicial organs to give effect to these provisions."[64]

At a minimum, the ambiguity of these sweeping provisions indicates a need for the Dispute Settlement Body (DSB) to elaborate on the kinds of procedures panels might adopt in cases involving developing countries and LDCs. Suggestions of procedures that might be helpful have already been raised in the context of negotiations about reforming the DSU. For example, pursuant to Article 4.10, the DSB might enable consultations to be held in developing countries to minimize the costs associated with travel and hiring counsel abroad.[65] To aid in enforcement, developing countries have proposed that the DSB allow monetary compensation (instead of suspension of concessions) and collective retaliation by all members to enforce recommendations.[66] There have been several proposals designed to compensate for the lack of resources to litigate, including proposals to have developed countries pay the costs of developing countries in cases where the developing country prevails, and proposals

---

[61] Hunter Nottage, *Developing Countries in the WTO Dispute Settlement System* 16 (Global Economic Governance Working Paper 2009/47, 2009); *see also* Frieder Roessler, *Special and Differential Treatment of Developing Countries Under the WTO Dispute Settlement System*, *in* THE WTO DISPUTE SETTLEMENT SYSTEM 1995–2003, 87, 89 (Federico Ortino & Ernst-Ulrich Petersmann eds., 2004) (discussing the use of Article 21.2). Panels have included developing country members, but not because of a particular request filed pursuant to Article 8.10. TRIPS RESOURCE BOOK, *supra* note 24, at 685.

[62] TRIPS RESOURCE BOOK, *supra* note 24, at 685.

[63] South Centre, *supra* note 45, at 19.

[64] Roessler, *supra* note 61, at 89.

[65] *See, e.g.*, Working Document, Negotiations on the Dispute Settlement Understanding: Proposal by the LDC Group, ¶ 3, TN/DS/W/17 (Oct. 9, 2002) [hereinafter Proposal by the LDC Group]; South Centre, *supra* note 45, at 31.

[66] *See* Proposal by the LDC Group, *supra* note 65, ¶¶ 13, 15.

to offer more training and funding in the area of legal assistance.[67] Other proposals would increase the litigation support available to developing countries by removing the impartiality requirement for experts provided by the Secretariat.[68] Some of these provisions were proposed in connection with the drafting of the DSU,[69] and some have been implemented. In 2001, for example, the WTO established the Advisory Centre on WTO Law, with the mission "to provide developing countries and LDCs with the legal capacity necessary to enable them to take full advantage of the opportunities offered by the WTO."[70]

One provision for special and differential treatment that has not received much attention is Article 24. Article 24.1 provides:

> At all stages of the determination of the causes of a dispute and of dispute settlement procedures involving a least-developed country Member, particular consideration shall be given to the special situation of least-developed country Members. In this regard, Members shall exercise due restraint in raising matters under these procedures involving a least-developed country Member. If nullification or impairment is found to result from a measure taken by a least-developed country Member, complaining parties shall exercise due restraint in asking for compensation or seeking authorization to suspend the application of concessions or other obligations pursuant to these procedures.

The first sentence of Article 24.1 is extraordinarily broad, mandating—not just permitting—that "particular consideration" be given to the "special situation" of LDCs "[a]t all stages of the determination of the causes of a dispute and of dispute settlement procedures." The remainder of Article 24.1 provides suggestions about ways in which such consideration might be ensured—for example, in restraint by members in raising matters and asking for compensation or sanctions against LDCs. LDCs have suggested strengthening this provision by requiring panels to affirmatively determine, in any suit against a least-developed country, whether the complainant exercised due restraint in bringing complaint against LDC, including whether the complainant should have called for assistance from the Director-General or used other means to settle the dispute.[71]

---

[67] Pham, *supra* note 26, at 364; South Centre, *supra* note 45, at 32.

[68] Proposal by the LDC Group, *supra* note 65, ¶ 21; South Centre, *supra* note 45, at 30.

[69] *See* Daniel H. Erskine, *Resolving Trade Disputes: The Mechanisms of GATT/WTO Dispute Resolution*, 2 Santa Clara J. Int'l L. 40, 80–81 nn.284–292 (2004).

[70] The Advisory Center on WTO Law's Mission, *available at* http://www.acwl.ch/e/about/about_us.html.

[71] Proposal by the LDC Group, *supra* note 65, ¶ 17.

Due restraint, however, is only one example of the "particular consideration" that might be afforded LDCs under the broad terms of Article 24.1. The phrase "[i]n this regard" indicates that what follows the first sentence satisfies but does not exhaust the "particular consideration" that might be offered to meet the needs of LDCs. The language of "[a]t all stages of the determination of the causes of a dispute and of dispute settlement procedures"—which must be given meaning by virtue of the principle of effective treaty interpretation followed by the Appellate Body[72]—is also far broader than the examples of initiating complaints and seeking remedies, thus indicating that this is a non-exhaustive list.

The fact that some of the activities discussed in Article 24.1 appear to be more aspirational than binding highlights the otherwise obligatory nature of the provision. The statement that states should exercise due restraint in raising issues against LDC member states, for example, appears to be a moral and not a legal obligation.[73] As Neils Petersen explains, "It is barely conceivable that a Member could be legally prevented from utilizing the dispute settlement procedure if a country had breached an obligation under the WTO regime."[74] Petersen argues that the obligation to consider the needs of LDCs in seeking compensation or the suspension of concessions, on the other hand, is expressed in prescriptive terms ("shall") and is thus a binding obligation.[75]

The first sentence of Article 24.1, which also uses the term "shall," expresses a mandatory obligation to treat LDCs differently during dispute settlement. This mandatory consideration to be afforded the least-developed countries explicitly embraces procedures used during adjudication. The article requires particular consideration both "[a]t all stages of the determination of the causes of a dispute" as well as "of dispute settlement procedures." The determination of the causes of a dispute occurs during adjudication, when the panel evaluates the reasons for the parties' dispute and their respective fault. Thus, this phrase specifically contemplates procedures that occur during the adjudicatory phase of the dispute settlement process.

---

72 Report of the Appellate Body, *United States—Standards for Reformulated and Conventional Gasoline*, AB-1996-1, WT/DS2/AB/R, at 23 (Apr. 29, 1996) ("One of the corollaries of the 'general rule of interpretation' in the Vienna Convention is that interpretation must give meaning and effect to all the terms of a treaty. An interpreter is not free to adopt a reading that would result in reducing whole clauses or paragraphs of a treaty to redundancy or inutility.").

73 Niels Petersen, *Article 24 DSU: Special Procedures Involving Least-Developed Country Members*, *in* WTO—INSTITUTIONS AND DISPUTE SETTLEMENT 563, 564 (Rüdiger Wolfrum et al. eds., 2006).

74 *Ibid.*

75 *Ibid.*

To the extent that there is ambiguity in the phrase "[a]t all stages of the determination of the causes of a dispute," the negotiating history of Article 24.1 also supports the interpretation that it applies to the adjudicatory phase. The genesis of the first sentence in Article 24.1 appears to have been a 1990 draft prepared by the Negotiating Group on Dispute Settlement. The first sentence in a section entitled "Special Procedures involving Least-Developed Contracting Parties" simply stated: "At all stages of dispute settlement procedures involving a least-developed contracting party, particular consideration shall be given to the special situation of least-developed countries."[76] This language was not present in proposals summarized by the Secretariat in 1988,[77] nor did it appear in a proposed draft text from 1988.[78] The sentence in the 1990 draft was carried over in expanded form in the Dunkel Draft, a draft proposed by Arthur Dunkel, Secretary General of the GATT in December of 1991 that eventually became the basis for the WTO agreements. Article 22.1 of the Dunkel Draft provided:

> At all stages of the *determination of the causes of a dispute* and of dispute settlement procedures involving a least-developed contracting party, particular consideration shall be given to the special situation of least-developed countries. In this regard, contracting parties shall exercise due restraint in raising matters under Article XXIII involving a least developed contracting party. If nullification or impairment is found to result from a measure taken by a least developed contracting party, complaining parties shall exercise due restraint in asking for compensation or seeking authorization to suspend the application of concessions or other obligations pursuant to Article XXIII:2.[79]

Article 22.1 of the Dunkel Draft was eventually codified with minor changes as Article 24.1 of the DSU.[80] By explicitly adding the phrase "the

[76] Negotiating Group on Dispute Settlement, *Draft Text on Dispute Settlement*, MTN.GNG/NG13/W/45, at 7 (Sept. 21, 1990).

[77] Note by the Secretariat, *Differential and More Favourable Treatment of Developing Countries in the GATT Dispute Settlement System*, MTN.GNG/NGl3/W/27 (June 30, 1988).

[78] Negotiating Group on Dispute Settlement, *Dispute Settlement Proposal*, MTN.GNG/NG13/W/30 (Oct. 10, 1988).

[79] The Dunkel Draft from the GATT Secretariat: Draft Final Act Embodying the Results of the Uruguay Round of Multilateral Trade Negotiations, S.19, GATT Doc. No. MTN.TNC/W/FA (Dec. 20, 1991) (emphasis added).

[80] With respect to the first sentence, Article 24.1 of the final text substituted "country Member" for "contracting party" and "country Members" for "countries."

determination of the causes of a dispute" to the text of this article, the Dunkel Draft, and all subsequent drafts, made clear that LDCs were to be provided with particular consideration during adjudication of the merits of those disputes. The addition of the second and third sentences on due restraint also made clear that these examples were illustrative only, and not exhaustive of the kind of consideration that might be afforded LDCs in dispute settlement.

B. Proposed Procedures for LDCs in TRIPS Disputes

The particular consideration owed LDCs under Article 24.1 may vary depending on the nature of the underlying dispute and the covered agreement under which it is brought.[81] In any WTO dispute, there are two operative treaties—the DSU and the covered agreement itself. The obligations and procedures relevant to any dispute must therefore be evaluated with reference to both treaties. Although some kinds of procedural protections might be appropriate regardless of the nature of the dispute, others may have the effect of altering the nature of the parties' obligations under the respective covered agreements. In discussing standards of review, for example, Andrew Guzman has argued that Article 11 of the DSU should be interpreted differently depending on the covered agreement at issue, noting that it "does not, and cannot, and should not prescribe a single standard of review for all cases."[82] As a result, it is important to evaluate what protections might be necessary in the context of each specific agreement.

In light of the burdens of strong intellectual property rights on LDCs and their need for maximum flexibility in implementing the provisions of the TRIPS Agreement, procedures establishing greater deference to the needs of LDCs would be appropriate for cases brought under that treaty. In particular, Article 24.1 provides a means to open up additional policy space for LDCs in using TRIPS flexibilities. There are three types of procedures that panels might apply to equalize the burden on LDCs—a more deferential standard of review, shifting the burden of proof on exceptions and limitations, and requiring complaining states to bring proof of injury to establish a prima facie case against an LDC. These procedures would

[81] *See* Andrew D. Mitchell, Legal Principles in WTO Disputes 265 (2008) (noting that the "the differing needs of developing countries in different situations and at different stages of development limit the utility of a general S&D principle").

[82] Andrew T. Guzman, *Determining the Appropriate Standard of Review in WTO Disputes*, 42 Cornell Int'l L.J. 45, 51–2 (2009).

help encourage LDCs to experiment with the flexibilities protected under TRIPS.

First, panels should use a highly deferential standard of review in TRIPS cases involving LDCs. During the negotiation of the TRIPS Agreement, developing and developed countries disputed the standard of review that WTO adjudicators should use with respect to complaints about violations of the TRIPS Agreement. Judith Bello, who was involved in the negotiations on behalf of the United States Government, recalls that the Bush administration's position with respect to TRIPS "was to empower dispute settlement panelists to scrutinize the measures or practices complained of closely, without undue deference for the member state's findings or determinations underlying them."[83] Developing countries, on the other hand, wanted to cabin the authority of the dispute settlement bodies, arguing that because the TRIPS Agreement required members to limit their sovereignty "more severely than the passive provisions" of the other covered agreements, it was necessary to provide a standard of review that detailed "the prerequisites under which a panel or the Appellate Body was obliged to respect decisions of the Members."[84] In the end, the parties were only able to agree on a standard of review for one of the covered agreements, the Anti-Dumping Agreement.[85]

Filling the gap left by the drafters, the panels in TRIPS cases have in practice established a very high standard of review by disregarding the purposes the state sought to achieve in using TRIPS flexibilities. In *U.S.–Copyright*, for example, the panel considered a challenge to two provisions of U.S. copyright law as inconsistent with Article 13, which allows exceptions and limitations to copyright that meet the requirements of that article. The panel focused nearly exclusively on the text of the treaty, relying on dictionary definitions and explicitly disregarding the purpose to be achieved by the exception.[86] Elsewhere, I have argued that when

---

[83] Bello, *supra* note 55, at 362.

[84] Kaiser, *supra* note 28, at 805.

[85] Agreement on Implementation of Article VI of the General Agreement on Tariffs and Trade, art. 17.6, Apr. 15, 1994, Marrakesh Agreement Establishing the World Trade Organization, Annex 1A, 1868 U.N.T.S. 201. In the absence of explicit agreement on a standard of review for the other agreements, WTO panels have looked to Article 11 of the DSU, which provides that panels "should make an objective assessment of the matter before it, including an objective assessment of the facts of the case and the applicability of and conformity with the relevant covered agreements." DSU, *supra* note 19, art. 11.

[86] *U.S.–Copyright*, *supra* note 38, ¶ 6.111 ("As regards the parties' arguments on whether the public policy purpose of an exception is relevant, we believe that the term 'certain special cases' should not lightly be equated with 'special purpose.'").

the obligations in the treaty, such as Article 13, impose context-specific standards rather than specific outcomes, panels should allow states to demonstrate why those standards are met by referencing the purposes they are designed to achieve.[87] For LDCs, panels should afford even more deference by adopting an "arbitrary and capricious" standard of review with respect to exceptions and limitations. Panels should not overturn the decision of an LDC balancing intellectual property rights with national policy goals unless it has no reasonable basis in fact or clearly violates the language of Articles 13, 17, and 30. For example, an action might violate Article 13 (which requires that the case be "special") only if there is nothing to distinguish it from other cases in which exceptions are not permitted. This approach would shift the focus of the panels from the question of whether the exception is "narrow in quantitative as well as a qualitative sense"[88] to whether the state has articulated a reasonable basis for the exception. Under this approach, then, panels would not only consider the purposes exceptions are designed to serve (already a change from current jurisprudence) but also view the LDC's articulated purpose with the greatest deference possible.

Second, additional protection for LDCs under Article 24.1 could be achieved by shifting the burden of proof on the applicability of exceptions and limitations. Under current jurisprudence, after the complaining state establishes a prima facie case that the defending state has violated a provision of the TRIPS Agreement, the burden shifts to the defending state to demonstrate that the challenged action was permitted under one of the exceptions and limitations protected under the agreement.[89] Additional deference might be afforded to efforts to tailor national policy by placing

---

[87] Land, *supra* note 3, at 471–4. Panels might consider whether an exception was proportional and narrowly tailored in evaluating whether it "unreasonably prejudiced" the interests of the rights holder under Article 13. *Ibid.* at 471. A panel might also consider whether an exception was designed to achieve human rights objectives in evaluating whether the case was "special" and the prejudice "unreasonable." *Ibid.* at 471–2.

[88] *U.S.–Copyright*, *supra* note 38, ¶ 6.109.

[89] *See, e.g.*, Panel Report, *Canada—Patent Protection of Pharmaceutical Products*, ¶ 7.16, WT/DS114/R (Mar. 17, 2000) (once the EC demonstrated a prima facie case of violation, the burden shifted to Canada "to demonstrate that the provisions of Sections 55.2(1) and 55.2(2) comply with the criteria laid down in Article 30"); *U.S.–Copyright*, *supra* note 38, ¶ 6.16 (noting that "it is for the European Communities to present a prima facie case that Section 110(5)(A) and (B) of the US Copyright Act is inconsistent with the provisions of the TRIPS Agreement" but that "the burden of proving that any exception or limitation is applicable and that any relevant conditions are met falls on the United States as the party bearing the ultimate burden of proof for invoking exceptions").

both burdens on the complaining state in situations in which a complaining state is challenging the use of a TRIPS flexibility by a LDC.[90] Once a defending LDC invokes a flexibility protected under the agreement—by, for example, arguing that its action is consistent with one of the explicit or implicit flexibilities embodied in TRIPS—that contention should be afforded a presumption of legitimacy. The burden should be on the complaining party to show that the challenged action is not in fact consistent with the agreement.

Third, panels could require that states that bring complaints against LDCs establish proof of injury as part of their prima facie case. Currently, a complaining state does not need to demonstrate that it has been harmed by the challenged action:

> [A] complaining Member does not need to produce evidence that a TRIPS-inconsistent domestic measure nullifies or impairs benefits conferred by the Agreement to that Member. It has no need to prove either that such an inconsistent measure has generated quantifiable damages. To the extent that an inconsistency with the TRIPS standards can be shown, there is automatically a *prima facie* presumption that such nullification or impairment has occurred.[91]

Although it is technically possible for a defending state to rebut the presumption of injury, it is practically impossible to do so.[92] Reversing the presumption of injury in cases brought by a developed against a least-developed country makes sense given the litigants' respective market positions. Failure of an LDC to conform its intellectual property law to the requirements of TRIPS is unlikely in many cases to result in harm to the developed country. As a result, it would seem only fair not to presume such harm in cases brought against LDCs and to require the developed state to make a showing of harm as part of its prima facie case.[93]

---

[90] It is also possible for a LDC to be a complaining state. This chapter is concerned with undue limits on LDC use of TRIPS flexibilities and thus focuses on LDCs as potential respondents.

[91] Carlos M. Correa, Trade Related Aspects of Intellectual Property Rights: A Commentary on the TRIPS Agreement 480 (2007); *see also* TRIPS Resource Book, *supra* note 24, at 665–6.

[92] Correa, *supra* note 91, at 480.

[93] The burden on the complaining state is also higher in cases of non-violation complaints. Under Article 26.1, the complaining state must "present a detailed justification in support of any complaint relating to a measure which does not conflict with the relevant covered agreement." DSU, *supra* note 19, art. 26.1. There is currently a moratorium on non-violation complaints under TRIPS. *See* Patricia Judd, *Toward a TRIPS Truce*, 32 Mich. J. Int'l L. 613, 633 n.110 (2011). This proposal, in contrast, requires only an additional showing of injury by the complaining state.

IV. CONCLUSION

Providing LDCs with an increased measure of authority to interpret the nature of their obligations under the TRIPS Agreement would serve as a safe harbor, assuring LDCs that if they actively engage in the process of tailoring their intellectual property policies to the local context, their efforts will be entitled to presumptive legitimacy. These changes would afford considerable leeway to LDCs in the context of TRIPS disputes. A challenged action by a LDC would be unlikely to violate the provisions of the TRIPS Agreement governing exceptions and limitations as long as the state were able to proffer any reasonable explanation for its decision. A complaining state would have to show injury before bringing suit against a LDC for a violation of TRIPS, and it would bear the burden of demonstrating the inapplicability of exceptions and limitations.

Although such special and differential treatment poses a risk to the perceived legitimacy of the system,[94] so does a system that does not attend to the unique challenges faced by LDCs in implementing the TRIPS Agreement. Interpretive statements subsequent to the conclusion of the WTO have stressed the importance of attending to the concerns of least-developed member states. The Decision on Measures in Favour of Least-Developed Countries, a Ministerial Decision adopted in conjunction with the agreement establishing the WTO and the TRIPS Agreement, provides that "[t]he rules set out in the various agreements and instruments and the transitional provisions in the Uruguay Round should be applied in a flexible and supportive manner for the least-developed countries."[95] LDCs are the least likely to benefit from the strong version of the intellectual property norms in the TRIPS Agreement and the most likely to suffer harm through the lack of flexibilities. Locating special and differential treatment in Article 24.1, which applies only to least-developed countries, offers the advantage of tailoring the greatest procedural protections to the countries that most need this flexibility.

---

[94] Pham, *supra* note 26, at 339 (explaining absence of concern for developing countries in language mandating revision of the DSU as a result of the fact that "dispute settlement is supposed to be a neutral, objective and fair process of strict legal interpretation, where favoritism, even for the weak, should be discouraged").

[95] Decision on Measures in Favour of Least-Developed Countries, ¶ 2(iii), LT/UR/D-1/3 (Apr. 14, 1994).

7. The IPT Project – proposals to reform the TRIPS Agreement*

Annette Kur and Marianne Levin

1. INTRODUCTION

When the TRIPS Agreement was concluded in 1994, it was welcomed by many as the ultimate breakthrough in long-standing efforts to elevate the threshold of international intellectual property (IP) protection.[1] Whereas negotiations under the aegis of the World Intellectual Property Organization (WIPO) had proven fruitless for many decades, the recalcitrant attitude assumed by developing and threshold countries towards enhanced standards lost momentum in the harsher climate of trade talks. The declared aim of the Uruguay Round (1986–1994) was to narrow the gaps between IP laws in various parts of the world.[2] Compared to the previous situation in international IP law, TRIPS thus triggered a "giant leap" in the area, entailing an unprecedented intensity of legislative efforts worldwide. However, it soon became obvious that TRIPS did not mark the end of IP history in any relevant regard. It turned out that the number of developing and threshold countries that actually profited from the deal struck in the WTO/TRIPS negotiations remained rather

* A synopsis of the current articles of the TRIPS text with the reformed proposals printed adjacently are presented as an Appendix to this chapter.

[1] The history of TRIPS has often been told. See for instance D. Gervais, The TRIPS Agreement, Drafting History and Analysis, 3rd ed., Sweet & Maxwell, 2008, p. 3 et seq.

[2] The preamble of the WTO Agreement (Marrakesh Agreement Establishing the World Trade Organization) also recognizes that Members' trade and economic relations "should be conducted with a view to raising standards of living, ensuring full employment and a large and steadily growing volume of real income and effective demand, and expanding the production of and trade in goods and services, while allowing for the optimal use of the world's resources in accordance with the objective of sustainable development, seeking both to protect and preserve the environment and to enhance the means for doing so in a manner consistent with their respective needs and concerns at different levels of economic development."

limited. For the large majority of poorer countries, hopes that acceptance of the conditions advanced by their industrialized counterparts would be rewarded by benefits deriving from increased trade flows and foreign direct investment were in vain.[3] Also, expectations were proven wrong that by including IP aspects into global trade talks, an end would be put to bilateral pressure and "blacklisting" of countries which, from the perspective of big trade nations or regions, did not live up to the required level of efficient IP protection. Vice versa, however, disappointment was also heavily felt on the side of developed nations, whose economies rely to a large extent on the market value of technological know-how and the output of information and entertainment industries. As is generally known, IP issues were included in the negotiation round leading to the WTO/TRIPS Agreement precisely because the sources of that wealth were arguably put in jeopardy by an increasing surge of counterfeit and pirated products polluting international trade flows. But if it was supposed to bring relief from rampant copying, TRIPS has not achieved its goal, at least not to a substantial degree and in a sustainable manner. The renaissance of bilateral agreements in the form of Free Trade Agreements (FTAs) or Economic Partnership Agreements (EPAs,) as well as attempts at concluding agreements such as ACTA[4] which are negotiated among a limited number of "willing nations", can be seen as a direct reaction to that widespread disappointment. On the other hand, such efforts reinforce the growing concerns and negative attitudes on the side of those who fear that the system is gradually spinning out of control, being infected by a chronic tendency to overrate the interest of proprietors vis-à-vis that of the public and third parties.

Indeed, in the eyes of many observers, TRIPS marks a culmination point in the sense that the broad public esteem previously commanded by IP was gradually lost. Fuelled by frustration of expectations raised with regard to the impact of IP on economic welfare, and resenting the restrictions imposed on communication and exchange of technology, deep skepticism towards the functioning of the system nowadays governs the perception of IP by large parts of the civil society, in particular when it comes to sensitive issues such as public health, nutrition, and dissemination of knowledge. IP

---

[3] For the reasons see e.g. K.E. Maskus & J.H. Reichman, The Globalisation of Private Knowledge Goods and the Privatization of Global Public Goods, 7 *Journal of International Economic Law*, 279 et seq. (2004).

[4] Anti Counterfeiting Trade Agreement, finalized on 3 December 2010 and signed by 33 states, including the EU and most of its Member States. After strong political protests, however, the European Parliament refused ratification, and ACTA is now off the agenda in the EU, with its fate in other states being uncertain.

is often seen as a mere tool for securing economic dominance of a few over a world of many, and as impeding rather than promoting a sound and sustainable socio-economic development.

It was before that backdrop, that the project conducted under the aegis of the Institute for Intellectual Property Law and Market Law (IFIM) at the Stockholm University in cooperation with the Max-Planck-Institute for Intellectual Property, Competition and Tax Law (MPI) in Munich under the title "Intellectual Property law in Transition" (IPT) set out, in the early years of the last decennium, to explore ways to re-establish the balance between different interests involved, where that equilibrium may have been distorted by a one-sided, inflexible approach towards IP on the global (as well as the domestic) level.[5] Of course, that endeavor is not unique – its goals are shared with a number of others working on comparable projects, or adding to the impressive wealth of academic contributions to the debate on contemporary challenges of IP. Like some other initiatives, which resulted in concrete proposals for amending and complementing the present corpus of international IP law,[6] it is the aim of the IPT project to contribute to the further development of international law in the area, so as not to remain confined to the ivory tower of academic discussions. And what was then more natural than to investigate, support and substantiate what could be "user-friendly amendments" to TRIPS, the "to date . . . most comprehensive multilateral agreement on intellectual property rights"?[7]

For clarification, it must be added at this stage that the short-term political prospects of that proactive approach are not overrated. Neither is it ignored that the world has moved on since 1994, when TRIPS was

---

[5] The project was initiated and led by IFIM's director, Marianne Levin, who was joined in her function as the group's chairperson by Annette Kur. Niklas Bruun, François Curchod, Antonina Engelbrekt-Bakardjieva, Henning Grosse Ruse-Khan, Frantzeska Papadopoulou, Jens Schovsbo and Andrea Wechsler were involved in the work as permanent or temporary project group members; Åsa Hellstadius acted as the group's secretary.

[6] See in particular the proposals made by B. Hugenholtz & R. Okediji, Conceiving an International Instrument on Limitations and Exceptions to Copyright, Final – Report 6 March 2008, available at: http://www.ivir.nl/publications/hugenholtz/limitations_exceptions_copyright.pdf; see also Declaration on a Balanced Interpretation of the "Three-Step Test" in Copyright Law', Joint project undertaken by the Max-Planck-Institute for Intellectual Property, Competition and Tax Law, Munich and Queen Mary College, University of London, 39 IIC, 707 – 713 (2008), also available at: http://www.ip.mpg.de/shared/data/pdf/declaration_three_step_test_final_english.pdf.

[7] http://www.wto.org/english/tratop_e/TRIPS_e/TRIPS_e.htm.

concluded, and that more "hot spots" have emerged on the IP trouble chart than those ensuing from TRIPS in its present form. Nevertheless, the TRIPS Agreement, with regard to its political genesis and ambitious content, still offers an obvious and prominent target for the criticism voiced against the international IP system as it exists today. Furthermore, even without an immediate chance for political implementation, consideration of amendments of TRIPS offers a welcome opportunity to address some of the urgently felt and widely articulated needs for readjustment of the system, or at least to offer some reasonable guidance to its interpretation, and to highlight, in a concise form, possible ways to overcome the perceived deficiencies, as will be pointed out in the following sections.[8]

2. GENERAL APPROACH AND STRUCTURE OF THE PROPOSAL: A BROADER PUBLIC INTEREST-BASED INTERPRETATION

The proposals made by the IPT project are concentrated mainly on Parts I (General provisions and basic principles) and II of the TRIPS Agreement (standards concerning the availability, scope and use of intellectual property rights), with special emphasis being placed in Part I on the objectives and principles, which are presently enshrined in Articles 7 and 8. Already in their current form, those articles – together with the preamble – are of seminal importance for an appropriate understanding of the TRIPS Agreement.[9] Based on Article 7, and in particular Article 8, it is possible, or even mandatory in certain cases, to interpret TRIPS provisions in the light of the broader public interest, taking account also of non-trade-related objectives, including not least such universal values as human rights.[10]

The amendments proposed by the IPT project elaborate upon the current wording of the objectives and principles, striving to clarify the actual breadth of their contents, and highlighting their function within the structure of the Agreement. In addition, further provisions are

[8] The footnotes made in the following refer primarily to chapters in A. Kur & M. Levin (eds.), Intellectual Property in a Fair Trade World, Edward Elgar, 2011 which presents the IPT proposal in its entirety.

[9] H. Grosse Ruse-Khan, Assessing the Need for a General Public Interest Exception in the TRIPS Agreement, in: A. Kur & M. Levin (supra, fn. 8). Ch. 4., p. 167 et seq.

[10] F. Papadopoulou, TRIPS and Human Rights, in A. Kur & M. Levin, (supra fn. 8), Ch. 6, p. 262 et seq.

proposed to be included in the first part of the Agreement: An overall "balancing clause" (Art. 8a), which builds on the concept and wording of the three-step test, and a competition clause (Art. 8b), formulating general guidelines for assessing the oft-disputed interface between intellectual property and competition ("antitrust") law.

It is submitted that already by fleshing out the objectives and principles in the manner proposed, the TRIPS Agreement would largely regain its capacity to provide a balanced framework for legislative and adjudicative activities that are able to find an adequate response to contemporary challenges. Nevertheless, it was felt that some adjustment was needed in Part II as well, in particular by spelling out expressly the limitations and exceptions which any legislation must incorporate in order to guarantee at least a minimum level of free or conditioned access for third parties to protected subject matter.

By thus embracing the concept of "substantive maxima"[11] or IP "ceilings",[12] the IPT project takes a deliberate step beyond the legal technique presently governing instruments of international IP protection, which are regularly based on the concept of minimum rights.[13] It was found that in a political climate where governments in industrialized countries still tend to pursue a markedly right holder-oriented approach, it is important to signalize that certain absolute boundaries for IP protection

---

[11] As far as can be seen, the term 'substantive maxima' and the concept to which it refers was first used by R. Dreyfuss, TRIPS – Round II: Should Users Strike Back, 71 *U. Chi. L. Rev.*, 21, 27 (2004); see also G.B. Dinwoodie The International Intellectual Property Law System: New Actors, New Institutions, New Sources. *Marquette Intellectual Property Law Review*, 205, at 214 (2006).

[12] For a comprehensive account see A. Kur & H. Grosse Ruse-Khan, Enough is Enough – the Notion of Binding Ceilings in Intellectual Property Conventions, in A. Kur & M. Levin (supra, fn. 8), ch. 8, p. 359 et seq.; A. Kur, International Norm-Making in the Field of Intellectual Property: A Shift towards Maximum Rules? [2009] WIPO Journal, 27–34.

[13] However, already at present, a few ceiling rules can be found in existing conventions, such as the exclusion of certain subject matter from copyright in Art. 2 (8) Berne Convention and Art. 9 (1) and 10 (2) TRIPS; do mandatory exceptions and limitations, see Art. 10 (1) Berne Convention and Art. 5*ter* Paris Convention. For full account of exceptions and limitations available under the Berne Convention, and of mandatory limitations in (other) in international Conventions, see Hugenholtz & Okediji (above, fn. 6, Annex A). In recent years, the concept of internationally mandatory ceilings meets with increasing attention; inter alia, it is reflected in the Draft Treaty on Facilitating Access to Published Works by Visually Impaired Persons and Persons with Printing Disabilities, scheduled to be concluded at a Diplomatic Conference in Marrakesh, 17–28 June, 2013; see http://www.wipo.int/dc2013/en/.

must be respected worldwide, so as to halt a potentially dangerous trend towards ever-stronger protection.

3. INDIVIDUAL PROVISIONS

3.1 Objectives and Principles: The Basic Formulae for Well-calibrated Protection

3.1.1 Objectives (Art. 7)

As was stated above, the changes proposed with regard to objectives and principles aim at fleshing out the contents of the provisions rather than suggesting changes in substance vis-à-vis the current text. Regarding Article 7, the main point of the suggestions made is to arrive at a better and more comprehensive reflection of the legal objectives impacting those areas for which TRIPS provides a normative framework. Hence, while the current text in its first part only makes reference to innovation and transfer of technology, wording is proposed which reflects the entire spectrum of policy goals to be aspired by a sound and thriving IP system, none of which should be regarded as per se inferior to others. In addition to the aspects presently mentioned, these concern cultural development and enhancement of creativity as well as the enhancement of competition and fairness in trade.

As a second part to be added to the present provision, it is further suggested to express in Article 7 the general rule that the protection granted should ideally be measured according to the contribution made to society. Such a rule is considered instrumental for a well-calibrated IP system: it should be avoided to grant broad and strong rights for innovations or creations that are of merely incremental character; likewise, it would have detrimental effects in the longer run if highly valuable achievements remain without sufficient compensation. Whereas overcompensation is likely to freeze sound and efficient competition and to produce high-transaction costs, insufficient compensation may result in disincentives for others to engage in creative or innovative activities.

The principle as such appears to be largely uncontroversial.[14] Its implementation in practice, however, gives rise to intricate questions. In particular, identifying and applying an appropriate yardstick according to which the societal benefits accruing from innovation or creation can be measured

[14] See for instance D. Gervais (above, fn.1), Art. 7, 2.71 refers to the same rules.

is likely to entail considerable difficulties. But this does not render such a rule totally meaningless: it needs to be recalled in this context that the impact of a provision such as Article 7 TRIPS is not the same as that of a hard and fast rule of law, like the minimum requirements for protection enshrined in Part II of the Agreement. Due to its position in Part I, as an expression of the objectives underlying the Agreement and informing its application, the provision rather provides for a principled guideline – an overarching concept towards which the IP system should be geared.

3.1.2 Principles (Art. 8)

The amendments proposed by the IPT project with regard to Article 8 are even less conspicuous. Nevertheless, they touch upon quite fundamental and sensitive issues. First, it is proposed to exchange the word "may" appearing in the present text of Article 8.1 by the somewhat stronger "should". The aim is to place more emphasis on the fact that the non-trade-related values mentioned in Article 8.1, such as public health and nutrition, are of seminal importance, not only in the meaning that Members' (relative) freedom to pursue those aims must be given special consideration, but also in the sense of imposing a "moral duty" on governments vis-à-vis their own population.[15]

Even stronger than that, a mandatory rule ("shall") is proposed with a view to the competition-related aims in Article 8.2. This is based on the proposition that the interest in well-functioning, unimpeded competition figures as an objective of primary importance for the establishment and maintenance of a sound IP system. Other than with regard to the general policy issues addressed in the first paragraph, it is estimated that to include features of competition law as a mandatory element into the WTO system would not demand major changes within the institutional framework. Instead, this should help countries without such a balancing instrument to better adapt the IP system to their national environment. It must be clarified in this context, however, that the intention would not be to prescribe in any detail which type of conduct should be regarded as falling under

---

[15] It was discussed in the project group whether one should not make observation of the goals mentioned in Art. 8.1 mandatory for TRIPS Members. However, if binding obligations relating to health, nutrition and other economic, social and cultural rights were included into TRIPS, this would have to proceed on a much broader scale, comprising inter alia alterations of the dispute settlement regime (e.g. concerning the right to file complaints, rights of participation, constitution of panels, etc.). It was therefore decided that in the present institutional framework, it would be more appropriate to emphasize the importance of the goals mentioned in a legally non-binding form.

Article 8.2. In that regard, the discretion left to members should not be curtailed to any substantial degree.[16]

Apart from that, changes are proposed that would impact the interaction between Article 8 on the one hand and the substantive provisions in Part II *et seq.* on the other. In the present text, the principles set out in Article 8 are qualified by the phrase "provided that such measures are consistent with this Agreement." At least initially, misgivings were nourished thereby that Article 8 in its entirety would be meaningless in case of a conflict, as the black letter rules in Part II of the Agreement would always take precedence.[17] Although those fears have been soothed to some extent by the Doha process, it remains true that parties relying on Article 8 in order to enact legislative measures pursuing relevant goals are placed at a procedural disadvantage insofar as they have to bear the burden of establishing that they still comply with TRIPS.[18] By suggesting to change the wording from "provided that such measures are consistent with this Agreement" to "*unless* such measures are *inconsistent* . . .," the proposal would reverse the structure and hence the burden it imposes. Following the amendment, it would be the party *contesting* the compatibility of certain measures with TRIPS that must establish its claim.

3.2 At the Core of the Proposal: The 'Balancing Clause' (Art. 8a)

3.2.1 General remarks

The newly promulgated Article 8a constitutes a core element in the proposal: the so-called balancing clause. Elaborating on the structure and wording of the three-step test, it is meant to provide guidelines for the legislature and the courts, and to assist in measuring out the 'wiggle room' that remains between the floor of substantive minimum requirements, and the ceiling established by the mandatory provisions proposed to be included in TRIPS Part II.

It is a crucial feature of proposed Article 8a that it develops a scheme of general, horizontal validity instead of distinguishing between the different

---

[16] The proposal therefore takes the form of an 'open ceiling'. On the oxymoronic character of that notion and its advantages and drawbacks, see A. Kur & H. Grosse Ruse-Khan, in A. Kur & M. Levin (supra, fn. 8), Ch. 8, 365, 369 et seq.

[17] On the structure of Art. 8 TRIPS in comparison with Art. XX GATT, see H. Grosse Ruse-Khan (above, fn. 9).

[18] This follows from the syntax of the clause, which must be interpreted in good faith in accordance with the ordinary meaning to be given to the terms (Art. 31 Vienna Convention on the Law of Treaties).

categories of IP rights.[19] By outlining the architecture for a sound and efficient balancing process that is capable of producing adequate results in all areas of IP alike, it is intended to lay open the general matrix to which all those areas must basically conform. The unitary approach thus endorsed requires that the constitutive features of the groundwork must be rather broad and robust – there is no place for fine-grained carvings. Accordingly, the overall structure of the provision as well as its details are of a fairly general and abstract nature; they do not address very specific concerns arising solely in individual areas.

To the extent that such concerns are urgent and important enough to warrant the introduction of mandatory limitations, they are encompassed by the respective provisions in Part II. It must be pointed out, however, that in the structure espoused by the IPT proposal, there is no proper place for limitations that are specific for certain areas, but in respect of which it would appear too demanding (and too much of a restriction on flexibility) to conceive of them as internationally mandatory rules. As a result, certain gaps are left where other instruments[20] and proposals[21] contain more detailed catalogues of specific provisions.

3.2.2 A modified version of the three-step test

3.2.2.1 The chapeau: general principles The most important element in proposed Article 8a is the *chapeau* of its second paragraph, which contains the basic elements of the modified version of the three-step test. By contrast to TRIPS, the provision basically takes a user-centered approach: whereas the three-step test is presently formulated as a (restricted) option for Members which they may or may not make use of, Article 8a takes the opposite approach by obliging Members to ensure that protected subject matter may be used without authorization of the right holder if and to the extent that the relevant conditions are fulfilled. Similar to what was pointed out above in connection with the general structure of Article 8, the effect is to reverse the burden of argument – unless it can be established, on the basis of the factors outlined in the article, that to grant such use would

---

[19] This is different from the Declaration on a Balanced Interpretation of the "Three Step Test" in Copyright (supra, fn. 6), which only relates to one specific area.

[20] For instance European directives with their usually rather detailed catalogue of (optional or mandatory) limitations.

[21] For instance, the proposal for a "European copyright code" elaborated by a group of European academics (the Wittem group), available at http://213.247.35.100/~copyrigh/index.php?websiteid=3".

unreasonably prejudice the interests of right holders, free access should prevail. Paraphrasing the popular metaphor often used in this context, the structure of the *chapeau* thus reflects the basic concept that limitations are not an island in an ocean of exclusivity, but that vice versa, freedom of access and use constitute the general rule, meaning that fully exclusive IP rights resemble an island in an ocean of freedom.[22]

Second, whereas the three-step test demands that exceptions and limitations are confined to "certain special cases"[23] or "limited exceptions"[24], no such requirement is mentioned in the chapeau of proposed Article 8a.2. The clause thus yields no basis for the narrow understanding of the three-step test which was endorsed in the three WTO panel reports concerning patent,[25] copyright[26] and trademark law.[27] According to the panels' interpretation, the criterion that exceptions must be "limited" or concern "special cases" imposes a quasi-quantitative restriction which does not leave room for a normative assessment. That, however, is bound to clash with the overall aim to undertake a full and comprehensive appraisal of the relevant provisions. It is more than just unfortunate – indeed, it is a major flaw in the structure of the three-step test as the panels have interpreted it – that it invites the dismissal of limitations as incompatible with TRIPS without any prior evaluation of the policy objectives motivating them.[28]

That being said, it must be emphasized nevertheless that the scope of limitations – their breadth and contents – should not be regarded as irrelevant. However, rather than treating the potential reach of a limitation as an initial requirement to be appraised in isolation before entering into a normative evaluation, this is an element to be considered within the

---

22 C. Geiger, Der urheberrechtliche Interessenausgleich in der Informationsgesellschaft', GRUR Int. 2004, 815, 818, 819; C. Geiger, Flexibilising Copyright – Remedies to the Privatisation of Information by Copyright Law', 39 IIC 178–97 (2008a) at 192–4; D. Voorhoof, Freedom of Expression, Parody, Copyright and Trademarks, in: J. Ginsburg & J. Besek (eds.), Adjuncts and Alternatives to Copyright, Proceedings of the ALAI Congress 2001, 2002, at 639.

23 In Art. 13 (copyright).

24 In Art. 17, 26.2 and 30 (trade mark, industrial design, and patent law).

25 Report presented on 17 March 2000, WTO Document WT/DS114/R – *Canada – patents*.

26 Report presented on 15 June 2000, WTO Document WT/DS160/R – *USA – copyright*.

27 Report presented on 15 March 2005, WTO Document WT/DS174/R.– *EC – GIs*.

28 For a more extensive elaboration on that point see A. Kur, in A. Kur & M.Levin (above, fn. 8), Ch. 5, 208, 224 et seq., with further references.

balancing process itself, as one factor informing the overall assessment of the appropriateness and proportionality of the contested measure in relation to the envisaged legal aims. In other words, rather than asking whether a provision is "limited" (or "special") in an absolute sense, the question is posed whether it is sufficiently limited for its purpose.

Next, the proposed amendment also modifies the second part of the three-step test by stipulating that for assessing whether the legitimate interests of the right holder would be unreasonably prejudiced, account must be taken of the normal exploitation of the right. Unlike the present wording of the test, it is therefore not suggested that if limitations and exceptions conflict with normal exploitation, this will (quasi-[29]) automatically result in a finding of incompatibility with TRIPS. By suggesting such automatism, the three-step test in its current form tends to become a source of immobility, rendering impossible any legal changes which would have more than minimal impact on the ways and means by which IP rights are, or could be,[30] exploited at the present point in time. In contrast, the IPT proposal only obligates legislatures to assess and measure the extent to which the pertinent forms of exploitation would become obstructed if certain modes of unauthorized use were declared admissible. The analysis then becomes part of the overall evaluation process: limitations permitting access to protected subject matter must be appraised, and must be justifiable, in full awareness of the way in which they affect modes of use that are presently considered as 'normal'.

Another difference resolves from the first paragraph of proposed Article 8a, which enunciates the general principles forming the overall framework for the balancing exercise. The provision sets forth that, in addition to taking due account of the objectives and principles in Articles 7 and 8, TRIPS Members must ensure that the protection granted under their laws and regulations must reflect a fair balance between private economic interests and the larger public interest in social and economic welfare as well as the interest of third parties. Due to the unitary character of the provision, third-party interests as well as the larger public interest are necessarily implicated in the assessment of limitations and exceptions concerning *all*

---

[29] At least for copyright, the wording of Art. 13 suggests that the finding of a conflict is indeed tantamount to incompatibility with TRIPS. The situation is somewhat different for patent and industrial design law, as incompatibility will only be found if the limitation at stake is found to be "unreasonably" conflicting. In trademark law, the second step is missing altogether.

[30] According to the copyright panel's interpretation, "normal exploitation" also encompasses forms of exploitation that are legally possible, without being presently used by the right holders. See *USA – copyright*, (supra, fn. 26), ¶ 6.188.

IP rights, including copyright. By contrast, the current version of Article 13 lacks any reference to public or third-party interests.

3.2.2.2 List of balancing factors In addition to the general outlines set forth in the *chapeau* of paragraph 2 and the overarching principles contained in paragraph 1, a list of individual balancing factors is enunciated in subparagraphs (a), (b) and (c) of paragraph 2. The list under (a) contains general principles to be weighed in favor of users' entitlement to get access to protected content. The policy issues addressed therein concern inter alia: use serving the exchange of ideas and opinions as well as the dissemination of information, use within the private sphere, and use which adds value to the subject matter involved. As the last factor in that list, reference is made to "serious cultural or social considerations." The purpose of that factor is to serve as an "umbrella clause", providing for a certain amount of built-in flexibility.[31]

The elements listed in subparagraph (b) are "neutral" in the sense that they may weigh in favor of both sides. First, reference is made to remuneration regimes or other forms of liability rules on the basis of which differentiated solutions may be fashioned instead of settling for an "all or nothing" approach. Thus, if statutory limitations are accompanied by reliable schemes securing adequate payment, this will regularly facilitate their acceptance.[32] Furthermore, it is set forth that special importance needs to be attributed to the personal interests of the original creators (as opposed to other right holders). This concerns primarily the interests of authors traditionally protected by Article 6^{bis}of the Berne Convention (*droit moral*), but it also includes other, more general interests.[33] For instance, this could become topical where authors are interested in a broad dissemination of

---

[31] Examples (in copyright) for which the last factor would be of relevance are found in limitations enabling access in copyright to protected content for disabled groups, like visually impaired persons and persons with printing disabilities (above, fn. 13) or limitations furthering the preservation of the cultural heritage, or provisions permitting the use of music in religious ceremonies, etc. In patent law, this concerns in particular limitations improving access to medicaments for the poor, and for providing a better calibration of research efforts into fields where new medication is actually needed.

[32] In the same vein, see the Declaration on a Balanced Interpretation of the "Three-Step Test" in Copyright, (above, fn. 6).

[33] For instance, the obstacles against free access for third parties to protected subject matter could be higher in a situation when the financial benefits to be derived from exclusivity or otherwise restricted access would accrue directly to the original creators than in the opposite case, i.e. when the additional gains would solely contribute to the purse of derivative right holders.

their works, without necessarily being interested in payment (e.g. authors of scientific papers), whereas those holding the right to publication are eager to maintain full exclusivity.[34] In that case, the personal interest of authors, this time coinciding with the interest of users, should be considered separately, instead of being merged for the purpose of balancing with those of the (differently motivated) derivative right holders.

Finally, subparagraph (c) obliges Members to carry out a proportionality test, so as to assess the extent and intensity of the use in relation to the protected right, and to measure the potential diminishment of the latter against the weight and urgency of the objectives pursued. This test corresponds to the exercise regularly undertaken by WTO adjudicating bodies when interpreting Article XX GATT[35]. Similar to that, a proportionality test is also applied by the European Court of Justice, when assessing the justifiability of obstacles to the free movement of goods: if such obstacles are found to be grounded on objectives which, as such, are capable of furnishing an acceptable motive for certain trade barriers, it must still be established that the same goal could not have been achieved by measures having less restrictive effects on cross-border trade.[36]

Basically the same scheme is also suggested here: even when a particular measure appears justifiable on the basis of one or several factors listed in Article 8a.2, the right to use protected subject matter should basically be limited to what is proportionate to the aspired goal.[37] Rather than expressing a novel rule, it is submitted that such a test is inherent in any sound and efficient balancing exercise.

3.3 Interface Between IP and Competition Law (Art. 8b)

It is one of the central points of criticism against the TRIPS Agreement in its current form that it merely strengthens IP law, whereas competition law as the obvious corollary to strong property rights remains unregulated

---

[34] Such discrepancy of interests is rather typical for publication of academic research results, and might call for specific solutions in the field; see R.M. Hilty, S. Krujatz; B. Bajon, A. Früh, A. Kur, J. Drexl, Ch. Geiger & N. Klass, (2009), European Commission Green Paper: Copyright in the Knowledge Economy, Comments by the Max Planck Institute for Intellectual Property, Competition and Tax Law, 40 IIC 309.

[35] Further on that, see H. Grosse Ruse-Khan, in A. Kur & M. Levin (above, fn. 8), Ch. 4,167, 188 et seq.

[36] The leading case is ECJ C-120/79 – Rewe/Bundesmonopolverwaltung für Branntwein (Cassis de Dijon), 1979 ECR 6349.

[37] See A. Kur, in A. Kur & M. Levin (above, fn. 8), Ch. 5, 246 et seq., where the same rule and its operation in the context of the three-step test are explained.

on the international level, with some rather weak exceptions.[38] Against that criticism, it could be argued that as TRIPS is concerned with the threat posed to international trade by increasing piracy and counterfeiting activities, internal regulations such as checking and balancing the conduct of powerful actors on domestic markets do not fall into its ambit. On the other hand, TRIPS goes far beyond what is needed to bolster the fight against international piracy and counterfeiting by imposing rather comprehensive rules with regard to the acquisition and protection of IP rights. It is therefore only consistent to go the entire way leading to a fully elaborated and fairly balanced legal system. In addition to the limitations of rights which are dealt with in Article 8a (above) as well as in the mandatory provisions set out in Part II, the IPT proposal therefore also chose to address the IP/competition interface, to the extent that it is of primary importance with regard to the IP environment.[39]

As a main rule, it is stipulated that Members are not only free, but also obliged,[40] to take action by imposing either individual remedies in the form of compulsory licenses, or by enacting legislation, in the following situations: (a) if use of a product which is protected by an IP right is indispensable for competition on the relevant market, unless the application of remedies would lead to clearly undesirable results; (b) if the exercise of an IP right constitutes an abuse of a dominant position. It is not ignored that the two cases may be often, or even regularly, overlapping; nevertheless, it was found important to make clear that even without any "fault" being found in the specific conduct of the proprietor in the first-mentioned situation, the fact alone that competition would be totally precluded if third parties could not get access to use of the IP right constitutes an irregularity against which measures should be taken, unless specific reasons exist for abstaining from legislative or administrative actions.

No further attempt is made to define in detail the criteria for finding e.g. abuse of a dominant position with regard to IP rights. The proposed provision contents itself with stating the general principle. This is deemed sufficient for the purpose of this proposal to highlight the general rule, in order e.g. to counter any attempts by interested stakeholders or trading partners to persuade (other) TRIPS Members, in the framework of bilateral

---

[38] This concerns Art. 8.2, Art. 31 and Art. 40 TRIPS.

[39] For a thorough analysis of the background and reasons for proposed Art. 8b see J. Schovsbo, Fire and Water Make Steam – Redefining the Role of Competition Law in TRIPS, in A. Kur & M. Levin (above, fn. 8), Ch. 7. P. 308 et seq.

[40] The approach complies with that towards Art. 8.2, which was also proposed to be changed into mandatory form.

agreements or otherwise, to introduce provisions granting immunity status to IP right against interferences on the basis of competition law.

3.4 Part II TRIPS: Mandatory Exceptions and Limitations

3.4.1 General remarks

As was stated above, the IPT project has undertaken to formulate concrete rules limiting the scope of rights conferred, as set out in Part II of the Agreement. The purpose of such "substantive maxima" or ceiling rules is two-fold: they would obligate TRIPS Members to pay respect in domestic legislation to the interests and legal position of IP users and the general welfare of their own citizens, (internal safeguard), and they would also make governments immune to pressure from other countries to introduce overly high protection standards in the framework of bilateral agreements such as FTAs (external safeguard). Apart from that, they would offer a way to concretize the boundaries of international IP norms, thereby creating a "safe haven" for user-friendly legislation. The importance of such safe havens should not be underestimated in view of the difficulties TRIPS Members are facing when trying to appreciate the space available for legislative measures limiting the availability and scope of IP protection. The ambiguity and restrictiveness of the approach reflected in the WTO panels' rulings on exceptions under TRIPS may have a deterring effect on those (developing) countries which aim to devise new exceptions corresponding to their individual situation and level of development.[41] Also from that perspective, international rules drawing a clearer and more concrete picture of what must definitely be accepted as a valid exception could be of some value.

On the other hand, it must not be ignored that the introduction of ceiling rules may have certain drawbacks. The most troubling aspect is that ceilings necessarily lead to a further curtailment of the sovereign policy space that countries presently enjoy in the field of IP. In order to ensure that this does not entail a simple and possibly dangerous transposition of the

---

[41] This applies also to countries with more experience in drafting exceptions when confronted with new technologies, modes of exploitation and business models relating to the utilisation of IP protected subject matter. One can compare the effect of the three-step test to what is referred to as "regulatory chill" or "freeze" effect in international investment law where certain investment protection standards in Bilateral Investment Treaties (BITs) may prevent the host country from introducing environmental or other public interests measures fearing that they might be challenged by investors as conflicting with these investment protection standards.

frequently criticized "one-size-fits-all" approach to the upper limits of IP law, an overly paternalistic attitude should be avoided. As a matter of principle, it should remain clear that countries must take upon themselves the primary responsibility for devising a comprehensive body of adequate rules. Based on that philosophy, it was decided in the IPT project that the proposals designed as maximum rules should be restricted to limitations and exceptions that are regarded as absolute "must-haves". Consequently, most of the proposals concern provisions that already form part of the laws in all or most TRIPS Member States. This also implies that while implementing the mandatory limitations would prevent IP legislation from becoming grossly imbalanced, it may often not be sufficient as such for achieving an optimal calibration of proprietor versus user interests. Therefore, each of the mandatory limitation clauses also sets out expressly, in a separate paragraph, that member states are free to implement more far-reaching exceptions and limitations, where this complies with the objectives and principles, or where the introduction of stronger limitations and exceptions is called for in the light of the balancing clause.

3.4.2 Copyright

3.4.2.1 Excluded subject matter: official works As a mandatory provision to be inserted in the copyright part of TRIPS, the IPT proposal suggests, in a paragraph added to Article 9, excluding from copyright protection official texts of a legislative, administrative or legal nature, and official translations of such texts. The wording is adapted from Article 2.4 Berne Convention, where the same exclusion is found as an optional rule.[42] The reason for making the exclusion of such works mandatory lies in the fact that the promulgation of official texts is essentially a task under public law, which must be fulfilled irrespective of the grant of any exclusive right. The utilitarian motive for granting copyright protection runs therefore void – there is no need to offer (additional) incentives for promoting creativity. Even from the natural rights' perspective, the connection between the personal author or authors and the work is regularly strongly attenuated by the public purpose it is intended to serve. And finally, the idea that official texts prepared in the course of legislation, administrative activities, and administration of justice should become

42 The wording in the English text of Art. 2.4 RBC is slightly different, as it refers to "legislative . . . and legal texts". However, it was found that the wording is not logical; furthermore, the French text, which is considered as prevailing in case of discrepancy uses the word "ou" (or) instead of "et" (and).

"property rights" of the persons producing such documents appears to clash with the very aim and function of such works.

3.4.2.2 Limitations and exceptions (Art. 13) Mandatory limitations restricting the scope of protection are proposed to be included in Article 13, thereby replacing the current version of the three-step test. First, in response to the fact that any meaningful communication under contemporary conditions requires some amount of copying as a technically necessary step in the process, such technically necessary acts should generally be declared permissible. The same applies to reverse engineering, to the extent it is indispensable for obtaining information needed to allow interoperability of communication tools and systems.

In addition, the provision addresses aspects of prime importance for the well-functioning of copyright regimes in the interest of users and society as a whole – quotations, news reporting, use for teaching and research, parody, and illustration for sales purposes. Regarding quotations, a limitation of mandatory character is already set out in the Berne Convention (Art. 10.1). Likewise, the Berne Convention acknowledges the privileged character of use for the purpose of teaching, and of news reporting as well as the related aspect of access to documents of public interest (see in particular Arts 10.2 as well as Arts 2.8 and 2bis Berne Convention). At least in part, implementing such rules appears as an undisputable command ensuing from the observation of fundamental human rights, such as the right to free speech, information, and education.[43] Free speech – albeit in the form of advertising and other commercial communication – in combination with aspects of free trade also account for the mandatory rule permitting illustration for the purpose of legitimate sales: although the principle of exhaustion does not form part of the TRIPS package,[44] it is basically uncontested that the proprietor of IP rights vested in tangible goods cannot control their further commercialization once they have been put on the (national) market by him or with his consent. In that situation, it should likewise not be possible to prohibit the announcement of such products for sale, and to accompany such announcements by illustrations showing the product itself, even if its appearance is basically protected under copyright.

Of course, it also needs to be observed in all those cases that account must be taken of the interests of the right holder as well as those of the

43 See Arts 19, 26 of the Universal Declaration of Human Rights (UDHR).

44 See Art. 6 TRIPS, which sets forth that with the exception of Arts 3 and 4, exhaustion issues cannot form the object of Dispute settlement proceedings.

author, which are likewise protected as fundamental rights.[45] The proposal therefore confines the mandatory limitations to what is necessary for achieving their very purpose, and it also ensures that the interests of right holders are safeguarded to a sufficient degree, by adopting wording from Article 10 Berne Convention.[46] As an additional protective element which is of particular relevance for the interests of personal creators, the proposal also paraphrases the aims and objectives underlying Article 6bis of the Berne Convention, by stating that the rights of the personal creator to have the work attributed to him or her and to oppose use that amounts to a massive and manifest mutilation of the work in its original form must be respected.

A further subparagraph in proposed Article 13 addresses specific acts of reproduction of works in public institutions for non-profit and non-commercial purposes.[47] This is based on the consideration that those institutions likewise play an indispensable role in the information society by preserving and contributing to the commonwealth of knowledge, and that their activities must therefore also be privileged to some degree. By contrast to the provisions previously mentioned (citation, news reporting, etc.), it is foreseen that member states may make the reproduction of works under this clause dependent on payment of remuneration.

Finally, the proposal also contains a general privilege for private copying. However, given that an internationally mandatory limitation of copyright with regard to private copying might actually erode the right vested in a protected work to a quite substantial degree – e.g. where the extent of private copying, and the circumstances under which it takes place, are uncontrollable in practice, with the consequence that large parts of the right holder's market would regularly be lost – it may be necessary to provide (at least) for adequate remuneration being paid to right holders, in order to comply with the general guidelines for limitations as are set out in Article 8a, paragraph 2.

3.4.3 Related rights (Art. 14)

Proposed Article 14.6 declares that the limitations set out in Article 13 are applicable *mutatis mutandis* with regard to related rights. In addition, it clarifies that to adopt rules modelled on the (other) limitations mentioned in the Rome Convention is generally considered to be in compliance with

---

[45] Art. 27 UDHR.

[46] The work must have been lawfully published, and it is only permitted to the extent which is necessary for the purpose.

[47] The clause is modelled on Art. 5.2 (c) of EU Directive 2001/29, where it is one of numerous optional limitations.

TRIPS. The system is similar to that already reflected in Article 14.6 TRIPS in its interplay with Article 15 of the Rome Convention, with the marked difference that (a) the limitations corresponding to those mentioned in Article 13 TRIPS are of a mandatory character, and (b) members are not bound by the restrictions in the Rome Convention, in particular as regards compulsory licenses. Even with the Rome Convention remaining untouched, this means that TRIPS Members not having adhered to it would retain greater freedom than at present to impose non-voluntary license schemes.

3.4.4 Trademarks

In trademark law, the concept of the rights conferred by a mark may already be sufficient as such to limit the possibility for right holders to unduly restrict commercial communication. If protection is confined per se to situations where the original function of a mark is actually jeopardized – i.e. when the same or a similar mark is used as a sign indicating the commercial origin of products or services originating from a third party who is unrelated to the trademark holder – the scope of protection will usually not go beyond what is necessary to protect the interests of right holders as well as those of consumers and honest trade. To an increasing extent, however, modern legislation takes a broader approach towards trademark protection to the effect that basically all modes of unauthorized use are considered to fall within the ambit of the proprietor's exclusive right.[48] In that situation, the need for the law to encompass adequately tailored limitations becomes more urgent.

As a general rule, proposed Article 17 exempts from trademark protection any use made for non-commercial purposes. This appears to reflect a principle applied already in the large majority of countries, where use "in the course of trade" or use "in commerce" is required as a prerequisite for raising claims against other parties' use of a mark. On the other hand, some countries have taken steps under criminal or administrative law to prohibit and impose sanctions for private use and possession of counterfeit goods, with the aim of laying waste the market for such merchandise.[49] The proposed clause would not preclude that possibility, as the measures taken in the framework of anti-counterfeiting strategies are anchored in

---

[48] For instance, according to ECJ decisions C-533/06 – O2/Hutchinson and C-487/07, L'Oréal/Bellure, reference to a competitor's mark in comparative advertisement generally falls into the ambit of trademark law.

[49] For France, see L. 716-10 Code de la propriété intellectuelle. For the application of the provision in practice see Cass. crim, 30 March 1994, Bull. crim. no 128.

a different context and operate on a different level than the provision on infringement.[50]

Article 17 further addresses the classical case of "fair use" made of descriptive terms, the use of marks in connection with commercializing legitimate goods or services, and use for other marketing purposes providing relevant information, in particular comparative advertising. Furthermore, use of trademarks in parody or satire is also mentioned as a form of use that must regularly be permitted, and the same applies to the possibility of using one's own personal name in order to identify one's business and/or the goods or services offered in that context. Here, aspects of fundamental rights are involved to some extent – this concerns in particular freedom of (commercial) speech; in addition, the possibility to identify the nucleus of one's business activities by one's own name can be understood as a manifestation of basically universally valid personality rights.

As a complement to the enunciation of mandatory limitations, proposed Article 17 also clarifies that use is only found permissible if and to the extent that it complies with honest practices in industrial and commercial matters. As is further stated, this means in particular that consumers must not be misled as to commercial origin.[51] Finally, Article 17.2 establishes as the baseline to be respected by any more far-reaching limitations that legislature might want to introduce, that the distinguishing character of the trademark must not be diminished or tainted in any substantial manner. In addition to establishing a barrier against misleading use, the clause is also of relevance for regulations subjecting the use of marks to certain requirements, such as use in connection with another sign, or with generic terms (see Art. 20 TRIPS). Proposed Article 17.2 reinforces the principle that if – and only if – the essential function of a trademark would be substantially jeopardized thereby, such measures would be irreconcilable with TRIPS.

3.4.5 Industrial designs

In respect of industrial designs, the IPT proposal suggests introducing a mandatory exception for private use. Other exceptions and limitations contained in the provision run parallel to those in copyright law, to the extent this appears as relevant for industrial design law. The provision also

---

[50] The same issue may arise in design and patent law, in case of horizontal IP legislation concerning anti-piracy measures and private behavior.

[51] That this is the core element of trademark protection under TRIPS is also emphasized in *EC – GIs* (above fn. 27), ¶ 7.644.

echoes the relevant parts of the qualifications contained in Articles 13 and 17, namely the obligation to indicate source, and the reference to honest commercial practices. In addition to that, another subparagraph was added in order to encompass obligations intended to safeguard freedom of traffic through air, sea and land, as presently regulated (with regard to patents) in Article 5ter of the Paris Convention, and as extended by Article 27 of the Convention on International Civil Aviation of December 1944 (Chicago Convention).[52]

3.4.6 Patents

3.4.6.1 Changes concerning patentable subject matter

3.4.6.1.1 GENERAL REMARKS Compared to other areas of IP, it is more difficult in patent law to arrive at a balanced protection system solely by adjusting the limitations and exceptions. One major source of discontent also lies in Article 27, which addresses the definition of patentable subject matter under international law. The IPT project has also therefore proposed a number of changes with regard to that article.

First and foremost, the critical discussions on Article 27 concern the fact that the article obligates TRIPS Members to grant patents "whether products or processes, in all fields of technology", thereby making it mandatory to introduce product patents in such sensitive fields as pharmaceuticals and agricultural products.[53] Inter alia, the argument was made that in spite of the fact that transition periods were granted to developing and least-developed countries (and were subsequently extended for the

---

52 Cf. Article 27 of the Chicago Convention:
Exemption from seizure on patent claims

> (a) While engaged in international air navigation, any authorized entry of aircraft of a contracting State into the territory of another contracting State or authorized transit across the territory of such State with or without landings shall not entail any seizure or detention of the aircraft or any claim against the owner or operator thereof or any other interference therewith by or on behalf of such State or any person therein, on the ground that the construction, mechanism, parts, accessories or operation of the aircraft is an infringement of any patent, design, or model duly granted or registered in the State whose territory is entered by the aircraft, it being agreed that no deposit of security in connection with the foregoing exemption from seizure or detention of the aircraft shall in any case be required in the State entered by the aircraft.
> (b)....

53 With the exception of plants, which, at the option of TRIPS Members, may only be subject to protection by a sui-generis regime: Art. 27.3 (b).

latter[54]), the obligation to grant product patents in all areas of technology basically denies developing countries the possibility to 'learn and grow by copying' during a certain phase of their development, thereby depriving them of a privilege which all industrialized countries have made ample use of in their own history. Before that background, it might be considered whether a revised form of TRIPS should remove the exigencies of the first sentence of Article 27.1, leaving it to members themselves to choose the right time to extend the patent regime to areas such as pharmaceutical products or other subject matter with specific importance for their own socio-economic development.

However, for several reasons such a radical step does not appear advisable. First, it seems too late anyhow for attempts to "turn back the clock" – most of the countries concerned have already brought their laws in accordance with Article 27.1, and for others, the current (or further) extension(s) of the transition period may be sufficient to take account of their specific needs. Second, there is indeed some substance to the argument that unlike previous times, when countries had full freedom to measure the size and speed of their own steps from pre-industrial to industrialized economy, the interferences with international trade possibly resulting from countries indulging in intense and prolonged "learning by copying"phases are much stronger in the world of today, with its interlinked markets, where goods can travel much easier and faster than ever before in history.

Rather than abandoning the basic principle set out in the first sentence of Article 27.1, the IPT proposal therefore settles for amendments in the second sentence: by deleting, in the phrase prohibiting discrimination, the references to fields of technology and to the aspect of whether goods are imported or produced locally, the proposed text gives broader discretion to TRIPS Members to differentiate between technological sectors, and to require that patents must be worked locally.

3.4.6.1.2 Discrimination as to field of technology Where fields of technology are concerned, it might be argued that *bona fide* differentiation is already possible under Article 27 TRIPS, in particular where public health or other urgent national concerns mentioned in the Doha Declaration are at stake. Nevertheless, the matter remains unclear, and

---

[54] The deadline for least-developed countries to introduce product patents for pharmaceuticals has been postponed to 2016. However, the effect of that extension was lost on the (substantial) number of WTO Members which had already previously renounced, on a "voluntary" basis, to making full use of the transition period.

guidance is lacking for situations when differentiation is not due to aspects of health or nutrition,[55] but rather to considerations of a technical or economic character. By omitting the reference to field of technology, the amended version of Article 27.1 would terminate any discussions resulting from those uncertainties. In addition, the changes would allow legislatures to go even further: as a matter of principle, it would be possible to develop patent legislation "à la carte", with provisions being tailor-made for individual areas of technology, as long as the minimum requirements for protection under TRIPS are met with regard to all of them. It is true that to grant such wide discretion does entail certain risks. On the other hand, it can hardly be expected that legislatures act irrationally and arbitrarily in matters of patent protection – and if they do, it is primarily a task for domestic politics to set them straight. International authorities should only become involved where arbitrary law making leads to discrimination on the basis of nationality, or where specific (foreign) national interests are given preference in relation to others. Both aspects are already reflected in Articles 3 and 4 TRIPS, which remain applicable and might arguably gain in importance after the proposed amendment.

3.4.6.1.3 Local working In view of the general approach underlying an agreement like WTO/TRIPS, which is intended to boost international trade and facilitate access to foreign markets it appears consequently as a matter of principle that discrimination is not allowed between imported goods and goods which are produced locally, as is stipulated in the second sentence of Article 27.1.[56] But although the argument as such makes sense, it fails to attribute sufficient weight to the specific importance and value of a local working requirement, not least for developing countries. Apart from the beneficial effect such requirements may have for foreign direct investment and the benefits this will entail for local employment rates and economic growth, it seems obvious that the "teaching effect" of a patent is typically deeper and more intense when it is worked in the local environment, than can possibly be achieved by simply studying the patent documents. Local working of patents thereby offers an inbuilt element of knowledge dissemination and technology transfer, and it thus complies exactly with the principles enshrined in Article 7 TRIPS. In that light, it seems inconsiderate to prohibit any such requirements simply because

[55] Expressly mentioned under Art. 2.1.

[56] The same aim is reflected in the principle of national treatment of goods, as set forth in Art. III.4 GATT: WTO Members may not discriminate against imported goods Cf. GATT (1947) panel on the US Manufacturing Clause, 15–16 May 1984 (L/5609-31S/74)

they necessarily imply, in a very specific, limited type of cases, an element of discrimination vis-à-vis imported goods.

3.4.6.2 Limitations (Art. 30) The objectives and structure of proposed Article 30 basically concur with those of the provisions on mandatory limitations in copyright, trademark, and design law. However, as to substantive contents, patent law poses specific problems. For copyright and trademark law, the proposed mandatory rules are basically meant to encapsulate those limitations that are uncontroversial, and already form part of a large majority of IP regimes. For instance, trademark use for descriptive purposes, or for honest commercial communication, is practically universally permissible.[57] For patent law, however, the situation is different – it is much harder to draw up a catalogue of limitations which are largely uncontroversial on the international level.[58] The question might therefore be asked whether the attempt to formulate a catalogue of mandatory limitations is too ambitious and premature, even for an academic project like IPT. On the other hand, the advantages for transparency and legal security typically ensuing from "ceiling rules"[59] are of relevance not least for patent law, and therefore provide sufficient justification for embarking on such a challenging endeavour.

As in the case of the other IP rights, the catalogue of limitations starts off with a mandatory exception for private acts undertaken for non-commercial purposes, following the general principle that IP rights (with some reservations for copyright) should not extend to the private sphere, in particular where this would only concern infringements of a *de minimis* character. Other mandatory limitations are primarily based on concerns that coincide with the general goal of the patent system to promote technical efficiency and knowledge. This applies in particular to the "research exception", which allows use to the extent necessary to study or test the functioning of the invention (reverse engineering) or experimentation on the invention to test or improve on it. Efficiency concerns as well as aspects of public health care underlie the rule permitting experiments

---

[57] This only applies to the principle as such; the extent to which those limitations may be used in practice may of course vary considerably.

[58] Valuable guidance can be found in the first (Anell) draft of TRIPS: it contained a tentative catalogue of limitations in patent law, which was later replaced by the three-step test (Art. 30). An inventory of limitations and exceptions currently applying in the Paris Convention Member States has been prepared under the aegis of the WIPO Standing Committee on the Law of Patents, WIPO Doc. SCP/15/3, at www.wipo.int/edocs/mdocs/scp/en/scp_15/scp_15_3-annex1.pdf.

[59] See above, section 3.4.1.

(development and testing) during the patent term in order to seek regulatory approval, as well as the mandatory exception proposed for extemporaneous preparation of drugs by pharmacists in case of prescriptions made in individual cases. Mandatory exceptions are further proposed for teaching purposes, for necessary repairs, and, as an element of justice balancing potential inequities ensuing from a first-to-file system, in favour of prior use. Another clause addresses (a limited form of) the so-called farmers' privilege. Lastly, the extensions of Article 5ter Paris Convention resolving from the Chicago Convention on Civil Aviation (see above, on design law) must also be applied under patent law.

In addition to the above-mentioned catalogue of specific exceptions, and quite importantly, proposed Article 30 includes a general limitation of patent scope for uses made with respect to functions that were not disclosed in the patent. The concept underlying that rule stems from the area of biotechnology, where – in spite of still existing divergences of view – it might be perceived as a welcome clarification of the pertinent situation, at least in the EU.[60] However, the principle that the scope of protection should be confined to what has been identified and disclosed in the patent does not only concern biotechnological patents; it was therefore formulated in a general manner, so as to apply in other areas as well, as technology may evolve. This is also consistent with the principle expressed in amended Article 7 (above) that the protection granted should ideally be measured according to the contribution made to society.

4. CONCLUSIONS

Among the many proposals which have been made to improve the balance currently existing in the international IP system, the IPT project seems to be the only one which has suggested a complete overhaul of critical points in the TRIPS Agreement. It is to be hoped that if not all, then at least some, of the proposals made can provide inspiration for a "TRIPS 2.0" version of the original, heavily right-holder oriented instrument at some – not too distant – point in time. As was shown by the Doha process and the amendments to which it has led, reforming TRIPS is possible, if the need arises, and if sufficient political support can be mustered. Furthermore,

[60] The fact that under European law, the scope of patents is limited by the function(s) which have been patented was confirmed by the ECJ in C-428/08 – Monsanto/Cefetra. The same decision confirmed that such an interpretation is not impacted by Art. 27 and/or 30 TRIPS.

as has been pointed out in this chapter, the changes do not have to be revolutionary – it would be helpful if the objectives to be achieved, and the principles to be observed, could find a fuller reflection in the relevant provisions, and could be linked somewhat closer to the interpretation of the black letter law found in Part II. In addition, it would be of seminal importance that either in TRIPS itself or in an accompanying instrument, guidelines for assessment of exceptions and limitations were given which ensured that a full and objective appraisal of such rules in view of their legal motives is undertaken, with the balancing exercise being based on the proportionality principle.

Whether or not time will be ripe some day to include mandatory limitations into TRIPS or other, special agreements like the presently pending draft Treaty on Access to Published Works by Visually Impaired People and People with Printing Disabilities[61] waits to be seen. Prospects are best where the matter pursued is of unquestionable moral appeal. It certainly also helps if the initiative is underpinned to some extent by matter-of-fact business interests – like the producers of Braille editions of protected works being eager to improve their chances to market their products in a large array of countries, without having to face a risk of marketing restrictions resulting from lacking limitations in domestic copyright laws.

The question remains whether the introduction of maximum rules into TRIPS would yield substantial improvements, in particular for developing countries. No uniform answer can be given to that; it certainly depends on the contents of the specific rule(s) envisaged. However, as a matter of principle, IP ceilings are not likely to provide a magic formula solving the problems presently encountered on the international level. As was stated above (3.4.1), mandatory ceilings would probably only be able to prevent gross imbalances, and would not include all elements which would be of relevance e.g. for developing countries to establish an optimally calibrated IP system. Furthermore, the potential of ceilings to "immunize" economically weak countries against pressure from others urging them, on a bilateral basis, to introduce TRIPS-Plus elements in their legislation would also be rather limited. Generally speaking, the problem with most TRIPS-Plus elements usually included in bilateral trade agreements is not that the provisions as such are excessive. For instance, it is not necessarily flawed to prolong the duration of copyright protection, or to accede to treaties such as the Madrid Protocol or the WIPO copyright treaties, or to protect plant varieties by patent law in addition to or instead of the *sui generis* plant variety protection regime, or

---

[61] Above, fn. 14.

to apply the WIPO Recommendations regarding trademark law, to name just a few typical examples. To prevent such commitments altogether by introducing mandatory rules therefore would not be a sensible option for international law in general. Nevertheless, commitments as those outlined above are of serious concern if and insofar as they are ill adapted to a country's individual situation and/or are likely to create conspicuous legislative and administrative burdens, and are accepted in hastened procedures without proper consideration of their economic impact and political consequences.

Rather than being caused by the (additional or stronger) IP protection as such, the discontent in those cases stems from the fact that regulations have been transplanted into an environment where they do not fit, and where they cause irritants and negative side effects. The roots of malfunctions of the system caused thereby rest in deficiencies of procedural fairness and the equal standing of the negotiating parties, which is first and foremost a political, and not a legal problem. However, at least in the longer run and in view of the growing density and complexity of international law making, the time may be ripe for embarking on an effort to address those issues too from a legal point of view. Although it appears an ambitious task, one might try to build an international agreement about rules addressing the validity and reach of, e.g., "unconscionable clauses" or similar phenomena due to manifestly unequal bargaining power of countries, in particular where an agreement establishes a trade-off between basically unrelated matters.[62] Whether and to what extent such an approach could be complemented by elements of the ceilings discussion – for instance by drawing up a general catalogue of users' rights, which, although not mandatory in a general sense, demarcate an area in which a country should not be obliged to make concessions to others – might be taken up for consideration at a later stage.

---

[62] For now, the VCLT only contains provisions on invalidation of treaties due to error, fraud, corruption of a representative, coercion, or conflict with *ius cogens* (Art. 48 – 53 VCLT).

APPENDIX

PART I GENERAL PROVISIONS AND BASIC PRINCIPLES

PART II STANDARDS CONCERNING THE AVAILABILITY, SCOPE AND USE OF INTELLECTUAL PROPERTY RIGHTS

1. Copyright and Related Rights
2. Trademarks
3. Geographical Indications
4. Industrial Designs
5. Patents
6. Layout-Designs (Topographies) of Integrated Circuits
7. Protection of Undisclosed Information
8. Control of Anti-Competitive Practices in Contractual Licences

PART III ENFORCEMENT OF INTELLECTUAL PROPERTY RIGHTS

1. General Obligations
2. Civil and Administrative Procedures and Remedies
3. Provisional Measures
4. Special Requirements Related to Border Measures
5. Criminal Procedures

PART IV ACQUISITION AND MAINTENANCE OF INTELLECTUAL PROPERTY RIGHTS AND RELATED *INTER-PARTES* PROCEDURES

PART V DISPUTE PREVENTION AND SETTLEMENT

PART VI TRANSITIONAL ARRANGEMENTS

PART VII INSTITUTIONAL ARRANGEMENTS; FINAL PROVISIONS

Members,

Desiring to reduce distortions and impediments to international trade, and taking into account the need to promote effective and adequate protection of intellectual property rights, and to ensure that measures and procedures to enforce intellectual property rights do not themselves become barriers to legitimate trade;

Recognizing, to this end, the need for new rules and disciplines concerning:

(a) the applicability of the basic principles of GATT 1994 and of relevant international intellectual property agreements or conventions;
(b) the provision of adequate standards and principles concerning the availability, scope and use of trade-related intellectual property rights;
(c) the provision of effective and appropriate means for the enforcement of trade-related intellectual property rights, taking into account differences in national legal systems;
(d) the provision of effective and expeditious procedures for the multilateral prevention and settlement of disputes between governments; and
(e) transitional arrangements aiming at the fullest participation in the results of the negotiations;

Recognizing the need for a multilateral framework of principles, rules and disciplines dealing with international trade in counterfeit goods;

Recognizing that intellectual property rights are private rights;

Recognizing the underlying public policy objectives of national systems for the protection of intellectual property, including developmental and technological objectives;

Recognizing also the special needs of the least-developed country Members in respect of maximum flexibility in the domestic implementation of laws and regulations in order to enable them to create a sound and viable technological base;

Emphasizing the importance of reducing tensions by reaching strengthened commitments to resolve disputes on trade-related intellectual property issues through multilateral procedures;

Desiring to establish a mutually supportive relationship between the WTO and the World Intellectual Property Organization (referred to in this Agreement as "WIPO") as well as other relevant international organizations;

Hereby agree as follows:

PART I
GENERAL PROVISIONS AND BASIC PRINCIPLES

Article 2
Intellectual Property Conventions

1. In respect of Parts II, III and IV of this Agreement, Members shall comply with Articles 1 through 12, and Article 19, of the Paris Convention (1967).

2. Nothing in Parts I to IV of this Agreement shall derogate from existing obligations that Members may have to each other under the Paris Convention, the Berne Convention, the Rome Convention and the Treaty on Intellectual Property in Respect of Integrated Circuits.

Article 2 [AMENDED]
Intellectual Property Conventions

1. [...] Members shall comply with Articles 1 through 12, and Article 19, of the Paris Convention (1967) and Articles 1 through 6, Articles 7 through 21 of the Berne Convention (1971) and the Appendix thereto.

2. Nothing in Parts I to IV of this Agreement shall derogate from existing obligations that Members may have to each other under the Paris Convention, the Berne Convention, the Rome Convention and the Treaty on Intellectual Property in Respect of Integrated Circuits.

Article 7
Objectives

The protection and enforcement of intellectual property rights should contribute to the promotion of technological innovation and to the transfer and dissemination of technology, to the mutual advantage of producers and users of technological knowledge and in a manner conducive to social and economic welfare, and to a balance of rights and obligations.

Article 7 [AMENDED]
Objectives

The protection and enforcement of intellectual property rights should:

(a) contribute, in a manner conducive to social and economic welfare:
   (i) to cultural development and the enhancement of creativity, taking due account of the larger public interest, particularly in education, research and access to information and knowledge for all;

(ii) to the promotion of innovation and technological progress, to the transfer of technology and to the dissemination of technology, information and knowledge;
(iii) to the promotion of competition and fairness in trade in the interests of creators, authors, inventors and other producers, traders and consumers;

(b) ensure, to the advantage of society as a whole, a balance of rights and obligations so that, in particular, the scope of the protection conferred by an intellectual property right corresponds to the contribution made to creativity and innovation.

Article 8
Principles

1. Members may, in formulating or amending their laws and regulations, adopt measures necessary to protect public health and nutrition, and to promote the public interest in sectors of vital importance to their socio-economic and technological development, provided that such measures are consistent with the provisions of this Agreement.

2. Appropriate measures, provided that they are consistent with the provisions of this Agreement, may be needed to prevent the abuse of intellectual property rights by right holders or the resort to practices which unreasonably restrain trade or adversely affect the international transfer of technology.

Article 8 [AMENDED]
Principles

1. Members should, in formulating or amending their laws and regulations, adopt measures necessary to protect public health and nutrition, and to promote the public interest in sectors of vital importance to their socio-economic and technological development, unless such measures are inconsistent with the provisions of this Agreement.

2. Members shall take appropriate measures, unless they are inconsistent with the provisions of this Agreement, [. . .] to prevent the abuse of intellectual property rights by right holders or the resort to practices which unreasonably restrain trade or adversely affect the international transfer of technology.

3. Members shall provide for the necessary infrastructure for adequate and efficient systems for acquisition and maintenance as well as for opposition, revocation and declaration of invalidity of intellectual property rights, taking into account their economic, financial and administrative constraints and their respective level of development, and provided that the procedures applied are not inconsistent with the provisions of this Agreement.

Article 8a [NEW]
Balance of Interests

1. Members shall take due account of the objectives and principles set out in Articles 7 and 8 when formulating or amending their laws and regulations. In doing so, they shall ensure that the protection granted reflects a fair balance between private economic interests and the larger public interest as well as the interests of third parties.

2. Members shall ensure that users may, without the consent of the right holder, use protected subject matter, provided that such use does not unreasonably prejudice the legitimate interests of the right holder, taking into due consideration the normal exploitation of the right.

(a) In particular, the following factors shall be taken into account for the admissibility of such use:
   (i) whether it contributes to the exchange of ideas and opinions;
   (ii) whether it contributes to the dissemination of information;
   (iii) whether it concerns the private sphere of the user;
   (iv) whether it results in the creation of value-added products and services;
   (v) whether it is justified by serious cultural or social considerations.

(b) The following factors shall also be taken into account:
   (i) to which extent the right holders and/or original creators are granted equitable and appropriate compensation under efficient and practicable mechanisms;
   (ii) whether the use recognises the dignity, the achievement and all the other personal interests of the original creator, be they moral or financial.

(c) In balancing the different factors, account shall be taken of the extent and intensity of the use, and whether it is proportionate to its objectives.

Article 8b [NEW]
Interface Between Intellectual Property Rights and Competition Law

1. For the purposes of maintaining a fair balance between intellectual property rights and free competition:

(a) Members shall provide for legislative or administrative measures, in particular, in the form of limitations of the rights or in the form of compulsory licences, if the use of the product protected by an intellectual property right is indispensable for competition in the relevant market, unless the application of such measures would have a significantly negative effect on the incentives to invest in research and development;
(b) Members should further provide for remedies if the use of an intellectual property right results in the abuse of a dominant position on the relevant market or in behaviour violating anti-trust principles.

2. To the extent that compliance with paragraph 1 depends on the establishment of an efficient system for control of competition, Article 8.3 shall apply *mutatis mutandis*.

PART II

STANDARDS CONCERNING THE AVAILABILITY, SCOPE

AND USE OF INTELLECTUAL PROPERTY RIGHTS

SECTION 1: COPYRIGHT AND RELATED RIGHTS

Article 9
Relation to the Berne Convention

1. Members shall comply with Articles 1 through 21 of the Berne Convention (1971) and the Appendix thereto. However, Members shall not have rights or obligations under this Agreement in respect of the rights conferred under Article 6*bis* of that Convention or of the rights derived therefrom.
2. Copyright protection shall extend to expressions and not to ideas, procedures, methods of operation or mathematical concepts as such.

Article 9 [AMENDED]
Protected Subject Matter

1. [Deleted]
2. Copyright protection shall extend to expressions and not to ideas, procedures, methods of operation or mathematical concepts as such.
3. Copyright protection shall not extend to official texts of a legislative, administrative or legal nature, and to official translations of such texts.

Article 13
Limitations and Exceptions

Members shall confine limitations or exceptions to exclusive rights to certain special cases which do not conflict with a normal exploitation of the work and do not unreasonably prejudice the legitimate interests of the right holder.

Article 13 [NEW]
Limitations

1. In accordance with Articles 7 to 8b, the protection conferred by copyright shall not extend to:

(a) reproduction for purely technical purposes, to the extent that this is necessary to enable communication and/or legitimate use;
(b) reverse engineering, where this is indispensable for obtaining the information necessary to achieve interoperability;
(c) use made for the purpose of:
  (i) quotation from a work which has already been lawfully made available to the public;
  (ii) illustration for teaching and/or scientific research;
  (iii) news reporting;
  (iv) illustration in order to provide information in connection with sales of goods that are legitimately commercialised on the market concerned;
  (v) parody;

to the extent that this is necessary for the relevant purpose, and notwithstanding the rights of the personal creator to have the work attributed to him or her and to oppose use that amounts to a massive and manifest mutilation of the work in its original form. In connection with such use, reference must be made to the source, unless that is impossible or manifestly inappropriate in view of the circumstances;

(d) acts of reproduction made by publicly accessible libraries, educational establish-ments, museums or archives which are necessary for these institutions to perform their tasks, provided that the use is not for direct or indirect economic or commercial advantage. Members may make repro-duction dependent on payment of fair remuneration to the rightholders.

2. Furthermore, the protection conferred by copyright shall not extend to personal use made in privacy, except for certain special cases where denial of protection would manifestly conflict with the principles set out in Article 8a.2, first sentence.

3. Members may further restrict the protection conferred by copyright subject to the provisions of Articles 7 to 8b.

Article 14
Protection of Performers, Producers of Phonograms (Sound Recordings) and Broadcasting Organizations

1. In respect of a fixation of their performance on a phonogram, performers shall have the possibility of preventing the following acts when undertaken without their authorization: the fixation of their unfixed performance and the reproduction of such fixation. Performers shall also have the possibility of preventing the following acts when undertaken without their authorization: the broadcasting by wireless means and the communication to the public of their live performance.

Article 14 [AMENDED]
Protection of Performers, Producers of Phonograms (Sound Recordings) and Broadcasting Organizations

1. In respect of a fixation of their performance on a phonogram, performers shall have the possibility of preventing the following acts when undertaken without their authorization: the fixation of their unfixed performance and the reproduction of such fixation. Performers shall also have the possibility of preventing the following acts when undertaken without their authorization: the broadcasting by wireless means and the communication to the public of their live performance.

2. Producers of phonograms shall enjoy the right to authorize or prohibit the direct or indirect reproduction of their phonograms.
3. Broadcasting organizations shall have the right to prohibit the following acts when undertaken without their authorization: the fixation, the reproduction of fixations, and the rebroadcasting by wireless means of broadcasts, as well as the communication to the public of television broadcasts of the same. Where Members do not grant such rights to broadcasting organizations, they shall provide owners of copyright in the subject matter of broadcasts with the possibility of preventing the above acts, subject to the provisions of the Berne Convention (1971).
4. The provisions of Article 11 in respect of computer programs shall apply *mutatis mutandis* to producers of phonograms and any other right holders in phonograms as determined in a Member's law. If on 15 April 1994 a Member has in force a system of equitable remuneration of right holders in respect of the rental of phonograms, it may maintain such system provided that the commercial rental of phonograms is not giving rise to the material impairment of the exclusive rights of reproduction of right holders.
5. The term of the protection available under this Agreement to performers and producers of phonograms shall last at least until the end of a period of 50 years computed from the end of the calendar year in which the fixation was made or the performance took place. The term of protection granted pursuant to paragraph 3 shall last for at least 20 years from the end of the calendar year in which the broadcast took place.
6. Any Member may, in relation to the rights conferred under paragraphs 1, 2 and 3, provide for conditions, limitations, exceptions and reservations to the extent permitted by the Rome Convention. However, the provisions of Article 18 of the Berne Convention (1971) shall also apply, *mutatis mutandis*, to the rights of performers and producers of phonograms in phonograms.

2. Producers of phonograms shall enjoy the right to authorize or prohibit the direct or indirect reproduction of their phonograms.
3. Broadcasting organizations shall have the right to prohibit the following acts when undertaken without their authorization: the fixation, the reproduction of fixations, and the rebroadcasting by wireless means of broadcasts, as well as the communication to the public of television broadcasts of the same. Where Members do not grant such rights to broadcasting organizations, they shall provide owners of copyright in the subject matter of broadcasts with the possibility of preventing the above acts, subject to the provisions of the Berne Convention (1971).
4. The provisions of Article 11 in respect of computer programs shall apply *mutatis mutandis* to producers of phonograms and any other right holders in phonograms as determined in a Member's law. If on 15 April 1994 a Member has in force a system of equitable remuneration of right holders in respect of the rental of phonograms, it may maintain such system provided that the commercial rental of phonograms is not giving rise to the material impairment of the exclusive rights of reproduction of right holders.
5. The term of the protection available under this Agreement to performers and producers of phonograms shall last at least until the end of a period of 50 years computed from the end of the calendar year in which the fixation was made or the performance took place. The term of protection granted pursuant to paragraph 3 shall last for at least 20 years from the end of the calendar year in which the broadcast took place.
6. Article 13 shall apply *mutatis mutandis* in relation to the rights conferred under paragraphs 1, 2 and 3. Reservations to the extent permitted by the Rome Convention are consistent with this Agreement. However, the provisions of Article 18 of the Berne Convention (1971) shall also apply, *mutatis mutandis*, to the rights of performers and producers of phonograms in phonograms.

SECTION 2: TRADEMARKS

Article 15
Protectable Subject Matter

Article 16
Rights Conferred

Article 17
Exceptions

Members may provide limited exceptions to the rights conferred by a trademark, such as fair use of descriptive terms, provided that such exceptions take account of the legitimate interests of the owner of the trademark and of third parties.

Article 17 [AMENDED]
Limitations

1. In accordance with Articles 7 to 8b, the protection conferred by a trademark shall not extend to:

(a) strictly non-commercial use;
(b) use in the course of trade:
  (i) for descriptive purposes, like indications concerning the kind, quality, quantity, intended purpose, value, geographical origin, the time of production of goods or of rendering of the service, or other characteristics of goods or services;
  (ii) in order to provide information in connection with sales of goods or services that are legitimately commercialised on the market concerned;
  (iii) for other marketing purposes providing relevant information, in particular comparative advertising;
  (iv) in a satirical or parodist manner, or in other modes of use covered by rules applying to freedom of speech and/or freedom of art in the Member concerned;
  (v) of a natural person's own name, in order to designate the goods or services originating from the business carried out by, or in cooperation with, that person, or to identify that business;

provided that such use is in accordance with honest practices in industrial or commercial

matters. In particular, use shall be deemed inadmissible that is likely to mislead the average consumer about the existence of a commercial link between the holder of the trademark and a third party.
2. Members may further restrict the protection conferred by trademarks subject to the provisions of Articles 7 to 8b, provided that this does not impair the capability of trademarks to convey correct and reliable information as to the commercial origin of goods or services.

Article 18
Term of Protection

Article 19
Requirement of Use

Article 20
Other Requirements

Article 21
Licensing and Assignment

SECTION 3: GEOGRAPHICAL INDICATIONS

Article 22
Protection of Geographical Indications

Article 23
Additional Protection for Geographical Indications for Wines and Spirits

Article 24
International Negotiations; Exceptions

SECTION 4: INDUSTRIAL DESIGNS

Article 25
Requirements for Protection

Article 26
Protection
1. The owner of a protected industrial design shall have the right to prevent third parties not having the owner's consent from

Article 26 [AMENDED]
Protection
1. The owner of a protected industrial design shall have the right to prevent third parties not having the owner's consent from

making, selling or importing articles bearing or embodying a design which is a copy, or substantially a copy, of the protected design, when such acts are undertaken for commercial purposes.

2. Members may provide limited exceptions to the protection of industrial designs, provided that such exceptions do not unreasonably conflict with the normal exploitation of protected industrial designs and do not unreasonably prejudice the legitimate interests of the owner of the protected design, taking account of the legitimate interests of third parties.

3. The duration of protection available shall amount to at least 10 years.

making, selling or importing articles bearing or embodying a design which is a copy, or substantially a copy, of the protected design, when such acts are undertaken for commercial purposes.

2. In accordance with Articles 7 to 8b, the protection conferred by industrial design rights shall not extend to:

(a) private acts for non-commercial purposes;
(b) acts of reproduction:
 (i) for the purposes of making citations or parodies, of teaching or of scientific research;
 (ii) in order to provide information in connection with sales of goods or services that are legitimately commercialised on the market concerned;

provided that such acts are compatible with honest practices in industrial or commercial matters and that reference is made to the source;

(c) acts referred to in Article 5ter of the Paris Convention (1967), which shall apply *mutatis mutandis* to industrial design rights, as well as acts referred to in Article 27 (b) of the Convention on International Civil Aviation of December 7, 1944[1*]. Those acts shall be permitted with regard to vehicles qualifying under Article 5ter (1) and (2) of the Paris Convention.

2a. Members may further restrict the protection conferred by industrial design rights subject to the provisions of Articles 7 to 8b.

3. The duration of protection available shall amount to at least 10 years.

SECTION 5: PATENTS

Article 27
Patentable Subject Matter

1. Subject to the provisions of paragraphs 2 and 3, patents shall be available for any inventions, whether products or processes, in all fields of technology, provided that they are new, involve an inventive step and are capable of industrial application.[5] Subject to paragraph 4 of Article 65, paragraph 8 of Article 70 and paragraph 3 of this Article, patents shall be available and patent rights enjoyable without discrimination as to the place of invention, the field of technology and whether products are imported or locally produced.

2. Members may exclude from patentability inventions, the prevention within their territory of the commercial exploitation of which is necessary to protect *ordre public* or morality, including to protect human, animal or plant life or health or to avoid serious prejudice to the environment, provided that such exclusion is not made merely because the exploitation is prohibited by their law.

3. Members may also exclude from patentability:

(a) diagnostic, therapeutic and surgical methods for the treatment of humans or animals;

(b) plants and animals other than micro-organisms, and essentially biological processes for the production of plants or animals other than non-biological and microbiological processes. However, Members shall provide for the protection of plant varieties either by patents or by an effective *sui generis* system or by any combination thereof. The provisions of this subparagraph shall

Article 27 [AMENDED]
Patentable Subject Matter

1. Subject to the provisions of paragraphs 2 and 3, patents shall be available, and patent rights shall be enjoyable without discrimination as to the place of invention, for any inventions, whether products or processes, in all fields of technology, provided that they are new, involve an inventive step and are capable of industrial application.

2. Members may exclude from patentability inventions, the prevention within their territory of the commercial exploitation of which is necessary to protect *ordre public* or morality, including to protect human, animal or plant life or health or to avoid serious prejudice to the environment, provided that such exclusion is not made merely because the exploitation is prohibited by their law.

3. Members may also exclude from patentability:

(a) diagnostic, therapeutic and surgical methods for the treatment of humans or animals;

(b) plants and animals other than micro-organisms, and essentially biological processes for the production of plants or animals other than non-biological and microbiological processes. However, Members shall provide for the protection of plant varieties either by patents or by an effective *sui generis* system or by any combination thereof. The provisions of this subparagraph shall be reviewed four years after the date of entry into force of the WTO Agreement.

[5] For the purposes of this Article, the terms "inventive step" and "capable of industrial application" may be deemed by a Member to be synonymous with the terms "non-obvious" and "useful" respectively.

be reviewed four years after the date of entry into force of the WTO Agreement.

Article 28
Rights Conferred

Article 29
Conditions on Patent Applicants

Article 30
Exceptions to Rights Conferred

Members may provide limited exceptions to the exclusive rights conferred by a patent, provided that such exceptions do not unreasonably conflict with a normal exploitation of the patent and do not unreasonably prejudice the legitimate interests of the patent owner, taking account of the legitimate interests of third parties.

Article 30 [amended]
Limitations

1. In accordance with Articles 7 to 8b, the protection conferred by a patent shall not extend to:

(a) private acts for non-commercial purposes;
(b) use to the extent necessary to study or test the functioning of the invention (reverse engineering) or experimentation on the invention to test or improve on it;
(c) experiments during the patent term made for purposes of seeking regulatory approval for the marketing of a product after the expiration of the patent;
(d) use of the invention for educational purposes;
(e) the extemporaneous preparation for individual cases in a pharmacy of a medicine in accordance with a medical (or dental) prescription or acts concerning the medicine so prepared;
(f) continued use of the invention by a third party that had used it bona fide, or had made serious preparations for that purpose, before the priority or filing date of the patent application;
(g) within reasonable limits and subject to the safeguarding of the legitimate interests of the patent owner, use by farmers for propagating purposes, on their own holdings, of the product of the harvest which they have obtained

by planting, on their own holdings, the protected variety;
(h) use of the invention to the extent necessary to repair an article, unless this amounts to reproduction of the patented invention;
(i) acts permitted under Article 17 (b) of the Convention of Civil Aviation of December 7, 1944*, with regard to vehicles qualifying under Article 5ter (1) and (2) of the Paris Convention.

2. In accordance with Articles 7 to 8b, the protection conferred by a patent shall not extend to use of the invention with respect to functions not disclosed in the patent.
3. Members may further restrict the protection conferred by patents subject to the provisions of Articles 7 to 8b.

SECTION 6: LAYOUT-DESIGNS (TOPOGRAPHIES) OF INTEGRATED CIRCUITS

SECTION 7: PROTECTION OF UNDISCLOSED INFORMATION

SECTION 8: CONTROL OF ANTI-COMPETITIVE PRACTICES IN CONTRACTUAL LICENCES

Article 40

1. Members agree that some licensing practices or conditions pertaining to intellectual property rights which restrain competition may have adverse effects on trade and may impede the transfer and dissemination of technology.
2. Nothing in this Agreement shall prevent Members from specifying in their legislation licensing practices or conditions that may in particular cases constitute an abuse of intellectual property rights having an adverse effect on competition in the relevant market. As provided above, a Member may adopt, consistently with the other provisions of this Agreement, appropriate measures to prevent

Article 40 [AMENDED]

1. Members agree that some licensing practices or conditions pertaining to intellectual property rights which restrain competition may have adverse effects on trade and may impede the transfer and dissemination of technology.
2. Members shall adopt, consistently with the other provisions of this Agreement, appropriate measures to prevent or control such practices, which may include for example exclusive grantback conditions,

* *For the text of Article 27 of that Convention see above, footnote to Article 26.2.*

or control such practices, which may include for example exclusive grantback conditions, conditions preventing challenges to validity and coercive package licensing, in the light of the relevant laws and regulations of that Member.	conditions preventing challenges to validity and coercive package licensing, in the light of the relevant laws and regulations of the Member concerned. Members may specify in their legislation licensing practices or conditions that may in particular cases constitute an abuse of intellectual property rights having an adverse effect on competition in the relevant market.
3. Each Member shall enter, upon request, into consultations with any other Member which has cause to believe that an intellectual property right owner that is a national or domiciliary of the Member to which the request for consultations has been addressed is undertaking practices in violation of the requesting Member's laws and regulations on the subject matter of this Section, and which wishes to secure compliance with such legislation, without prejudice to any action under the law and to the full freedom of an ultimate decision of either Member. The Member addressed shall accord full and sympathetic consideration to, and shall afford adequate opportunity for, consultations with the requesting Member, and shall cooperate through supply of publicly available non-confidential information of relevance to the matter in question and of other information available to the Member, subject to domestic law and to the conclusion of mutually satisfactory agreements concerning the safeguarding of its confidentiality by the requesting Member.	3. Each Member shall enter, upon request, into consultations with any other Member which has cause to believe that an intellectual property right owner that is a national or domiciliary of the Member to which the request for consultations has been addressed is undertaking practices in violation of the requesting Member's laws and regulations on the subject matter of this Section, and which wishes to secure compliance with such legislation, without prejudice to any action under the law and to the full freedom of an ultimate decision of either Member. The Member addressed shall accord full and sympathetic consideration to, and shall afford adequate opportunity for, consultations with the requesting Member, and shall cooperate through supply of publicly available non-confidential information of relevance to the matter in question and of other information available to the Member, subject to domestic law and to the conclusion of mutually satisfactory agreements concerning the safeguarding of its confidentiality by the requesting Member.
4. A Member whose nationals or domiciliaries are subject to proceedings in another Member concerning alleged violation of that other Member's laws and regulations on the subject matter of this Section shall, upon request, be granted an opportunity for consultations by the other Member under the same conditions as those foreseen in paragraph 3.	4. A Member whose nationals or domiciliaries are subject to proceedings in another Member concerning alleged violation of that other Member's laws and regulations on the subject matter of this Section shall, upon request, be granted an opportunity for consultations by the other Member under the same conditions as those foreseen in paragraph 3.

PART III

ENFORCEMENT OF INTELLECTUAL PROPERTY RIGHTS

SECTION 1: GENERAL OBLIGATIONS

Article 41

1. Members shall ensure that enforcement procedures as specified in this Part are available under their law so as to permit effective action against any act of infringement of intellectual property rights covered by this Agreement, including expeditious remedies to prevent infringements and remedies which constitute a deterrent to further infringements. These procedures shall be applied in such a manner as to avoid the creation of barriers to legitimate trade and to provide for safeguards against their abuse.
2. Procedures concerning the enforcement of intellectual property rights shall be fair and equitable. They shall not be unnecessarily complicated or costly, or entail unreasonable time-limits or unwarranted delays.
3. Decisions on the merits of a case shall preferably be in writing and reasoned. They shall be made available at least to the parties to the proceeding without undue delay. Decisions on the merits of a case shall be based only on evidence in respect of which parties were offered the opportunity to be heard.
4. Parties to a proceeding shall have an opportunity for review by a judicial authority of final administrative decisions and, subject to jurisdictional provisions in a Member's law concerning the importance of a case, of at least the legal aspects of initial judicial decisions on the merits of a case. However, there shall be no obligation to provide an opportunity for review of acquittals in criminal cases.
5. It is understood that this Part does not create any obligation to put in place a judicial system for the enforcement of

Article 41
Enforcement Procedures
[HEADLINE ADDED]

1. Members shall ensure that enforcement procedures as specified in this Part are available under their law so as to permit effective action against any act of infringement of intellectual property rights covered by this Agreement, including expeditious remedies to prevent infringements and remedies which constitute a deterrent to further infringements. These procedures shall be applied in such a manner as to avoid the creation of barriers to legitimate trade and to provide for safeguards against their abuse.
2. Procedures concerning the enforcement of intellectual property rights shall be fair and equitable. They shall not be unnecessarily complicated or costly, or entail unreasonable time-limits or unwarranted delays.
3. Decisions on the merits of a case shall preferably be in writing and reasoned. They shall be made available at least to the parties to the proceeding without undue delay. Decisions on the merits of a case shall be based only on evidence in respect of which parties were offered the opportunity to be heard.
4. Parties to a proceeding shall have an opportunity for review by a judicial authority of final administrative decisions and, subject to jurisdictional provisions in a Member's law concerning the importance of a case, of at least the legal aspects of initial judicial decisions on the merits of a case. However, there shall be no obligation to provide an opportunity for review of acquittals in criminal cases.
5. It is understood that this Part does not create any obligation to put in place a judicial system for the enforcement of

intellectual property rights distinct from that for the enforcement of law in general, nor does it affect the capacity of Members to enforce their law in general. Nothing in this Part creates any obligation with respect to the distribution of resources as between enforcement of intellectual property rights and the enforcement of law in general.

intellectual property rights distinct from that for the enforcement of law in general, nor does it affect the capacity of Members to enforce their law in general. Nothing in this Part creates any obligation with respect to the distribution of resources as between enforcement of intellectual property rights and the enforcement of law in general.

Article 41a [NEW]
Remedies Against Mala Fide Use of Intellectual Property Rights

Members shall provide for proportionate, efficient and deterrent remedies against *mala fide* use of intellectual property rights, in particular the making of unjustified threats.

Article 41b [NEW]
Jurisdiction and Choice of Law in Transborder Conflicts in Intellectual Property Matters

1. Members shall ensure that, subject to compliance with principles of due process and of fair balance between the interests of the parties, the rules applied with regard to jurisdiction in transborder conflicts in intellectual property matters do not unduly hamper an efficient pursuit of justice.
2. Members shall ensure that the rules applied with regard to choice of law in transborder conflicts in intellectual property matters pay due respect to the territoriality principle, thereby acknowledging the sovereign power of other Members to regulate, within the boundaries of obligations resulting from international agreements, the law governing acquisition, scope and content of intellectual property rights with regard to their respective territories. As a matter of principle, this results in the application of the law of the country for which protection is sought (*lex protectionis*).
3. Derogation from *lex protectionis* shall only be permitted:

   (a) on the basis of an agreement between the parties, to the extent acceptable in view of the specific nature of intellectual property rights;

(b) to the extent that, due to the ubiquitous nature of an infringement, the application of *lex protectionis* would seriously impede a fair and efficient enforcement of intellectual property rights.

Article 70
Protection of Existing Subject Matter

1. This Agreement does not give rise to obligations in respect of acts which occurred before the date of application of the Agreement for the Member in question.
2. Except as otherwise provided for in this Agreement, this Agreement gives rise to obligations in respect of all subject matter existing at the date of application of this Agreement for the Member in question, and which is protected in that Member on the said date, or which meets or comes subsequently to meet the criteria for protection under the terms of this Agreement. In respect of this paragraph and paragraphs 3 and 4, copyright obligations with respect to existing works shall be solely determined under Article 18 of the Berne Convention (1971), and obligations with respect to the rights of producers of phonograms and performers in existing phonograms shall be determined solely under Article 18 of the Berne Convention (1971) as made applicable under paragraph 6 of Article 14 of this Agreement.
3. There shall be no obligation to restore protection to subject matter which on the date of application of this Agreement for the Member in question has fallen into the public domain.
4. In respect of any acts in respect of specific objects embodying protected subject matter which become infringing under the terms of legislation in conformity with this Agreement, and which were commenced, or in respect of which a significant investment was made, before the date of acceptance of the WTO Agreement by that Member, any Member may provide for a limitation of the remedies available to the right holder as to the continued performance of such acts after the date of application

Article 70 [Amended]
Protection of Existing Subject Matter

1. This Agreement does not give rise to obligations in respect of acts which occurred before the date of application of the Agreement for the Member in question.
2. Except as otherwise provided for in this Agreement, this Agreement gives rise to obligations in respect of all subject matter existing at the date of application of this Agreement for the Member in question, and which is protected in that Member on the said date, or which meets or comes subsequently to meet the criteria for protection under the terms of this Agreement. In respect of this paragraph and paragraphs 3 and 4, copyright obligations with respect to existing works shall be solely determined under Article 18 of the Berne Convention (1971), and obligations with respect to the rights of producers of phonograms and performers in existing phonograms shall be determined solely under Article 18 of the Berne Convention (1971) as made applicable under paragraph 6 of Article 14 of this Agreement.
3. There shall be no obligation to restore protection to subject matter which on the date of application of this Agreement for the Member in question has fallen into the public domain.
4. In respect of any acts in respect of specific objects embodying protected subject matter which become infringing under the terms of legislation in conformity with this Agreement, and which were commenced, or in respect of which a significant investment was made, before the date of acceptance of the WTO Agreement by that Member, any Member may provide for a limitation of the remedies available to the right holder as to the continued performance of such acts after the date of application

of this Agreement for that Member. In such cases the Member shall, however, at least provide for the payment of equitable remuneration.

5. A Member is not obliged to apply the provisions of Article 11 and of paragraph 4 of Article 14 with respect to originals or copies purchased prior to the date of application of this Agreement for that Member.

6. Members shall not be required to apply Article 31, or the requirement in paragraph 1 of Article 27 that patent rights shall be enjoyable without discrimination as to the field of technology, to use without the authorization of the right holder where authorization for such use was granted by the government before the date this Agreement became known.

7. In the case of intellectual property rights for which protection is conditional upon registration, applications for protection which are pending on the date of application of this Agreement for the Member in question shall be permitted to be amended to claim any enhanced protection provided under the provisions of this Agreement. Such amendments shall not include new matter.

8. Where a Member does not make available as of the date of entry into force of the WTO Agreement patent protection for pharmaceutical and agricultural chemical products commensurate with its obligations under Article 27, that Member shall:

(a) notwithstanding the provisions of Part VI, provide as from the date of entry into force of the WTO Agreement a means by which applications for patents for such inventions can be filed;

(b) apply to these applications, as of the date of application of this Agreement, the criteria for patentability as laid down in this Agreement as if those criteria were being applied on the date of filing in that Member or, where priority is available and claimed, the priority date of the application; and

of this Agreement for that Member. In such cases the Member shall, however, at least provide for the payment of equitable remuneration.

5. A Member is not obliged to apply the provisions of Article 11 and of paragraph 4 of Article 14 with respect to originals or copies purchased prior to the date of application of this Agreement for that Member.

6. Members shall not be required to apply Article 31 to use without the authorization of the right holder where authorization for such use was granted by the government before the date this Agreement became known.

7. In the case of intellectual property rights for which protection is conditional upon registration, applications for protection which are pending on the date of application of this Agreement for the Member in question shall be permitted to be amended to claim any enhanced protection provided under the provisions of this Agreement. Such amendments shall not include new matter.

8. Where a Member does not make available as of the date of entry into force of the WTO Agreement patent protection for pharmaceutical and agricultural chemical products commensurate with its obligations under Article 27, that Member shall:

(a) notwithstanding the provisions of Part VI, provide as from the date of entry into force of the WTO Agreement a means by which applications for patents for such inventions can be filed;

(b) apply to these applications, as of the date of application of this Agreement, the criteria for patentability as laid down in this Agreement as if those criteria were being applied on the date of filing in that Member or, where priority is available and claimed, the priority date of the application; and

(c) provide patent protection in accordance with this Agreement as from the grant of the patent and for the remainder of the patent term, counted from the filing date in accordance with Article 33 of this Agreement, for those of these applications that meet the criteria for protection referred to in subparagraph (b).

9. Where a product is the subject of a patent application in a Member in accordance with paragraph 8(a), exclusive marketing rights shall be granted, notwithstanding the provisions of Part VI, for a period of five years after obtaining marketing approval in that Member or until a product patent is granted or rejected in that Member, whichever period is shorter, provided that, subsequent to the entry into force of the WTO Agreement, a patent application has been filed and a patent granted for that product in another Member and marketing approval obtained in such other Member.

ANNEX TO THE TRIPS AGREEMENT

1. For the purposes of Article 31*bis* and this Annex:

(a) "pharmaceutical product" means any patented product, or product manufactured through a patented process, of the pharmaceutical sector needed to address the public health problems as recognized in paragraph 1 of the Declaration on the TRIPS Agreement and Public Health (WT/MIN(01)/DEC/2). It is understood that active ingredients necessary for its manufacture and diagnostic kits needed for its use would be included[1];

[1] This subparagraph is without prejudice to subparagraph 1(b).

(c) provide patent protection in accordance with this Agreement as from the grant of the patent and for the remainder of the patent term, counted from the filing date in accordance with Article 33 of this Agreement, for those of these applications that meet the criteria for protection referred to in subparagraph (b).

9. Where a product is the subject of a patent application in a Member in accordance with paragraph 8(a), exclusive marketing rights shall be granted, notwithstanding the provisions of Part VI, for a period of five years after obtaining marketing approval in that Member or until a product patent is granted or rejected in that Member, whichever period is shorter, provided that, subsequent to the entry into force of the WTO Agreement, a patent application has been filed and a patent granted for that product in another Member and marketing approval obtained in such other Member.

(b) "eligible importing Member" means any least-developed country Member, and any other Member that has made a notification[2] to the Council for TRIPS of its intention to use the system set out in Article 31*bis* and this Annex ("system") as an importer, it being understood that a Member may notify at any time that it will use the system in whole or in a limited way, for example only in the case of a national emergency or other circumstances of extreme urgency or in cases of public non-commercial use. It is noted that some Members will not use the system as importing Members[3] and that some other Members have stated that, if they use the system, it would be in no more than situations of national emergency or other circumstances of extreme urgency;

(c) "exporting Member" means a Member using the system to produce pharmaceutical products for, and export them to, an eligible importing Member.

2. The terms referred to in paragraph 1 of Article 31*bis* are that:

(a) the eligible importing Member(s)[4] has made a notification to the Council for TRIPS, that:

---

[2] It is understood that this notification does not need to be approved by a WTO body in order to use the system.

[3] Australia, Canada, the European Communities with, for the purposes of Article 31bis and this Annex, its member States, Iceland, Japan, New Zealand, Norway, Switzerland, and the United States.

[4] Joint notifications providing the information required under this subparagraph may be made by the regional organizations referred to in paragraph 3 of Article 31bis on behalf of eligible importing Members using the system that are parties to them, with the agreement of those parties.

(i) specifies the names and expected quantities of the product(s) needed[5];
(ii) confirms that the eligible importing Member in question, other than a least developed country Member, has established that it has insufficient or no manufacturing capacities in the pharmaceutical sector for the product(s) in question in one of the ways set out in the Appendix to this Annex; and
(iii) confirms that, where a pharmaceutical product is patented in its territory, it has granted or intends to grant a compulsory licence in accordance with Articles 31 and 31*bis* of this Agreement and the provisions of this Annex[6];

(b) the compulsory licence issued by the exporting Member under the system shall contain the following conditions:
(i) only the amount necessary to meet the needs of the eligible importing Member(s) may be manufactured under the licence and the entirety of this production shall be exported to the Member(s) which has notified its needs to the Council for TRIPS;
(ii) products produced under the licence shall be clearly identified as being produced under the system through specific labelling or marking. Suppliers should distinguish such products

---

[5] The notification will be made available publicly by the WTO Secretariat through a page on the WTO website dedicated to the system.

[6] This subparagraph is without prejudice to Article 66.1 of this Agreement.

through special packaging and/or special colouring/shaping of the products themselves, provided that such distinction is feasible and does not have a significant impact on price; and

(iii) before shipment begins, the licensee shall post on a website[7] the following information:

— the quantities being supplied to each destination as referred to in indent (i) above; and

— the distinguishing features of the product(s) referred to in indent (ii) above;

(c) the exporting Member shall notify[8] the Council for TRIPS of the grant of the licence, including the conditions attached to it.[9] The information provided shall include the name and address of the licensee, the product(s) for which the licence has been granted, the quantity(ies) for which it has been granted, the country(ies) to which the product(s) is (are) to be supplied and the duration of the licence. The notification shall also indicate the address of the website referred to in subparagraph (b) (iii) above.

3. In order to ensure that the products imported under the system are used for

---

[7] The licensee may use for this purpose its own website or, with the assistance of the WTO Secretariat, the page on the WTO website dedicated to the system.

[8] It is understood that this notification does not need to be approved by a WTO body in order to use the system.

[9] The notification will be made available publicly by the WTO Secretariat through a page on the WTO website dedicated to the system.

the public health purposes underlying their importation, eligible importing Members shall take reasonable measures within their means, proportionate to their administrative capacities and to the risk of trade diversion to prevent re-exportation of the products that have actually been imported into their territories under the system. In the event that an eligible importing Member that is a developing country Member or a least-developed country Member experiences difficulty in implementing this provision, developed country Members shall provide, on request and on mutually agreed terms and conditions, technical and financial cooperation in order to facilitate its implementation.

4. Members shall ensure the availability of effective legal means to prevent the importation into, and sale in, their territories of products produced under the system and diverted to their markets inconsistently with its provisions, using the means already required to be available under this Agreement. If any Member considers that such measures are proving insufficient for this purpose, the matter may be reviewed in the Council for TRIPS at the request of that Member.

5. With a view to harnessing economies of scale for the purposes of enhancing purchasing power for, and facilitating the local production of, pharmaceutical products, it is recognized that the development of systems providing for the grant of regional patents to be applicable in the Members described in paragraph 3 of Article 31*bis* should be promoted. To this end, developed country Members undertake to provide technical cooperation in accordance with Article 67 of this Agreement, including in conjunction with other relevant inter-governmental organizations.

6. Members recognize the desirability of promoting the transfer of technology and capacity building in the pharmaceutical sector in order to overcome the problem faced by Members with insufficient or no manufacturing capacities in the pharmaceutical sector. To this end, eligible importing Members and exporting Members are

encouraged to use the system in a way which would promote this objective. Members undertake to cooperate in paying special attention to the transfer of technology and capacity building in the pharmaceutical sector in the work to be undertaken pursuant to Article 66.2 of this Agreement, paragraph 7 of the Declaration on the TRIPS Agreement and Public Health and any other relevant work of the Council for TRIPS.

7. The Council for TRIPS shall review annually the functioning of the system with a view to ensuring its effective operation and shall annually report on its operation to the General Council.

APPENDIX TO THE ANNEX TO THE TRIPS AGREEMENT

Assessment of Manufacturing Capacities in the Pharmaceutical Sector

Least-developed country Members are deemed to have insufficient or no manufacturing capacities in the pharmaceutical sector.

For other eligible importing Members insufficient or no manufacturing capacities for the product(s) in question may be established in either of the following ways:

(i) the Member in question has established that it has no manufacturing capacity in the pharmaceutical sector;

or

(ii) where the Member has some manufacturing capacity in this sector, it has examined this capacity and found that, excluding any capacity owned or controlled by the patent owner, it is currently insufficient for the purposes of meeting its needs. When it is established that such capacity has become sufficient to meet the Member's needs, the system shall no longer apply.

8. Access to genetic resources and benefit sharing: The Nagoya Protocol in the light of the TRIPS Agreement

Linda Briceño Moraia

I. INTRODUCTION

Access to and utilization of genetic resources express the tension between two different interests: one of the entity who exercises sovereignty over genetic resources located in a given territory and the one of third parties seeking access to those resources in order to undertake scientific research. The Rio Convention on Biodiversity[1] and the Nagoya Protocol[2] link access to the subsequent sharing of the benefits arising from the exploitation of the resources, in order to promote the transfer of technology and the spread of the associated knowledge among the so-called *industrialized countries* and *developing countries*. In this framework, the interest of the

[1] *Convention on Biological Diversity*, opened for signatures at Rio de Janeiro on 5 June 1992 and entered into force on 29 December 1993 (hereinafter CBD). It was given effect in Italy through Law No. 124 of 14 February 1994 (Official Gazette No. 44 of 23 February 1994).

[2] *Nagoya Protocol on Access to Genetic Resources and the Fair and Equitable Sharing of Benefits Arising from their Utilization to the Convention on Biological Diversity* (hereinafter the Protocol), UNEP/CBD/COP/DEC/X/1 of 29 October 2010. For an updated list of the States having signed, ratified the Protocol, as well regarding acceptance, approval or accession, see http://www.cbd.int/abs/nagoya-protocol/signatories/ At present, the Nagoya Protocol still has not been signed by USA. In accordance with its Article 32, the Protocol was opened for signature from 2 February 2011 to 1 February 2012 at the United Nations Headquarters in New York by Parties to the Convention. It was open for signatures not to only by the Contracting Parties to the Convention on Biological Diversity but also by those that are not Party thereto (chief among which the USA, which have not signed it). The Protocol will enter into force on the 90th day after the date of deposit of the 50th instrument of ratification, acceptance, approval or accession (Article 33).

owner of the resources and that of the users are not in contrast, but they appear to be complementary.

The implementation of these rules shall be in accordance with the obligations stemming from other international sources of law, and in particular with the patent provisions contained in the TRIPS Agreement.[3] This is stressed by the Rio Convention itself, which provides that genetic resources are subject to the sovereignty of the country that they are located in[4] but at the same time it clarifies that "in the case of technology subject to patents and other intellectual property rights, such access and transfer shall be provided on terms which recognize and are consistent with the adequate and effective protection of intellectual property rights".[5]

II. OBJECTIVE AND SCOPE OF THE NAGOYA PROTOCOL

The Nagoya Protocol was adopted at the Tenth Conference of the Parties to the Convention on Biological Diversity.[6] The treaty's objective is to implement the provisions of the Rio Convention on access to, and utilization of, genetic resources and traditional knowledge.[7] More precisely, its aim is to guarantee an equitable sharing of the benefits deriving from the utilization of resources, ensuring also that the access thereto and the transfer of technology is informed by the principles of *fairness* and *equity*.[8]

---

[3] *Agreement on Trade-Related Aspects of Intellectual Property Rights, Annex IC of the Marrakech Agreement Establishing the World Trade Organization*, signed in Marrakech on 15 April 1994 (hereinafter the TRIPS Agreement". See articles 27–34.

[4] Article 3 CBD.

[5] Article 16.2 CBD.

[6] *Conference of the Parties to the Convention on Biological Diversity, Tenth Meeting*, Nagoya, Japan, 18–19 October 2010.

[7] In fact the Preamble to the Protocol recalls "that the fair and equitable sharing of benefits arising from the utilization of genetic resources is one of three objectives of the Convention" and recognizes "that this Protocol pursues the implementation of its objective within the Convention". See also article 15 CBD and article 3 of the Protocol.

[8] "[F]air and equitable sharing of benefits arising from the utilization of genetic resources", see article 1 of the Protocol. See also article 1 CBD, which provides that:

> the objectives of this Convention, to be pursued in accordance with its relevant provisions, are the conservation of biological diversity, the sustainable use of its components and the fair and equitable sharing of the benefits arising out of the utilization of genetic resources, including by appropriate access to genetic

From this standpoint, the Nagoya Protocol stresses the need to take into consideration all rights over those resources, to promote the conservation of biodiversity and the sustainable use of the relevant components.[9]

Also from a terminological standpoint the Protocol refers to article 2 of the Rio Convention, though expanding its scope. First, it clarifies what is meant by the "utilization of genetic resources", defining the uses that are relevant for the purposes of the application of the Protocol. It extends also to research and development activities conducted on the genetic and/or biochemical composition of genetic resources, including those implying the use of biotechnologies.[10] After referring to the definition of biotechnologies already included in the Rio Convention, article 2(e) of the Protocol defines the term "derivative" as "a naturally occurring biochemical compound resulting from the genetic expression or metabolism of biological or genetic resources, even if it does not contain functional units of heredity".

Genetic resources of human origin are excluded from the scope of application of the Rio Convention.[11] However, it should be noted that reference is made to "human pathogens" in the following part of the Preamble to the Protocol: "mindful of the International Health Regulations (2005) of the World Health Organization and the importance of ensuring access to human pathogens for public health preparedness and response purposes".[12]

---

resources and by appropriate transfer of relevant technologies, taking into account all rights over those resources and to technologies, and by appropriate funding.

[9] Further to article 1 of the Protocol:

The objective of this Protocol is the fair and equitable sharing of the benefits arising from the utilization of genetic resources, including by appropriate access to genetic resources and by appropriate transfer of relevant technologies, taking into account all rights over those resources and to technologies, and by appropriate funding, thereby contributing to the conservation of biological diversity and the sustainable use of its components.

[10] Article 2(c) of the Protocol.

[11] See *Bonn Guidelines on Access to Genetic Resources and Fair and Equitable Sharing of the Benefits Arising out of their Utilization*, 1 C, (COP 6, Decision VI/24).

[12] *Infra*, Section IV.1.

III. THE CORRELATION BETWEEN ACCESS TO GENETIC RESOURCES AND BENEFIT SHARING

Access to genetic resources is subject to a twofold condition: to the so-called *prior informed consent* and to the *mutual agreement* on benefit-sharing terms. The informed consent shall be given by the State in whose territory the genetic resources are located[13] and by the indigenous and local communities that have such a right.[14] Therefore, the latter and those who seek access must agree on how to share the benefits arising from the utilization of the resources: in fact, both the Protocol and the Convention state that benefit sharing must be "on mutually agreed terms",[15] that is, through private agreement governed by domestic law.[16] Article 6(g) of the Protocol provides that the terms shall be expressed in writing and it sets out their minimum content, i.e. "(i) a dispute settlement clause; (ii) terms on benefit-sharing, including in relation to intellectual property rights; (iii) terms on subsequent third-party use, if any; and (iv) terms on change of intent, where applicable".[17]

This mechanism is designed to guarantee remuneration for the Party that holds rights on the resources[18] and hence it makes access subject to

---

[13] Further to article 6.1 of the Protocol "access to genetic resources for their utilization shall be subject to the prior informed consent of the Party providing such resources that is the country of origin of such resources or a Party that has acquired the genetic resources in accordance with the Convention, unless otherwise determined by that Party". The text therefore repeats the content of articles 15.3 and 15.5 of the Rio Convention on the definition of the Contracting Party providing the resources.

[14] Article 6.2 of the Protocol affirms that "[i]n accordance with domestic law, each Party shall take measures, as appropriate, with the aim of ensuring that the prior informed consent or approval and involvement of indigenous and local communities is obtained for access to genetic resources where they have the established right to grant access to such resources".

[15] See article 5 of the Protocol and article 15.4 CBD.

[16] *N. Boschiero*, *Le biotecnologie tra etica e principi generali del diritto internazionale*, in *N. Boschiero* (ed.), *Bioetica e biotecnologie nel diritto internazionale e comunitario – Questioni generali e tutela della proprietà intellettuale*, Turin, Giappichelli, 2006, 84.

[17] See article 6.3(g) of the Protocol.

[18] The correlation between access to the resources and the related benefit sharing can also be found in other parts of the Protocol, which concern both the preliminary authorization stage and the *final* stage aimed at ensuring compliance with the relevant legislative and/or regulatory provisions.

As regards the preliminary stage, the Protocol obliges the Parties to set up a competent authority in charge of issuing at the time of access "a permit or its equivalent as evidence of the decision to grant prior informed consent and of the subsequent sharing of the benefits. Article 5.1 of the Protocol states that the latter should also relate to "subsequent applications and commercialization". In any case, the provision alludes not only to *monetary* benefits in a strict sense but also to the advantages stemming from the transfer of technology and collaboration in R&D.[19] To ensure that the system outlined in the Protocol does not encounter obstacles to its concrete application, it appears necessary:

---

the establishment of mutually agreed terms, and notify the Access and Benefit Sharing Clearing-House accordingly" (see article 6.3(e) of the Protocol). That permit should constitute a veritable "internationally recognized certificate of compliance", apt to prove compliance with the domestic provisions on the obtaining of consent and the establishment of "mutually agreed terms". Article 17.4 of the Protocol sets out the minimum information that the certificate shall contain, which include "(g) confirmation that mutually agreed terms were established" and "(h) confirmation that prior informed consent was obtained". As regards the necessity to ensure compliance with the provisions on access, the Protocol obliges the Parties to take appropriate, effective and proportionate steps "to provide that genetic resources utilized within its jurisdiction have been accessed in accordance with prior informed consent and that mutually agreed terms have been established". With the corollary that access cannot be considered valid when it has been granted in the absence of "mutually agreed terms", and the measures envisaged in such cases by the Parties can be considered as thus being applicable. See article 15.1 and 17.3 of the Protocol.

[19] The Annex to the Protocol gives a list of examples of "monetary and non-monetary benefits" that could be used to ensure an equitable sharing of the benefits. Among the monetary benefits, worthy of note are "(d) payment of royalties", "(e) licence fees in case of commercialization", "(h) research funding", "(i) joint ventures" and "(j) joint ownership of relevant intellectual property rights". In any event, even those included among "non-monetary benefits" are susceptible to having an impact on the economic development of the countries' providers of genetic material. For instance, "(a) sharing of research and development results", "(b) «collaboration, cooperation and contribution in scientific research and development programmes, particularly biotechnological research activities, where possible in the Party providing genetic resources", "(c) participation in product development", "(d) access to scientific information relevant to conservation and sustainable use of biological diversity, including biological inventories and taxonomic studies", "(f) transfer to the provider of the genetic resources of knowledge and technology under fair and most favourable terms, including on concessional and preferential terms where agreed, in particular, knowledge and technology that make use of genetic resources, including biotechnology, or that are relevant to the conservation and sustainable utilization of biological diversity", "(m) research directed towards priority needs, such as health and food security, taking into account domestic uses of genetic resources in the Party providing genetic resources" and "(q) "joint ownership of relevant intellectual property rights".

i) to guarantee that the procedure for obtaining consent does not act as a disincentive to investment in the related R&D;
ii) in case of patents, to coordinate the provisions of the Convention and the Protocol with those governing the exercise of intellectual property prescribed by the TRIPS Agreement ;
iii) to promote the sharing of the benefits in the form of transfer of technology and collaboration in R&D.

IV. OBTAINING OF CONSENT: THE NEED TO HARMONIZE THE REGULATORY REQUIREMENTS

The Protocol provides that domestic legislation is to lay down the criteria and procedures for seeking informed consent and involving the indigenous and local communities. Therefore every Party shall provide for clear, precise and transparent regulation, suitable to guarantee the non-arbitrariness of the procedure.[20] To that end, the Protocol only encourages the development and use of voluntary codes of conduct, guidelines, best practices and standards.[21]

Failure to achieve a uniform legislative framework at international level could hinder the attainment of the Protocol's aims and lead to imbalances in the dynamics of international trade. Consider, for example, where a given resource can be found at the same time in two countries having different procedures for the obtaining of consent: one particularly detailed and complex and the other much more simple. Presumably, the Party adopting the latter procedure will attract investment from those interested in gaining access to the specific resource, thereby discouraging access to the one located in the other country. But this runs the risk of undermining one of the Convention's objectives, namely, that of promoting the conservation of biodiversity and the sustainable use of its components.[22] And indeed, in case domestic legislation on access differs significantly from one country to another, this could lead also to the indiscriminate exploitation

---

[20] See articles 6.3(a) and 6.3(b) of the Protocol.

[21] Article 20 of the Protocol.

[22] See article 1 CBD: "The objectives of this Convention, to be pursued in accordance with its relevant provisions, are the conservation of biological diversity, the sustainable use of its components and the fair and equitable sharing of the benefits arising out of the utilization of genetic resources [. . .]". See also article 1 of the Protocol, which refers to "thereby contributing to the conservation of biological diversity and the sustainable use of its components".

of resources located in a given geographic area. By contrast, identifying uniform criteria on the obtaining of consent could have contributed to the harmonization of the Parties' procedures without jeopardizing "the sovereign right to exploit their own resources pursuant to their own environmental policies" that article 3 of the Rio Convention recognizes.[23]

In general, procedures for obtaining consent could thus act as a disincentive for investment in scientific research on genetic resources, slowing down innovation in the relevant sectors of application.[24] Moreover, the Protocol itself seems to recognize that the procedures adopted by member States could hinder access to the resources, and article 8(a) recognizes to the Parties the possibility to adopt simplified measures on access on the grounds of the "non commercial" nature of the scientific research purposes.[25] On the other hand, it has been highlighted that in many

---

[23] See also the Preamble to the Protocol: "The Parties to this Protocol [. . .] reaffirming the sovereign rights of States over their natural resources and according to the provisions of the Convention".

[24] See *N.P. De Carvalho*, *The TRIPS Regime of Patent Rights*, The Netherlands, Kluwer Law International, 2010, 245, 247, 248.

> As found in the International Cooperative Biodiversity Groups (ICGB) program, a number of constraints and complexities contribute to the time it takes to conclude an ABS agreement: national governments without focal points and clear procedures; the requirements of legal staff involved in complex negotiations; the time required to get sign off from senior and busy management in companies; community outreach and consultation, and the need to follow traditional decision-making practices and timelines; and university or research institution policy deliberation,

Secretariat of the Convention on Biological Diversity, *Access and benefit-sharing in practice: trends in partnerships across sectors*, Montreal, Technical Series No. 38, 2008, 25.

[25] See article 8(a) of the Protocol to the effect that

> each Party shall create conditions to promote and encourage research which contributes to the conservation and sustainable use of biological diversity, particularly in developing countries, including through simplified measures on access for non-commercial research purposes, taking into account the need to address a change of intent for such research.

However, even this provision risks remaining devoid of any practical importance because nowadays research is mainly undertaken by firms, which by definition pursue commercial aims. It should be noted that a recent Decision (IX/14) of the Conference of the Parties to the CBD stressed the need to undertake "more in-depth analysis of new open-source-based modes of innovation, as well as other additional options to intellectual property rights". In this regard see *P. Oldham & S. Hall*, *A European Patent Indicator for Access to Genetic Resources and Benefit-Sharing*, Report to the European Environment Agency EEA/BSS/08/012, ESRC

cases it may not be easy to draw a clear line between "non-commercial" and "commercial" research activities, and therefore providers may be concerned about the potential abuses of this simplified procedure by user States.[26] The possibility of expediting the procedures for obtaining consent has been envisaged also by subparagraph (b) of article 8 in cases of national emergencies "that threaten or damage human, animal or plant health, as determined nationally or internationally".[27]

IV.1 Access to Human Pathogens

The Preamble of the Protocol inter alia affirms as follows: "The parties to this Protocol [. . .] Mindful of the International Health Regulations (2005) of the World Health Organization and the importance of ensuring access to human pathogens for public health preparedness and response purposes." The question is whether such a recognition could open the way to a broad interpretation of article 8(b), and more precisely in the sense of permitting access to human pathogens in cases of "present or imminent emergencies that threaten or damage human, animal or plant health". However, access to human pathogens cannot be grounded on the Protocol because it lies outside its scope of application.[28] First, the Protocol does

---

Centre for Economic and Social Aspects of Genomics (Cesagen), Lancaster University (UK), 87, 88; *P. Oldham, An access and benefit sharing commons? The role of commons/open source licenses in the international regime on access to genetic resources and benefit sharing*, Discussion Paper, ESRC Centre for Economic and Social Aspects of Genomics (Cesagen), 2; *R. Jefferson, Science as social enterprise: the CAMBIA BiOS Initiative*, Innovations, Fall 2006, 13. The Center for the Application of Molecular Biology to International Agriculture (CAMBIA) is an Australian research institute that has adopted an *open licensing* approach to foster the dissemination of biological material.

[26] *Kamau, E.C., B. Fedder, and G. Winter, The Nagoya Protocol on Access to Genetic Resources and Benefit Sharing: What is New and What are the Implications for Provider and User Countries and the Scientific Community*? (December 21, 2010). Law & Development Journal (LEAD), Vol. 6, No. 3, 2010. Available at SSRN: http://ssrn.com/abstract=2178975

[27] Article 8(b) of the Protocol provides that each Party shall:

> pay due regard to cases of present or imminent emergencies that threaten or damage human, animal or plant health, as determined nationally or internationally. Parties may take into consideration the need for expeditious access to genetic resources and expeditious fair and equitable sharing of benefits arising out of the use of such genetic resources, including access to affordable treatments by those in need, especially in developing countries.

[28] See, however, *EU Council Conclusions on Convention on Biodiversity (Nagoya)*, 14 October 2010, Luxembourg, whereby the Council in paragraph 27

not provide a definition of human pathogen. And since the Convention and the Protocol are not concerned with genetic resources of human origin,[29] the expression used could be understood as referring to "non-human genetic resources found in humans".[30] But even in this case there would be incompatibilities with the provisions of the Protocol, which do not seem capable of being extended to human pathogens without overly stretching their meaning. For example, it would be unclear as to how reference to the "country of origin" could be construed given that the pathogen would be present in human beings.

On the other hand, the reference to human pathogens could be explained in light of article 4.2 of the Protocol, further to which "nothing in this Protocol shall prevent the Parties from developing and implementing other relevant international agreements, including other specialized access and benefit-sharing agreements, provided that they are supportive of and do not run counter to the objectives of the Convention and this Protocol". The rules on access to and the utilization of those genetic resources do not seem capable of being stretched so as to fall within the Nagoya Protocol,[31] but they could well be the subject matter of a different specific agreement. At the same time the Protocol should be implemented "in a mutually supportive manner" with the *International Health Regulations* by virtue of article 4.3.

"stresses that this ABS Protocol must not interfere with the work of the relevant international organisations and agreements such as WHO, IPPC and OIE, while keeping pathogens within its scope", in http://www.eu-un.europa.eu/articles/en/article_10202_en.htm. Therefore, it would seem to interpret the reference to *human pathogens* in the Preamble to the Protocol as meaning that they fall within its scope of application.

[29] See article 2 CBD whereby "Genetic resources" are defined as "genetic material of actual or potential value" and "Genetic material" as "any material of plant, animal, microbial or other origin containing functional units of heredity".

[30] "(e.g. HIV, H5N1, virus, malaria parasite)", See Secretariat of the Convention on Biological Diversity, *Access and benefit-sharing in practice: trends in partnerships across sectors*, Montreal, Technical Series No. 38, 2008, 27.

[31] In this sense see World Health Organization – Report of the Open-Ended Working Group of Contracting Parties, *Pandemic Influenza Preparedness: sharing of influenza viruses and access to vaccines and other benefits*, EB 128/4, 12 January 2011, Principle 12, "recognizing that influenza pathogens do not fall within the scope of the Convention on Biological Diversity or the Nagoya Protocol".

V. ACCESS, BENEFIT-SHARING AND PATENT RULES: POSSIBLE INTERFERENCE WITH THE TRIPS AGREEMENT

Where the R&D on the genetic material[32] leads to an invention which is new, involves an inventive step and is capable of industrial application, the user of the genetic resources could decide to apply for a patent. In those cases the Nagoya Protocol could interfere with the TRIPS Agreement.[33] It should be highlighted that the latter exhaustively lists only the substantive requirements for patentability, in other words, the characteristics that the claimed invention must have in order to gain access to patent protection, while it does not contain (unlike the CBE and the UPOV) an exhaustive list of the grounds of invalidity.[34] The TRIPS Agreement does not prevent the Members from introducing new validity requirements for patents, such as the need to comply with access rules foreseen by the Protocol.[35]

TRIPS rules must be coordinated with the ones related to the

---

[32] For an analysis of the issues associated with traditional knowledge see *H. Hullrich*, *Traditional knowledge, biodiversity, benefit-sharing and the patent system: romantics v. economics?*, EUI Working Paper Law No. 2005/07; D.J. *Gervais*, *Traditional Knowledge & Intellectual Property: A TRIPS-Compatible Approach*, in *Michigan State Law Review*, 137 *et seq*., 2005, available at http://ssrn.com/abstract=507302; *G. Van Overwalle*, *Holder and user perspectives in the traditional knowledge debate: a European view*, in *R. McManis* (ed.), *Biodiversity and the Law – Intellectual Property, Biotechnology and Traditional Knowledge*, Earthscan, London, 2007, 354.

[33] With regard to marine genetic resources see *S. Trevisanut* and *A. Bonfanti*, *Intellectual Property Rights Beyond National Jurisdiction: Outlining a Regime for Patenting Products Based on Marine Genetic Resources of the Deep-Sea Bed and High Seas* (June 2011). Available at SSRN: http://ssrn.com/abstract=1861020 or http://dx.doi.org/10.2139/ssrn.1861020.

[34] *R. Romandini*, comment to the Italian Law on Biotechnological Inventions (Legge 22 febbraio 2006, n. 78), in L.C. Ubertazzi, *Commentario breve allee leggi su proprietà intellettuale e concorrenza*, Cedam, 2007, 1388. See *N.P. de Carvalho*, *Requiring Disclosure of the Origin of Plant Genetic Resources and Prior Informed Consent in Patent Applications Without Infringing the TRIPS Agreement: The Problem and the Solution*, in *2 Wash. U.J.L. & Pol'Y* 372, 379–89, 2000.

[35] "[I]t has increasingly become a common practice of nations to condition the granting of patents for inventions using their resources on providing evidence of compliance with national ABS laws". *Ni, Kuei-jung*, *The Incorporation of the CBD Mandate on Access and Benefit-Sharing into TRIPS Regime: An Appraisal of the Appeal of Developing Countries with Rich Genetic Resources. Asian Journal of WTO & International Health Law and Policy*, Vol. 1, No. 2, 2006, 441, available at http://ssrn.com/abstract=1017531.

enforcement of benefit-sharing provisions,[36] otherwise there could be a contrast between the mentioned Treaties.[37] For example, the measures taken by a Party may conflict with domestic legislation on the exercise of intellectual property rights adopted in conformity with the TRIPS Agreement. The Protocol does not govern such situations: while awaiting their possible definition at international level, the Parties would have to identify solutions that are not in contradiction with rules protecting intellectual property rights. In fact, article 4.2 of the Protocol should be implemented "in a mutually supportive manner with other international instruments".

In this framework, it could be useful to think which instruments among those already offered by the TRIPS Agreement could be used by the Parties. More precisely, Member States may introduce further rules regarding possible measures in case the user does not comply with the benefit-sharing method established "on mutually agreed terms".[38] These provisions could be compatible not only with the Protocol, which does not lay down exhaustive rules, but also with the TRIPS Agreement. As a matter of fact, the latter grants Members a degree of flexibility to meet certain social, economic or environmental needs, which may conflict with an unconditional observation of the rules regulating the exercise of exclusive rights. Regarding patents, the relevant provisions are contained in articles 30 and 31 of the TRIPS Agreement.

Subject to the conditions indicated,[39] article 30 of the TRIPS Agreement permits domestic legislation to grant third parties a right to use patented technology for reasons of fundamental public interest such as food and health protection.[40] Among the national emergencies which may warrant

---

[36] See articles 15–18 of the Protocol.

[37] See *P. Stoll, J. Busche & K. Arend* (eds), *WTO – Trade-Related Aspects of Intellectual Property Rights*, The Netherlands, 2009, 512.

[38] It should be noted that in practice "joint ownership of patents by providers and users is thus complex, rare, and expensive, although examples exist", Secretariat of the Convention on Biological Diversity, *Access and benefit-sharing in practice: trends in partnerships across sectors*, Montreal, Technical Series No. 38, 2008, 33.

[39] Article 30 of the TRIPS Agreement: "Members may provide limited exceptions to the exclusive rights conferred by a patent, provided that such exceptions do not unreasonably conflict with a normal exploitation of the patent and do not unreasonably prejudice the legitimate interests of the patent owner, taking account of the legitimate interests of third parties."

[40] *Doha Declaration on the TRIPS Agreement and Public Health*, November 2001, where it is affirmed that the Agreement "can and should be interpreted and implemented in a manner supportive of WTO Members' rights to protect public health and, in particular, to promote access to medicines for all". In this regard see

an exception pursuant to article 30 of the TRIPS Agreement, could be included the situation where "the exercise of those rights and obligations would cause a serious damage or threat to biological diversity" (article 3 *bis*.1 of the Protocol). In this case the third parties would coincide with indigenous and local communities that had granted access to the genetic resources and associated traditional knowledge.[41] This exception could be invoked also to deal with situations that frequently affect developing countries, the main providers of genetic resources.[42] As a matter of fact, the problems related to nutrition and access to essential drugs concern precisely those sectors mainly characterized by R&D activities "on the genetic and/or biochemical composition of genetic resources, including through the application of biotechnology as defined in Article 2 of the Convention".[43]

However, article 30 of the TRIPS Agreement does not seem to allow recognizing rights of use to indigenous and local communities outside cases of national emergencies, such as those involving "a serious damage or threat to biological diversity". The need to ensure an equitable sharing of the benefits arising out of the utilization of the resources does not appear sufficient to warrant an exception to exclusive rights pursuant to article 30. As a matter of fact, there could be a conflict with the prohibition in article 27 of the TRIPS Agreement against discrimination on the basis of the field of technology that the invention belongs to.[44] Further to this

---

F.M. Abott, J. Reichman, The Doha's Round public health legacy: strategies for the production and diffusion of patented medicines under the amended TRIPs provisions, in *Journal of International Economic Law*, Vol. 10, No. 4, 2007, 929 *et seq.*

[41] See articles 5.2 and 5.4 of the Protocol.

[42] *P.K. Yu, The objectives and principles of the TRIPS Agreement*, in *Houston Law Review*, 2009, 995.

[43] Article 2(c) of the Protocol.

[44] Article 27 of the TRIPS Agreement states:

> subject to the provisions of paragraphs 2 and 3, patents shall be available for any inventions, whether products or processes, in all fields of technology, provided that they are new, involve an inventive step and are capable of industrial application. Subject to paragraph 4 of Article 65, paragraph 8 of Article 70 and paragraph 3 of this Article, patents shall be available and patent rights enjoyable without discrimination as to the place of invention, the field of technology and whether products are imported or locally produced.

In this regard see *N.P. De Carvalho, The TRIPS Regime of Patent Rights*, The Netherlands, Kluwer Law International, 2010, 279; *G.B. Dinwoodie, R.C. Dreyfuss, Diversifying without discriminating: complying with the mandates of the TRIPS Agreement*, in *13 Mich. Telecomm. Tech. L. Rev.* 445 (2007), available at http://www.mttlr.org/volthirteen/dinwoodie&dreyfus.pdf; *B. Kahin, Patents and*

provision Members may not exclude from patentability inventions or may not restrict or jeopardize the exercise of rights under a patent by reason of the fact that the invention belongs to given field of technology. From this standpoint also the exceptions under article 30 are subject to the prohibition in article 27.[45] Therefore, the introduction of an exception to exclusive rights aimed at ensuring an equitable sharing of the benefits arising out of the utilization of genetic resources could be in contrast with the prohibition above mentioned. Moreover, such a provision could also breach article 4.1 of the Protocol to the extent that it would mean that the Rio Convention prevailed over the TRIPS Agreement. Matters might be different in a case where the genetic resources and the associated traditional knowledge would be considered as an expression of "cultural heritage".[46]

Moreover, article 31 of the TRIPS Agreement allows one to resort to compulsory licensing in exceptional circumstances. Indeed, the 2001 Doha Declaration on the TRIPS Agreement and Public Health has reiterated Members' powers "to grant compulsory licenses and the freedom to determine the grounds upon which such licenses are granted".[47] In this

---

Diversity in Innovation, in *13 Mich. Telecomm. Tech. L. Rev. 389* (2007), available on http://www.mttlr.org/volthirteen/kahin.pdf.

45 See *Canada – Patent Protection of Pharmaceutical Products*, Report of the Panel adopted on 7 April 2000, WT/DS114/R, of 17 March 2000.

46 See the following part of the Preamble to the Protocol: "further recognizing the unique circumstances where traditional knowledge associated with genetic resources is held in countries, which may be oral, documented or in other forms, reflecting a rich cultural heritage relevant for conservation and sustainable use of biological diversity". See *R.M. Hilty, Rationales for the legal protection of intangible goods and cultural heritage*, Max Planck Institute for Intellectual Property, Competition & Tax Law Research Paper Series No. 09–10 20, and the literature cited therein; *D. Convay-Jones, Safeguarding Hawaiian traditional knowledge and cultural heritage: supporting the right to self-determination and preventing the commodification of culture*, in *Howard Law Journal* 2005, Vol. 48, No. 2, 737.

47 Doha Declaration, paragraph 5(b). As a matter of fact, paragraph 6 envisions a system of compulsory licensing "that would enable any country needing medicines at lower prices than those charged by local patentees to seek assistance from other countries able and willing to produce the drugs for export purposes, without interference from the patentee in either country". Following lengthy negotiations this solution was incorporated into the *Decision of 30 August 2003 on Implementation of Paragraph 6 of the Doha Declaration on the TRIPS Agreement and Public Health*, adopted by the WTO General Council in order to facilitate access to patented medicines by those countries with insufficient or no manufacturing capacity. It should become final following an amendment to the TRIPS Agreement currently under discussion, known as article 31bis (see WTO General Council, *Proposal for a Decision on an Amendment to the TRIPS Agreement*, doc. IP/C/41, 6 December 2005). See *J.H.* Reichman, *Compulsory licensing of patented*

context the need to guarantee the equitable sharing of the benefits arising out of the utilization of genetic resources could warrant recourse to that tool.[48] More precisely, the indigenous or local communities' right to use the patent could be recognized within the framework of compulsory licenses dictated by reasons of public interest pursuant to article 31(b) of the TRIPS Agreement. And thus the following preconditions would have to be met: i) the access to the genetic resources led to an invention that was patented; ii) there is a national emergency or other situation of "extreme urgency" in the provider country under article 31(b) or the need to assure the development of a production sector of vital importance under article 8 of the TRIPS Agreement (in particular, the equitable sharing of benefits and the conservation of biodiversity in light of the Nagoya Protocol). iii) The conditions of benefit-sharing established "on mutually agreed terms" have not been respected. As a matter of fact, it seems that it would be possible to resort to the instrument of compulsory licenses only if the equitable sharing of the benefits could not be guaranteed on mutually agreed terms. And within this context, the Parties should adopt all the measures necessary to encourage the definition of an agreement.[49]

By allowing access to and utilization of the resources, indigenous or local communities provide the material on which the R&D will be carried out

---

pharmaceutical inventions: evaluating the options, 248 and 249, in http://scholarship.law.duke.edu/cgi/viewcontent.cgi?article=2747&context =faculty_scholarship.

[48] On this point see also *G. Ghidini*, *Equitable Sharing of Benefits from Biodiversity-Based Innovation: Some Reflections under the Shadow of a Neem Tree*, in *J.H. Reichman* and *K. Maskus*, *International Public Goods and Transfer of Technology under a Globalized Intellectual Property Regime*, Cambridge, 2005, 701. Resorting to compulsory licensing could be facilitated on a practical level by setting up competent national authorities, whose designation is required by article 13.2 of the Protocol. Indeed, on the basis of that same article "competent national authorities shall, in accordance with applicable national legislative, administrative or policy measures, be responsible for granting access or, as applicable, issuing written evidence that access requirements have been met and be responsible for advising on applicable procedures and requirements for obtaining prior informed consent and entering into mutually agreed terms".

[49] For example, through forms of "joint ownership of relevant intellectual property rights", see the Annex on "Monetary and Non-Monetary Benefits", subparagraph j) (monetary benefits) and q) (non-monetary benefits). On so-called *collective ownership of IP rights* in the TRIPS Agreement see *D. Gervais*, *Traditional knowledge and intellectual property: a TRIPS compatible approach*, in *Michigan State Law Review*, 2005, 149. In general on this topic see *G. Ghidini*, *Equitable Sharing of Benefits from Biodiversity-Based Innovation: Some Reflections under the Shadow of a Neem Tree*, in *J.H. Reichman* and *K. Maskus*, *International Public Goods and Transfer of Technology under a Globalized Intellectual Property Regime*, Cambridge, 2005, 697.

on and which could lead to an invention. Indeed, considering the access to the resources *previously* granted and in the light of the remunerative function served by compulsory licenses, the *subsequent* payment of adequate remuneration pursuant to article 31(h) would not seem to be necessary. Compulsory licenses *at zero royalty rates* are not unheard of in the praxis: for example, they have been granted to limit or correct anti-competitive behaviors.[50] Moreover, the use of *royalty free licenses* has occurred also when agreement has been reached on how to share the benefits.[51]

VI. ARE COMPULSORY LICENSES THE PROPER MEANS TO ENSURE BENEFIT-SHARING?

The remedy envisaged by article 31 of the TRIPS Agreement does not appear to be the best means through which the benefit sharing between the parties involved is guaranteed, that is the Party that grants access and the patentee.[52] In particular, it does not seem that they would obtain the same benefits that could stem from mutual agreement as to the terms governing the exploitation of resources.

First, it is necessary to consider that article 65 of the TRIPS Agreement requires developing countries to meet rather tight deadlines in implementing

---

[50] In particular, the reference is to the US practice where compulsory licensing is a tool that has often been used to remedy anticompetitive behavior. See *J. Love, Remuneration guidelines for non-voluntary use of a patent on medical technologies*, WHO/TCM/2005.1, available at http://www.who.int/medicines/areas /technical_cooperation/WHOTCM2005.1_OMS.pdf, 18 and 29.

[51] Consider for example the partnership between *Diversa Corporation, Kenya Wildlife Service (KWS)* and the *International Centre of Insect Physiology and Ecology (ICIPE)* in Kenya:

> the company retains intellectual property rights over any product that it develops, provided that ICIPE and KWS have the option of a royalty free license that allows them to research, develop and otherwise make use of any products or inventions developed from the material supplied within the jurisdiction of the Republic of Kenya (but not beyond this jurisdiction) (Case study 2; Lettington, 2003).

Secretariat of the Convention on Biological Diversity, *Access and benefit-sharing in practice: trends in partnerships across sectors*, Montreal, Technical Series No. 38, 2008, 33.

[52] In these terms but with reference to access to essential drugs, see *G. Ghidini, Developing countries' access to patented essential drugs. Are compulsory licenses the optimal means?*, in *Estudios sobre propiedad industrial e intelectual y derecho de the competencia. Colleccion de trabajos en homenaje a Alberto Bercovitz Rodriguez*, Barcelona, 2005.

the provisions of the Agreement,[53] although for "least developed countries" (hereinafter "LDCs") the 2001 Doha Declaration has extended to 2016 the deadline for implementing the provisions regarding patents on pharmaceutical products.[54] As stressed in the literature, these are very short deadlines that do not take into account the specific features of the economic and legal systems of each country. In fact, adapting domestic law to the model enshrined in the TRIPS Agreement could well require periods of time that vary depending on the different local situations.[55] The

---

[53] Article 65 of the TRIPS Agreement, "Transitional Arrangements":

1. Subject to the provisions of paragraphs 2, 3 and 4, no Member shall be obliged to apply the provisions of this Agreement before the expiry of a general period of one year following the date of entry into force of the WTO Agreement.
2. A developing country Member is entitled to delay for a further period of four years the date of application, as defined in paragraph 1, of the provisions of this Agreement other than Articles 3, 4 and 5.
3. Any other Member which is in the process of transformation from a centrally-planned into a market, free enterprise economy and which is undertaking structural reform of its intellectual property system and facing special problems in the preparation and implementation of intellectual property laws and regulations, may also benefit from a period of delay as foreseen in paragraph 2.
4. To the extent that a developing country Member is obliged by this Agreement to extend product patent protection to areas of technology not so protectable in its territory on the general date of application of this Agreement for that Member, as defined in paragraph 2, it may delay the application of the provisions on product patents of Section 5 of Part II to such areas of technology for an additional period of five years.
5. A Member availing itself of a transitional period under paragraphs 1, 2, 3 or 4 shall ensure that any changes in its laws, regulations and practice made during that period do not result in a lesser degree of consistency with the provisions of this Agreement.

[54] Article 66 of the TRIPS Agreement, "Least-Developed Country Members":

1. In view of the special needs and requirements of least-developed country Members, their economic, financial and administrative constraints, and their need for flexibility to create a viable technological base, such Members shall not be required to apply the provisions of this Agreement, other than Articles 3, 4 and 5, for a period of 10 years from the date of application as defined under paragraph 1 of Article 65. The Council for TRIPS shall, upon duly motivated request by a least-developed country Member, accord extensions of this period.
2. Developed country Members shall provide incentives to enterprises and institutions in their territories for the purpose of promoting and encouraging technology transfer to least-developed country Members in order to enable them to create a sound and viable technological base.

[55] See *G. Ghidini, Innovation, Competition and Consumer Welfare in Intellectual Property Law*, Edward Elgar, Cheltenham, 2010, 252 *et seq.*

use of compulsory licenses could thus turn out to be *anachronistic* having regard to the state of implementation of the TRIPS Agreement in some LCDs, who are the main providers of genetic resources.[56] These countries could thus prefer alternative forms of benefit sharing, appropriate to assure the effective transfer of technologies and scientific knowledge.[57]

Secondly, compulsory licenses are not an advantageous tool for patentees either: they deprive the patentee of the possibility of choosing the entities to establish commercial relations with and they bind her/him to predetermined terms and conditions that do not reflect specific needs that from time to time may arise.[58] For example, consider the compulsory licenses that are granted at so-called *zero royalties rates*: the Parties concerned may well prefer solutions that allow them to share the benefits over a short period, using so-called *up-front payments*. In particular there are models of sharing that do not necessarily imply a limitation of exclusive rights: for example, the parties could sign cooperation agreements for the undertaking of scientific research activities in the country providing the resources[59]. This option is contemplated in the Protocol, both in article 23 regarding the transfer of technology and in the Annex setting out a range of "non-monetary benefits".

---

[56] "A country issuing a compulsory license avoids the payment of royalties to the patent holder; but issuing a compulsory license will only be cost-effective if that country is able to either buy or produce the drugs at a lower cost", see *B.M. Salama & D. Benoliel, Towards an Intellectual Property Bargaining Theory: The Post-WTO Era*, in *University of Pennsylvania Journal of International Economic Law*, Vol. 32, No. 1, p. 265, 2010, paragraph 2.2.2.1., available at http://ssrn.com/abstract=1353286. See also *W.A. Kaplan & R. Laing, Local Production: Industrial Policy and Access To Medicines* 1 *(World Bank, HNP Discussion Papers, 2005)*, cited therein.

[57] *N.P. De Carvalho, The TRIPS Regime of Patent Rights*, Kluwer Law International, The Netherlands 2010, 281 and 282.

[58] "[T]he imposition of a compulsory license (or government use) 'reduces' the patentee's position to little more than that of a simple rentier", see *G. Ghidini, Innovation, Competition and Consumer Welfare in Intellectual Property Law*, Edward Elgar, Cheltenham, 2010, 256.

[59] See section 1.2(b) of the Annex to the Protocol, giving as an example of a non-monetary benefit "collaboration, cooperation and contribution in scientific research and development programmes, particularly biotechnological research activities, where possible in the Party providing genetic resources".

VII. TRANSFER OF TECHNOLOGY: A REAPPRAISAL OF THE LOCAL WORKING REQUIREMENT

The Nagoya Protocol seeks to promote the spread of knowledge deriving from scientific research as advocated in articles 15, 16, 18 and 19 of the Rio Convention. Article 23 of the Protocol obliges the Parties to cooperate in R&D programs, including in the biotechnological sector, as a means to achieve the transfer of technology from so-called industrialized countries to developing ones and especially to the LCDs. Moreover, it provides that "where possible and appropriate, such collaborative activities shall take place in and with a Party or the Parties providing genetic resources", in other words, the country or countries of origin of such resources or those that have acquired the genetic resources in accordance with the Convention. The reference to the place where those activities shall be undertaken would seem to hark back to the so-called *local working requirement*, originally included in the 1883 Paris Convention[60] but subsequently abandoned by the TRIPS Agreement.[61] It refers "to the condition that the patentee must manufacture the patented product, or apply the patented process, within the patent granting country".[62] Various authors on more than one occasion have stressed that this provision could facilitate transfer of technology from industrialized countries to developing ones, arguing that it would be compatible with the TRIPS Agreement *de jure condendo*. More precisely, the reintroduction of the local working requirement would satisfy systemic needs consistent with the objectives and principles expressed in articles 7 and 8 of the TRIPS Agreement.[63]

---

[60] Article 5 of the 1883 *Paris Convention*:

> (1) The importation by patentee into the country where the patent has been granted of articles manufactured in any of the States of the Union shall not entail forfeiture of the patent.
> (2) Nevertheless, the patentee shall remain under the obligation to exploit his patent in accordance with the laws of the country into which he introduces the patented articles.".

[61] See article 27.1 of the TRIPS Agreement, in the part providing that "patents shall be available and patent rights enjoyable without discrimination as to the place of invention".

[62] *G. Van Overwalle, Regulating protection, preservation and technology transfer of biodiversity-based drugs. Patents, contracts and local working requirements under the microscope*, in *H. Ullrich* and *I. Govaere, Intellectual Property, Public Policy, and International Trade*, Brussels, *College d'Europe studies*, P.I.E. – Peter Lang, 2007, 113.

[63] On the local working requirement and for criticism on its abandonment in relations between industrialized countries and least developed countries, see *G.*

In this context, further support could come from a combined reading of articles 16.2 and 16.5 of the Rio Convention, article 23 of the Protocol and article 7 of the TRIPS Agreement[64]. Article 16 of the Convention concerns access to and the transfer of technology, with paragraphs 2 and 5 addressing situations in which the technology is subject to patents and other intellectual property rights: on the one hand, access and transfer should be on terms consistent "with the adequate and effective protection of Intellectual Property Rights" while, on the other hand, the Contracting Parties must cooperate at national and international level to ensure that "such rights are supportive of and do not run counter to its objectives". At the same time, article 7 of the TRIPS Agreement recognizes that the protection of intellectual property rights should contribute to the promotion of the transfer of technology "in a manner conducive to social and economic welfare and to a balance of rights and obligations". In this context, article 23 of the Protocol seems to suggest a possible tool through which the various interests at stake could be balanced, and it would allow one to achieve a result similar to that which could be attained through the local working requirement. As a matter of fact, the main difference between the latter solution and the one suggested in the Protocol stays only in the temporal moment it refers. More precisely, article 23 of the Protocol concerns R&D activities which, eventually, may lead to the granting of a patent on the invention carried out. "Local working requirement" refers to the stage of the subsequent exploitation of a patent. In any case, the chances that collaborative activities take place in the country of origin of the resources is subject to the mutual agreement of the Parties,[65] with the risk that the aims pursued by the provision will remain solely theoretical; for this

---

Ghidini, On TRIPS' Impact on "Least Developed Countries": A Tale of Double Standards?, in *Queen Mary Journal of Intellectual Property*, 2011, forthcoming, and the literature cited therein. The author points out that "in this context, the abandonment of the requirement to work the patent locally curtails the spill-over of advanced technological skills, and hence the sharing by least developed countries of both the patented technologies and the know-how that typically accompanies them". See also *M. Halewood, Regulating patent holders: local working requirements and compulsory licenses at International Law*, in 35 *Osgoode Hall Law Journal*, 1997, 245 *et seq.*

[64] Article 7 of the TRIPS Agreement: "The protection and enforcement of intellectual property rights should contribute to the promotion of technological innovation and to the transfer and dissemination of technology, to the mutual advantage of producers and users of technological knowledge and in a manner conducive to social and economic welfare, and to a balance of rights and obligations.".

[65] The provision does however include the qualification "where possible and appropriate".

reason, consideration should be given to the opportunity of reintroducing the local working requirement into the TRIPS Agreement.

VIII. THE RELATIONSHIP BETWEEN THE RIO CONVENTION AND THE TRIPS AGREEMENT IN THE LIGHT OF THE NAGOYA PROTOCOL

The entry into force of the Protocol raises the question of how the relationship between the Rio Convention and the TRIPS Agreement could evolve and whether it might be possible to extend TRIPS normative boundaries to cover also the subject of biodiversity.[66] As a matter of fact, paragraph 19 of the Doha Declaration stresses the importance of clearly defining the relationship between the TRIPS Agreement and Convention.[67] The main positions expressed by the literature can be summarized as follows:

i) there is a conflict between the two instruments, and in particular it is linked to the absence within the TRIPS Agreement of provisions on prior informed consent and benefit-sharing. In this framework, this opinion suggests to consistently amend the TRIPS itself;[68]

---

[66] *Kuei-jung Ni, The incorporation of the CBD mandate on access and benefit-sharing into TRIPS regime: an appraisal of the appeal of developing countries with rich genetic resources*, in *Asian Journal of WTO & International Health Law and Policy*, Vol. 1, No. 2, September 2006, 433 *et seq*., available at http://ssrn.com/abstract=1017531. With special reference to the protection of traditional knowledge see amongst many *D. Gervais, Traditional knowledge and intellectual property: a TRIPS compatible approach*, in *Michigan State Law Review*, 2005, 161.

[67] Paragraph 19 of the Doha Declaration:

> We instruct the Council for TRIPS, in pursuing its work programme including under the review of Article 27.3(b), the review of the implementation of the TRIPS Agreement under Article 71.1 and the work foreseen pursuant to paragraph 12 of this declaration, to examine, inter alia, the relationship between the TRIPS Agreement and the Convention on Biological Diversity, the protection of traditional knowledge and folklore, and other relevant new developments raised by members pursuant to Article 71.1. In undertaking this work, the TRIPS Council shall be guided by the objectives and principles set out in Articles 7 and 8 of the TRIPS Agreement and shall take fully into account the development dimension,

11 November 2001, WT/MIN(01)/DEC/1, available at http://www.wto.org/english/thewto_e/minist_e/min01_e/mindecl_e.htm.

[68] On the advantages of introducing a mandatory obligation on the patent applicant as part of the norms of disclosure see *Joseph, R.K., International Regime on Access and Benefit Sharing: Where are We Now?* July 5, 2010), in *Asian*

ii) there is no conflict and both the TRIPS Agreement and the Convention can be "implemented in a mutually supportive manner". This view is based on the assumption that the two treaties cover different matters and pursue different aims;
iii) there is a possible conflict between the TRIPS Agreement and the Convention, and it should be solved so that the two instruments can be "implemented in a mutually supportive manner".[69]

The debate regarding the interference between the TRIPS Agreement and the Rio Convention could be integrated by an analysis of article 4 of the Protocol concerning the relationship with other international agreements. First, the opening sentence of article 4.1 replicates article 22.1 of the Convention: the provisions of the Protocol do not affect the rights and obligations deriving from any other international agreement except where the exercise of those rights and obligations would cause a serious damage or threat to biological diversity.[70] The second sentence of article 4.1 provides that the paragraph is not intended to create a hierarchy between this

---

Biotechnology and Development Review, Vol. 12, No. 3, 82, 2010. See also the position of Perù, *L. Briceño Moraia, Risorse genetiche, traditional knowledge e brevettabilità dell'invenzione. Le richieste di tutela del Perù*, in *Dir. Comm. Int.*, 3–4, 2006, 863 *et seq*.

[69] On the relationship between the Convention on Biological Diversity and the TRIPS Agreement, see *amplius D. Gervais*, *The TRIPS Agreement: Drafting History and Analysis*, London, Thomson Reuters, 2008 and the literature cited therein. See also *M.B. Rao, M. Guru, Biotechnology, IPRs and Biodiversity*, Pearson, Dorling Kindersley, 2007, 82 *et seq*.; *M.I. Jeffery QC., Intellectual property rights and biodiversity conservation: reconciling the incompatibilities of the TRIPS Agreement and the Convention on Biological Diversity*, in *B. Ong* (ed.), *Intellectual Property and Biological Resources*, Marshall Cavendish Academic, 2005, 185 *et seq*.; Note by the Secretariat, *The relationship between the TRIPS Agreement and the Convention on biological diversity: summary of issues raised and points made*, IP/C/W/368, 8 August 2002; *Communication by the European Communities and their member States on the relationship between the Convention on Biological Diversity and the TRIPS Agreement*, 3 April 2001.

[70] Analogously to article 22.1 CBD, article 4.1 of the Protocol provides as follows:

> The provision of this Protocol shall not affect the right and obligations of any Party deriving from any existing International agreement, except where the exercise of those rights and obligations would cause a serious damage or threat to biological diversity. This paragraph is not intended to create a hierarchy between this Protocol and other international instruments.". Article 22.2 of the Convention further provides that "Contracting Parties shall implement this Convention with respect to the marine environment consistently with the rights and obligations of States under the law of the Sea.

Protocol and other international instruments. At the same time, article 4.2 provides that the Parties may develop and implement other relevant international agreements provided that they do not run counter to the objectives of the Convention and the Protocol.[71] Reference is also made to other possible specialized agreements concerning genetic resources. And this provision should be coordinated with article 4.4 recognizing the general principle whereby specialized rules *ratione materiae* derogate from general rules.[72] In addition, article 4.3 states that:

> this Protocol shall be implemented in a mutually supportive manner with other international instruments relevant to this Protocol. Due regard should be paid to useful and relevant ongoing work [. . .], provided that they are supportive of and do not run counter to the objectives of the Convention and this Protocol.[73]

In this framework, the Protocol seems to offer an opportunity for adhering to the position mentioned in subparagraph iii) above on the relationship between the Rio Convention and the TRIPS Agreement. More precisely, even though due regard should be given to relevant ongoing work at international level, instead of focusing only on a possible reform of the TRIPS Agreement member States should first try to achieve those objectives at a national level, implementing the rules stemming from different international instruments in a "mutually supportive manner".

---

[71] Article 4.2 provides as follows: "Nothing in this Protocol shall prevent the Parties from developing and implementing other relevant International agreements, including other specialized access and benefit-sharing agreements, provided that they are supportive of and do not run counter to the objectives of the Convention and this Protocol."

[72] Article 4.4 affirms that:

> This Protocol is the instrument for the implementation of the access and benefit-sharing provisions of the Convention. Where a specialized International access and benefit-sharing instrument applies that is consistent with, and does not run counter to the objectives of the Convention and this Protocol, this Protocol does not apply for the party or Parties to the specialized instrument in respect of the specific genetic resource covered by and for the purpose of the specialized instrument.

[73] One could think of the efforts made by the WTO to review the TRIPS Agreement in line with the aims expressed in the Doha Declaration.

IX. CONCLUSIONS

The Nagoya Protocol aims to promote a mechanism for the dissemination of technical knowledge based on an access-sharing tradeoff whose terms are to be established on a "mutually agreed" basis. In order to ensure the effectiveness of that system, first and foremost it is necessary to regulate possible conflicts between the rules set forth in the Rio Convention and the Protocol and those contained in the TRIPS Agreement. In fact, neither the Protocol nor the TRIPS Agreement include exhaustive provisions in this regard. In particular, the two treaties may interfere in case one Party does not comply with the provisions regarding sharing of the benefits arising from the utilization of genetic resources. Analyzing the boundaries of the TRIPS Agreement, it would seem possible to resort to compulsory licensing under article 31. Nonetheless, this instrument does not seem to guarantee an effective balance between the different interests at stake. Instead, the Protocol suggests a possible different approach, encouraging Parties to mutually agree on a different stage. More precisely, collaborative activities could take place in the country of origin of the genetic resources, as advocated by article 23 of the Protocol.[74] This provision is not binding; in any case, it evokes the local working requirement, which appears to be coherent with the aims and principles set out in article 7 and 8 of the TRIPS Agreement and in the 2001 Doha Convention. *De jure condendo*, the reintroduction of the local working requirement within the TRIPS Agreement itself could bring to an effective balance between the relevant interests, and in a way consistent with the principle whereby the Protocol and Convention "shall be implemented in a mutually supportive manner". Otherwise, in the absence of changes to the framework governing intellectual property rights, the provision contained in the Protocol risks to remain devoid of any practical value.

---

[74] Through mutually agreed terms, the Parties could thus provide that "in the case of technology subject to patents and other intellectual property rights, such access and transfer [. . .] shall take place in and with a Party or the Parties providing genetic resources".

9. The illusion of TRIPS Agreement to promote creativity and innovation in developing countries: Case study on Kenya

James Otieno Odek

INTRODUCTION

International trade increasingly involves a diverse array of products in which ideas and knowledge play a part. The products range from high-technology products such as new medicines and computer processors, to creative material like films and music, to low-technology products such as brand names and designs.[1] The 21st century has unveiled unparalleled growth in knowledge-based products with unique human resource didactic and pedagogy skills required for countries to be competitive in their trade relations. These trends observed in national economic growth have one thing in common: they are fuelled by the creativity and inventiveness of mankind. The seed and gem of these remarkable trends is the human intellect – the knowledge ensconced in the human mind – intellectual property (IP). IP law makes property out of knowledge. Any country that does not harness and improve its knowledge base to leverage its creativity and innovation for socio-economic development and trade relations will be left behind.[2] Knowledge is key

[1] Antara Dutta & Siddharth Sharma, "Intellectual Property Rights and Innovation in Developing Countries: Evidence from India" World Bank, 2008, at p 2.

[2] Scientific and technical knowledge is the knowledge that leads to innovation. To be termed scientific, a method of inquiry must be based on gathering observable, empirical, logical and measurable evidence subject to specific principles of reasoning. Scientific knowledge consists of collection of data through observation and experimentation and formulation of testing hypothesis. It is this scientific and technical knowledge that countries should acquire and nurture for creativity, inventiveness and innovation.

to leveraging innovation, competitiveness and economic and political power.[3]

At the multilateral level, issues of innovation and creativity are part of IP rights whose guiding principles are in the WTO TRIPS Agreement.

The TRIPS Agreement envisages that the protection and enforcement of IP rights should contribute to the promotion of technological innovation and to the transfer and dissemination of technology.[4] In formulating their national laws and regulations, countries may adopt measures necessary to promote sectors of vital importance to their socio-economic and technological development.[5] The Agreement further stipulates that developed country Members shall provide incentives to enterprises and institutions in their territories for the purpose of promoting and encouraging technology transfer to least-developed country (LDC) Members in order to enable them to create a sound and viable technological base.[6] Developed country Members shall provide on request technical and financial cooperation in favour of developing countries and LDC Members. It is argued that the benefits of the TRIPS Agreement lie in full implementation. So long as developed, developing and least-developed countries do not all implement the provisions of TRIPS; no tangible benefit should be expected from the Agreement. The global politicization of TRIPS negotiations is a hindrance to creativity and innovation in developing countries.

The argument in this chapter is that the provisions of the TRIPS Agreement are an illusion that cannot spur technology transfer, creativity and innovation in developing and least developed countries. This argument is premised on the reality that IP laws are one of the means through which governments manage ownership, availability and use of ideas and technologies and the distribution of profits they generate.[7] IP laws have a bearing on a range of critical and often competing areas of public policy,

---

[3] Knowledge is the expertise and skills acquired by a person through experience or education. It includes the theoretical understanding of a subject and what is known in the particular field. It encompasses awareness or familiarity of a fact or situation. It is the confident understanding of a subject with the ability to use it for a specific purpose. Knowledge is the sum of what has been perceived, discovered or learned. When added to the power of reasoning, knowledge is esoteric and metaphysical. Plato stated that in order to count as knowledge, a statement must be justified, true and believed.

[4] Article 7 of the TRIPS Agreement.

[5] Article 8 of the TRIPS Agreement.

[6] Article 66 (2) of the TRIPS Agreement.

[7] Carolyn Deere, The Implementation Games – The TRIPS Agreement and the Global Politics of Intellectual Property Reform in Developing Countries, Oxford University Press, New York 2009 at p 5.

from industrial and health to cultural, agricultural and educational policy. IP laws can impact on international competitiveness, the pace and focus of innovation and affordable access to new technologies, knowledge and creative works.

In order to discuss the issues identified above, this chapter is divided into two parts. Part One is a conceptual discourse on the basic framework underpinning the TRIPS Agreement. The part explores the multilateralization of IP principles and standards and emphasizes the relationship between the TRIPS Agreement and promotion of creativity and innovation. Part Two is a case study on Kenya's national innovation system; it underscores the need for a coordinated national innovation system and strategy in promoting creativity and innovation.

1. MULTILATERALIZATION OF INTELLECTUAL PROPERTY STANDARDS IN TRIPS AGREEMENT

The TRIPS Agreement recognizes the underlying public policy objectives of national systems for the protection of IP, including developmental and technological objectives. Recognition is also given to the special needs of the least-developed country members in respect of maximum flexibility in the domestic implementation of laws and regulations in order to enable them to create a sound and viable technological base.[8]

Prior to the coming into effect of TRIPS, national governments had policy space and various flexibilities relating to the scope and coverage of IP within their national jurisdictions. The advent of TRIPS saw the emergence of global minimum standards on IP. The TRIPS Agreement reflects the movement and imposition of IP standards from developed to developing countries. It embodies the transplant of developed country IP norms to developing and least-developed countries. Prior to TRIPS, most existing international treaties allowed countries a national discretion to determine their own IP standards. TRIPS introduced substantive minimum standards that hitherto did not exist, for example, TRIPS specifies that all countries must expand the scope of copyright protection to software and original data compilations (data bases) and to provide rental rights for sound recordings, film and computer programs.[9] TRIPS requires the protection of software as literary works but is silent on matters regarding the permissibility of reverse engineering of software and activities undertaken

[8] Preamble to the TRIPS Agreement.
[9] Article 11 of the TRIPS Agreement.

to make different software interoperable. From a development perspective, reverse engineering can be a useful way to improve innovation and competition in the software industry.[10]

Multilateralization of IP under the TRIPS Agreement is viewed as a milestone in norm setting and standards in IP protection. The TRIPS Agreement incorporates the basic IP principles embodied in the Paris and Berne Conventions.[11] During TRIPS negotiations, industry lobbyists persuaded their governments to wage protracted campaigns against developing countries that did not wholly embrace the standards incorporated in TRIPS. With hindsight, TRIPS represents a victory for multinational corporations in their pursuit of stringent IP enforcement mechanisms.[12] Developing countries resisted incorporation of IP into the WTO system arguing that TRIPS would consolidate corporate monopolies over the ownership of ideas and exacerbate the north-south technology gap. It was argued that stronger IP rights would harm their developmental prospects and that developing countries were ill equipped to harness any purported benefits that might inure from the TRIPS Agreement.

In the area of patents, TRIPS provides a minimum 20-year protection period.[13] The Agreement espoused a detailed scope of patent protection including a requirement that patents be available in all fields of technology and processes without discrimination.[14] TRIPS requires national patent laws to confer on patent holders exclusive rights for product and process

---

[10] Carolyn Deere, The Implementation Games – The TRIPS Agreement and the Global Politics of Intellectual Property Reform in Developing Countries, Oxford University Press, New York 2009 at p 92.

[11] Article 2 of the TRIPS Agreement. Paris Convention for the Protection of Industrial Property (1967); and the Berne Convention for the Protection of Literary and Artistic Works (1971).

[12] Facing cuts to their profits margins, foreign export markets and also domestic market share, US industries complained that competitors were riding on their R&D investments. They called on the US Government to help halt imitation and reverse engineering abroad. Like-minded leaders of major US corporations mobilized to consolidate a US agenda for a trade-based conception of IP rights and to integrate IP into the international trade policies. Key actors included the International Intellectual Property Alliance, the Pharmaceutical Manufacturers Association, the Chemical Manufacturers Association, the National Agricultural Chemicals Association, the Motor Equipment Manufacturers Associations, the International Anti-Counterfeiting Coalition and the Semiconductor Industry Association. See Carolyn Deere, The Implementation Games – The TRIPS Agreement and the Global Politics of Intellectual Property Reform in Developing Countries, Oxford University Press, New York 2009 at pp 46–7.

[13] Article 33 of the TRIPS Agreement.

[14] Article 27 of the TRIPS Agreement.

patents. Governments are to provide negative rights to prohibit certain acts from being undertaken without the owner's consent. TRIPS requires governments to ensure that their laws provide for enforcement of IP rights and to make available procedures to ensure that private IP right holders can take effective action against IP infringement. Countries are required to establish enforcement procedures that are fair, transparent and expeditious.[15] TRIPS also calls on governments to intervene directly to help enforce the private rights of IP holders including through border measures. However, it must be noted that TRIPS does not impose an obligation to establish a distinct judicial system to enforce IP rights. Further, many of the key terms in the Agreement such as "effective action", "expeditious remedies" or "adequate remuneration" have not been defined. This ambiguity combined with Article 1 enables Members to implement TRIPS in accordance with their own legal system and practice and leaves countries with room for discretion in the area of enforcement.[16]

With regards to IP administration, WTO Members are to establish a special industrial property service and a central office for administration of patents, utility models, industrial designs and trademarks. For most developing and least-developed countries, putting these legal reforms into action requires commitment of new financial resources, increased managerial, technical and legal expertise as well as improved organizational capacity, infrastructure and management procedure.[17] The envisaged adjustment costs are not provided for in TRIPS and each individual country is expected to shoulder the burden of these costs. To developing and least-developed countries, such adjustment costs would compete with other priorities including health, education and food security needs of the country.

More than a decade after the coming into effect of the TRIPS Agreement, most developing countries (particularly in Africa) have yet to realize an increase in technology transfer through licensing or a spur in innovative and creative activity within their borders. It is noteworthy that TRIPS does not harness and leverage resources for financing and building relevant institutional government agencies in developing countries for IP administration. Nor does it mobilize and harness resources needed to develop relevant legal expertise and to shoulder the opportunity cost of developing and least-developed countries employing scarce human resource capital to administer IP rules. TRIPS does not address the social,

---

15 Article 41 of the TRIPS Agreement.

16 Carolyn Deere, The Implementation Games – The TRIS Agreement and the Global Politics of Intellectual Property Reform in Developing Countries, Oxford University Press, New York 2009 at p 95.

17 Ibid, at pp 67–8.

institutional, administrative and adjustment costs required for implementing the Agreement.

From the perspective of developing African countries, this chapter argues that the TRIPS Agreement is an illusion and a failed promise to spur technology transfer, creativity and innovation in developing and least-developed countries. This argument is premised on the following observations:

(i) In most developing and least-developed countries, especially the African states, the IP laws and principles applicable have no local cultural or legal roots. The implication is that the IP legal regime has no synergy with indigenous or local production systems and supply chain management. In most of the African countries, western conceptions of privately held IPRs reflect pre-colonial commercial legal arrangements and any post-colonial IP arrangement is a feature of the colonial administration and production patterns. In Africa, the first encounter with IP laws was through the colonial master of either Britain or France and the colonial powers laid the foundations for an enduring influence on the legal development on how IP was perceived and understood. For example, in 1911, the UK transplanted its copyright law throughout its empire including East Africa and Nigeria. The UK 1949 Patent Law was likewise transplanted to the colonies. The UK Trade Marks Act was transplanted to the colonies. France also applied its own IP laws to its colonies in Africa and until 1962, the French National Institute for Intellectual Property (INPI) served as the central IP authority for French colonial Africa.

    Across Africa, colonial IP laws embodied concepts alien to the many traditional and indigenous approaches to the stewardship of ideas, knowledge and innovation and did little to incorporate them. The colonial administrators did not have much regard to the traditional knowledge systems of the colonies because such systems did not serve the commercial interest of the colonial power. The colonial IP law was not inclined to build innovation and technological capacity in the colonies but to set up IP registration systems to serve colonial commercial interest. The IP administration was not geared towards building an IP culture or developing IP expertise. For example, in francophone Africa, France provided the legal experts and expertise from the metropole while in anglophone Africa, the emphasis was on socializing the legal profession to create an English legal culture and this practice rarely extended to IP which was generally administered from London.

In the TRIPS framework, the implication of colonial IP system is that developing countries and Africa in particular have limited IP expertise to appreciate technical discussions and analytical implication of the IP normative framework. Most African and developing country delegations are comprised of generalist officials from national trade ministries or Permanent Missions in Geneva rather than IP specialists. The negotiators lack IP culture and finesse and the legal mastery of the technical details and implications necessary to engage substantively in IP discussions. Negotiation fatigue is a common feature for African delegations.[18] The root cause of this state of affairs is the colonial background to IP administration and absence of an IP culture. Example of ramifications of this state of affairs is in the field of traditional knowledge and genetic resources. The broader use of traditional knowledge and genetic resources raises the prospects that they may play an important role in driving growth in developing countries. The main issue is how this prospect might be realized. The effectiveness of IPRs in this regard depends on local capabilities to engage in market production and exchange and negotiate and establish the right legal infrastructure and enforcement.[19] This capability is lacking in most developing countries.

(ii) The normative framework of the TRIPS Agreement reflects globalization and politicization of TRIPS negotiations and most provisions in the Agreement are tilted towards appropriation of knowledge rather than transfer and diffusion of technology. TRIPS specifically recognizes that IP rights are private rights and there is no enforceable obligation to transfer and diffuse technology.

(iii) Ideational power as a factor in global IP discourse is weak among developing and least-developed countries and the consequence is that during TRIPS negotiations, no convincing argument is made to address the *sine qua non* for creativity and innovation which is the identification and strengthening of the national innovation systems in developing and least-developed countries.

(iv) Technology transfer and innovation provisions in TRIPS Agreement are not enforceable but are best-endeavour clauses. Endeavour provisions do not facilitate creativity and innovation.

---

18 Ibid, at p55.

19 Emmanuel Hassan, Ohid Yaqub, Stephanie Diepeveen, "Intellectual Property and Developing Countries – A Review of Literature", (2010) RAND EUROPE at www.rand.org at p xvi.

(v) The institutional framework of the TRIPS Agreement i.e. the TRIPS Council, has proved ineffective in norm creation as relates to issues germane to developing countries. Experience shows that normative issues that are dear to developing and least-developed countries have not seen the light of day under TRIPS Council. The debate surrounding review of Article 27 (3) of the TRIPS Agreement is a case in point. Likewise, the stall in discourse on extension of geographical indication protection beyond wines and spirits is another example.

(vi) TRIPS does not prohibit countries from bilaterally or regionally raising IP standards. The result has been that developing and least-developed countries have been boxed into accepting TRIPS-plus obligations and diluting flexibilities contained in the TRIPS Agreement.

(vii) TRIPS is premised on a false assumption that "one size fits all". The minimum standards of the TRIPS Agreement makes this assumption while ignoring that the immediate costs of TRIPS implementation for developing countries outweighs the nebulous and uncertain dogma that IP protection attracts foreign investment and is an incentive to creativity and innovation. The presence of flexibility provisions in the Agreement does not negate the general assumption that one size fits all.

The illusion that the TRIPS can promote innovation can aptly be demonstrated through analysis of issues that are ignored under the Agreement. The following discussions identify the issues ignored.

Technology Diffusion and Dissemination under TRIPS Agreement

Harnessing technological progress is a key priority to boost economic growth and improve living standards.[20] In an open economy, technological progress is driven either by technology diffusion or technology creation (innovation). In developing and least-developed economies, technology absorption (technology transfer) can drive economic growth.[21]

The TRIPS Agreement provides that the protection and enforcement of IP rights should contribute to the promotion of technological innovation and to the transfer and dissemination of technology.[22] To realize

---

20 Ibid, at p xiv.

21 Ibid, at p xv.

22 Article 7 of the TRIPS Agreement.

the objectives of TRIPS for the benefit of transfer of technology, TRIPS provides that developed country Members shall provide incentives to enterprises and institutions in their territories for purpose of promoting and encouraging technology transfer to least-developed country Members in order to enable them create a sound and viable technological base.[23] To augment this provision, developed country Members shall provide, on request and on mutually agreed terms and conditions, technical and financial cooperation in favour of developing and least-developed country Members. Such cooperation shall include assistance in the preparation of laws and regulations on the protection and enforcement of IP rights as well as on the prevention of their abuse, and shall include support regarding the establishment or reinforcement of domestic offices and agencies relevant to these matters, including the training of personnel.[24]

Developing countries have stressed the need for international rules that facilitate diffusion of knowledge and transfer of technology. The trend in the TRIPS institutional framework has been towards appropriation and privatization of knowledge rather than transfer and dissemination of knowledge. This trend is explicitly recognized in TRIPS through the article recognizing that IP rights are private property.[25] Efforts to modify the Berne Convention to take into account educational and developmental needs of developing countries have failed to succeed. Despite this, the scope of copyright protection has increased to include software protection, use of internet and domain name protection.

In the patent field, strict adherence to patent rules is emphasized and efforts to liberalize the use and application of compulsory licensing for the benefit of developing countries have not yielded much. The Protocol to Amend the TRIPS Agreement and the Decision of 30th August 2003 is a further proof that the flexibility provisions in the TRIPS Agreement are not responsive to developing country needs. Both Rwanda and Canada being countries that have utilized the decision of 30th August 2003 agree that whereas the objectives of the decision were noble, the implementation is weary and a disincentive to countries.

The stifling of technology transfer and dissemination is further witnessed through increased bilateralism and regionalism in IP protection. Since the mid 1980s, the US and EU have used a combination of unilateral pressure and forum shifting from bilateral agreements to multilateral standard setting and then back to bilateralism as a way of securing trade

---

[23] Article 66 (2) of the TRIPS Agreement.
[24] Article 67 of the TRIPS Agreement.
[25] Preamble to the TRIPS Agreement.

concessions from developing countries.[26] This bilateralism and regionalization of IP norm-setting negotiations operate outside the TRIPS institutional framework ostensibly to strengthen the appropriation of IP and to limit knowledge transfer and technology diffusion. The TRIPS Agreement legalizes the bilateral approach through its Article 1 where it is stated that "Members may, but shall not be obliged to, implement in their law more extensive protection than is required by this Agreement, provided that such protection does not contravene the provisions of this Agreement". An ex-EU Trade Commissioner candidly admitted, albeit with reference to the EU approach to Free Trade Areas: "We always use bilateral free trade agreements to move things beyond WTO standards. By definition, a bilateral trade agreement is "WTO plus". Whether it is about investment, intellectual property or trade instrument."[27]

The picture that emerges from recent trends is that higher and higher standards of IP protection are being globalized with little attempt to build into these standards provisions on transfer and diffusion of technology.[28] Likewise, no provisions are being made for financial and infrastructural support to set up viable national innovation systems in the developing countries signatory to the Free Trade Agreements (FTAs). Carlos Correa writes that a number of developing countries have agreed or are in the course of negotiating FTAs in order to attain perceived commercial advantages.[29] As a result, they have been bound to accept standards of protection of intellectual property rights that go beyond what they had consented to at the multilateral level. Dutfield states that the FTAs extend patents and copyright to new kinds of subject matter; eliminating or narrowing permitted exceptions, introducing new TRIPS-mandated IPR rules and ratifying new WIPO treaties containing TRIPS plus measures.[30]

---

[26] Ruth Mayne, "Regionalism, Bilateralism and TRIPS plus Provisions on Public Health: The Threat to Developing Countries" UNDP November 2004, at p 1.

[27] Jarkata Post, 9th September 2004 "Singapore Issues" Part of EU's Trade Agenda: Lamy.

[28] Examples of TRIPS-plus provisions include extension of the patent protection period beyond 20 years to take into account any delays in granting the patent, new restrictions on registering generic drugs, new restrictions on use of existing clinical trial data by generic companies, new restrictions on compulsory licensing and new restrictions on parallel imports as well as TRIPS plus enforcement agenda.

[29] Carlos M. Correa, Trade Related Aspects of Intellectual Property Rights: A Commentary on the TRIPS Agreement. Oxford University Press, Oxford, 2007.

[30] Graham Dutfield (2005), "Turning Knowledge into Power: Intellectual Property and the World Trade System", *Australian Journal of International Affairs*, **59 (4)** 533–47 at p 535.

These bilateral and regional approaches to IP negotiations do not contain enforceable provisions for technology transfer and diffusion.

Globalization and Politicization of TRIPS Negotiations

Intellectual property law making is a political process in which particular conceptions of rights and duties are institutionalized, policy shift takes place and new disputes emerge. The globalization and politicization of TRIPS debates have operated as disincentives to ensuring that inbuilt flexibilities in the TRIPS Agreement are effective in promoting creativity and innovation. Presently, TRIPS is the centrepiece of the global system of rules, institutions and practices governing the ownership and flow of knowledge, technology and other intellectual assets.[31] The TRIPS implementation process has become an intense political game. The playing field is a global political arena in which countries fight to amend, twist and duck the TRIPS rules.[32] Two teams are the key players: one for the rich countries, the other for the poor countries both teams flanked by multinational companies and Non Governmental Organizations (NGOs) respectively. The teams engage in global-wide struggles to influence both international IP rules and IP reforms in developing countries.

To help build domestic industries, some businesses and enterprises lobby for weak IP regimes that enable them to copy, imitate and adapt foreign technologies. Consumers and public health advocates frequently appeal for weaker patent rights to make products such as medicines cheaper. Weak IP levels mean that governments can still exercise considerable discretion over the level and form of IP protection available within their borders. To promote the availability of educational materials, librarians and educators frequently promote fair use exceptions to copyrights.[33]

On the other hand, knowledge-intensive industries lobby for stronger patent protection to protect their investments in research and development. Creators, artists and authors in cultural industries sometimes call for stronger copyright protection the same as those companies that invest in them. During TRIPS negotiations, the world's largest companies had a socio-economic stake in the outcome. The global pharmaceutical industry, the commercial seed industry and the global software and entertainment industries demonstrated that they had a direct stake in the negotiations. In

---

[31] Carolyn Deere, The Implementation Games – The TRIPS Agreement and the Global Politics of Intellectual Property Reform in Developing Countries by Oxford University Press, New York 2009 at p 1.

[32] Ibid, at p 204.

[33] Ibid, at p 7.

many of these industries, a handful of companies monopolize markets and their business models depend on securing IP protection.[34]

From 1999, developing countries sought to use the review of TRIPS Article 27.3 (b) as an opportunity to clarify their options regarding *sui generis* systems of plant variety protection, narrow the scope of patentability and add provisions that would require disclosure of the origin of genetic materials. Developing countries further highlighted tensions between TRIPS and the Convention on Biological Diversity (CBD). CBD requires signatories to protect and support the rights of communities, farmers and indigenous peoples over their biological resources and systems of knowledge and requires equitable sharing of benefits arising from their use. Developing country determination to address concerns related to Article 27 (3) (b) became globalized by several NGOs. Bio-piracy arguments were raised, supported by developed country granting patents on products such as basmati rice, maca, neem, hoodia, turmeric and ayuhuasca which patents are based on genetic material from developing countries.[35]

Efforts to review the provisions of TRIPS Article 27 (3) (b) to produce standards on biodiversity and food security have not been successful under the TRIPS framework. Developing countries objective to review TRIPS Article 27 (3) (b) to prohibit patenting of life forms and recognition of broader CBD principles has been frustrated through globalization of TRIPS politics.[36]

Role of Non Governmental Organizations in TRIPS Debates

The globalization of TRIPS politics has taken place due to increasing role and influence of NGOs in IP discourse in Geneva. The participation of NGOs in global debates on TRIPS began in the late stages of the Uruguay Round. From 1993 to 1995, NGOs such as Third World Network (TWN), Health Action International (HAI) and GRAIN published concerns about the implications of TRIPS on development, public health and farmers. A plethora of international NGOs such as Oxfam, Action Aid, the Quaker

---

[34] Ibid, at p 9.

[35] Ibid, at pp 115–25.

[36] Despite the foregoing, a number of developing countries provide protections for traditional knowledge (TK), folklore and cultural heritage. In the African region, Angola, Namibia, South Africa and the OAPI countries have all included some protections for cultural heritage and folklore in their laws. The ARIPO countries have signed the Swakopmund Protocol on Protection of Traditional Knowledge, Folklore and Cultural Expressions. The Protocol is a legal instrument to safeguard, foster and promote African TK and folklore.

Geneva Secretariat, MSF among others have contributed to vigorous and politicized debates on IP issues relating to food, agriculture, seed, health and biotechnology. NGOs working in other sectors have influenced the direction on IP discourse in education, software programming, libraries, privacy and free speech. For example, the US academic community in the field of copyright has fought the expansionism in the copyright sector.

The presence of so many NGOs in the IP debate has provided a scope of alliance between developing countries and this has led to globalization of TRIPS in a political context. The consequence is that the position of most developing countries in TRIPS Council is informed by research conducted by NGOs. The effectiveness of the developing countries (supported by NGO research) in the TRIPS Council has been a major factor contributing to bilateralism and regional approach to IP issues by the dominant western countries.[37] The reality to developing and least-developed countries is that they operate in a paradigm dominated by the US, EU, international NGOs and international business interests. The developing countries are encircled in an IP standard-setting process. This encirclement is reinforced by the absence of clear substantive instructions and oversight from national capitals and several Geneva-based diplomats have taken the lead and filled the void by devising and advancing national positions. In many cases, communication between Geneva and national capitals is very weak and the prospects of consultations limited. The net result is that positions of developing countries are sometimes not consistent over time and in some cases the positions and perspectives vary across issues and international forum and reflect views of NGOs.[38] Such non-coordinator approach cannot lead to negotiated principles and rules that promote creativity and innovation.

The increasing role of NGOs in IP debate is evidenced by various political strategies used by the NGOs to advance their respective interests. The array of strategies used includes conferences, high-profile campaigns, appeals to the international media and outreach through e-mail listings. Informal collaborations with government negotiators in Geneva are also adopted as a strategy by the Geneva-based NGOs. They also reach out to NGOs in developed countries to galvanize global and regional networks.[39]

---

[37] Ruth Mayne, "Regionalism, Bilateralism and TRIPS plus Provisions on Public Health: The Threat to Developing Countries" UNDP November 2004, at p 1.

[38] The Implementation Games – The TRIPS Agreement and the Global Politics of Intellectual Property Reform in Developing Countries by Carolyn Deere, Oxford University Press, New York 2009 at pp 115–22.

[39] Ibid, at pp 115, 134–5.

Competing and at times complementing the NGOs are pro-IP business-related industry actors that are active in global IP debates. These include:

(a) multi-sectoral business associations such as the International Chamber of Commerce (ICC).
(b) sectoral or multi-sectoral business associations dedicated specifically to promoting IP protection such as International Intellectual Property Alliance (IIPA).
(c) sectoral business associations such as the Pharmaceutical and Research Manufacturers and the Business Software Alliance.
(d) expert associations that bring together IP attorneys and
(e) industry backed think-tanks and research centres such as the US based International Intellectual Property Institute (IIPI) and Innovative Economic Centre.[40]

In terms of target countries, industry groups focus on those countries that pose the greatest threat to their commercial interests. They also target countries that serve as transit points for infringing goods. In the small countries, the strategy is that by securing strong IP laws, the larger more competitive and less malleable developing countries would be isolated. Further, with stronger IP laws, the smaller and weaker countries would be less likely to resist new TRIPS-plus multilateral agreements and their vote could help close deals. An example of this is from the World Intellectual Property Organization (WIPO) where potential opposition to new international copyright protection was neutralized by securing TRIPS-plus terms of copyright protection at the national level in numerous commercially marginalized countries.[41] In the copyright field, a key industry objective is to extend the scope of IP protection to new areas, to increase protection for copyright industries in the context of the internet and to strengthen enforcement in the face of mounting manufacture of pirate and counterfeit products. Industry is also pushing for stronger customs control.

The politicization of TRIPS at the global level is also reinforced by internal politics within the US and the EU. There has been tension between the European Commission and the European Parliament and between them and among the EU members about the appropriate EU perspective in global IP negotiations and IP protection in developing countries. In addition, global European NGOs put pressure on national and European policy makers to desist from pushing TRIPS-plus reforms

40 Ibid, at pp 115–6.
41 Ibid, at p 116.

in developing countries. In the US, the Departments of State of Commerce and Health as well as US Trade Representative (USTR) and US Patent and Trademark Office (USPTO) and the Office of the President all intervene on global IP issues.[42]

The degree of engagement by national legislatures and the public debate on IP issues influence executive or legislative reforms in the implementation of the TRIPS Agreement. In most developing countries, there is an absence of public debate on IP issues and this explains the limited use of TRIPS flexibilities. On issues relating to public health, public interest NGOs participate in influencing legislative outcomes. This has been noticeable in Kenya and South Africa.

Noting that there are various government agencies dealing with IP issues in most developing countries, a notable feature is the absence of internal government coordination on IP decision making. There is lack of coordination between the external and internal faces of government and limited coordination of external IP relations and no mechanism to coordinate regional IP arrangements.

Globalization of IP politics has also been influenced by WIPO. WIPO's prominence in global IP discourse flows from its role as administrator of some 23 IP treaties and their financial arrangements. The Organization's pro-IP influence is facilitated by its technical authority, extensive global network of IP professionals, close relationship with national IP offices and the considerable budget it has allocated for IP outreach, training and capacity building. The technical influence of WIPO Secretariat is widely observed in diplomatic circles. WIPO staff general share a pro-IP perspective and technical expertise and they have organizational and financial resources to project these.[43] The authority of WIPO vis-à-vis developing countries has consolidated the perception among many national officers that WIPO's advice is imbued with neutrality. From 2004, the push for a Development Agenda placed WIPO at the centre of IP stand-off between developed and developing countries. The effect of WIPO's influence has played a role in shaping the political

---

[42] Ibid, at p 118.

[43] It has been stated that WIPO through its recruitment of experts, promotes and sustains internationally a jurisprudence of IP that isolates IP from use as a regulatory tool in relation to development issues in health, environment, food and agriculture. WIPO instead fosters an Anglo-American-German jurisprudential game in which developing countries are the most marginal of marginal players. See "IPR Agents Try to Derail OAU Process", GRAIN, June 2001, available at http://www.graon.org/publications/oan-en.cfm.

dynamics of global IP perspectives.[44] Most African IP offices have been beneficiaries of technical assistance, training, institutional support, IT infrastructure or other services provided by other international donors. This support enabled IP offices to undertake a range of activities including public awareness, training and the modernization of IP and administration systems. The effect of the technical assistance given has been to create a pro-IP culture in the recipient countries.

Ideational Power as a Factor in Global IP Discourse

Ideation is the ability to create ideas. Ideational power is vital to explaining the participation and influence of a country in global IP discourse. Ideation power is sought to influence, alter or build: (a) expertise, know-how and institutional capabilities on IP matters (b) understanding, beliefs and discourses on IP issues (c) scrutiny and weighing up of ideas and concepts and (d) to frame issues and agenda pertinent to IP discourse.

Ideational power, just as economic power, is critical in promoting a compliance-plus or pro-development IP agenda at international level. It is also a primary vehicle for the countervailing efforts to criticize IP perspectives. The ideational power influences and determines how governments understand their TRIPS obligations and options, supporting particular kinds of expertise, persuading officials of the pros and cons of stronger IP protection and shaping a country's perception of the political climate and room for maneuver. The specific mechanisms used to exert ideational power include creation of knowledge communities, framing issues, monitoring and capacity building. The strategy used to influence others includes drawing on an array of governments, NGOs, industries, academics, technical experts, and having access to and sharing information, influencing media and harnessing public opinion to exert the ideational power.

Developing and least-developed countries have a limited stock of ideational power and knowledge communities. There is a dearth of framing acumen and limited human resource capacities for IP discourse. These attributes are essential if the TRIPS Agreement is to be effective in promoting creativity and innovation.

Knowledge communities are like-minded epistemic communities of experts, academics and public officials. Each draws on distinct set of ideas and assumptions which enrich IP perspectives and help in framing

---

[44] The Implementation Games – The TRIS Agreement and the Global Politics of Intellectual Property Reform in Developing Countries by Carolyn Deere, Oxford University Press, New York 2009 at p 142.

IP issues. Framing is deployed as a tool to set agenda, influence debate and outcomes. Frames are used to influence, distort and alter communications with the hope of setting and dominating the terms of the debate and determining what stakeholders should be arguing about. Framing is used to fix meanings, build shared understandings and influence how challenges are defined and represented. This legitimizes and motivates particular kinds of collective action and impacts on what kinds of solutions are adopted in particular policy debates.[45] To respond to the various strands of the pro-IP debates, NGOs and other actors use counter-framing to reframe IP debate to facilitate discourse from public interest perspective. Monitoring is a tool used to pressure individual countries to influence their perspectives.

Capacity building in developing and least-developed countries is critical to unlocking the potential of TRIPS to spur creativity and innovation. The scope of capacity building is from legislative and policy advice to training and human resource development as well as administrative and institutional competencies. Conferences and seminars are a tool to advance specific agenda and perspectives on IP. The depth of government expertise on IP issues and administrative competence of government institutions as well as the ability to maintain control of national IP offices is critical. Across Africa, the colonial era left most countries with very weak expertise on IP and weak or non-existent IP offices. At the time TRIPS was negotiated, most African IP offices were dormant and few local businesses or innovators made use of the IP system. National governments devoted few resources to the operation of IP offices. Decision making was constrained by a deep lack of technical knowledge or policy experience in IP issues. In general, IP law was perceived as a technical issue rather than one central to a range of public policy goals. This led to most governments delegating negotiations to a small number of technocrat staff in the IP offices. Lack of depth and specialized knowledge on IP policy in other government agencies meant that IP offices monopolize IP discourse. With limited human resource capacities, there has been uneven capacity of developing country governments to provide substantive policy direction and oversight of their IP officers. The result is that most IP offices adopt a TRIPS compliance-driven approach rather than a development-oriented IP approach.[46]

In the context of weak IP expertise and policy-making vacuums in most developing and least-developed countries, donor efforts to build capacity

45 Ibid, at p 169.
46 Ibid, at p 200.

and provide technical advice has had significant impact on TRIPS implementation. Within developing countries, the line between national and international interest groups is often blurred. National interest groups often have alliances with international counterparts that shape their perspectives and activities. In the face of a proliferation of the forum in which IP policy issues are discussed, fragmentation and contradictions in developing country position is evident. Coordination and communication among and within developing countries is weak and weak communication and consultation between various government ministries and departments has led to a divergent and fragmented approach. This fragmentation is exacerbated by the growing number of bilateral IP agreements and different NGO actors with conflicting interests and perspectives.

In addition to ideation, international pressures such as trade threats and diplomatic intimidation and bilateralism have had a decisive effect on developing and least-developed country positions in IP discourse.[47] For instance, the US used its enormous market as a powerful source of bargaining and used credible threats to break resistance of hard-line developing countries in the TRIPS negotiations at the WTO – India, Brazil, Argentina, Cuba, Egypt, Nicaragua, Nigeria, Peru, Tanzania and Yugoslavia – resulting in the signing of the TRIPS Agreement in 1994.[48] The US strategy implied that if free trade progress became stalled globally – where any one of the 148 WTO economies has a veto – then the US would move ahead regionally and bilaterally. Poor countries have tended to sign the FTA trade deals for political reasons, because they are desperate for greater access to the vast US market and they may not fully realize what they are signing away.

TRIPS and Promotion of Creativity and Innovation

The TRIPS Agreement envisages that as the Agreement is being implemented, creativity and innovation in countries is promoted. However, no substantive obligation is placed on countries to promote innovation. This chapter analyzes the significance of innovation and discusses what promoting innovation entails. From the analysis, it is apparent that TRIPS does not make provision for creating essential attributes required to promote creativity and innovation.

---

47 Ruth Mayne, "Regionalism, Bilateralism and TRIPS Plus Provisions on Public Health: The Threat to Developing Countries", UNDP November 2004, at p 3.

48 Ibid, at p 3.

The essence of innovation is revealed by its latin root "*nova*" or new. The antithesis (opposite) of innovation is imitation. TRIPS ignores that in most countries, innovation is preceded by imitation.[49]

Innovation is the introduction of a new thing or method.[50] In elaborate terms, innovation is the embodiment or synthesis of knowledge in original, relevant and valued new product, processes or services.[51] In business terms, innovation is the commercial exploitation of ideas.[52]

Innovation is a process that must be driven, motivated and provoked.[53] It is not a simple process of investment in fundamental research leading to commercialization by far-sighted management in industry. Such a view of innovation stresses the supply side of policy initiatives and not demand-driven innovation. The TRIPS Agreement ignores the demand side of innovation. A holistic appreciation of innovation examines both the demand and supply side factors in creativity. Demand drives innovation.

Innovations are the product of the creative interaction of supply and demand. The supply side is reflected through R&D expenditure. Demand side is reflected by consumer taste and market size.[54] A large market is an incentive to conduct research on consumer goods. A large market offers an incentive to increase R&D expenditure. Firms in a large market have an opportunity to cover the high fixed costs of R&D

---

[49] In most developed countries, innovation was preceded by imitation particularly in the pharmaceutical sector. Initial growth of pharmaceutical industries in UK, Switzerland and India was accomplished through weak IPR laws on product patents. Lack of product patents allowed process innovation to take place which gave companies ability to enter and dominate generic drug markets. Once the drug making processes were mastered, the nascent pharmaceutical companies invested in R&D for drug development.

[50] Jean-Eric Aubert and Aisling Quirke of the World Bank Institute define innovation as the diffusion of a product, process or practice which is new in a given context (not in absolute terms. It includes use of available technology, setting of a new industry or plant. See Jean-Eric Aubert and Aisling Quirke, "How to promote innovation in developing countries," , World Bank Institute, PREM Week, 2005.

[51] Harvard Business Essentials "The Innovator's Toolkit", Harvard Business Press, Massachusetts, 2009 at p 2.

[52] Andy Bruce & David Birchall, Innovation – Fast Track to Success, FT Prentice Hall Publishers, 2009, at p 5.

[53] Schumpeter defines innovation as the "carrying out of new combinations" which he resolves into five different types namely: the introduction of a new product; the introduction of a new method of production (process); the opening of a new market; the opening of a new source of supply; and the carrying out of a new organization of any industry.

[54] Antara Dutta & Siddharth Sharma, "Intellectual Property Rights and Innovation in Developing Countries: Evidence from India" World Bank, 2008, at p 24.

necessary for innovation. Demanding and adventurous consumers drive innovation by providing firms with incentives to enter new markets and creating pressures on firms to improve their products and services. The demand-side drivers of innovation include public procurement procedures, technical standards, information disclosure in patent applications, awareness building and support for private demand through increasing disposable income. Regulations and standards effect innovation by the pull-through effect and diffusion of advanced products technology, services and processes. By encouraging industry to converge on common standards, innovation is promoted.[55] It must be noted that standards if introduced too early or designed too prescriptively, can lock an industry into a given technology and truncate the search for potentially new and competitive alternatives.[56] The TRIPS Agreement ignores the demand side of innovation. For example, strong IPRs are important for the pharmaceutical innovation, but only where there is a strong market. IPRs are of value to commercial product and technology developers only if a viable market can be created.[57]

In addition to ignoring the demand side of innovation, TRIPS has no substantive provisions on promoting innovation. Promoting innovation is not about technical assistance to explain what a patent is, what a trademark is, what is copyright or what IP rights are or what flexibilities are available under the TRIPS Agreement or training on legislative advice and drafting. Such an approach is simplistic, theoretical, and unrealistic and demonstrates a lack of appreciation of what innovation entails.

Promoting innovation involves setting up an innovation strategy and implementing the strategy to generate creativity, innovative products and processes and new service delivery models. The TRIPS Agreement does not address these issues. Promoting innovation entails putting in place an effective national innovation system that generates ideas,

---

[55] Standards have been shown to be a powerful vehicle for transmission of business knowledge and innovative practices and there is a strong statistical association with productivity and growth. UK DTI Economics Paper No. 12, "The Empirical Economics of Standards" 2005 available at http://www.berr.gov.uk/files9655.pdf.

[56] For a discussion on the interface between IP and Standards, see Xuan Li, "Intellectual Property, Standards, and Anti-Competitive Concerns: Trends, Challenges and Strategic Considerations" in How Developing Countries Can Manage Intellectual Property Rights to Maximize Access to Knowledge, South Centre, February 2009 at pp 27–55.

[57] Emmanuel Hassan, Ohid Yaqub, Stephanie Diepeveen, "Intellectual Property and Developing Countries – A Review of Literature", (2010) RAND EUROPE at www.rand.org at p xvi.

creativity and inventiveness. It entails establishing a national innovation framework and infrastructure that produces a self-sustaining and indigenous innovation system. It involves a paradigm shift to set up a critical mass of knowledgeable, skilled, analytical, abstract thinking and problem solving workforce.

The challenge many developing and least-developed countries face is to promote innovation. Promotion of innovation entails the following activities:

- Codification of knowledge, which is the feedstock for new ideas.
- Interpretation of codified knowledge using existing skills as a starting point or instrument to decode ideas, which are being studied, or used leading to improved skills.
- Fostering systems of innovation and competence building.
- Explaining how to recognize innovation opportunities.
- Explaining how to commercialize innovation.
- Setting up innovation incubation centres.
- Removing barriers and facilitating technology diffusion, acquisition and adoption.
- Identifying technology diffusion tools and setting up technology diffusion observatory units.
- Identifying funding opportunities for prototype development and commercialization of innovation.
- Linking innovators to industry.
- Understanding the S-curve of innovation.
- Presentation of how to protect innovations.
- Explaining the role of innovation in a business enterprise.
- Explaining linkages within the national innovation system.
- Demonstrating how innovation determines socio-economic development.
- Formulating a national innovation strategy.
- Promoting strategic utilization of intellectual property to promote socio-economic development.
- Nurturing a knowledgeable and analytical workforce.
- Providing infrastructure and physical facilities and equipment for research and innovation.
- Incentivising creativity and inventiveness.

The TRIPS Agreement does not address any of the issues raised above in relation to promotion of creativity and innovation. Insofar as promoting innovation is concerned, TRIPS is an illusion and a mirage. The IP regime embodied in the TRIPS Agreement is not an effective mechanism for promoting innovation.[58] Countries that aim to promote creativity and innovation should not anchor their aspirations on the TRIPS Agreement.

Other than lacking effective provisions on promoting innovation, TRIPS has no provision to harness the sources of innovation for creativity and inventiveness. The TRIPS Agreement does not provide a framework to harness the sources of innovation for the benefit of developing and least developed countries. Analysis of sources of innovation reveals that none of the identified sources are mentioned in TRIPS Agreement and there is no substantive provision to ensure that these sources are utilized for the benefit of developing and least developed countries.

The first and primary source of innovation is basic research. Other sources are:

(i) Creative application of tried and tested technologies.
(ii) Design in developing innovative products and services.
(iii) Design of new methods for delivery of public services.
(iv) Diffusion and absorption of foreign or international innovations.
(v) Infusion and utilization of comments and ideas from users of products and services. Users are increasingly innovating independently or in collaboration with businesses or in the co-creation of public services.
(vi) Sharing information between universities, suppliers, competitors and other companies.
(vii) Technology transfer.
(viii) Franchising.
(ix) Mergers and acquisitions.

Boxes 9.1 and 9.2 below show the link between innovation and development and the difference in the nature of science, technology and innovation policies. The TRIPS Agreement has privatized knowledge and does not address link between innovation and development as well as the link between IP, innovation and technology.

---

[58] Antara Dutta & Siddharth Sharma, "Intellectual Property Rights and Innovation in Developing Countries: Evidence from India" World Bank, 2008, at p 6.

BOX 9.1 INNOVATION AND DEVELOPMENT

- Innovation in a developing context includes continuous improvement in product design and quality.
- Changes in organization and management routines, creativity in marketing and modifications to production processes that bring costs down.
- Increase efficiency and environmental sustainability.
- The ability to manage a portfolio of partnerships, to form linkages and to learn through them.
- As opposed to the focus on novelty that is central to the concept of invention and a key criterion for patenting, innovation is a broader concept.

Source: Banji Oyelaran-Oyeyinka and Padmashree Gehl Sampath, "Innovation in African Development – Case Studies of Uganda, Tanzania and Kenya" A World Bank Study Paper March 2007 at pp 10–11.

BOX 9.2 SCIENCE, TECHNOLOGY AND INNOVATION POLICIES

Science Policy: objective is the production of scientific knowledge

- To manage and fund the accumulation of knowledge in relation to natural phenomenon by the creation and support of appropriate organizations-research labs and universities.

Technology Policy: objective is the commercialization of technical knowledge

- To manage and fund the accumulation and application of practical knowledge needed for particular productive activities, including transfer of technology from overseas and transfer of scientific knowledge into wealth creation.

Innovation Policy: objective is improvements in the overall performance of the economy

To foster the transfer of science and technology knowledge into application by ensuring that necessary complementary resources (capital finance) are available, by supporting entrepreneurship and by protecting intellectual property rights. The focus of innovation policy is on the interaction between actors and their institutional and policy context that influences their innovative behaviour and performance.

Source: Banji Oyelaran-Oyeyinka and Padmashree Gehl Sampath, "Innovation in African Development – Case Studies of Uganda, Tanzania and Kenya" A World Bank Study Paper March 2007 at pp 10–11.

TRIPS and National Innovation Systems

The TRIPS Agreement does not make provision for the establishment of national innovation systems but focuses on the creation of domestic IP administration offices and enforcement mechanism.[59] It is argued that by focusing on establishment of domestic IP administration offices, TRIPS does not facilitate the establishment of viable and sustainable national innovative systems in developing and least developed countries that are prerequisite to creativity and innovation.

A national innovation system is that structure that encourages and leads people to be creative and innovative. Figure 9.1 below illustrates the major components of a National Innovation System (Source: Arnold & Bell, 2001).

A national innovation system is "the network of institutions in the public and private sector whose activities and interactions develop, build up, initiate, import, modify and diffuse technologies."[60] It is a system whose elements and relationships interconnect in the production, diffusion and use of new and economically useful knowledge and is either located within or rooted inside the borders of a country. The system encompasses the set of institutions whose connectivity determine the innovative performance of national firms.[61]

---

[59] Articles 41 and 42 of the TRIPS Agreement.

[60] Christopher Freeman (1987), Technology and Economic Performance: Lessons from Japan, Pinter, London. See also OECD, National Innovation Systems Report 1997, and Box 1 at p 10.

[61] Banji Oyelaran-Oyeyinka and Padmashree Gehl Sampath, "Innovation in African Development – Case Studies of Uganda, Tanzania and Kenya" World Bank Study Paper March 2007 at page 12.

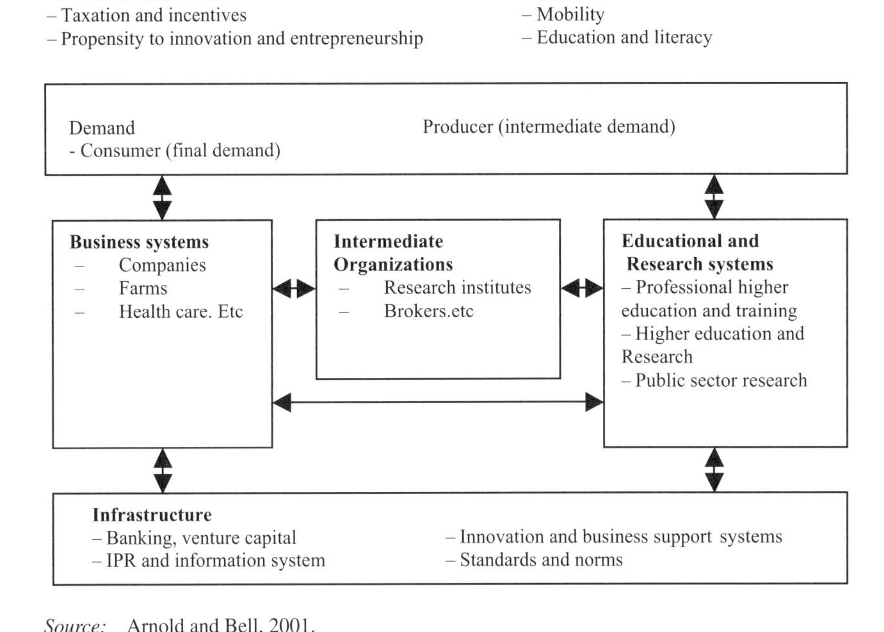

Source: Arnold and Bell, 2001.

Figure 9.1 Major Components of a National Innovation System

In a broad sense, the national innovation system is the institutions, their incentive structures and their competencies that determine the rate and direction of technological learning (or the volume and composition of change generating activities) in a country. It is the system that leads to creation and articulation of new ideas for innovation.[62] The system includes

[62] Ideas are the fuel and catalyst for innovation; they are the cornerstones for innovation. However, by itself, an idea benefits no one. Innovative ideas emanate from various sources. Some come from a flash of inspiration, others are accidental but most result from a conscious, purposeful search for opportunities to solve problems or please customers. Thomas Edison stated that invention is 1 percent inspiration and 99 percent perspiration. There are six recognized sources of new ideas namely:

(i) New knowledge;
(ii) Customers' ideas and direct customer participation;
(iii) Lead users;
(iv) Empathetic design;

the set of distinct institutions which jointly and individually contribute to the development and diffusion of new technologies and which provide the framework within which governments form and implement policies to influence the innovation process.

For policy makers, an understanding of the national innovation system can help identify the leverage points for enhancing innovative and creative performance and overall economic competitiveness. It can assist in pinpointing mismatches within the system both intra- and inter-institutions. Understanding of the national innovation system helps to improve networking among the actors and institutions in the system and identify and absorb technologies that are most valuable in the context.

An innovation system should not be confused with the IP system. The IP regime of a country is not the national innovation system. The IPR regime is but a subset or component of the national innovation system and not vice versa. Enacting IPR laws per se does not lead to creativity and innovation. The IPR laws are on a piece of paper – a piece of paper *de facto or de jure* cannot innovate – it is the people who create and innovate. However, noting that the patent system contains technological information, for the IPR regime to be an effective part of the national innovation system, there is need for a country to develop its expertise in the field of patent informatics – that is, software-based techniques for interrogating patent databases to extract relevant data for more detailed analysis and interpretation.[63] As part of the national innovation system, the patent informatics should be able to spot new and emerging technologies.

The TRIPS Agreement has no provision to facilitate the establishment of viable national innovation systems in developing and least-developed countries. In its technology transfer provisions, TRIPS does not address issues of incremental or radical innovation in developing and least-developed countries.[64] No incentive system has been inbuilt as part of

---

(v) Invention factories or skunk works and
(vi) Open market of ideas.

[63] "Implementing the Race to the Top", Lord Sainsbury's Review of Government's Science and Innovation Policies, UK Department for Innovation, Universities & Skills at pp 22–3.

[64] Incremental innovation exploits existing forms of technology. It either improves on something or reconfigures an existing technology. In this sense, it is innovation at the margins. These are new-use innovations. By contrast, radical innovation is something new to the world, a departure from existing technologies or methods. The term breakthrough and discontinuous are often used as synonyms for radical innovation. In industry, incremental and radical innovations go hand in hand. The course of innovation is generally characterized by long periods of incremental innovation punctuated by infrequent radical innovation. Radical

TRIPS flexibilities. There is no financial component accompanying the innovation and technology transfer provisions of TRIPS. There are no infrastructural support provisions and business support mechanisms engrained within TRIPS to spur commercialization of innovation. The inescapable inference is that for developing and least-developed countries to have viable domestic national innovation systems, they must look outside the TRIPS framework.

Further, the TRIPS Agreement does not address the flow and diffusion of information and technology among people, enterprises, institutions and countries that are pivotal to the innovative process. The flow of information and technology is essential considering that innovation is the result of a complex set of relationships among actors in the system, which includes enterprises, industry, plant and animal breeders, universities, private or non-governmental research institutes, end users and government research institutes.

The TRIPS Agreement does not address any of the above issues and hence it is a mirage to expect TRIPS to promote innovation and technology diffusion.

Recommendations for Developing Countries with Regard to International IP Debates

For developing and least-developed countries to effectively participate in international IP debates, and to realize the goal of promoting creativity and innovation, several pro-active policy measures need to be put in place.

First, the countries should formulate a national IP policy and strategy outlining clear policy strategies and how the country seeks to leverage IP rights for its socio-economic development.

Second, each country should enhance its institutional and human resource capacity for ideation. Due to their weakness in ideation power and limited financial and technical resources, developing and least-developed countries should consider pooling their resources by means of a more formal structure.

Third, developing and least-developed countries should be wary of TRIPS-plus binding commitments undertaken through bilateral and

---

innovation takes place in R&D labs or in the minds of scientists or entrepreneurs. They usually take a long time to germinate and develop. Their appearance in the market place (few make it to that point) is both infrequent and generally unpredictable. Incremental innovation takes place during intervals or gaps in radical innovation with competing technological variants, each with different operating principles.

regional trade agreements. The bilateral arrangements are likely to introduce distortions in the global trade relations due to the higher levels of IP protection and diminish the significance of TRIPS flexibilities.

Fourth, each country should develop and implement a national innovation strategy with clear incentives for promotion of creativity and innovation. In this regard, developing and least-developed countries should bear in mind that the IP framework in the TRIPS Agreement cannot promote innovation and creativity. Sustainable innovation and creativity requires pro-active domestic initiatives.

Fifth, in collaborating with international NGOs, developing and least-developed countries must identify their own national interests and priorities and should not blindly imbibe and emulate NGOs perspectives.

Sixth, developing and least-developed countries should expect fewer concessions from developed countries in matters relating to IP norm creation. The symbolic rather than real value and nature of transitional periods and the special and differential treatment in the context of IP must be appreciated.

Seventh, developing and least-developed countries need political will and strong leadership from the top. Presently, there is a façade of political backing from capitals that is imaginary and not realistic. No negotiators can hope to muster support from other countries on difficult issues involving disagreement, if there is suspicion that no political will exist in the capital.[65]

Eighth, developing and least-developed countries should strengthen their delegations to multilateral IP forum. The practice is that they send representatives from IP offices who have technical knowledge of patent and trademark administration but have no knowledge of IP as a tool of regulatory and development policy. Such officers cannot raise heterodox views about IP and development. There is need for country delegations that have analytic skills to generate and evaluate debates and lay emphasis on IP and development.

Ninth, developing countries need to shape their IP laws to promote development generally and to keep in mind some of the negative impacts of overly generous IP protection. For example, patenting of technologies needed to conduct research can provide an incentive for research but can also inhibit research which needs to make use of those protected technologies.

---

[65] S.P. Shukla, Indian Ambassador to the GATT at that time quoted in Agriculture in "Dunkell's Draft of GATT – A Critical Analysis", Third World Network, 1993, at p 6.

Tenth, developing countries must understand and appreciate that innovation is not only about IP but is also dependent on a host of other factors such as levels of skill/education and infrastructure among others.

2. CASE STUDY ON KENYA'S NATIONAL INNOVATION SYSTEM

This chapter underscores the significance of a national innovation system in promoting creativity and innovation. This part adopts Kenya (a developing country) as a case study of a national innovation system. The synergies between various actors in the system are highlighted and this part recommends the need for a national innovation strategy to promote creativity and innovation.

A country that does not understand and recognize its national innovation system is like an individual who has HIV-AIDS virus without knowing he is unwell – such a person shall surely die without understanding the cause of death.

Kenya's national innovation system is centred on several actors including:

(i) Public research institutes.
(ii) Public and private universities.
(iii) Non-governmental research institutes.
(iv) Private sector commercial enterprises.
(v) Plant and animal breeders.
(vi) Individual scientists and private research firms.
(vii) Jua kali sector.
(viii) Intellectual property regulatory authorities such as the Kenya Industrial Property Institute (KIPI), the Kenya Copyright Board and the Kenya Plant Health Inspectorate Services (KEPHIS) and the Pharmacy and Poisons Board.
(ix) National standards organizations such as the Kenya Bureau of Standards.
(x) Government ministries such as the Ministry of Education (with respect to the national education curricular); the Ministry of Science and Technology with regard to the Science, Technology and Innovation policy; Ministries of Trade and Industrialization with regard to value addition strategy, SME participation as well as national industrialization policy. The Ministries of Agriculture and Health with regard to putting science into agriculture and

developing appropriate public health policies more particularly with respect to intellectual property issues. The Ministry of Finance/Treasury has a role in relation to fiscal incentives that promote innovation and allocation of resources for research and development and prototype development.

(xi) The Presidency and Cabinet with regard to providing political will and policy direction for creating an innovative and creative knowledge based economy.

(xii) External development partners with regard to funding and their respective national policies on technology transfer and foreign direct investment.

(xiii) Regional and multilateral actors in relation to regional or multilateral intellectual property and technology transfer regimes.

Innovation and Research Institutions in Kenya

There are two categories of research institutions involved in innovation in Kenya. The first are those state corporations whose core mandate is to conduct basic research. The second category relate to all other non-public institutions that conduct research.

The state corporations whose core mandate is to conduct research include:

(i) Coffee Research Foundation
(ii) Tea Research Foundation
(iii) Kenya Industrial Research and Development Institute – KIRDI
(iv) Kenya Agricultural Research Institute – KARI/Kenya Trypanosomiasis Research Institute – KETRI
(v) Kenya Medical Research Institute – KEMRI
(vi) Kenya Forestry Institute – KEFRI
(vii) Kenya Marine and Fisheries Institute – KEMFRI
(viii) Kenya Sugar Research Foundation – KESREF
(ix) Kenya Seed Company
(x) Institute of Primate Research
(xi) Pyrethrum Board of Kenya
(xii) National Council for Science and Technology – NCST
(xiii) Horticultural Crops Development Authority – HCDA
(xiv) National Environmental Management Authority – NEMA
(xv) Kenya Wildlife Service – KWS

The mandate and succinct activities of each of the above state corporations is discussed hereunder.

Coffee Research Foundation

Coffee research in Kenya dates back to 1908 when the colonial government appointed the first coffee entomologist. Coffee Research Station (CRS) was later established in 1944 at Jacaranda Estate near Ruiru. In 1994, the CRS was incorporated as the Coffee Research Foundation being a company limited by guarantee under the Companies Act. The Foundation has its headquarters at Ruiru with research stations at Koru, Kitale, Kisii and Meru. The objective of the Foundation is to promote research into and investigate all problems relating to coffee and such other crop system of husbandry as are associated with coffee.

The Coffee Research Foundation has its laboratories at Ruiru, a plantation named "Azania" in Juja and four sub-stations and several demonstration plots. There are seven core research divisions: Plant Pathology (coffee berry disease, leaf rust and bacterial blight), Coffee Breeding, Agronomy, Chemistry and Processing, Crop Physiology, Entomology and Agricultural Economics.

The breeding of new varieties for disease resistance is a major research activity for the Foundation. The Foundation has established a plant-breeding section whose goal is to develop cost effective and sustainable coffee production technologies that enhance yield and quality. The section has been able to develop coffee-berry disease and rust-resistant varieties. A particularly successful new variety is Ruiru 11, which has proven itself impervious to coffee-berry disease.

Tea Research Foundation

The Tea Research Foundation is responsible for research and development of new tea varieties. It conducts research into diseases that affect the tea industry. The Foundation has been able to introduce six clones of hybrid between the Asam variety and the *Cambod-C Sinensis* variety and *Assanica* tea. The Assam variety is predominant in Kenya while the Assanica is predominant in China. Further, in April 2009, a new tea variety, which can realize three to four times more than the ordinary crop, was released by the Foundation. The variety is known as TRFK 306/1. The new tea is rich in *anthocyamin* which is an antioxidant. Antioxidants confer health benefits since they protect cells from damage. A total of 100,000 purple tea cuttings of the new variety have been distributed to farmers.[66]

[66] Nairobi, Daily Nation Newspaper 8th April 2009.

Kenya Industrial Research Development Institute (KIRDI)

KIRDI's origin lies in the colonial period, when in 1942, the East African Industrial Research Organization was established to develop local industries, with the objective of relieving shortages brought about by World War II. KIRDI employs approximately 270 persons in Nairobi, where facilities consist of several workshops, laboratories and offices. KIRDI's statutory mandate includes:

- Identifying and developing appropriate process and product technologies to suit the local market and export potential;
- exploring options to substitute imported raw materials and intermediate goods with indigenous materials;
- designing, developing and adapting machinery, tools, equipment and instruments and processes suitable for introduction and use in the rural areas;
- developing suitable treatment/recovery processes and devices to reduce environmental hazard created by industrial wastes and effluents;
- setting up pilot plants where necessary to demonstrate the efficacy of industrial technology; and
- acting as consultants to industry in the provision of industrial information and technical services and, if necessary, to commercialize the relevant research findings.

In fulfillment of the mandate, KIRDI has four divisions: Analytical and Testing, Design and Engineering, Process and Product Development and Project Studies and Development (primarily market research). KIRDI has a mechanical workshop, a leather technology laboratory, a ceramics laboratory and workshop, a microbiology laboratory and a chemical laboratory. Funding for KIRDI comes from three sources: the Government of Kenya, foreign donors and to a lesser extent consulting fees and charges.

Kenya Agricultural Research Institute (KARI)/ Kenya Trypanosomiasis Research Institute (KETRI)

KARI was established in 1979 as a semi-autonomous government institution under the Science and Technology Act. Following the collapse of the East African Community in 1977, the new Institute took over the research activities of the East African Agricultural and Forestry Research Organization and the East African Veterinary Research Organization. Recently, the Kenya Vaccines Production Institute (KEVEVAPI) and the Kenya Trypanosomiasis Research Institute (KETRI) have been integrated into KARI.

From 1985 to date, KARI with the support of government and donors has been able to release over 146 improved varieties of food and horticultural crops including maize (22), wheat (18), grain legumes (32), Irish potatoes (6), sorghum and millets (20), flowers (42) and tissue culture bananas.

To enhance its plant breeding research, the KARI Seed Unit was established in 1997. The responsibilities include developing sustainable organization structure for producing, processing, marketing and distribution of good-quality breeder, pre-basic and basic seed and maintaining all pre-released and released parental lines, populations and varieties as well as vegetatively propagated planting materials. The Seed Unit is helping the informal sector to produce high-quality farm-saved open pollinated variety seed by training seed producers. The Seed Unit disseminates knowledge and technologies and catalyzes the process of outreach and adoption of agricultural technologies and sustainable funding initiatives.

In terms of production, from October 1997 to December 2002, the total amount of certified seed (maize, sorghum, pearl millet, beans, cowpea, green gram and pigeon pea) produced by the KARI Seed Unit included 457 tons of breeder, pre-basic and basic seeds (crops adopted to semi-arid lowlands). In addition, 2,730 (50 kg bags) of pre-basic and basic seed potato; 188,000 seedlings, 71 (50 kg bags) of arabicum and tuberose flower seed; 41,000 corns and 209,000 cornels; 143,000 flower stems and 150,440 cuttings of cassava were produced.

In livestock research, KARI has produced 18 livestock vaccines and diagnostic kits. Five hundred dual-purpose Sahiwal bulls have been availed for breeding and 800 Sahiwal/Friesian crossbred were availed to farmers for improved adaptability and dairy production in semi-arid and arid lands. KARI has established the Veterinary Vaccines Production Centre to produce high-quality, affordable veterinary vaccines for local and export markets. The Centre under the name KEVEVAPI was established as a State Corporation in June 1990. The Centre has a Vaccine Production Laboratory at Embakasi and a Vaccine Production Unit in Kabete.

Kenya Medical Research Institute (KEMRI)

The Kenya Medical Research Institute is a leading medical research centre in Kenya and Africa. KEMRI has numerous research centres that focus on specific areas of national and/or strategic importance. Each of these centres has attracted a cadre of competent scientists. Prominent among the centres is the Centre for Biotechnology Research and Development, Centre for Clinical Research, Centre for Microbiology Research, Centre for Respiratory Diseases Research, Centre for Traditional Medicine and

Drug Research, Centre for Infectious and Parasitic Diseases, and Centre for Public Health Research and Centre for Virus Research.

In addition to the centres, KEMRI has research programs that oversee research activities at the Institute. Presently, the four programs are the Infectious Diseases Control Research program; Parasitic Diseases program; Epidemiology, Public Health and Health Systems Research program; and the Biotechnology and Non-Communicable Diseases Research program. The focus of the biotechnology program includes the development and promotion of modern biotechnological techniques in molecular biology for production of pharmaceuticals, biological and other applications for use in the promotion of health. KEMRI has developed several medical kits and vaccines under its programs.

Kenya Forestry Research Institute (KEFRI)

The Kenya Forestry Research Institute was established in 1986 under the Science and Technology Act to carry out research in forestry and allied natural resources. The Institute has focused on problem-oriented research and has a staff component of about 1,000. The Institute has adopted a multi-disciplinary research approach and decentralized research activities to facilitate improved interaction and linkages with the local users.

Kenya Marine and Fisheries Institute (KEMFRI)

Section 4 of the Science and Technology Act defines the research mandate of KEMFRI. The Institute is empowered to carry out research in marine and freshwater fisheries, aquatic biology, aquaculture and environmental chemistry as well as ecological, geological and hydrological studies. KEMFRI has focused its research on fish population dynamics, isolating suitable fish species as well as collecting and disseminating scientific information on fishery resources. The areas of research include utilization of fish by-products, identification of species for fish culture adaptable to local conditions, disease control methods and valorization of the 200-mile Exclusive Economic Zone.

KEMFRI has several programs to realize its mandate. These include the aquaculture program on hatchery development and production of quality seed, genetics and selective breeding. The natural products program focuses on extraction and identification of bioactive compounds suitable for biomedical and nutritional research.

Kenya Sugar Research Foundation (KESREF)

The core function of KESREF is the development and dissemination of customer-oriented demand-driven technologies for maximized production and profitability of sugar cane and related crops; enhancement of factory performance and efficiency as well as utilization and value addition of milling co-products.

To achieve its core objectives, KESREF has five departments, namely, crop development, agricultural engineering, milling and processing, economics and biometrics and technology transfer.

A key research output from KESREF has been the development and release of new varieties of sugar cane. In 1992, three new cane varieties were released. In 1998 four varieties were released while in 2002, six varieties were released. In the year 2007, six varieties were released, namely EAK 73-335, KEN 82-62, KEN 82-472, KEN 83-311, KEN 85-83 and D 8484.

Kenya Seed Company

The Kenya Seed Company is a State corporation whose mandate is to conduct research, promote and facilitate production of high yielding better quality certified seed to farmers and stakeholders and to enhance food self-sufficiency in the country.

The company was incorporated in 1956 to promote the use of improved strains of pasture seed that was developed by the National Agricultural Research Station at Kitale. In 1958, the company started to produce commercial sunflower for the European bird feed market. In 1963, the company introduced hybrid seed maize production. Seed wheat was produced in 1971 to provide certified seeds to farmers who previously relied on low-quality farm saved seed. In 1979, the company acquired Simpson and White Law, a company that was dealing in horticultural seeds and introduced the brand name "Simlaw Seeds". The core function of Simlaw Company is selling and marketing of high-quality horticultural seeds. In the same year 1979, Kenya Seed incorporated Kibo and Mt Elgon Seed companies in Tanzania and Uganda respectively as a market expansion strategy.

Kenya Seed Company has produced seed varieties for pasture, maize, wheat, barley, sorghum, sunflower and horticulture. For pasture, Kenya Seed has introduced varieties for rhodes grass *(chloris gayana);* forage sorghum and leguminous grasses. For maize *(zea mays)* the Company has introduced a wide variety of certified maize seed suitable for all agro-ecological zones of the East African region. Highland maize varieties as well as transitional and dry land agro-ecozone varieties have been introduced. The Katumani Composite B variety is significant in this context. It is a fast-growing, open-pollinated variety and is a drought-escaping variety for marginal areas. The Dry Land Agro-Ecozone (DLC1) is a variety for arid and semi-arid lands. For sunflowers, Kenya Seed has continued to produce new varieties for the export market; of significance is the hybrid sunflower for oil extraction.

Under the Simlaw brand, Kenya Seed has improved indigenous vegetables. Seeds have been developed for black nightshade (managu); spider plant (saget) and amaranthus (terere) which are highly nutritious.[67]

Institute of Primate Research

The origin of the Institute of Primate Research is connected to the life and times of Louis Seymour Bazett Leakey. Today, the Institute is under the National Museums of Kenya. It is a World Health Organization collaborating centre for research in reproductive biology, infectious diseases and ecology/conservation. It has a fully equipped surgical complex, quarantine facility and laboratory. It has over 500 primates, mainly baboons.

At the Institute, reproductive research is applied to endometriosis, assisted reproduction and prevention of heterosexual transmission of HIV and includes investigation on immuno-contraceptives and placental retroviruses. The reproductive research capacities of the Primate Institute include: video laparoscopic surgical equipment, surgical experience, endometrial biopsies and uterine flushes, ovarian stimulations, laparoscopic oocyte aspiration, sperm assessment and hormonal analyses in baboon blood as well as *in vitro* culture.

The Institute of Primate Research has in the recent past enhanced collaboration with other Kenyan gynecologists' at the level of KEMRI, Kenyatta National Hospital and the Aga Khan Hospital to develop clinical infertility services including low-budget, high-quality In-Vitro Fertilization (IVF) in Nairobi. The logic behind this initiative is that the Kenyans trained in non-human primate embryology and IVF would be natural partners to develop human IVF in Kenya.

Pyrethrum Board of Kenya

Pyrethrum Board of Kenya is a state corporation charged with the responsibility of overseeing production, processing and marketing of pyrethrum in Kenya. As a crop, colonial farmers introduced pyrethrum in Kenya in 1920 and the governance of the industry was in the private sector until 1980 when the State Corporations Act was established to govern all state corporations including the Pyrethrum Board.

When the State Corporations Act was passed in 1980, political appointees joined the directorship and management of the Pyrethrum Board. These appointees had no knowledge of the crop. The directors and managers ran down the Pyrethrum Board and pyrethrum industry. Farmers uprooted the crop due to delayed and at times non-payment for

---

[67] See Daily Nation Newspaper, Nairobi, 25 October 2010.

pyrethrum delivered. Cases of theft of pyrethrum stocks were rampant in the 1980s while managers engaged in corruption. As farmers abandoned crop, the Board closed offices. Since 2008, there have been attempts by government to revitalize the pyrethrum industry and appoint new directors. The mismanagement of the Pyrethrum Board and industry implied that no research and new varieties were introduced in Kenya. The practical result is that new synthetic pyrethrins from developed countries entered the market further spelling doom to the pyrethrum industry in Kenya.

National Council for Science and Technology (NCST)

The National Council for Science and Technology is a statutory body established in 1977 under the Science and Technology Act. The NCST is not a research institute. The functions of the Council are to determine the priorities for scientific and technological activities in Kenya. The Council's role is to advise the government on the National Science Policy including assessment of the requisite financial resources, and to ensure the application of results of scientific activities to the development of agriculture, industry and social welfare in Kenya. This particular function relates to promotion of innovation and technology diffusion. The Council is also mandated to ensure cooperation and coordination between various agencies involved in the machinery for making the national science policy.

The Council also has an advisory role with regard to the application of results of research; transfer of technology into agriculture and industry; training of scientific and technical manpower; scientific research and technology funding and science education at all levels. The Council has interpreted these roles to include promoting and popularizing science and technology culture in the country.

In order to discharge its mandate, the NCST has eight specialist Committees, namely: Agriculture and Allied Sciences; Biological Sciences; Environmental and Earth Sciences; Health Science; Industrial Science; Information and Communication Science; Physical and Nuclear Sciences and Social Science. The specialist committees comprise a Council member and five to ten other specialists in the particular science field. The Committees provide advice on details of research programs and projects. In addition, they implement identified research priorities arising from the national science policy. The Committees also assess the financial, human resources and facilities required. The Committees disseminate research findings and coordinate research activities in their respective scientific field.

Horticultural Crops Development Authority (HCDA)

The Horticultural Crops Development Authority is mandated to facilitate the development, promotion, coordination and regulation of the horticultural industry in Kenya. It is not a research institute. One of its coordination functions is to organize smallholders into production and marketing groups through contract farming by implementing the code of conduct thus improving producer-buyer linkages. The Authority also promotes local utilization and consumption of horticultural products.

The Authority's mandate includes improving productivity through demonstrations of new technologies and introducing new crop varieties. The Authority also collaborates with research and training institutions to generate new technologies and develop quality standards for produce in the local market. These functions have a bearing on technology transfer, adaptation and technology diffusion and innovation within the horticultural sector.

National Environmental Management Authority (NEMA)

The National Environmental Management Authority has a role to play in innovation with regards to biodiversity conservation. This is more pertinent with regard to NEMA Regulations on Access and Benefit Sharing, biodiversity assessment and integration of biodiversity concerns into development planning.

Under the Conservation of Biological Diversity and Resources, Access to Genetic Resources and Benefit Sharing Regulations of 2006,[68] any person who intends to access genetic resources in Kenya should apply to NEMA for an access permit. The holder of an access permit is required to inform the Authority of all discoveries from research involving genetic resources and/or intangible components thereof. The holder of an access permit is required to facilitate the active involvement of Kenyan citizens and institutions in the execution of activities under the permit. The facilitation includes enjoyment of both monetary and non-monetary benefits arising from the right of access granted and use of genetic resources. The monetary benefits include research funding, joint ventures and joint ownership of relevant IP rights. Non-monetary benefits include participation in product development, collaboration, cooperation and contribution in scientific research and development programs and strengthening capacities for technology transfer to Kenya as well as institutional capacity building.

---

[68] Kenya Gazette Supplement No. 84 of 1 December 2006.

Kenya Wildlife Service (KWS)

The Kenya Wildlife Service is a State Corporation charged with the responsibility of wildlife conservation in Kenya. The Service controls several national and game parks where in-situ biodiversity exists. To the extent that KWS controls access to part of Kenya's biodiversity, the institution has a role to play with regards to innovation.

Recently, Novozymes and KWS entered into an agreement on biological diversity with effect from May 2007. The agreement is in line with the principles of the United Nations' Convention on Biological Diversity (CBD). Together, Novozymes and KWS have initiated a collaboration to characterize Kenyan microbial diversity from specific biological niches. As part of the project, Novozymes will train Kenyan students in taxonomy, isolation and identification of microorganisms. Furthermore, Novozymes will transfer advanced technology to Kenya, including knowledge of how to collect and isolate microorganisms and how to characterize microbial diversity.

The agreement gives Novozymes the right to make commercial use of Kenya's microbial diversity in return for financial compensation and local institutional capacity building. Under this agreement, if Novozymes commercializes products developed on the basis of microbial strains isolated as part of the collaborative project, KWS will receive a milestone payment and a running royalty from sales. Furthermore, Novozymes has been granted rights on similar terms to commercially make use of specific strains isolated in Kenya, which are already in Novozymes' possession. One minor product has already been marketed based on one of these strains

Public Universities, Polytechnics and Innovation in Kenya

In Kenya, publicly funded basic research has been concentrated in public universities. These are:

(i) University of Nairobi
(ii) Kenyatta University
(iii) Moi University
(iv) Egerton University
(v) Jomo Kenyatta University of Agriculture and Technology (JKUAT)
(vi) Maseno University and
(vii) Masinde Muliro University of Technology

There are a number of non-university academic institutions including national polytechnics that undertake research, particularly innovational research. The national polytechnics are Kenya Polytechnic in Nairobi, Mombasa Polytechnic, Eldoret Polytechnic and Kisumu Polytechnic. Other notable institutions include the Kiambu Institute of Science and Technology, Rift Valley Institute of Science and Technology and the Kimathi Institute of Science and Technology in Nyeri as well as the Kenya Industrial Training Institute (KITI) at Nakuru. Other middle-level technical institutes include Kaiboi Technical, Migori Technical Institute, Ramogi Institute of Advanced Technology (RIAT-Kisumu) and Mawego Technical Institute as well as the Department of Industrial Training (DIT).

At Kenyatta University, the Appropriate Technology Centre (ATC) is the leader in innovation. The Centre receives funding from external agencies such as the Intermediate Technology Development Group, German Technical Cooperation (GTZ) and UNICEF. The Centre in collaboration with KENGO developed a famous cooking stove, the Kenya Ceramic Jiko, as well as other minor products. Internally, the ATC is divided into seven subject areas namely: agriculture, manufacturing, renewable energy, construction, water technologies, biomass and stove testing, and transport. The staff component at ATC has varied from a low of 25, of whom 14 were technically trained, to a high of 42, of whom 25 were technically trained. Recent fluctuations in staffing numbers are high, in large part because of a dearth of financing. Foreign assistance has ceased and the primary funding is from Kenyatta University of which over 80 per cent is expended on wages and salaries. Operating under such constraint, the ATC's further contribution to the development of appropriate technologies has been minimal.

At the University of Nairobi, the Faculty of Science (including Veterinary Agriculture) and the Medical School (including the College of Health Sciences) are the core to innovation and have links with foreign institutions. These faculties receive large donations. However, despite the foregoing, patent applications and grants to the University of Nairobi is negligible. Trademark registrations or utility model certificates in favour of the University of Nairobi is also negligible.

Moi University, Masinde Muliro University as well as all other public and private universities in Kenya reveal the same trend. Innovation measured by the number of patent applications and patent grants is non-existent. Polytechnics and technical training institutions exhibit the same pattern. Inference may be drawn that little innovation is taking place at public universities, polytechnics and technical institutions. It would appear that these publicly funded institutions devote more attention to basic teaching and training rather than research and development.

Impact of university research on industrial innovation in Kenya

The efficacy of university research is measured by how industry absorbs research findings by producing new products or processes based on university research. Industry regards as successful interaction with research institutes that undertake projects with a higher degree of sophistication than was available in the industry.

In Kenya, university-industry linkage has been ad hoc, sporadic and unsuccessful with no concrete university policy to promote and guide the linkages. The universities are good at research but poor at its exploitation.[69] Most of the universities have made efforts to set up linkage or international relations offices but the innovative impact of such offices is yet to be seen. For example, the University of Nairobi has an office for International Relations and Linkages. Other than vetting contracts and concluding collaboration agreements, the innovative impact of the office has not been measured.

Impediments to university–industry linkages in Kenya There are various impediments to industry-university linkages in Kenya. Research institutes and universities seldom appreciate what industry requires, and conflicts of interest abound. Universities and research institutes focus on basic research while industry requires new products and processes. Attitudinal factors and industry's lack of in-house research capabilities contribute to low university–industry linkages. Attitudinal factor is reflected in the belief by researchers that industry is interested in their work while on the part of industry the attitude is that nothing good comes from universities and research institutes. This contemptuous attitude is further aggravated by industry perception that university graduates are more theoretical than practical. Such a mindset does not foster linkages. Due to the industry perception, there is reluctance by industry to support and fund research at universities and in the rare cases of support, industry would want to direct what research is to be conducted and when to do it.

An additional factor that dictates the low levels of industry–university linkages is the priority of each party. The Kenyan experience shows that universities and research institutes are predominantly concerned with their internal problems of staffing, finance and expansion. On the other hand, industry is preoccupied with lack of adequate markets, institutional rigidities, inefficient infrastructure and poor regulatory framework. Industry

[69] "Implementing the Race to the Top", Lord Sainsbury's Review of Government's Science and Innovation Policies, UK Department for Innovation, Universities & Skills at p 16–17.

is rarely aware that there is local scientific research capacity that may provide plausible solutions to their problems.

Table 9.1 below lists types of unsuccessful links that involved the University of Nairobi, revealing that eight (47.1 per cent) of the 17 unsuccessful interactions at the university were with subsidiaries of Multi National Corporations (MNCs) and six (35.3 per cent) were with large-scale firms (LSF).[70] There was only one unsuccessful link involving an informal-sector entrepreneur. Individual members of staff carried out three of the projects.

From the field survey conduct, Table 9.2 below highlights some of the impediments to industry-university linkages.

In the Kenyan context, the Jomo Kenyatta University of Advanced Technology (JKUAT) has tried to address university–industry linkage in various ways. The University now has a policy where all students must undergo industrial attachment; it is compulsory for each lecturer to spend some time on attachment in a relevant industry so that they are acquainted with changing trends in their fields; the University has developed an IP policy that motivates the innovators by giving them a percentage of profits made from commercialization of their innovations; the University has signed a number of memorandum of understanding with various companies to commercialize their innovations and the University has established a policy to train small artisans and to sublet production of components of its innovation products. The University has also set up a commercial company known as JKUAT Enterprises that assist innovators to commercialize their innovations.

The JKUAT established an Innovation Fund in 2005 to support the generation and application of new ideas and skills that will lead to production of new products, processes and services. The Fund supports inter alia research outputs projects with potential for commercial value and setting up demonstration plots and/or pilot plants.

Another example of linkage between university and innovation process is through the SUCAPRI initiative. SUCAPRI is an acronym for "Strengthening of university capacity for promoting, facilitating and teaching rural innovation". The project is funded by the European Union and Implemented by the ACP Secretariat. The project is a network of teaching and research staff in Makerere University (in Uganda) and four

---

[70] The Table is reproduced from a paper written by Henry M. Bwisa and Alex R. Gacuhi titled "An Investigation into Factors that Influence the Diffusion and Adoption of Inventions and Innovations from Research Institutes and Universities in Kenya" ATPS Working Paper No. 19 – September 1999.

Table 9.1 Description of unsuccessful interactions at the University of Nairobi

Description of project	Department or unit	Company (category)[a]
Research-support mechanisms		
Research collaboration on *Matricaria chamomilla* L. project	Chemistry	Dawa Pharmaceuticals Ltd (MNC)
Proposed research project on salt and soda quality	Industrial Research and Consultancy Unit	Magadi Soda plc (MNC)
Extension of research project on sand analysis for cement production	Civil Engineering	Bamburi Portland Cement Co Ltd (MNC)
Knowledge-transfer mechanisms		
Kenya car project	Central administration	Naciti Engineers Ltd (LSE)
Student attachment, participation in 2nd Conference on University–Industry Cooperation Workshop in Chemistry	Chemistry	Dawa Pharmaceuticals Ltd (MNC) CPC Industrial Products Ltd (MNC) East Africa Industries Ltd (MNC) Kenya Breweries Ltd (LSE) Magadi Soda plc (MNC)
Technology-transfer mechanisms		
Energy auditing in a large dairy	Food Technology and Nutrition	Kenya Cooperative Creameries (LSE)
Foundry technology for local enterprises project	Mechanical Engineering	African Marine and General Engineering Works (LSE)
Engineering consultancy on refurbishment of existing foundry	Mechanical Engineering	African Marine and General Engineering Works (LSE)
General-cooperation mechanisms		
Attempts to form a national forum for university–industry interactions	Central administration	Kenya Assn of Manufacturers (NGO)
Coopted membership of the University–Industry Links Committee	Central administration	Naciti Engineers Ltd (LSE)
General cooperation on Unesco-sponsored projects	Chemistry	Dawa Pharmaceuticals Ltd (MNC)
General cooperation on the development and dissemination of low-cost building materials	Housing and Building Research Institute	Undugu Society, Metal Workshops (NGO) Shelter Works (ISE)

Source: Field survey, 1991/92.
[a] ISE, informal-sector entrepreneur; LSE, large-scale enterprise; MNC, (subsidiary of) multinational company; NGO, nongovernmental organization.

Table 9.2 Barriers to institute–industry interactions (mean responses)

Impediments to interactions	University[a] (n = 12)	Industry[a] (n = 16)
The orientation of the institute's research toward basic research is a mismatch with industry's needs for new and improved products	2.53 (3)	2.53 (2)
The need for the institute to publish research results is in conflict with industry's needs for protection of its trade secrets	3.35 (7)	3.44 (9)
Research performed by institutes is generally more expensive than in-house research	3.65 (9)	3.44 (9)
The institute often does not understand what industry needs in the way of product-oriented research or industry's need to maximize profits as return on investment	3.29 (5)	2.39 (1)
Legal matters regarding the institute's research inhibit the commercialization of these innovations	3.77 (10)	3.59 (10)
National industrial property policies hamper relationships	3.82 (11)	4.06 (12)
National research institutes are unable to efficiently undertake industry-sponsored applied research	3.47 (8)	3.03 (5)
Collaborations could affect the normal research environment and processes	4.35 (12)	3.97 (11)
Industry is reluctant to support national research institutes in basic research	2.24 (1)	3.03 (5)
Industry lacks its own in-house research capabilities	3.06 (4)	2.83 (4)
Attitudinal factors create a generalized culture gap and lack of understanding	2.41 (2)	2.83 (3)
Distance is a factor – some activities depend on close proximity between collaborators	3.29 (5)	3.36 (8)

Source: Field survey, 1991/92.

Notes: n, number of respondents; numbers in parentheses refer to the ranking of the determinants by order of importance.
[a] Significance conversion table: 1.49 or less, dominant; 1.50–2.49, very significant; 2.50–3.49, significant; 3.50–4.49, occasionally significant; 4.50 or over insignificant.

universities in Kenya (Nairobi, Egerton, Kenyatta and Jomo Kenyatta). The aim is to strengthen the capacity of the five universities to participate in decentralized national agricultural research system and to prepare professionals with the competencies needed to promote agricultural rural innovation. The goal is to establish a core team of change agents in each of the universities and link these with other key stakeholders in the field of rural innovation who can then jointly develop and promote agricultural innovation. The core team is to be linked with the International Centre for Development Oriented Research in Agriculture in the Netherlands which will improve teaching practice and research in rural innovation process.

Intellectual Property Portfolio of Public Universities in Kenya

Table 9.3 below is a concordance of patent applications received at the Kenya Industrial Property Offices emanating from public universities in Kenya.

Analysis of Kenya's National Innovation System

An overview of Kenya's national innovation system shows that the country has established an institutional framework for a self-sustaining indigenous capacity to innovate and invent technologies. Innovation strategy, funding for R&D and adequate human resource technical capacity is lacking. However, from public universities, there is limited empirical data to show that the research findings are exploited and that society is benefiting from research expenditure in public universities. There is little systematic data on innovation from public universities and there are major gaps in understanding the roles of users, consumers and other social actors in the innovation process. There is no automatic connection between areas of potential strength (or weakness) and policy actions. Some innovation policies aim to build on areas of strength to maximize economic and social returns; others aim to address areas of weakness.

Strength of Kenya innovation system

There are, however, numerous areas of strength in Kenya's innovation system. These include:

Existing legal and institutional framework for recognition, protection and enforcement of intellectual property rights The legal framework that rewards innovation is the IP system. Kenya has enacted legislation for the protection of patents, trademarks, industrial designs, utility models, copyright and plant breeders' rights. In addition, common law protects trade secrets. Computer programs and data are also protected. Kenya is a member of numerous regional and multilateral IP agreements. The country has domesticated the WTO TRIPS Agreement, the WIPO Paris Convention for Protection of Industrial Property and the Copyright Treaties. These legal regimes provide a solid framework for protection of creative and innovative products and processes. The national legal

Table 9.3 Patent applications from local universities as at 16/07/2009

No	Status	Application No	Filing Date	Registration No	Registration Date	Applicant	Title
1	Withdrawn	KE P 1993 96	06/07/1993 0:00			University of Nairobi	Products from *melia volkensii* for insect and tick control
2	Not granted	KE P 2004 408	07/04/2004 0:00			Moi University	An electro-coagulation method for colour removal in wastewater or water with low power consumption.
3	Granted	KE P 2004 420	22/07/2004 0:00	220	05/07/2006	Egerton University	
4	Abandoned	KE P 2006 490	12/05/2006 0:00			Jomo Kenyatta University of Agriculture And Techno	A trap for controlling bont ticks in pastures
5	Awaiting substantive examination	KE P 2008 735	05/04/2005 13:05			Moi University	An electro-coagulation method of colour removal in wastewater or water with low power consumption.
6	Not granted (awaiting correction of defects)	KE P 2008 784	13/08/2008 12:55			Maseno University	African indigenous vegetable products with prolonged shelf life.
7	Awaiting substantive examination	KE P 2008 795	15/09/2008 11:02			Moi University	Agro-chemical waste water use as fertilizer
8	NA Awaiting correction of defects	KE P 2009 922	11/06/2009 12:05			Kenyatta University	Compositions for attracting blood-feeding insects.
9	NA Awaiting correction of defects	KE P 923	11/06/2009 12:05			Kenyatta University	Repellant compositions for blood-feeding insects.

framework establishes administrative and institutional regulatory structures for recognition and enforcement of the IP rights. The Kenya Industrial Property Institute, the Copyright Board of Kenya and the Kenya Plant Health Inspectorate Services are institutions charged with granting IP rights. With regard to enforcement, the Anti-Counterfeit Act of 2009 establishes a legal regime to combat piracy and counterfeit.[71]

An example of positive impact of the legal framework in promoting innovation and technology diffusion can be glanced from the plant variety protection system. The international plant breeders' protection regime started to operate in Kenya in 1997. Since Kenya's accession to the UPOV 1978 Convention (in 1999), there has been significant increase in the number of varieties developed and released.[72] There has also been increased introduction of foreign varieties particularly in the horticultural sector, which contribute to diversification and support of competitiveness in the industry. Increased introduction of foreign germplasm in the form of new, protected varieties has been evidenced. This has also impacted positively on the increase in the number of Kenyan-bred varieties of agricultural crops with improved performance such as pest and disease tolerance, nutritional qualities, early maturity and tolerance to abiotic stresses.

Existing infrastructural and institutional research capability Kenya has numerous public research institutes charged with responsibility to conduct research in specific fields. These institutes have institutional and administrative capability to conduct research. Some of the institutes have physical and laboratory facilities that if well utilized, should result in innovative products rolling on to market shelves. The facilities and equipment at KEMRI, KARI, KIRDI, KEPHIS, the Numerical Machine Complex as well as the Kenya Bureau of Standards compare well to state of the art. This is not to mention the facilities available in public universities and other research institutes like the Coffee and Tea Research Foundations and the Institute of Primate Research. Physical survey reveals that Kenya has basic and applied research facilities that are critical to dovetailing the country into the innovation path.

Promulgation of a Science, Technology and Innovation (STI) Policy Kenya already has a National Science Policy. Recently, the Cabinet has approved

---

[71] The Act came into force on 7th July 2009.

[72] UPOV Report on the Impact of Plant Variety Protection, UPOV (International Union for the Protection of New Varieties of Plants) 2005 at pages 85–86.

the formulation of a Science, Technology and Innovation (STI) policy. In addition, the formulation of a national IP policy and strategy is underway. All these policy initiatives are strengths that enable Kenya to take and implement strategic measures to strengthen and enhance its national innovation system. The proposed STI policy provides for incentives to innovation. It also has provision for research and innovation fund. The role of public universities and research institutions in promoting innovation is underscored. The policy aims to incorporate the teaching of intellectual property in the educational curriculum of the country.

Enhanced awareness of IP and innovation in public and private universities and polytechnics Traditionally, public universities and polytechnics in Kenya understood their primary function to be teaching. Research was a secondary objective and undertaken as end in itself and a ticket towards career progression giving rise to the slogan "publish or perish" among the faculty.

From the year 2000, the Kenya Industrial Property Institute has undertaken a deliberate and concerted effort to raise the level of IP awareness in public universities and national polytechnics. The universities have been sensitized on the need to formulate university IP policy. In addition, they have been encouraged to adopt the slogan "research to invent". Universities have now adopted an IP culture and have come up with University IP policies. The University of Nairobi, Moi University, Kenyatta University and Jomo Kenyatta University for Advanced Technology all have individual IP policies. The universities are in the process of establishing technology/science parks to promote commercialization of their research findings. Technology licensing officers have also been recruited. Deliberate efforts to enhance university-industry linkages are also being undertaken. The foregoing initiatives are a positive strength in Kenya's innovation system.

Existing collaboration initiatives with foreign and non-governmental research institutes Public universities and research institutes in Kenya have established linkages and networks with foreign and other external research agencies. Such collaboration initiatives are a fertile ground for technology transfer and diffusions. Collaboration provides an opportunity for Kenyan scientists to access the latest technical and scientific knowledge, equipment and funding that are crucial in the innovative cycle. Examples of collaborative linkages in Kenya's research institutions abound. For example, KARI has developed linkages with the Tropical Soil Biology & Fertility; International Institute of Tropical Agriculture; International Potato Research Centre; International Institute of Biological Control;

International Maize and Wheat Improvement Centre (IMWIC) and the International Livestock Research Institute among others.

The Institute of Primate Research at the National Museums of Kenya has collaboration with John Hopkins University; the World Health Organization; Rutgers University; Kenya Wildlife Service; Anderson Cancer Centre; Coriell Institute (USA); Southwest Foundation for Biomedical Research and University of Texas Health Sciences Centre.

The University of Nairobi has collaborative agreements with Western Michigan University; Washington School of Medicine and Faculty of Medicine of the University of Toronto among others.

The Kenya Medical Research Institute (KEMRI) has collaborations with British Medical Research Council; Wellcome Trust Foundation; Walter Reed Army Institute of Medical Research (WAIR); Nagasaki University Institute of Tropical Medicine; Medical Research Council of South Africa and the Suez Canal University of Egypt among others.

Existing technology and policy research organizations Effective implementation of a national technology and innovation strategy requires analysis of the policy framework that underpins realization of the strategy. Kenya has numerous private sector (civil society) organizations that conduct public policy analysis. Some of these specifically target public policy and technology. The African Centre for Technology Studies (ACTS), the Kenya National Academy of Science and the African Technology Policy Studies Network (ATPS) among others are a case in point. On the government side, the Kenya Institute of Public Policy and Research Analysis (KIPPRA) is at the forefront in examining IP impact in the country. The Kenya Energy and Environment Organization (KENGO) has been able to develop ceramic jiko (cooking stove) for rural and urban low-income families.[73] The new stove uses up to 50 per cent less fuel wood and it reduces cost of fuel while decreasing cooking time.

The studies undertaken from such organizations are strength in Kenya's innovation system to the extent that such studies evaluate the impact of policy on innovation.

Presence of inter-governmental research organizations Kenya is host to several inter-governmental research organizations. Examples are the International Livestock Research Institute (ILRI), International

[73] KENGO is an indigenous NGO membership organization established in 1982 to promote grassroots organizational involvement in renewable energy, environmental management and community development.

Crop Research Institute for the Semi-arid Tropics (ICRISAT), and the International Centre of Insect Physiology & Ecology (ICIPE). These international research organizations employ Kenyan scientists and contribute towards the development of human resource capacity in the country. The experience gained through learning-by-doing is also enhanced taking into account the state-of-the-art equipment in these inter-governmental research organizations.

For example, ICRISAT has bred a new variety of pigeon peas, which require little rain, no fertilizer, and is drought resistant. The variety can be harvested twice a year and the crop matures in three months. ICRISAT has disseminated the technology to local plant breeders in various parts of Kenya.[74] The new pigeon pea variety was developed through cross-pollination and can tolerate high temperatures.

The headquarters of ICIPE are in Nairobi. ICIPE is engaged in tropical science for development. Together with partners, ICIPE searches for effective prevention, security, sustainable livelihoods, good health and sustainable tropics. ICIPE's four major divisions – human health, animal health, plant health and three research departments – play a role in contributing to chemical ecology, molecular biology and biotechnological science. ICIPE's objective is to help alleviate poverty, ensure food security, protect the environment and conserve and make better use of natural resources. As part of Kenya's national innovation system, ICIPE's scientists and laboratories contribute to innovation and human resource capacity building in the country.

The International Livestock Research Institute (ILRI) works at the crossroads of livestock bringing high-quality science and capacity building to bear on poverty reduction and sustainable development. ILRI is a non-profit-making non-governmental organization with headquarters in Nairobi. ILRI employs innovation system approach to enhance effectiveness of its research. ILRI conducts research in five themes – targeting research and development opportunities, enabling innovation, improving market opportunities, using biotechnology to secure livestock and people as well as research on livestock and the environment. ILRI is funded by more than 60 private, public and government organizations. Some donors support ILRI with program funds while others finance individual research projects.

Existing human resource and skill development In order to establish an innovative, knowledge-based economy, there must be investment in

---

[74] See Sunday Nation Newspaper, Nairobi – Kenya, 9th August 2009 at p 3, "New Pigeon Pea Variety Boosts Food Security".

education, skills, technical competence, know-how and the health of the population. Kenya has a functioning educational system, which has worked well to increase the level of literacy. This trained human resource capital is a strength in the national innovation system. The number of graduating students from local universities has been increasing and this provides a base for establishing a knowledge-based economy. The number of engineers, medical doctors, scientists and other professionals has also been increasing.[75] The challenge has been to provide them with their tools of trade and the industrial exposure to sharpen skills acquired in the classroom and to enable experience to be acquired through learning by doing.

Kenya has a pool of indigenous citizens who can be used as a seeding point towards innovation. However, this pool of trained human resource is threatened by the brain drain scourge, unattractive remuneration packages and lack of merit in career progression. There is also the question of limited research grants and failure to appreciate that successful research requires time, patience and money. These fundamentals must be addressed. In the educational curricular, there is need to shift focus to increasing numeracy skills as well as inculcating the culture of empirical and analytical thinking. New didactic and pedagogical skills for a digital economy need to be adopted.

The health of the population as a human resource capital and people as source of ideas must not be overlooked. A healthy population is a reliable and sustainable human-resource base for innovation in a country. A healthy population lives longer and the country benefits from the training, skills and experience acquired over time. An unhealthy population implies a dying population and this means an undependable, unproductive and inexperienced human-resource base. The rate of inflow of new, skilled population and the regeneration rate of an unhealthy population is high. Such a regeneration rate means there is no accumulation and increase in the number of technical manpower and skilled competencies in the country. In Kenya, evidence shows that it is the educated, trained and skilled personnel who are succumbing to the HIV-AIDS pandemic,[76] and who are contributing to the brain drain. This reduces the technically competent human-resource base that could launch the country into a sustainable innovation path. In Kenya, as at 2003, it was estimated that 6.7 per cent of the adult population is living with HIV/AIDS and of this 65 per

---

[75] As of 1990, Kenya had 16,241 scientists and 45,962 technicians. This number has been increasing. See UNESCO Statistical Year Book 1990, Table 5.2 and 5.17.

[76] See 7th edition of AIDS in Kenya Report that indicates a HIV prevalence rate of 8 per cent in adult women and 4 per cent in adult men.

cent were adult women and 57 per cent adult male. In 2001, the percentage of young men between 15–24 years living with HIV/AIDS was 4.8–7.2 per cent.[77]

Other strengths in Kenya's innovation system include the existence of the jua kali sector and increasing appreciation of the role of innovation in national development. Individual researchers and innovators also exist in Kenya who, if motivated and given financial support in commercialization, can assist promoting creativity and innovation in the country.

Examples of innovative Kenyans include Mr Pascal Katana and Mr Jeremiah Murimi who as fourth-year students of electrical and information engineering at the University of Nairobi designed a smart mobile phone charger which is powered by the dynamo of a bicycle.[78] The device converts the heat generated in the dynamo into electricity that is used to charge the phone, it has a capacitor that stores and controls the current while a voltage stabilizer reduces the current from the dynamo. No charging can take place unless the bicycle is being pedalled.

Weakness of Kenya's innovation system

Kenya's national innovation system suffers from a myriad of weaknesses some of which have been identified as:

Meagre public expenditure in basic research Public investment in R&D is weak in Kenya. At the core of a knowledge- and technology-based economy is public expenditure on research. This reflects the public good characteristics of fundamental scientific research and the spillover externalities generally accepted as emanating from R&D. In Kenya, public expenditure in research as base for national innovation is meagre. In addition, there is limited relationship between public expenditure on research and diffusion of public research findings into economic impact that go towards wider transmission and development of knowledge in technologically intensive sectors of the economy. There is no evidence that public research in Kenya is contributing to the stock of knowledge in the economy. The science budget is low in real and nominal terms. Empirical data on public expenditure in R&D is discernible when it is noted that less than 1 per cent of the country's GDP is spent on research. In addition, over 80 per cent of the budget of public universities and research institutes

[77] See National AIDS Control Council of Kenya: www.nacc.or.ke/; UNAIDS Kenya Country Page: www.unaids.org/en.

[78] See Nairobi Daily Nation Newspaper, 22nd July 2009, "Expect More Calls from the Village".

go towards operation and maintenance budget and are not utilized for research and innovation.

Limited exploitation of publicly funded research and limited technology diffusion from research base The meagre public funds spent on R&D has not yielded any tangible transfer and absorption of technology to the market place. There is no evidence that publicly funded research has given rise to a new product or process in Kenya. From the non-existent patent grants to insignificant number of patent applications from public universities, there is no evidence of universities commercializing results of research. An exception to the foregoing statement relates to expenditure on plant breeding. There is evidence that new plant varieties have been developed and disseminated from public research institutions.

One of the reasons for limited exploitation of publicly funded research is the lack of communication between scientists and industry. Scientists need to communicate better to improve the uptake of advancing technologies. Most Kenyan scientists are cocooned in laboratories – churning out findings but neglecting to pass them on to consumers.[79] Scientists should recognize that their poor communication skills are a problem. Universities and research institutes should make use of the mass media to inform the public about their discoveries. It is recommended that institutions should be measured in success by counting the number of people who are successfully using research findings. This shall highlight that the value of science lies in its rate of transfer to the end user.

Universities and public research institutions are not information sources There is poor uptake of research products from research institutes and public universities by industry. Lack of clear policy, limited or non-existent funding for research and apathy among universities to develop applied research has resulted in a lukewarm relationship between industry and the universities.[80] Empirical data shows that businesses in Kenya use other businesses, customers, suppliers, collaborators and competitors as sources of their innovative activities. The ratio of businesses stating that universities and research institutes are an important source of innovative activities is fictional in Kenya. No business has reported or documented a high level of knowledge exchange with institutions of

[79] See Nairobi Daily Nation 27th January 2009 "Scientists Failing to Communicate".

[80] See Daily Nation, 20th May 2009, "Missing Link between Industry and Universities".

higher learning, research institutes or other similar providers of scientific expertise. There is no evidence of indirect knowledge flow through publications, operation of consultancies, codified standards and movement of people from university to industry. Lack of research at universities and poor linkage to industry is one of the biggest obstacles to industrial growth in Kenya, it should be realized that industrial development hinges on the linkage between government, industry and research institutions. Unless there is a clear link in the role of each, how they work together cannot be defined.

Limited number of creative and innovative people New ideas rarely come as a flash of inspiration to a lone, genius inventor, they come from how people create, combine and share their ideas. Kenya's capacity to unlock and harness the talent, energy and imagination of all individuals is crucial to making innovation stronger and more sustainable.

As a country, Kenya thrives on importing and distributing other country's innovative products. The country depends less on technical and apparatus imitation and copying; and even less on reverse engineering. The existence of a skilled, inquisitive and analytical population is a *sine qua non* for creativity and innovation. The absence of an inquisitive and experiential (experimentation) culture in Kenya implies that technology is not embraced but is feared.

The effects of an innovative people are self-reinforcing: innovative businesses are attracted to highly skilled and creative workforces and in turn, innovative people are drawn towards exciting and challenging career opportunities. Innovative people generate new ideas that require skilled people to implement and exploit them. In Kenya, trained personnel can only undertake basic scientific research. The stock of the country's scientists is the bedrock of the country's potential innovators.

Absence of incentive structure to facilitate innovation Innovation is not a happenstance event. It involves research and requires time and money. It involves the sweat of the brow. Without an incentive system to encourage, motivate and reward those who take time to innovate, the innovation process cannot attract a critical mass of knowledgeable persons. The few who are attracted will do so for personal and not societal gain. Recognizing that the optimum gain and returns for an individual is much lower than the optimum aggregate gain for society, the absence of an innovation incentive system generates sub-optimal returns to society.

In the Kenyan context, there is no coherent innovation incentive system. Any incentives that there are, while appearing to be deliberate, have no positive impact in promoting innovation. For instance, under the

Industrial Property Act of 2001, the Minister may waive patent application fees in relation to inventions that are of public interest. Such a provision is *ex post facto* to the extent that it is premised on the fact that the creativity and inventiveness has already taken place. An incentive system must be *ex ante a priori* to the innovation. There is no record in Kenya that the Ministerial waiver has been used. The implication is that whereas the waiver exists in law, it is yet to yield practical effect.

A further example is the research fund in NCST. The fund is available to promote scientific research in the country, but there is no empirical data to demonstrate that the existence of the research fund is an incentive to innovation. Despite the increasing number of applicants for research grants from the NCST, what the country requires is innovative products on market shelves. At fiscal level, it can be argued that the duty free importation of scientific equipment and other capital goods into Kenya is an incentive to innovation through provision of tools and equipment. Admittedly, such fiscal incentives may spur innovation but the primary consideration in granting the duty free importation is industrial development and technology transfer. The fiscal incentives have not been designed and skewed towards providing incentives to innovators. In the educational sector, there is no deliberate effort to nurture a culture of creativity and inventiveness. The education curricular is not empirical and analytical; the human resource skill being trained is passive, inactive and geared towards fearing technology and anathema to reverse engineering; there is very limited experiential learning in Kenya's education curricular; and the education system is premised on cramming and passing examination rather than on inquisitorial and experiential training.

The practical effect in the Kenyan context is that there is no systemic arrangement to provide incentives for innovation. The process of innovation has been relegated to a happenstance event with individual drive. Such an approach to innovation is sub-optimal and unrealistic. The country needs to put in place deliberate measures that provide incentives and reward to innovators. These measures must be practical, physical, fiscal and complementary and not merely legal principles in written law.

No political will to support innovation as key to a knowledge-based economy Creating a knowledge-based economy involves a deliberate and conscious effort on the part of government. It involves a radical shift in policy, attitude, and funding priorities as well as a change in the educational and vocational curriculum of a country. It requires integrating science and abstract thinking into the daily lives of the citizenry. Such a radical policy shift can only take place if there is political goodwill and determination to steer the country into a knowledge-based economy. The shift and its impact can neither be achieved nor felt overnight. It requires long-term, sustained commitment. Absence of sustained political will implies that the paradigm shift cannot be successfully undertaken.

In Kenya, there is a demonstrable lack of political will. This is evidenced by limited resource allocation to support R&D. Obsolete equipment, run-down and mismanaged existing research institutions are a further demonstration of a lack of political will, as are the absence of an innovation fund, failure to compel universities to research to invent and the absence of innovation recognition and award schemes. The appointment of politically correct but technically incompetent directors to run scientific research institutes is lack of foresight as well as lack of political will. Above all, there is no noticeable, practical, deliberate, political effort to create a knowledge-based economy.

No coordinated institutional and administrative structures to promote innovation A national innovation system has many actors and stakeholders. Without coordinating the activities of the multifarious actors to achieve a common purpose, the innovation process will be fragmented and will focus on incremental firm level innovation. There is need for a focal institution to be charged with responsibility for driving the national innovation system and implementing the national innovation strategy. In Kenya, the various actors in the innovation system are not coordinated. The actors perform their roles without reference to each other and without recognizing that each is a cog in the wheel of innovation. Any attempt at coordination has been met with territorial and functional (jurisdictional) turf wars. There is no designated coordinator or driver to push the innovation wheel and give bearing to determine the speed and direction of the wheel. Where there is no leader, no targets are set and nothing gets done. This is the sorry state of innovation in Kenya.

No legal framework to promote and guide innovation An effective national innovation system should be based on a legal framework. The framework should provide incentives and rewards for innovation and creativity. Such a regime creates certainty as regards the rights and obligations of the individual researcher vis-à-vis the research institute. The legal regime can also be used to allocate resources for R&D. The framework can establish the institutional and administrative mechanism for promoting creativity and innovation. The legal framework should designate responsibility for promoting innovation and provide legal synergy among the actors in the innovation system. In Kenya, there is no legal framework to promote and guide innovation.

No conscious and deliberate effort to sow, inculcate and nurture an innovative population A creative and innovative population is critical to the establishment of an indigenous and self-sustaining innovation system in a country. To have such a population, deliberate efforts should be made to instill and nurture creativity and inventiveness in the people. The first step is to ensure that the educational curriculum of the country encourages inquisitive minds and problem-solving techniques. Abstract and analytical thinking should be promoted. The role of science, mathematics and experimentation should be enhanced. In the Kenyan context, presently, there is no IP in the educational curricular in basic, secondary and a majority of the tertiary institutions. There is need to review the education curricular to raise IP awareness and to inculcate empirical and innovative thinking.

Inappropriate technology in the "jua kali" sector The term "jua kali" literally means "hot sun". In Kenya, the term colloquially refers to working in the open sun without a shade. It also refers to the sector employing people who work in the open. Many a time it is stated that the "jua kali" sector is the nerve centre of Kenya's industrialization. Millions of Kenyans work in small businesses as artisans, mechanics and vendors in the open without shade and shelter. Many of these artisans and mechanics use entrepreneurial ingenuity and initiative to create jobs for others. They are a dynamic lot and have boundless levels of energy. The artisans have developed skills in wood, metal work and motor vehicle repair as mechanics. They have skills in modification and adaptation of equipment. Some artisans are adept at making simple hand-held tools. They have improvised tools such as welding machines and alternators for their trade and some are beginning to make mechanized tools. A majority of jua kali products include furniture, jembes (hoes), wheelbarrows and sufurias (cooking pots). Apart from timber, a common raw material in the jua kali sector is scrap metal.

The government has put hope in this sector as a potential source of innovators for Kenya. Funds have been set aside and spent to try and modernize the sector as a pool for indigenous future industrialists in the country. However, despite the modernization efforts, the sector still deals in scrap metal which is being flattened in the old-fashioned way – manual pounding and flattening using charcoal or fuel wood for melting. The artisans place scrap metal in a furnace, get it out when red hot, hold it with wet cloths so that it does not burn and then hit it to flatten it many times before it cools off. They repeat the same procedure until the desired result and shape is obtained several hours after enduring sweat, boundless energy and loud bangs. It has been argued that how can an enterprise of manual loud bangs endure competition from mass-produced, automated, tested and standardized products?

At present, products from the jua kali sector include sufurias, metal boxes, jembes, koroboi lamps and furniture. Few of the jua kali artisans have been able to produce industrial, standardized products. Some of the large jua kali entrepreneurs have ventured into machine-tool making and automated their production processes. The jua kali sector needs to be given a technological leap and its artisans trained in management skills.

The existing structure, organization and technology utilized in the jua kali sector portrays a weakness in Kenya's innovation system. If the jua kali sector is to provide a pool of innovators for Kenya, there is need for deliberate effort to automate the sector and to train the artisans in technology diffusion and absorption skills. Technology management skills need to be imparted to the artisans. They have proved that they have the capability to absorb technology and if such capabilities are enhanced with relevant tools, the sector may start producing innovative and competitive products. The sector can also play a role in producing innovations that fulfill the relative novelty criteria and obtain utility model protection. The sector is also good at modification and adaptation of existing technology and designing of artifacts. The artisans should be trained in automating production processes, pricing and relevance of cost-cutting technology. In this context it would be sensible to emulate the 4K MSE 2030 Initiative.

The 4K MSE 2030 Initiative is a program formed by Kenya Industrial Property Institute (KIPI), Kenya Industrial Research and Development Institute (KIRDI), Kenya Bureau of Standards (KEBS) and the Kenya National Federation of Jua-Kali Association (KNFJKA). The 4K program aims to assist the MSEs in unlocking their potential in mass production of quality goods, creating wealth and jobs through technology transfer and design, IP rights, quality use of standards, and R&D. The creation of forward and backward linkages and viable business activities from supply of raw materials through manufacturing to accessing global markets is a goal.

Unfavourable public service/civil service work culture Most of the institutions with mandates to promote innovation in Kenya employ civil servants who show signs of civil service work culture, which is synonymous with low productivity, insensitivity to deadlines, low quality of service, no customer focus, resistance to individual performance evaluation, slow and hesitant to make decisions and with a preference for numerous committee meetings giving recommendations rather than bold decision making. It shows a lack of business plans, bureaucratic decision making process, a lack of principle in making decisions but a deference to political correctness, a lack of skills to formulate technical and financial proposals, a slow recruitment process and hesitance in identifying and replacing non-performing officers.

Other negative aspects of the public service culture in Kenya can be identified as including the practice of hoarding information and data on the mistaken assumption that the practice makes the officer relevant and provides security of tenure. Within the public service, there is an imbalance between risk and reward for innovation. Officers have a choice whether or not to innovate. Typically, the costs of deciding not to innovate are small or non-existent, the status quo is usually a defensible option because the costs of not innovating may not be visible. There is a lack of skills to innovate and systemic resistance to change and reform in the public service; business as usual and old ways cannot easily be relinquished. The knowledge and experience required to simulate innovative services is lacking. Service innovation requires deep tacit knowledge and skills stored in "communities of practice". A further handicap in the public service culture in Kenya is the weakness in spreading good practice. The process of diffusing knowledge and spreading knowledge is not systematic. There is no delivery structure that gives incentives for efficiency. There is a lack of managerial skills to innovate. Further the civil service has an additional negative culture that lays emphasis on procedure rather than outcome. Fixation to process rather than output has relegated decision making to mechanical routine work rather than measurable output-impact based decision making. This culture has given rise to the concept of "senior clerical officers" where senior technical officers are preoccupied with procedural issues rather than providing technical and analytical output-based advice. In addition, the low levels of personal emoluments in public service has given rise to a culture within the service where the "government is to be eaten or exploited for personal gain". Working for the government or in public service is viewed as a means to freely access, acquire and exploit public resources – customer focus or public service is rarely viewed as a service to the citizenry. The government officers have become embodiment of officialdom and red tape to the citizenry rather than promoters of creativity and innovation.

The foregoing culture in public service is a major impediment to creativity and innovation in Kenya the more so when it is considered that the government through its officers has a role to play in the innovation process.

Over reliance on external donor funds in some public research organizations Policy support for innovation by the state and state run agencies is critical to ensure a well-functioning, macro-economic climate as well as a micro-economic environment where innovation can flourish. Most researchers at universities complain of lack of research funds and initiative to support and direct relevant research. Most public research institutions and state regulatory agencies do not have an innovation policy and the requisite funding to implement the policy. In some cases, there is an extraordinary reliance on external donors to fund for research; this means that ongoing innovative activities hardly represent the true national potential. KARI, KEMRI and ILRI are outstanding examples on over-reliance on external funding to drive innovation. The donor largely dictates the field of research and ownership of the accruing IP rights.

Weak systemic linkages for interactive learning The various public agencies and research institutions in Kenya involved in innovation, mostly work in isolation without formal linkages and incentives to foster them. The linkages and interactions between the various actors in the system of innovation are very weak owing to a lack of coherent policy that supports innovation and a lack of organizational and individual trust among researchers.[81] There is a wide range of actors with diverse policy and legal instruments that are not well coordinated and who do not serve the interest of local innovation. Incentives for the development of an indigenous private sector capacity need to be introduced. Indigenous entrepreneurship is stifled by policies that make it cheaper to import finished products rather than import components and domestically assemble them. The local pharmaceutical sector is a sterling example where taxes on importing components and manufacturing drugs locally is higher than what is charged for finished pharmaceutical products. Lack of domestic credit is another aspect that is detrimental to local entrepreneurship.

Absence of employer-training culture and low business demand for skills in some parts of the economy Employer's investment in training is not taken seriously in Kenya, where it exists, it is for relatively short duration and is not of the intensity required to upgrade workforce competences to spur creativity and innovation. A majority of employers provided no training for employees but rely on job training, which focuses on current productivity and not innovation. Technical competencies and skills are demands derived in the market. Where there is demand for a specific skill, an employment opportunity is created. The approach of most Kenyan

---

[81] Banji Oyelaran-Oyeyinka and Padmashree Gehl Sampath, "Innovation in African Development – Case Studies of Uganda, Tanzania and Kenya" World Bank Study Paper March 2007 at p 45.

firms to recruiting fresh graduates and using on-the-job training with no employer training, demonstrates that there is lack of an innovation strategy. The focus is on current productivity and not future, low-cost competitive productivity. Low demand for new and upgraded skills implies low ambitions for the business and existence of a business strategy based on low-value segments of product markets. The inference is that most of the firms in Kenya do not seek to innovate but are trapped in low skills equilibrium to serve and produce low-end market products.

Threats to innovation in Kenya

Having analyzed the strengths and weakness of Kenya's national innovation system, it is worth stating that there are threats to successful innovation in the country. The threats include:

- Infringement of existing IP rights – Kenya has an IP rights system, which adopts the absolute novelty standard for patentability and plant varietal protection. The country is a member of the PCT and Madrid Registration systems and a signatory to the Paris Convention for the Protection of Industrial Property, Berne Convention and the TRIPS Agreement. Research and innovative activity in Kenya must take into account that there could exist IP rights that must be respected. An example to note is the KEMRI use of interferon for making of KEMRON tablets for HIV-AIDS medication. KEMRI had not obtained the consent of the patent holder for interferon and the IP rights proved to be one of the factors that prevented the successful launch of KEMRON.
- Competition from well-established and tried technologies is a threat in commercializing innovation – successful innovation demands that the new product must appeal to the public and either replace existing products and technologies or give higher product utility to consumers. The new product must also be price competitive. In Kenya, any innovative product must ensure that it is price competitive and generates utility to consumers. The threat arises from the fact that western companies with established technologies can easily perfect a local innovation and with their capacities for mass production and well-established distribution channels, they can easily swamp and override local innovators. For example, the Kenyan students who made a bicycle mobile telephone charger face the threat from Nokia and Samsung who have designed mobile handsets that have a solar charger on the screen. The customer utility of a bicycle charger compared to a handheld mobile telephone with solar charger will determine the success of the bicycle charger.

- The need to avoid reinventing the wheel is a major threat to Kenyan innovators. Time and resources should not be wasted to reinvent and reproduce existing innovations. Reinventing the wheel is not prudent utilization of scarce resources. The threat arises from the fact that with limited technical knowledge and expertise in the country, research can be undertaken in the mistaken belief that it is ground-breaking research only to find that the research that appeared original and ground breaking is not original because of ignorance about existing prior art on the part of the researcher and the funding authority.

Recommendations to improve Kenya's creative and innovative capacity

In order to enhance Kenya's innovative capacity, the following measures (among others) need to be undertaken:

- Put in place a national innovation policy and strategy.
- Raise the country's human resource skill and competence levels and enhance opportunities for innovation.
- Put in place an innovation fund to support businesses to raise their innovation potential. The fund should be aimed at supporting targeted pathfinder projects to unlock the talent of the workforce to drive innovation through partnership and knowledge exchange.
- Establish a national skills academy in every sector of the economy.
- Develop a higher-level skills strategy to provide an overall framework for driving up the higher-level skills that contribute to innovation in business.
- Devise and implement a Train to Gain as well as Apprenticeship programs.
- Establish a Skills Council to identify national skills gap which inhibit innovation.
- Promote High Performance Working Practices to increase value added in business.
- Establish a Science and Innovation Network as well as technology parks and a technology diffusion observatory unit.
- Develop and implement a strategy for technology transfer and diffusions.
- Establish a National Innovation Index to measure innovative performance of the country.
- Broaden knowledge transfer between research institutions and businesses. Research industry linkage should deliberately be fostered.
- Establish a Public Service Innovation Laboratory. The laboratory will try new methods for uncovering, stimulating, incubating and

evaluating the most radical and compelling innovations in the public services.

- Identify innovative places. Innovation does not take place everywhere. Innovation tends to cluster in particular locations whether urban or rural and such clusters need to be identified. The clusters mean that innovative organizations can be close to their market and thereby be able to anticipate demand driven innovation of the future. This spatial nature of innovation must be recognized and harnessed.
- Prioritize innovation and technology through The National Economic and Social Council (NESC).
- Establish a centralized innovation promotion and coordination agency.
- Generate high-level commitment and capture and drive political will for innovation by establishing a cabinet innovation hub.

10. Public sector information, intellectual property data and developing countries

Marco Ricolfi

1. A NEW INNOVATION PARADIGM

One way to look at the history of innovation and creativity in the last two centuries is to account for how the ingenuity of individual innovators was gradually replaced by the organized, systematic and formalized effort of corporate entities. These may have been either private businesses or public research centers and universities, the latter having an inclination towards basic research as much as the former specialize in applied research and development (R&D). In both cases, the original paradigm of Benjamin Franklin-like individual creativity took a back seat while the later, management- and organization-based paradigm took center stage.

The case can be made – and is indeed being made[1] – that in the last two decades a third, entirely novel, network-driven paradigm of innovation and creativity has been emerging. The possibility of a myriad of cooperative research enterprises, which use the web as an instrument to bring together vast data sets accumulated by the different players, has become a reality. This distributed intelligence and the ecosystems in which

[1] Sometimes in specialized areas (*see* J.H. Reichman & P. Uhlir, *A Contractually Reconstructed Research Commons for Scientific Data in a Highly Protectionist Intellectual Property Environment*, in 66 *Law & Contemp. Probs.* 2003, 315 ff. and A.K. Rai, J.H. Reichman, P.F. Uhlir & C. Crossman, *Pathways Across the Valley of Death: Novel Intellectual Property Strategies for Accelerated Drug Discovery*, in VIII *Yale Journal of Health Policy, Law, and Ethics*, 2008, 1 ff., in connection with scientific data and drug discovery) or in more generalized ways (*see* L. Lessig, *Remix. Making Art and Commerce Thrive in the Hybrid Economy*, The Penguin Press, 2008, 117 ff.; Y. Benkler, *Sharing Nicely: On Shareable Goods and the Emergence of Sharing as a Modality of Economic Production*, 114 *Yale L.J.* 2004, 272 ff.). Also for additional references *see* M. RICOLFI, *Making Copyright Fit for the Digital Agenda*, forthcoming.

it thrives are the subject matter of a number of forward-looking studies, which seem to suggest that radically new rules and governance mechanisms are required for an innovation paradigm which is so different in its functioning from the ones which antedated it.[2]

We do not know much, as yet, of this third paradigm. One of its features is apparent at first sight, however. Network-driven cooperative projects are hungry; more specifically they are hungry for data sets as comprehensive, reliable, and robust as possible, to be sifted, parsed, matched and combined with other data sets. The raw data for web-based cooperation no longer are the restricted, or even proprietary, data on which firms used to base their research. Particular data in the public domain, if appropriately collected, stored and combined using the computational firepower of digital networks, may not only go into the preparation of novel products and services but additionally supply unprecedented insights to contribute to tackling the multiple challenges of our age, from unsolved health issues to climate change, from the erosion of biodiversity to the preservation of cultural heritage.

In this chapter it is submitted that among the raw data for which digital networks are hungry there is an essential ingredient: public sector information (PSI), that is the data sets which governments and public sector bodies collect, generate, organize and use while carrying out their institutional tasks.[3] First, it examines these data and the uses to which they can be put in the context of the novel paradigm of innovation and creativity hinted at above. Thereafter the role which PSI may play in specific connection with developing countries will be considered and finally, some current topics concerning PSI in this specific perspective will be discussed.

---

[2] An overview of the knowledge commons and of the literature relating to it is to be found in C. Hess & E. Ostrom, *Introduction: An Overview of the Knowledge Commons*, in Charlotte Hess & Elinor Ostrom (eds.), *Understanding Knowledge as a Commons. From Theory to Practice*, MIT Press, Cambridge-London, 2007, 3–26.

[3] For an overview of the main features and issues of the area the work of G. Aichholzer & H Burkert (eds.), *Public Sector Information in the Digital Age. Between Markets, Public Management and Citizens' Rights*, Edward Elgar, Cheltenham, 2004 still is fundamental. *See* also D. Robinson, H. Yu, W.P. Zeller & E.W. Felten, *Government Data And The Invisible Hand*, in 11 *Yale J.L. & Tech.* 2009, 160 ff.; E. Derclaye, *Does the Directive on the Re-use of Public Sector Information affect the State's database sui-generis right?*, in J. Gaster, E. Schweighofer & P. Sint P., *Knowledge Rights – Legal, societal and related technological aspects*, Austrian Computer Society, 2008, 137 ff.; M.M.M. Van Eechoud-B. Van der Wal, *Creative Commons Licensing for Public Sector Information – Opportunities and Pitfalls*, January 2008, available at SSRN: http://ssrn.com/abstract=1096564; P. Uhlir, *Policy Guidelines for the Development and Promotion of Governmental Public Domain Information*, UNESCO, Paris, 2004.

2. PUBLIC SECTOR INFORMATION (PSI): WHAT ARE WE TALKING ABOUT?

It is a common experience that it is quite difficult to convey the meaning of what is in fact understood under the label of PSI. It is the personal experience of the author that the difficulty may be even greater when a European Intellectual Property (IP) lawyer is listening.

In order to give a feeling of what is contained herein, just to a short inventory of a few examples of PSI data sets will be examined.

Geographic information, in the form of maps, aerial photographs, post-code information, tags to the above, which all have become popular over the last few years thanks to GoogleMaps and Google Earth,[4] is collected and generated in connection with a number of public tasks, including military purposes (usually the best maps are military). However, it may also be employed to help vehicles' navigation along any given route, as well as the delivery of physical goods at any given address. This is only the starting point; as the detail of the information has been enhanced by combining different data sets, it has also gone into multiple applications, including of late helping to counter forest fires and saving lives in the recent Australian devastation.

Land data, sometimes referred to as cadastral information, serve the essential purpose of identifying real estate ownership. The information assembled in this collection may also be put to several additional uses; among other purposes, it may enable lenders and businesses to assess counterparty risk, on the basis of updated knowledge concerning the extent and value of assets owned by the debtor and therefore on their creditworthiness.

Metadata concerning museums and archives at any given location, by identifying works and items available at any given location, as well as the images of the same, no doubt serve the purpose of managing and preserving the artifacts collected in these institutions. However, the same information, when digitized and made available over the net, may also

---

[4] And which in many countries are, at least in part, the backbone of several public services and the tool for the supply of a number of value-added services: for an illustration of the outline of the dynamics of the sector in the UK and of the tensions surfacing in it *see* Review Board of the Advisory Panel on Public Sector Information APPSI, Report 30 April 2007 and Office of Public Sector Information, Report on its Investigation of a complaint (SO 42/8/4): Intelligent Addressing and Ordnance Survey, 13 July 2006. The two Reports are available at http://www.appsi.gov.uk/review-board/review-SO-42-8-4.pdf and at http://www.nationalarchives.gov.uk/documents/so-42-8-4.pdf.

stimulate tourism, to the extent a given location, on top of having other attractions, is shown to be a repository of valuable items.

The collection and preservation of meteorological data, of increasing detail and accuracy, has become one of the basic functions of Western public administrations in the last century and a half. The same data may at the same time be the basis for added value services, when private providers combine and match it with different information sets coming from other sources, to provide individually tailored weather bulletins or guidance for harvesting management. It may be interesting to note that the same data may also have a separate and additional "value" in a totally different perspective: they may turn out to be valuable in a public debate concerning climate change and in the forming of policy choices in this area, as well as in the public debate over them. Indeed, PSI may give crucial contributions not only to added value services, but to broader societal goals, usually referred to under the catchwords "e-government" and "e-democracy".

These examples may be limited and sketchy. They are however sufficient to make two points.

First, they explain why the wealth of information collected, generated and preserved by governments and public sector bodies is a veritable minefield. The value of the individual information obtained by them may approximate nil, if separately considered; but this changes when the data accumulate, are integrated, organized and verified. The value may be greatly enhanced when data sets are available over a period of time, possibly over a long period of time, stretching over a decade or a century; this is even more so, if it is to be expected that even in the future the same kind of data will be made available in similar formats.[5] It is difficult to be sure that these data are collected in a way which is totally unbiased and neutral; even public bodies have their own agendas and may be inclined to overestimate or underestimate certain figures, as we all know when we refer to data going into forming consumer price indexes or unemployment tallies. However, at least a certain degree of neutrality is to be expected, in view of the necessities of the public function entrusted to the relevant public body. Land Registrars could not carry out their task of keeping records of land transactions and being able to identify who owns what at any given time, if they were not totally accurate in their recording of any given parcel of land and of the person or entity that may from time to time own it.[6]

---

[5] For a fuller treatment of these qualities of PSI *see* H. BURKERT, *The Mechanics of Public Sector Information*, in G. Aichholzer & H. Burkert (eds.), *Public Sector Information in the Digital Age*, quoted above at note 3, 7 ff.

[6] We should also consider that the whole point of PSI is that it is "dual" or "multiple" use information. The difficulties of the notion of "dual use" have been

Now, on the basis of this kind of information, mathematical models may be tried and developed to test possible correlations and to supply extrapolations, which may in turn provide novel insights, to the delight of several researchers,[7] to the benefit of several constituencies of users and possibly also to the profit of savvy and forward-looking service providers.

Second, these examples account for the extreme difficulty of any attempt to figure out what exactly is the value which may be extracted from the from time-to-time relevant data sets. Nobody had thought of the enormous potential of GoogleMaps, until Google started providing them.[8] Indeed, there are infinite possibilities of matching and combining disparate data sets. It is not to be expected however that either governments or researchers may have *ex ante* a perfect or even reasonably accurate knowledge on the possible uses of the information deriving from all the possible matching and combination exercises. These possibilities remain to a large extent unfathomable, until the exercise is in fact taken up by somebody who has a specific reason (or, may be, incentive) to try doing so and to go to all the trouble (and costs) that are required to build the necessary tools and applications. The hidden value of any non-obvious combination of data sets may be revealed only when decentralized decisions to invest in their exploration have been taken and carried out. The minefield analogy crops up again here: there is value only if you dig; and you dig only if you have an incentive to do so.

This is why, when we try to imagine what is the value, for end user, for added-value service providers, and for society at large, linked to collecting, generating, preserving, disseminating, matching and combining data sets, in ways which have not yet surfaced, the reply is (and has to be): who knows? This does not mean that it is not worthwhile trying to locate and

---

explored by weapons-control regulations, intended to develop a framework to identify components and chemical substances which may either go into peaceful, civilian uses or be considered "weapon-grade" (spent uranium being one of the best-known examples). When public-sector originated PSI is put to a second or third use, different from the one for which it was originated or collected, it may well be that the bias which may be in the original data is no longer relevant, e.g. because what is of concern is the variation rather than the absolute amount; or may be adjusted (by discounting the expected rate of bias).

[7] Such as S.D. Levitt & S.J. Dubner, *Freakonomics. A Rogue Economist Explores the Hidden Side of Everything*, Penguin Books, 2nd ed., 2006.

[8] The story is actually a bit more complicated: as indicated by R. Stross, *Planet Google. One Company's Audacious Plan to Organize Everything We Know*, Free Press, New York, London, Toronto and Sydney, 2008, several start-ups had been thinking about the idea, when Google purchased them to develop and implement the concept on a global scale.

"mine" the hidden trove. Indeed, it is well known that large digital businesses do have "PSI evangelists", keeping track of any activities, including governmental, which are likely to generate appropriate data sets. This is an effort likely to be rewarded, not only in the long run but in a time-horizon relevant to the decision-making of business, which after all are entities interested in revenue streams available in the foreseeable future. It may also be noted that it would pay, for society at large, also to have "public sector evangelists"; except that, it should be argued, their job should be about which data should be made accessible for re-use by private players, rather than which data should be directly re-used by the public sector itself. In other words, PSI evangelism in the public sector should be about rules concerning data sets, not about data sets as such.

3. PSI AND INTELLECTUAL PROPERTY: THE US AND THE EU

The economic relevance of PSI in the US and in Europe is very different. Value-added services based on PSI account for over 7 percent of GNP in the US; the share is much smaller in Europe. There are obvious reasons which explain the difference. The US from the onset adopted liberal rules on re-usability of PSI, following the principle whereby no copyright attaches to governmental data. This principle entails two corollaries: no payment is required for re-using PSI and no strings are attached to PSI made available by the public sector.[9] This is why the acronym PSI has no currency in the US: there the expression "open data" is much more to the point.

Europe is different, or, to put it bluntly, totally different. PSI attracts copyright protection, if and to the extent it may qualify as a "work" under general copyright definition; which is a quite usual occurrence in connection with, say, maps or digital images of museum artifacts. Whatever data fail to qualify for copyright protection is likely to trigger database rights,[10] which, in any event, provide a separate second layer of IP protection also for copyright-protected works.[11]

This explains why your average European IP lawyer can hardly conceive

[9] For more details *see* H. BURKERT, *The Mechanics of Public Sector Information*, quoted above at note 3, 8 ff.

[10] See E. DERCLAYE, *Does the Directive on the Re-use of Public Sector Information affect the State's database sui-generis right?* above at note 3.

[11] See E. DERCLAYE, *Does the Directive on the Re-use of Public Sector Information affect the State's database sui-generis right?* above at note 3.

that PSI is re-usable. Be it Queen's copyright or *droit d'auteur* over works, we are accustomed to the idea that, as a rule, what belongs to the State may not be re-used short of specific permission and only on the terms and conditions mandated by the sovereign. Consequentially, we are not much surprised to learn that in Europe there are so called "trading funds", which are public entities established with the specific task of extracting the maximum profit on behalf of the sovereign out of PSI. As if it were normal that re-users, who are usually citizens who have already paid their fair amount of taxes to fund museums, military maps, meteorological services and Land Registers, should pay all over again a specific fee to access and re-use the same data which they themselves funded to begin with.[12]

This does not mean that PSI cannot be re-used in the EU. Only re-use is much more complicated and costly. If a public sector body decides – or is mandated by law – to make its PSI accessible, it must also set the terms and conditions (usually in the form of a license) under which the copyright and database-protected items are re-usable.[13] The EU faces an additional difficulty: how can a pan-European cross-border service take off, if the terms and conditions promulgated by one Member State do not seamlessly overlap with the terms and conditions adopted by other Member States? Imagine that the license in Member State A authorizes "tagging" of maps with data on tourist attractions, whereas Member State B does not. This simple divergence is sufficient to prevent the emergence of a multi-State service.

The EU has tried to overcome these shortcomings – and the resulting competitive disadvantages vis-à-vis the US – by means of a EU Directive, 2003/98/EC on the re-use of public sector information (PSI Directive), which is at this time subject to an impact assessment with a view to amending it. Of course a Directive may help; but only up to a point. If and to the extent the baseline of PSI information is copyright and database protection, harmonization, however comprehensive and deep running it may be, is bound to face an additional hurdle: the rule on which all IP protection is based, territoriality, forces providers and finally end-users to comply with as many IP laws as the number of the Member States involved.

---

[12] Fortunately, this charging policy is currently subject to discussion and possibly revision: see D. Newbery, L. Bently & R. Pollock, *Models of Public Sector information provision via Trading Funds*, Study commissioned jointly by the Department for Business, Enterprise and Regulatory Reform (BERR) and HM Treasury, 2007.

[13] For the UK *see* http://www.nationalarchives.gov.uk/information-management/uk-gov-licensing-framework.htm; for the Netherlands http://www.rijksoverheid.nl/ last visited March 7, 2011.

For completeness sake, it be should added that in regulating PSI the EU has not shied away from dealing with the implications at the level of privacy and data protection laws. This may sound as an additional complication of EU PSI regulation, considering the much more cavalier attitude US law shows in the same areas. But this is not certain; as the intersection between PSI and privacy indeed is a very, very hard nut to crack, it may still be that EU will turn out to have done the right thing to face the issue straight into the eyes. This may in the long run turn out to be a competitive advantage for Europe.

4. DEVELOPING COUNTRIES AND PSI

As far as the author knows, PSI legislation does not reach beyond the US and Europe although the author is aware of an initiative sponsored by UNESCO and by the Council of Europe to examine the feasibility for Maghreb States (Algeria, Morocco and Tunisia) to adopt legislation concerning access to public documents. However, access is only the preliminary step to re-use. The right to access, usually provided for by Freedom of Information Acts (FoIAs),[14] certainly is important in and by itself to secure transparency of governments and accountability of public decision-makers. In the perspective of re-use, however, access is a necessary step (no re-use can even be conceived of information which is not available to begin with),[15] but not a sufficient one: a given piece of information may not be incorporated into a value added service, even though it is accessible, unless its re-use is authorized by law or contract.

Therefore, a broad task is before developing countries in an area which may turn out to be very promising for their cultures, economies and societies. In this connection, developing countries may find themselves in a scenario which is somewhat unprecedented for them. While it often happens that the hands of developing countries are tied by international IP Covenants, including TRIPs,[16] this is not the case with PSI. Article

---

[14] On which *see* E. DERCLAYE, *The Legal Protection of Data Bases. A Comparative Analysis*, Edward Elgar, Cheltenham, 2008, 13 ff.

[15] Notice however that not all the countries which provide re-usability of PSI have open access legislation: the US, the UK and Sweden do; other European countries do not (*see* E. DERCLAYE, *The Legal Protection of Data Bases. A Comparative Analysis*, Edward Elgar, Cheltenham, 2008, 13 ff.).

[16] For examples and additional references *see* M. RICOLFI *Is There an Antitrust Antidote Against IP Overprotection within TRIPs?* in 10 *Marquette Intellectual Property Law Review*, 2006, 305 ff.

9 TRIPs incorporates by reference the Berne Convention;[17] but Article 4(2) of the latter gives ample leeway to Members to provide, as well as to rule out, copyright protection for "legislative, *administrative* and judicial documents";[18] where the notion of "administrative documents" may be very broadly conceived. In turn, database protection under Article 10.2 TRIPs is sketchy at best.

It would therefore appear that developing countries have a totally free hand in determining the IP status of data which are candidates to become PSI. This may give them a chance to leapfrog developed countries in designing the architecture of PSI re-use. Indeed, economic history taught us over half a century ago that late joiners may have distinct advantages over initiators.[19] Moreover, it is not true that there are pre-set steps in the development either of economies or of legal institutions[20] so that it is always possible to learn from the mistakes incurred in other jurisdictions.

The author's knowledge about developing countries and about PSI is not sufficient to presume to be in a position to give advice on which PSI design is optimal for which developing countries. However, a few notes may be informative.

5. TWO SETS OF LEGISLATIVE OPTIONS

In the previous paragraphs the two models of approach to PSI were contrasted, where the more liberal US attitude was compared to the more hands-on, regulatory approach of European jurisdictions.

It should not be taken for granted that one is superior to the other. No doubt the EU approach enables a greater control of PSI re-use than the US one. There may be good grounds to leave to governments some degree of control over re-use, considering that whatever freedoms in this area may be desirable may also be granted via contracts, rather than by law. Additionally, some degree of control may in turn allow for charging

---

[17] Berne Convention for the Protection of Literary and Artistic Works, Sept. 9, 1886 as last revised at Paris, July 24, 1971 [hereinafter Berne Convention].

[18] Italics added.

[19] *See* the influential work of A. GERSCHENKRON, *Economic Backwardness in Historical Perspective, A Book of Essays*, Cambridge, Massachusetts, Belknap Press of Harvard University Press, 1962, criticizing W.W. ROSTOW's orthodox view according to whom economic take off required going through preset steps (*see The Stages of Economic Growth*, in 11 *Economic History Review*, 1959, 1 ff.).

[20] This is an accepted proposition now, based on the theory of so-called path-dependence (for a brilliant formulation of which *see* M.J. ROE, *Chaos and Evolution in Law and Economics*, in 109 *Harvard Law Review*, 1996, 640 ff.).

policies which enable raising revenue out of PSI-based, added value services, which may at some point prove handy for cash-strapped governments. It is however also true that there may be too much of a good thing and that EU Member States may be a bit overdoing the control thing.

The reverse may also apply to the US model, which, no doubt, is very liberal, to the point we may question whether it is not too liberal (e.g. at the interface between PSI and privacy).

There is no reason, therefore, to recommend the adoption of one model over the other. The following is therefore confined to dealing with two sets of issues; the first one is bound to come up whichever model is chosen; the other one specifically concerns the EU model and therefore situations where one country might decide to opt for it.

The following deals with the issues which are common to both models.

A) One major issue is about formats and interoperability. If data sets are to be re-used; and they are to be re-used by private players in ways which cannot be anticipated *ex ante*, then the formats should be as re-use friendly as possible. Only open, machine-readable formats should be selected, leaving it to the freedom of re-users downstream to match and interface without limitations. Proprietary formats, i.e. formats which are based on software or other IP which is privately owned, are not interoperable and should therefore be avoided. Once concerns about formats and interoperability are dealt with, data should be made available without worrying too much about their presentation. As Tim Berners Lee said a while ago, "raw data now!" should be the guiding principle. After all, governments are not in the business of providing admirable portals; their mission in this connection consists in giving back to taxpayers the data which they collected, generated and stored away with taxpayers' money.[21]

B) There is a cost in moving from paper, analog information to digital data sets. This cost may be worth incurring, e.g. because the public task itself is liable to require the move from analog to digital. This is not always the case, however. Public institutions like museums and archives may still carry out their original function, of receiving visitors in physical premises, even though no digitization is undertaken. Digitization may, quite reasonably, rank very low in the priorities of

[21] *See* D. Robinson, H. Yu, W.P. Zeller & E.W. Felten, *Government Data And The Invisible Hand*, quoted above at note 3, who at 161 refer to the engineering principle of separating the provision of data from the job of allowing the interaction with them.

countries which face issues of malnutrition, health, epidemics and the like. In such cases the private sector may be called in; it may even wish to be involved, for a number of reasons (as mentioned earlier, network driven projects are hungry for information; text, images, audiovisual data all enable computational experiments which may lead the way to the next big thing). Public Private Partnerships (PPP) have fared rather well in some contexts; however, the private side may overuse the argument if contributing money to a joint project to secure exclusivity over the outcome. Reasonable compromises may be worked out, though. The EU High Level Group on the Digital Libraries Initiative has recommended that exclusivity does not extend beyond a certain period of time, say three to five years. Possibly other solutions may be found; but the problem may not be neglected.

Turning to the EU model, it should be borne in mind that this approach is bound to raise a number of specific issues, which should be considered separately.

A) If IP protection for PSI is provided, then it should belong entirely to the government itself. It would be a nightmare if private contractors supplying products or services to the public sector, which may include IP protected data sets, were to retain rights over the data themselves. They would be in a position to block decisions to make available PSI downstream, may be decades after their job was finished. It might be considered whether procurement rules are to be adopted, which provide that all IP over data is automatically vested in the public entity paying for the product or service which incorporates the same data. Also governmental employment contracts might require a default rule thought along these lines. Fortunately enough, ownership rules are again an area in which neither Berne Convention nor TRIPs create specific obligations.
B) As earlier indicated, if PSI is IP protected, it may still be made available to private service providers and re-users under licensing terms. If this is the case, then the concerns about interoperability, which were earlier raised in connection with technical interoperability, will also extend to legal interoperability. In this regard, it should be considered that data sets of one kind may be mixed, matched and combined with data sets of a different kind. Re-use which is allowed under the license for data sets of the first kind cannot be remixed with data sets of the second kind, unless the conditions totally overlap. The same applies to cross-border services. A way out is the creation of a single set of cross-sectoral and regional licensing terms.

C) A special case of the former issue concerns the choice between commercial and non-commercial licenses. An apparently strong case may be made for choosing a license for PSI content which rules out the possibility of authorizing commercial re-use of the same (e.g. by resorting to a Creative Commons NC license).[22] The idea behind this initial reaction might be as follows. Public money has been spent on the generation, collection, maintenance of these data sets; now, all is fine and well if this PSI is disseminated as widely as possible to enable study, research, entertainment and the like. But enabling these goals is clearly possible even if the authorization to access and re-use is under a NC license, i.e. limited to non-commercial uses. Conversely, it might be argued, it does not make sense that PSI generated with taxpayers' money is appropriated by profit-making entities to build on it a proprietary product and service and sell on the market goods and services based on it. This line of argument is plausible at first glance; and is in fact adopted by a great number of well-meaning civil servants, who intend "to avoid that public data are 'resold' by private businesses", but probably misguided if we stop to think a bit further and this on at least two accounts.[23]

First, the concept of chain of authorizations should be considered. No-profit institutions, like Wikipedia and other aggregators of information and cultural content, undoubtedly contribute a great deal to the dissemination of knowledge, information, culture. However, they do so because the content they make available is accessible downstream without restrictions as to the commercial or non-commercial nature of re-use; the reason of the great success of Wikipedia and organizations and projects, such as Project Gutenberg, Open Street Map and the like, is that they make anything they put together available to anybody without strings attached. To do so, however,

---

[22] On Creative Commons in connection with PSI *see* M.M.M. VAN EECHOUD & B. VAN DER WAL, *Creative Commons Licensing for Public Sector Information – Opportunities and Pitfalls*, quoted above at note 3. On Creative Commons licenses in general *see* M. RIMMER, *Digital Copyright and the Consumer Revolution*, Edward Elgar, Cheltenham, 2008, 269 ff.; B.F. Fitzgerald, J.M. Coates & S. M. Lewis (a cura di), *Open Content Licensing: Cultivating the Creative Commons*, Sydney University Press, 2007; N. ELKIN-KOREN, *What Contracts Cannot Do: The Limits of Private Ordering in Facilitiating A Creative Commons*, in 74 *Fordham L. Rev.* 2005, 375 ff.; M. VALIMAKI & H. HIETANEN, *The Challenges of Creative Commons Licensing*, in *Cri* 2004, 173 ff.

[23] For a more complete treatment of the issue *see* M. Ricolfi, post http://www.epsiplatform.eu/guest_blogs/re_use_licenses_commercial_or_non_commercial_this_is_the_question.

Wikipedia and its likes have to make sure that the content they incorporate is free to begin with; the flipside of the coin is that Wikipedia cannot incorporate content which would otherwise be splendid in complementing or illustrating its store of knowledge any time the same comes with restrictions as to the commercial nature of the intended re-use.[24] Therefore, if consideration is not confined to the first re-users but also to the subsequent ones, it can clearly be seen that in this specific case NC licenses can end up greatly restricting dissemination. A moment's reflection, will lead to the realization that when there is no content on Wikipedia, this means that what is restricted is not only commercial re-use, but availability on Wikipedia for whatever end and purpose. Full stop.

Second, once the costs necessary to generate, collect and maintain PSI are incurred, it does not make any difference whether the re-user makes a profit from re-use. No marginal cost is incurred by the PSI holder just because there is an additional re-user. If the latter is smart enough to create a business model which enables her to combine this input with other inputs and make money out this, nice for her. Nothing is taken away from the public. Of course, there would be a disadvantage to the public if the re-user is able to obtain monopoly or even market power through the use of PSI created by public funds. This may indeed happen in a number of ways, e.g. because the PSI based data set goes into a wider one which is protected by the *sui generis* database right also in connection with its "substantial parts", the data set is migrated to a proprietary format and/or technical protection measures are applied to it. This unwanted outcome would result if PSI generated through public money were made available on terms of exclusivity. But this is a good reason to avoid exclusivity, not commercial use.[25]

---

24 Incidentally, this is the reason why no pictures are available to showcase a great many Italian monuments and buildings.

25 It also is possible that the re-user combines publicly funded PSI with proprietary content; and secures a dominant position on the strength of the combination of the two complementary items. Economists would suggest that, if this is the case, there would be an incentive for new entrants to create and offer competitive complementary data sets; that is, if the publicly funded PSI is made available to all comers, without exclusivity. Of course, it may also happen that a re-user possessing market power controls so many important assets which are complementary to PSI, that the chances of a competitive challenge to such a powerful incumbent are slim. This is a possibility; but it is arguable that this occurrence is an externality which should be taken care by regulation, e.g. by means of antitrust enforcement or by application of the so-called doctrine of essential facilities. It is likely that the

D) Finally, even though a charging policy remains possible in this context, it should be considered with great caution. A default rule in favor of free re-use might be appropriate; also the provision for recovery of marginal costs of distribution or dissemination could be a viable option in some cases; it should be considered, however, that a profit maximization policy has given poor results both in terms of downstream wealth creation and for purposes of revenue raising.[26]

This may not be much by way of a Bible for designing re-use policies in developing countries. The author, however, hopes that, as a beginning, it may still do.

---

adoption of licenses preventing commercial re-use of PSI would make the matter worse. Indeed, if PSI data sets were made available only on the condition that they are used non-commercially, it might happen that this restriction turns out to be more detrimental to firms intending to enter the market than to an entrenched business leader, who may have the means to generate the data sets it needs by itself. In such a context, NC licenses would make matters worse, not better.

[26] Empirical evidence to this effect is to be found in P. Weiss, *Borders in Cyberspace: conflicting public sector information policies and their economic impact*, in G. Aichholzer-H. Burkert (eds.), *Public Sector Information in the Digital Age*, above note 3, 137 ff.

Index